Also by the Same Authors

———

Human Biological Development

HUMAN
PSYCHOLOGICAL
DEVELOPMENT

ELIZABETH LEE VINCENT

PROFESSOR OF HUMAN DEVELOPMENT AND BEHAVIOR
CHATHAM COLLEGE

PHYLLIS C. MARTIN

PROFESSOR OF BIOLOGY AND CHAIRMAN OF HUMAN
DEVELOPMENT AND BEHAVIOR, CHATHAM COLLEGE

Illustrated by

WILLIAM A. OSBURN, M.M.A.

THE RONALD PRESS COMPANY • NEW YORK

Library of Congress Catalog Card Number: 61-8416

Preface

The essential purpose of this book is to give the student a better understanding of the sequences of psychological development and of the principles underlying them—in himself and in other human beings. Our thesis is that the psychological self can exist only in a body, and that intellect and personality are affected by and in turn affect the body.

Throughout our chapters, we have attempted to guide, enlighten, and reassure the student. We hope that he will come to "feel" as well as "think" psychological development. The content and organization of the chapters are based upon a number of years of teaching a general education course to freshmen and sophomores in a liberal arts college. *Human Psychological Development* is the second of two books which have grown out of this course. The first book, *Human Biological Development* (also published by The Ronald Press Company), concentrates on the human aspects of biological development.

In *Human Psychological Development*, it will be noted, we have given the adolescent years a considerable amount of space, in recognition of the interest of men and women students in both the period of growth they have recently left and the period in which they now find themselves. Our telescoping of fifty to sixty years of adult life into three chapters is the result of many experiments in interesting young people in the psychological challenges and rewards of these seemingly distant years.

Since knowledge of psychological development at every age is helpful to all who are interested in gaining insights into human behavior, this book may be useful to many whose classroom days are behind them. It is an introduction to the subject and does not presume previous subject-matter background.

The end-of-chapter "Suggestions for Further Discussion" stem directly from the questions that have repeatedly been asked in our own classes. They mirror the student's personal experience or his eager wish to solve some personal problem and, often, represent simply the wish to know. It has also been our experience that the use of supplementary readings tends to enliven class discussions. Our "Suggestions for Further Study," at the close of each chapter, have been chosen so that only a limited number of reference works are needed.

Documentation in the text has been kept to a minimum, and supporting references will be found as a Bibliographical Supplement in the Appendix. A Film Supplement, also in the Appendix, lists important film sources and offers chapter-by-chapter suggestions of films useful in connection with the topics discussed. Although the films are described briefly, it is suggested that the instructor preview them to assure maximum benefit from their screening.

We are grateful to William A. Osburn, M.M.A., for his imaginative interpretations of our suggestions for many of the illustrations. We are indebted to the W. B. Saunders Company for permission to pattern Fig. 5–8 after an illustration in Arey's *Developmental Anatomy*. Figure 4–3 is reproduced from *A Baby Is Born*, published by the Maternity Center Association, New York City, with their permission, and we wish to thank the Association for their cooperation. The photographs appearing in Figs. 5–4, 5–5, 5–10, 6–3, 6–4, 6–5, 8–2, 8–3, 8–4, 8–5, 13–2, 13–3, 13–4. 14–1, 14–2, and 14–3 are from H. Armstrong Roberts and have been used with his permission.

We are indebted to our several readers and to Dr. Albert Martin, Jr., for many helpful suggestions concerning the manuscript, and to our intelligent and patient typist, Lee Fowler.

ELIZABETH LEE VINCENT
PHYLLIS C. MARTIN

Pittsburgh, Pennsylvania
February, 1961

Contents

HUMAN PSYCHOLOGICAL DEVELOPMENT

CHAPTER I

An Inclusive View

Why Study Psychological Development?

The study of psychological development throughout life is of interest to anyone who wonders why people are what they are and why they do what they do. Many things said in this book are familiar to the close observer of human life, because people of all races and cultures have growth experiences in common. Yet every individual is different from every other individual, and ways of doing things differ from one culture to another and from one individual to another. No two lives are exactly the same.

No one can know all about human beings. It is hoped, however, that in this course the student will widen his knowledge about how people grow psychologically and about what is known of the forces that make each individual develop as he does.

Throughout history the various cultures have passed from one generation to another their ideas about what man is, why he is as he is, what he might become, and how best to rear children in the pattern of these ideas. It is only in the last two hundred years, and particularly in the last fifty years, that systematic attempts have been made through carefully recorded observation and controlled experimentation to discover the basic laws which underlie human development. These studies have revealed some of the factors which determine the course of human development, and have attempted to find what can be done to reduce aberrations and abnormalities on the one hand and to encourage optimal development on the other hand. As a result, medical science and public health measures have greatly decreased fatal and debilitating diseases. Studies of physiology have produced the knowledge by which health at all ages may be improved. Psychology, sociology, and allied sciences are discovering basic principles in human behavior which make it possible to improve human welfare.

Life Expectancy Today

Life expectancy differs in various areas of the world. The average life expectancy for babies born in the United States in 1955 is 69.6 years: for boys it is 66.3 years; for girls 73.6 years. This means that half of the boys born in 1955 in the United States may expect to live for 66.3 years or longer; half of the girls for 73.6 years or longer. It has been estimated,[169] that average life expectancy in the world in the early Bronze Age was 18 years. During the first century B.C. it was about 22 years; during the Middle Ages, 33 years; and between 1700 and 1800 A.D., 35 to 40 years. By 1900 in the United States, it had increased to 49.2 years. There are still many countries in the world, however, in which more than one half of the population suffers from critical nutritional shortages and where the average life expectancy is only 40 years.[105]

The rapid increase in life expectancy since 1900 has resulted from reductions in the mortality rate. Infant mortality in most countries of the world has decreased [34] because of improved prenatal, obstetrical, and pediatric care. General mortality rates have decreased as a result of improved public health and nutrition. Much of the change has come from the partial triumph over such childhood diseases as scarlet fever, measles, diphtheria, and whooping cough. Contributing, too, has been the relative success of the battle against once major killers such as typhoid fever, malaria, cholera, smallpox, pneumonia, and influenza. Although the death rate has decreased, generally speaking, it has done so in spite of a considerable increase in diseases common to people in the older age brackets. Such old-age diseases, for example, are cardiovascular-renal (heart-blood-vessel-kidney) diseases, tuberculosis, and cancer. Since deaths from many childhood diseases have been almost eliminated, it is possible for many more people to survive to the age when the "old-age diseases" attack.

Population Pressures

Desirable as the extension of life may seem, it poses certain problems. Left to herself, nature is prolific, but she weeds out the defective and the weak along the way. In countries where birth rates tend to be high, but where public health protection and nutrition are poor, maternal and infant death rates are high, as are death rates throughout the life span. The struggle for existence is rigorous, and life expectancy is relatively short. In spite of high death rates and of a relatively short life span in such countries, the demands of the population on the food supply are so great that death from malnutrition is common, and the need for outlets into other living spaces is a pressing one.

In the United States, where as recently as the turn of the twentieth century there seemed to be no end to the unused fertile lands, population growth is now a matter of concern. In 1940, some 132 million people lived in the United States; by 1960, the number had increased to over 180 million. It is estimated that if this rate of increase is maintained, the United States alone in 1980 will have some 200 million people. In 1900, if a man felt "hemmed in" because he could see the smoke of a neighbor's house ten miles away, he could easily find another fertile spot where he could see no sign of a neighbor's abode. Today the eastern part of the United States, from Boston to Washington, D.C., is an almost unbroken concentration of buildings and paved streets. Traffic problems, crowded schools, noise and hurry, and the crowding of homes are seriously affecting physical as well as emotional health. The United States itself is becoming typical of the total world picture. The United Nations in 1957 estimated that the world population was growing at the rate of 5,000 people every hour, or 44 million every year—a number larger than the total current population of France. The provision of adequate space for every individual is now man's most pressing problem.

Why Do We Live?

There are people who expect life to be an easy, unobstructed path of comfort and fun; they are resentful when anything disagreeable happens or when effort is required of them. In contrast, there are those who find that life consists of birth and death with plentiful trouble between. Actually, for many of us, life turns out to be an experience somewhere between these extremes.

One list of criteria [124] for personality maturity (which has to do with accepting life as it is) includes the following statement: "The well-adjusted person does not try to change the fact that life is an endless struggle." However, this same list includes these statements:

"The well-adjusted person enjoys attacking and eliminating obstacles to his development and happiness after he is convinced they are real, not imaginary obstacles," and "The well-adjusted person participates with pleasure in experiences belonging to each successive age level."

Jersild [91] discusses life as a form of striving. According to one point of view, the growing child's activity is directed solely by the need to overcome obstacles that lie in his way. The child acts only because of frustrations, problems, irritants, or other conditions that upset his inner equilibrium and cause him discomfort, such as hunger, obstacles in his physical environment, and being kept from doing as he pleases. This activity may be called *negative striving*.

Jersild also discusses an opposite point of view: that living involves *positive striving*. The individual is seen to be endowed with an urge to discover, to mobilize, and to use his inner resources. He is motivated, not solely to avoid pain and to conquer obstacles, but rather to gain something, to fulfill and to express something, to use his capacities for doing, thinking, feeling, and sharing with others. Thus he seeks, strives for, and struggles toward self-fulfillment.

Jersild goes on to point out that physical growth often involves growing pains. Every hurdle in development involves a hazard, every gain is made at a price. For example, as the child learns to walk, he walks not only into new pleasures but into new troubles. If he develops imagination which enables him to look ahead and to anticipate future pleasures and satisfactions, he becomes able to worry about what the future may bring. The more the adolescent can stand on his own feet, the more decisions he has to make and the more responsibilities he has to take. Struggle, from this point of view, is a feature of life and the source of much of its strength. An individual cannot develop his full potential in a protected environment. He must be active, and sometimes deeply fulfilled. But he must sometimes get hurt, and many times must encounter difficulties which he can either run away from, thus losing momentum in his growth, or tackle squarely and thereby increase his strength and wisdom.

Heredity

In the past, many people have believed that we are what we are solely because of the particular genes (the hereditary particles) that we receive at our conception. When we are born, the reasoning went, we have the makings of all that we shall ever be, and what happens to us thereafter makes little if any difference. On the other hand, there have been those who have said that we are what we are almost entirely because of the things that happen to us after we are born. These people have maintained that each experience affects us by way of our nervous systems, and because it does, it affects everything that follows in life: that we become what we are because of what we have experienced. Most psychologists and biologists today, however, think that we are what we are because of the interaction of our heredity and the various environmental factors and experiences that come our way, either as the result of circumstances or of our own initiative.

Our heredity comes to us from our ancestors (see Fig. 1-1) through two minute cells, the *egg*, not as large as the typical period on a printed page, from the mother, and the *sperm*, much smaller than the egg, from the father. The two cells, sometimes called the *germ cells*, contain the chromosomes, which are aggregations of particles called *genes*. These genes are believed to be the bearers of heredity from generation to generation. For some time, observers have thought that they could count 24 chromosomes in the germ cells, but more recent evidence makes it likely that 23 is the accurate number. In any case, each chromosome in the egg has a partner in the sperm; hence, the fertilized egg contains pairs of chromosomes and therefore pairs of genes. The fertilized egg carries within it all the potentialities, physical and psychological, that the developed individual can ever have. These potentialities are determined at the instant of conception by the particular egg and the particular sperm that happen to unite in the uterine tube of the mother-to-be.

If all goes well, the fertilized egg divides into more cells, and the rudiments of all the systems—the skin, nervous, digestive, circulatory, skeletal, muscular, genito-urinary, endocrine, and breathing systems —are differentiated within the first ten weeks following conception. At birth, all the systems are either already functioning or will be ready to function when needed.

One of the many traits that are determined at the moment of conception is the sex of the individual. One pair of the chromosomes is known to affect sex. These chromosomes are designated, for convenience, as X and Y. All eggs carry an X; sperms carry X or Y. If the fertilized egg carries XX, it develops into a female; if XY, into a male. Of a number of sex differences in growth and development,

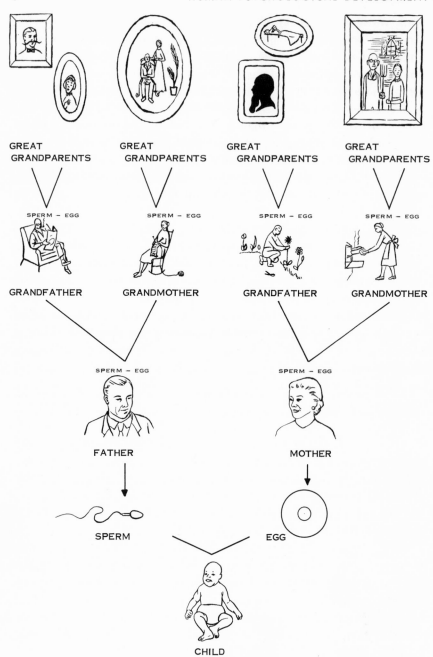

Fig. 1–1. Sperm and egg, the hereditary bridge between generations.

one is a difference in viability, females on the whole having a greater viability than males. For example, it is estimated from a study of abortions that about 120 male conceptions occur for every 100 female conceptions. Approximately 106 boys are born for every 100 girls. Thus we see that mortality between conception and birth is substantially higher for males than for females. Between birth and four weeks of age the excess of male over female deaths is 40 per cent. During the first year of life, the excess of male deaths is 33 per cent. The differential death rate of males and females continues through childhood. Although the difference becomes less marked after the adolescent years, it remains throughout life. Even though there are 106 boys to 100 girls at birth, the death rate is such that females gradually overtake males in numbers by around age 20, after which their numbers exceed those of males. This excess of females is about 3.5 per cent from age 30 to about age 60, when it increases sharply. At age 70 there are 10 per cent more women than men, and at age 80 there are 20 per cent more women than men.

There are other hereditary differences connected with sex which we shall have occasion to refer to in subsequent chapters.

Environment

Environment is all the conditions, circumstances, and influences, internal and external, that affect the development and behavior of living beings. It affects us in both general and specific ways. Factors such as geographical location and climate have affected the long-time development of the human species, as is evidenced by the fact that although civilizations have flourished in many kinds of geographical location, historically the temperate zones have produced the dominant civilizations of both ancient and modern times. Today, due to greatly improved means of enriching the soil, irrigation, and selecting species of plants and animals best suited to particular regions, better food can be grown in what were formerly less favorable situations. With modern methods of preserving food, the vitamin content can be retained. As a result, with modern methods of transportation, the people of most countries are now less dependent than previously upon the quality of soil and climate in their local situations.

The *effect of climate* on physical health is well known. Climate also affects our ambition and verve. An opportunity to get out-of-door exercise is important not only because of the effect of such exercise on the strength and health of the body, but also because it is one of the most effective means of releasing emotional tension. These factors ultimately make a difference in personality development. Competent observers recognize the effect of a sense of physical well-being on mental alertness as well as upon type of mood. Climatic changes also affect vitality and mood, a buoyancy of mood tending in many people to be associated with clear, dry weather, a mood of lassitude or even of depression tending to be associated with dark days and high humidity.

The most important environmental factor outside of nutrition and general health is the home. As a general rule, parents supply not only the genetic inheritance but also the physical and psychological home, and provide the first impact of the social and cultural inheritance upon the individual. If the biological parents do not supply the home, it is usually supplied either by adopting parents or by an institution for homeless children. The *physical home* may be a hovel or a palace. It may be unwholesome, or a home planned for health; a place where all the family must endure life in a single room, or one in which there is adequate privacy for individual pursuits. The *psychological home* may be one in which consideration of others, mutual cooperation, and love predominates; or it may be torn with strife and antagonisms, with crosscurrents of selfishness and struggles for domination. Whatever its physical condition and psychological atmosphere, psychologists are agreed that in the home are laid the foundations of physical and emotional health or the lack of it in one's lifetime.

The *neighborhood,* which represents the next environmental factor experienced by most children, provides influences which reinforce, or conflict with, but in any case extend those of the home. Crowded or spacious, sordid or beautiful, physically and psychologically wholesome or unwholesome, the neighborhood makes its mark on the growing body and personality. In it the quality of schools, churches, and other social institutions contributes to or interferes with growth and development of the body, mind, and personality. What the other children are like, how they conceive of themselves in relation to the things and persons around them, and how they behave are probably even more influential than schools and other institutions in molding the habits, feelings, thoughts, and attitudes of the growing child.

As the individual moves out of childhood, through adolescence into adulthood, the *vocation* or profession he chooses and trains for, enters, and spends his life in has an effect not only upon the kind of life he leads but also upon the kind of person he becomes. The *person he marries* and shares the most intimate and prolonged personal contact in his life span has a marked effect upon his development. Next to the influence of the parents during the periods of infancy, childhood, and adolescence, the husband or the wife is the most effective environmental influence upon the shaping of the personality.[53] The *friends* that one chooses in childhood, adolescence, and in adulthood exert a certain influence upon the interests pursued, the individual ideas attained, and the quality of purpose and practices throughout life. As Fig. 1–2 shows, the individual is the result of the interaction of many factors which exert a variety of influences upon him. In the long run, however, no matter what the inheritance and the early environment has been, the individual has opportunities to react in his own way, to determine from within himself much of what he does with his abilities, how much he leans on the strengths of his early life, and how much he overcomes or counters its weaknesses. Living beings are constantly renewing themselves. From earliest embryonic development, cells are wearing out and being replaced. What was gives way to what is; this in turn leads to what is to be. At every stage of adolescence and adulthood, the individual has opportunities to renew himself as a person, to change habits and attitudes, and to grow in psychological stature.

DIFFERENTIAL GROWTH PATTERNS

Although we frequently think of growth as increase in size, when the term refers to human beings it is not restricted to size or mass. Growth goes on at varying rates and for different lengths of time in the emotional, social, intellectual, and spiritual areas of the personality, as well as in the physical body.

The Physical Body

The greatest and speediest growth of the physical body occurs between conception and birth, the weight during this period increasing six billion times. In mass, however, 95 per cent of the adult weight is acquired between birth and adulthood. Growing is not

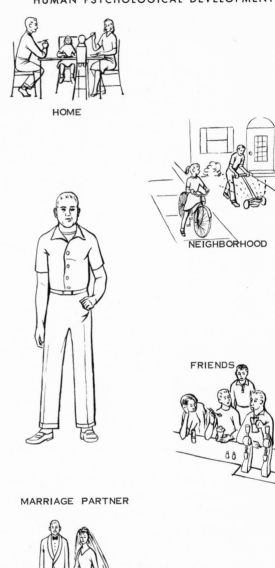

HOME

GEOGRAPHIC LOCATION
(CLIMATE)

NEIGHBORHOOD

VOCATION

FRIENDS

MARRIAGE PARTNER

Fig. 1–2. Environmental factors influence the development of the individual.

limited to the preadult years, of course. The physical body, as Fig. 1–3, line 1 shows, reaches its maximum height around 15 to 20 years of age; for girls the maximum is reached earlier than it is for boys, who occasionally continue to grow even at 21 or 22 years of age. This is about one-fifth to one-fourth of the life span. Weight usually stabilizes at about this time; if the individual is not careful about diet and exercise in the years of middle adulthood, weight may increase,

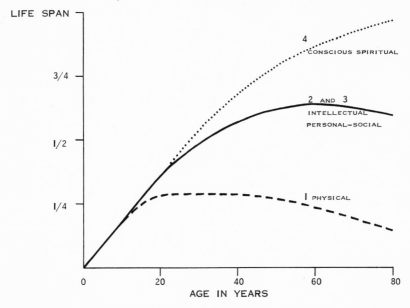

Fig. 1–3. Optimum development and decline in different areas of life.

resulting in the "middle-aged spread." Strength and coordination of muscles increase if they are put to enough of the right kind of use. Swimmers, tennis players, and golfers, for example, may continue to develop skills well into the twenties or thirties. If they continue to use such skills, the body responds with continuing strength and coordination well into middle adulthood, even though endurance lessens. For most people who get adequate exercise the decline of physical abilities is much slower than was the rise.

Intelligence and Intellectual Development

Intelligence, as measured by tests, reaches a ceiling of speed in skills such as reading, simple mathematical calculations, and rote memory at around 18 to 20 years of age. In breadth of knowledge and experience, and in depth and soundness of judgment, however, intelligence may continue to develop to around 35 to 40 years of age, as Fig. 1–3, line 2, shows. For some people, development continues even to ages 65 to 70. Even more than the body, the mind responds to continued training, and goes on to a continuously higher peak of ability until middle adulthood. This does not mean that a low ability can be made into a higher one by training, but rather that whatever ability the individual has inherited can reach its greater actuality by training and usage. Wide individual differences exist in ultimate ceilings. Those endowed with lower intellectual ability, even with the best training, reach their ceilings at an earlier date as well as a lower level. Students of intellectual development [12, 214] agree that people with superior intellectual ability, if they continue to study and to practice, generally continue to develop in intellectual power until middle life, maintaining a high level of performance (barring emotional or other interference) until later life, and declining more slowly than the average.

Personality

Personality development involves emotional, social, and spiritual growth and follows much the same pattern as intellectual development. Innate abilities in this area differ somewhat. There are, for example, differences in the physiological behavior of the nervous system and of the endocrine glands which to some extent determine the amount of energy available. The vitality of the body, along with its general health and appearance contributes to personal-social development. Influential as training and experience are in the development of intellectual ability, they are even more so in the development of personal-social ability. For the great majority of people, personality patterns established as results of infant and childhood experiences are likely to remain the predominant ones throughout life.

Some adolescents and young adults, however, awaken to the fact that changes in personality are possible. With this awakening may come a determination to direct the personality into more desirable patterns. With an increasing understanding of themselves, they face defects and weaknesses in their personalities and work courageously to correct them; they survey and evaluate their assets and proceed to develop them toward their maximum possibilities. With patience and continuing determination they carry their personal-social behavior beyond patterns typical of childhood into patterns desirable for adult life. When this occurs, personal-social ability continues to develop, and new abilities emerge well into middle life, as shown in Fig. 1–3, line 3.

Interrelations Between Areas

Body, intellect, and personality work closely together. The interrelationships between physical and psychological aspects of growth and development are close and pervasive. The state of the body affects both the efficiency of the intellect and the arousal and control of emotions. The emotional state is reflected in posture, tone of voice, ability to concentrate, and in disposition. Intellect, emotions, and body are what an industrialist might refer to as "a closely woven corporation," meaning that each branch of the business is important to and is affected by the others. Serving somewhat as the board of directors of this "corporation" is that part of the individual referred to by psychoanalysts as "the ego." By the ego, is meant that part of the personality which is concerned with conscious, intentional "purpose," by which one adapts to changing circumstances. In brief, the ego organizes experience. To the extent that favorable conditions have resulted in an ego that is strong and sound, the ego exercises control over future experience.[229]

Conscious Spiritual Development

Figure 1–3, line 4, calls our attention to conscious spiritual development and shows the optimum of such development. The development of an ego which as life goes on enables the individual to gain increasing insight into the relationships of human and other life and the inanimate universe is what we refer to here as spiritual development. A figure, of course, cannot tell the whole story. Some people do very little spiritual growing at any stage of their lives. In general, however, most people achieve some spiritual development. Life itself teaches something, opportunism or humanism, bitterness or acceptance, hedonism or true happiness. Whatever one's concept of spiritual growth is, it is evident that (as in the areas of physical and

intellectual development) many people never develop their full
spiritual ability.

Development Includes Both Growth and Decline

Figure 1–3 shows another fact: that the course of human development from conception to death includes both growth or emergence
of abilities and their decline. Development and decline proceed to
some extent simultaneously. During infancy and early childhood
growth predominates, but decline has already begun in the constant
wearing out of tissues and cells.[232] The loss of teeth in childhood and
their replacement by permanent teeth is one of the more obvious
examples of these simultaneous processes. Predominance of growth
over decline continues in most people until around forty years of age,
after which decline begins to exceed growth and emergence. The
situation with intelligence is not so obvious. Before his first birthday,
the individual possesses all the *neurons* (cells of the nervous system)
that he will ever possess. If his learning ability is low, he learns most
of what he is going to learn fairly early in life. If, however, his ability
is superior and his motivation high, his development and learning
continue for many years. His mental decline begins later and proceeds more slowly than it does in a person with less ability.

The same is true of conscious spiritual development. As in each of
the separate areas of development, people differ in spiritual ability
and in the use they make of it. According to most religions, the
spiritual worth of the individual has nothing to do with his ability; it
is the use he makes of the ability he has that counts.

In general, as we view the picture of growth and decline, we see
that the possibilities for continuing emergence and growth to high
ceilings of development increase through sequences: from the
physical through the intellectual, and the personal-social to the
spiritual. There are individual differences in ability in each of these
areas, and differences in the extent to which individuals develop the
abilities they have. In general, the less able person in any or all of
these areas, even with the best effort, reaches a lower ceiling and
declines earlier and more quickly than does the person of average
ability; both are surpassed by the person of superior ability (if, of
course, he uses and develops it) who grows over a longer time,
reaches higher ceilings, maintains them longer, and hence declines
later and more slowly than do the others.

Developmental Tasks

At each period of life we tend to be, in part at least, what we were and did in the preceding periods. What we do and experience in each period contributes to or detracts from what we are and what we can do in the succeeding periods. Havighurst [78] has clarified this idea in an interesting way. He conceives of each period of growth and development as being accompanied by certain tasks, which if accomplished contribute to success in the next period, and if not accomplished make development in the next period more difficult. He defines a developmental task as *"a task which arises at or about a certain period in the life of the individual, successful achievement of which leads to his happiness and to success with later tasks, while failure leads to unhappiness in the individual, disapproval by society, and difficulty with later tasks."* Although there is the possibility that his statement may be excessively dogmatic, it does serve a useful purpose in helping us to see why the life ahead of us is less difficult if we achieve certain levels of development as we go through the years.

Growth Periods

It is evident, then, that life and growth do not stand still at any age. The individual is continually changing, forever leaving what he has been and becoming someone different. Growth and development move forward in fairly clear-cut phases, each of which has certain characteristic aspects. This fact is so evident to students of human development that there is general agreement on the rough boundaries of the various phases of growth and development.

The *prenatal* period extends from conception to birth, during which time development from the fertilized egg to the complicated organism capable of living outside the mother's body takes place. The developmental tasks of the prenatal period are the attainment of adequate body size and form; the development of an adequately functioning skin, nervous system, circulatory system, skeleton, muscles, urinary system, and endocrine glands; of a digestive system and a breathing apparatus ready to function at birth; and of a reproductive system that indicates definite maleness or femaleness.

The period of *infancy* lasts from birth to about two years of age. Some of the tasks of this period are developing the postural controls which lead to walking, beginning the control of waste elimination, and beginning to relate oneself to other people.

Early childhood lasts to about six years of age. Some of the tasks of this period are increasing the control of body skills, learning to talk, completion of the control of waste elimination, beginning to adjust to people beyond the immediate family, beginning the development of emotional control, and beginning the development of a conscience.

Later childhood lasts from about six years to the onset of puberty. The word "puberty" comes from the Latin noun *pubes*, meaning "hair," and refers to the condition and age of the person when hair begins to appear under the arms and at the base of the abdomen in both sexes, and on the face in males. In this period some of the tasks are adjusting to school, improving the physical skills necessary for ordinary games, adjusting to the gang or play group, increasing emotional control, and further developing a conscience and a scale of values.

Puberty occurs as a rule in the early teens, *early adolescence* follows in the middle teens, and *later adolescence* in the later teens, often extending into the first years of the twenties. In adolescence, the tasks are accomplishing biological maturity, accepting one's physique as well as one's masculine or feminine role, establishing independence from parents and other adults, developing new relations with age-mates of both sexes, desiring and achieving socially responsible behavior, selecting and preparing for an occupation and thus achieving assurance of economic independence, preparing for marriage and family life or for the single life, and expanding one's conscious values in harmony with a sound philosophy of life.

Early adulthood extends from the early twenties into the early forties. The usual tasks are getting started and established in an occupation, selecting a mate and learning to live with him (her) or establishing a way of living as a single person. If the adult is married, he (or she) takes part in establishing and managing a home and in rearing children. Further tasks are accepting civic responsibility, finding a congenial social group, and continuing spiritual development.

Middle adulthood extends from the middle forties into the middle sixties. The usual tasks are accomplishing the biological changes of middle age, adjusting to other changes of middle age, continuing to carry full responsibility in one's occupation; if married, continuing to relate oneself to one's spouse as two developing individuals and assisting teen-age children to become responsible adults; adjusting to aging parents, achieving adult civic and social responsibility, and continuing personal and spiritual growth.

Later adulthood extends from the middle sixties to death. In this period the tasks are adjusting to declining strength, preparing for retirement from one's occupation, for the reduced income that often accompanies retirement, and, if married, for the eventual death of the spouse; establishing suitable physical and psychological living conditions, developing new recreational interests, establishing an explicit affiliation with one's own age group, making a conscious effort to retain one's physical and psychological flexibility, and continuing spiritual development.

SOME PRINCIPLES OF GROWTH

If we as individuals are to grow and be helpful in promoting the growth of others, we need some guiding principles. Many years of research in human development have revealed the following general principles by which growth proceeds:

Development Is Both Growth and Change

The body, for example, grows in size and changes in proportions and in ability to function. A small child is not a miniature adult; he is different in proportions and in strength, but even more so in the skills he can perform. The number of things that he can comprehend and do increases. The quality and complexity of the tasks that he can perform also increase.

Growth and Development Proceed as a Result Both of Inner Maturation and of Learning

By *maturation* is meant that process of inner growth and development by which the physical and psychological potentials of the individual move toward their maximum possibility. It is a sort of ripening. For example, all of the neurons for the lifetime are present by the end of the first year of life, but their connecting extensions grow as the trunk and limbs grow. During infancy and early childhood many of them lack the outer (*myelin*) sheath without which they cannot carry nerve impulses. Until these extensions (*nerves*) have reached a certain stage of development, the infant cannot control certain muscle groups such as those involved in coordinating the eyes. Until the bones and muscles of the back and legs have reached a certain stage of strength and ability to coordinate, he cannot sit, or stand, or walk. Until the growing child has attained a certain degree of maturation in the total nervous system, he cannot exercise control enough to turn distractibility into concentration of attention, nor can he remember or reason. Maturation may, perhaps, best be understood if we define it as including *any (normal) change which occurs as the individual grows older which is primarily dependent upon inherent growth factors rather than upon practice and experience.*

Learning, on the other hand, proceeds as the result of practice and experience. Learning occurs most efficiently when the person is sufficiently mature for that particular learning experience. When the person is ready, learning not only can take place, but, if permitted and encouraged at that particular time, takes place with greater efficiency than is possible at any other time in the growth cycle. If an attempt is made to force learning before the individual is sufficiently mature, results are minimal. If, on the other hand, the child is deprived of experiences when he is ready and eager for them, we may find later, when he is encouraged to learn, that he has become less able to learn or even has become indifferent about learning.

When a person is mature enough for a given learning experience, and if he is given suitable opportunities to learn, he practices with persistence and derives pleasure from his accomplishment. This urge to use recently matured abilities is compelling in the young child, who finds their use so rewarding that he frequently expresses his delight by throwing back his head and laughing as he experiences a new sensation or makes a new discovery. This urge is still a lively motivator in the older child who endlessly practices throwing a baseball, for example, or skating, or diving, or doing stunts on his bicycle, and who exults in showing off his latest accomplishment. Similarly, the late adolescent may, for example, practice at bridge playing, dramatics, or sports.

Development Follows a Pattern: It Is Regular, Orderly, and Predictable

Gesell [63] says that "each child sits before he stands; he babbles before he talks; he fabricates before he tells the truth; he draws a circle before he draws a square; he is selfish before he is altruistic; and . . . is dependent before he achieves dependence on self." All children control the musculature of the head and upper trunk before they control that of the lower trunk and legs. Control of larger muscles occurs before control of most of the finer muscles. Children play with other children as individuals before they can play an organized game in a group.

The major sequences of growth proceed in this predictable fashion. If we understand what the steps of growth are, we can see from a child's appearance and behavior what stage of development he is in, and can predict what steps lie ahead. Thus we can help him to prepare for next steps or, if need be, to make up steps he has missed.

The Tempo of Growth Is Uneven

Although the stages of growth occur in a regular, orderly and predictable sequence, the tempo of growth is uneven. Even though growth in the long run is forward and continuous, there are spurts, leveling-off periods, even occasional regressions in the growth process. Physically, for example, the infant grows with great rapidity compared with his rate of growth in the early childhood period, which in turn is rapid in comparison with the relatively slow rate of growth in the later childhood years. About the time of puberty, there is a relatively sudden spurt of physical growth, some boys growing as much as six to eight inches in one year and some girls almost as much. Again, in adolescence there is a tapering off until the individual reaches his adult height.

The changes in pace of the intellectual rate of development are less obvious, but they do occur. As in physical growth, the rate of acquisition of new intellectual abilities in the infant is extremely rapid. Much happens in the later childhood period, especially as the child enters school and formal training of the intellect is given substantial amounts of time and attention. At puberty, what appears to be a lag in intellectual development often occurs, and a drop in school grades is characteristic of the period. This happens because at this time a great deal of energy is being used in physical growth and experience. Another example of this can be seen in the twelve- to fourteen-months-old child who finds upright locomotion so exciting that he concentrates his full attention on it and seems, for the time being, to forget the words he has recently acquired in his vocabulary. He soon picks up momentum in vocabulary development, however, just as the adolescent in time returns to concentration on his school work.

Each Individual Grows at His Own Rate

Usually each individual passes through each of the major developmental stages, and experiences the changes in tempo of growth in each of the developmental areas; the sequences and the accelerations and decelerations are the same for all people. However, each individual passes through these sequences and varying tempos at his own rate, arriving at his own peculiar quality of development and performance.[19, 163] Child development specialists speak of slow growers, average growers, and fast growers, meaning that some children take a longer time, others a shorter time to pass through the growth stages than do most children. Figure 1–4 shows the general distribution of

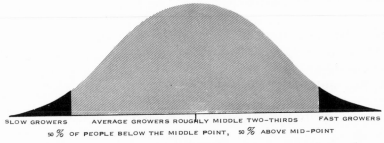

SLOW GROWERS   AVERAGE GROWERS ROUGHLY MIDDLE TWO–THIRDS   FAST GROWERS
50 % OF PEOPLE BELOW THE MIDDLE POINT, 50 % ABOVE MID–POINT

Fig. 1–4. Distribution of individual differences in rate of growth.

individual differences in this growth pace. The illustration indicates that about 50 per cent of the population lies below and about 50 per cent above the midpoint of the base line. In such a normal probability curve about two-thirds of the population is represented as being in the middle or average range, and about one-sixth at either side. The standards for growth in each of the different areas are based upon the usual or average achievements, translated as a rule in terms of age. Thus, we refer to physical height-age or weight-age, to mental-age, to social-age, meaning by "age" that height or weight, or that set of intellectual accomplishments or social achievements which on the average characterizes each chronological age.[163] Those who grow faster or more slowly in any area are said to be accelerated or retarded respectively in that area of growth.

Although on the whole people are fast, average, or slow in all areas of their growth, it is characteristic of any given individual that he is somewhat faster or slower in one area than in another. Even fast growers may prove to move more slowly, for example, in physical than in the intellectual areas, or vice versa. Slow and average growers show comparable unevenness, but, in general, move within the category of average or slow. So, too, the fast growers usually stay within the range of faster-than-average in all areas.

A few people are exceptionally uneven, being, for example, average in one area, and slow in another. It is unusual for the unevenness to occur in more than two areas, the fast grower being perhaps average but never slow in another area, the slow grower being perhaps average but never fast in another area. Although there is a popular notion that nature compensates abilities, such sayings as "beautiful but dumb" or "slow in the head, fast in the feet" being frequently heard, abilities are usually correlated. Studies show [12, 213, 214] that mentally gifted children are as a rule also fast in physical development, superior in health and appearance, and outstanding in social leadership. Feeble-minded children are likely to be abnormally slow in physical and social as well as in intellectual growth.

There are certain differences between the sexes in rate of growth in the different areas. Boys, for example, grow a little faster physically than girls at all stages except during puberty. From conception to birth, boys gain a little more than girls, and boys are born slightly longer and heavier than girls. They retain this lead until about nine years of age, when the girls forge ahead in both height and weight until about fourteen years, when the boys again take the lead, to keep it throughout the rest of the life span. Girls consistently run ahead of boys at all stages of language development, and usually make a smoother adjustment to school than do boys.

Rate and Pattern May Be Modified

Although the innate impulse for growth is strong, and even though the pattern sequence is fairly definite for all children, both the rate and the exact pattern may be changed by the child's internal or external environment. Such factors as climate or public hygiene may modify growth in whole populations. The quality of the child's home, of nutrition, rest, opportunity for play, psychological challenge, security in affection, and sound or unsound discipline are all important in determining how fast and how far the child's potentials are developed.

Prolonged deprivation in nutrition and other health needs may or may not lead to prolonged illness, but they do affect height and weight gains and general vitality.[19] Prolonged deprivation in the psychological areas or critical disasters in the home or in the family may noticeably affect the child's disposition and psychological vitality and may result in serious personality maladjustments. Conversely, optimal environments may promote maximum growth and development of both physical and psychological potentials.

Growth Aspects Are Interrelated

It is doubtless evident by now that all aspects of growth are interrelated. The body is the place in which the intellect and the personality develop. Its well-being is their well-being; healthy, vigorous, and flexible, it serves as an avenue for their expression and for experiences that are essential to their growth. Unhealthy, lazy, or rigid, it receives stimuli poorly and impedes growth of intellect and personality. Rested, well-fed, and exercised, the body contributes to peace of mind, efficient functioning of the intellect, and evenness of disposition. If the body is fatigued or ill, underfed, or under-exercised, the control of temper, fear, anxiety, and other destructive emotions is reduced. These emotions, in turn, affect the digestive, circulatory, eliminative, and other functions of the body and interfere with the free flow of neural associations in the brain.

Emotions and Growth

We have said little about emotions as such. Webster defines emotion as "a departure from the normal calm state of an organism of such nature as to include strong feeling, an impulse toward open action, and certain internal physical reactions; any one of the states designated as fear, anger, disgust, grief, joy, surprise, yearning, etc."

This concept of emotion is recognizable to most people. It is not so generally known, however, that emotion involves certain physiological reactions. Violent emotion affects parts of the nervous system and certain of the endocrine glands. The results may be increased rate of breathing and of the heart beat, constriction of blood vessels, increased contraction of the muscles, and changes in the function of the brain. These bodily accompaniments of vigorous emotion probably served as a means of protecting primitive man from danger in that they mobilized his body for fighting or for running away.

Basically this is what happens today under vigorous emotional reactions such as those involved in anger or fear. The body behaves as if it were preparing for vigorous physical action. The heart pumps more blood to the skeletal muscles used in fighting or running, and into the lungs, liver, and other organs concerned with the release of energy. Action is reflex and immediate, vigorous and physical, rather than intellectually controlled. Thought processes are arrested and digestion is slowed down.

What happens in the emergency situations involving strong emotion happens as pervasively, though less dramatically, in many situations that do not concern immediate physical survival. Under conditions of moderate fear, anxiety, or anger, the various systems mentioned are similarly although less drastically affected. As a result, growth and development of the individual in all areas is somewhat handicapped, at least temporarily.

SUMMARY

John E. Anderson,[5] for many years head of the Child Welfare Research Center at the University of Minnesota, has said:

> What manner of thing is the person whom we study from birth on to maturity? . . . It is a complex system moving forward in time by growing in complexity and size. . . . It receives much stimulation from the outside world and reacts to that stimulation in many and varied ways. As it grows, it contacts a wider and wider range of objects and persons; its ability to solve problems increases; it builds up many habits and skills; it gains in knowledge and self control. It is a complex manifold of many characteristics and potentials which together make up the total shape or form we call a human being.

> The human system has been described in terms of two levels; first as a physio-chemical machine which takes in food and converts it into action and waste products, and second as a sensory-neuromuscular mechanism which takes in stimulation and converts it into behavior by channeling the energy developed in the physio-chemical system into specific responses.

This course in psychological development is concerned with the individual from conception to death. It studies his emergence from helplessness and follows him through about twenty years of physical growth; it sees him assume his full responsibility which he carries for about forty to forty-five years, and it sees him passing on his responsibility to the next generation as his abilities decline. The course views the typical lifetime as one in which each normal individual takes more from society than he gives for the first fifteen or twenty years and for the last ten to fifteen years of life. For forty or forty-five years he gives more to society than he takes, because he makes up not only for his own non-productive years but also for those who are not normal and who cannot contribute to society or even care for themselves. He also hopes, in general, to better conditions for his fellow men.

Man proceeds from birth to death through certain developmental periods, each of which has its characteristic tasks to be accomplished. If he fails to accomplish them, he carries them over into his next period, in what some psychologists refer to as "unfinished business." His unfinished business not only may make the tasks of that period more difficult to achieve but may also distort his personality to some extent. If the tasks of each period are accomplished well, the individual moves forward with full momentum, free to use his abilities to the optimum. Hence, he is relatively happy at each stage of his development, even including the later stages of slowing down and decline.

SUGGESTIONS FOR FURTHER DISCUSSION

1. Look up the latest edition of *Statistical Abstract of the United States* for figures on death rates, birth rates, and life expectancy. Compare these with those given in this chapter. What do the trends seem to be? What are the implications of your findings?

2. Look up the same figures in the latest edition of *The Demographic Yearbook*, for several other countries. What implications can you draw from these?

3. Call to mind three or four people you know of ages 6 to 12; 20 to 30; 40 to 50; 65 to 75 or over. Where do they fit in the curves in Fig. 1–3?

4. How do you think emotions have affected the development of each of the three people you know the best?

5. Have some members of the class select readings from the list below for report to and discussion by the class. Report also excerpts from current newspapers and magazines that are relevant to the content of this chapter.

REFERENCES FOR FURTHER STUDY

DANIEL, R. S. *Contemporary Readings in General Psychology*. Boston: Houghton Mifflin Co., 1959. Selections: p. 26, Are the sexes really equal? p. 27, facts about mental deficiency; p. 28, concerning nature and nurture of genius; p. 44, a biologist looks at human nature; p. 46, a physical basis of mind: a philosopher's symposium; p. 49, What will your child be like? p. 59, When is human nature predetermined? p. 60, recent advances in the prediction and control of behavior.

DENNIS, W. *Readings in Child Psychology*. Englewood Cliffs, N.J.: Prentice-Hall Inc., 1951. Selection VI–4, a survey of studies of identical twins reared apart.

DEWEY, R., and HUMBER, W. J. *The Development of Human Behavior*. New York: The Macmillan Co., 1951. Ch. 2, human nature's interactive variables: three factors of (1) biological heritage, (2) environment, and (3) personality interact to develop human nature. Illustrative case.

DULANY, D. E., JR. (ed.). *Contributions to Modern Psychology*. New York: Oxford University Press, 1958. Selection 1, heredity and environment.

MARTIN, P. C., and VINCENT, E. L. *Human Biological Development*. New York: The Ronald Press Co., 1960. Ch. 2, Tables 2–1 and 2–2, summary of physical development from conception through old age; Ch. 2, the mechanisms of heredity; Ch. 12, how emotion is associated with endocrine and autonomic nervous system action.

MUNN, N. L. *The Evolution and Growth of Human Behavior*. Boston: Houghton Mifflin Co., 1955. Ch. 2, foundations of development: cells, chromosomes, genes; hereditary transmission; the nature and significance of environmental conditions. Ch. 7, basic factors in the behavorial development of children: maturation; learning; conditioned responses; conditioning applied to children.

OLSON, W. C. *Child Development* (2d ed.). Boston: D. C. Heath & Co., 1959. Ch. 1, an overview of child development.

SEIDMAN, J. M. *The Child: A Book of Readings*. New York: Holt, Rinehart & Winston, Inc., 1958. Selections: p. 1, a proposed reorientation of the heredity-environment controversy; p. 7, the conditioning of the human fetus *in utero;* p. 49, antecedents of aggression and effects of frustration in doll play; p. 54, inadequate masculine physique; p. 64, the discovery and encouragement of exceptional talent.

THORPE, L. P., and CRUZE, W. W. *Developmental Psychology*. New York: The Ronald Press Co., 1956. Ch. 2, problems and methods in the study of developmental psychology.

For film suggestions see Film Supplement, in the Appendix.

CHAPTER 2

Primary Influences on Development and Behavior

PHYSICAL FACTORS

Prenatal Development

The heredity of an individual begins to take effect immediately following fertilization. The normal fertilized egg divides and subdivides numerous times. Its stored food supply is rapidly exhausted. Having moved down the *Fallopian (uterine) tube,* the developing embryo establishes a maintenance system in the mother's uterine wall, from which it receives nutrients and oxygen, and through which its wastes pass into its mother's blood. As Fig. 2–1 shows, the normal maintenance system soon develops as a placenta, a sac, and an umbilical cord. Its efficiency is one of the factors that determine the quality of future growth. The quality of the placenta, sac, and cord is largely dependent upon the genes received by the fertilized egg at conception. If the development of the maintenance system is defective, the embryo may die. If it proceeds normally, the well-nourished embryonic body takes shape and the various systems form, and either begin to function prenatally, or prepare to function at birth, or when they are needed after birth.

Birth

Birth itself is a factor in development. Where modern prenatal and obstetrical care is available, birth has become far less of a hazard to the mother and child than it once was. Normal babies who have developed for at least seven months in the uterus have a good chance for life, but the closer to full term (about 266 days) birth occurs, the greater is the baby's chance for surviving outside the mother's body.

Efficiency of Body Systems

Most babies are born well formed and with their systems functioning normally. Only one live birth in 50 presents obvious external defects, but internal defects occur somewhat more frequently. Let us

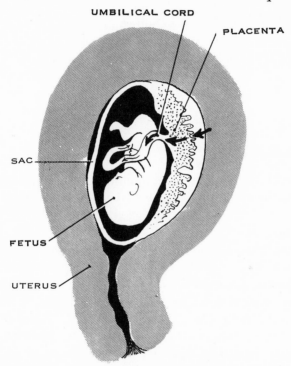

Fig. 2–1. The human embryo and its normal maintenance system.

assume, however, that a baby is well formed and that his systems are all functioning normally. This being the case, he eats, digests, breathes, eliminates wastes, cries, moves his muscles, and sleeps. The adequacy or inadequacy of his systems become apparent only as he grows and meets the tests of living. As new foods are added to his diet, for example, he may react unfavorably to some of them. His reactions may or may not be serious enough to interfere with his growth. His breathing apparatus may prove to be unusually susceptible to infection. Not only during his growth years but throughout life, the efficiency of his systems assists or interferes with the adequate functioning of his body, intellect, and emotions. Obviously, the length of life itself is affected by the way the systems perform.

Sensory Equipment

The different kinds of sensory equipment are not all equally well developed at birth. The sense of touch is the best developed, the senses of taste and smell are functioning to a certain extent, but the senses of sight, hearing, and equilibrium are functioning at only a rudimentary level. The baby is actually deaf at birth and for a few days thereafter. In the first weeks of life, the child is likely to appear to be without sensory defect. He may well be; but it is not unusual for sensory defect to become apparent as time goes on. The newborn or very young infant does not see and hear sufficiently well, for example, to warrant definite predictions concerning these senses. In all cases, of course, the individual must in time learn to interpret his various sensations.

Efficient sensory equipment is important although not essential to life. If one sense is defective from birth, the otherwise normal child compensates for the defect to some extent by greater development of the other senses.

Good sight is associated with alertness to objects in the environment and to the increasingly discriminating responses to them. It is also associated with freedom of movement in total body activity. The young child who continually bumps into or stumbles over things, or who seems less skillful in the use of his hands as he reaches for objects than is usual for children of his age, may have some visual defect. Such defects may be hereditary or they may result from infections and other environmental factors.

The child's ability to hear loud noises is apparent within a few days after birth. However, his reactions to sounds in the lower tonal range do not become clearly evident for some weeks. Some children remain subnormal in hearing without the handicap being detected for several years. The young child's ability to compensate for hearing deficiencies through efficient use of sight often proves adequate to keep the deficiency from becoming evident to any but trained observers. The United States Office of Education estimates that about 400,000 children in the United States have hearing impaired to the degree that they would benefit from special classes or schools, if these are available. Deafness, either total or partial, results from many causes, some kinds being hereditary, others being the result of diseases such as measles.

Visual and auditory defects, particularly, are handicaps to development in the infancy and childhood periods, since sight and hearing reinforce touch as major avenues for learning. Even with the compensations by way of another sense, children handicapped in these two senses require special training if their intellectual and personal-social development is to proceed satisfactorily. If the child is deficient in both of these senses, he lives under a very serious handicap to learning and to freedom of movement. Helen Keller was the first such child to receive the training needed to develop what, in her case, proved to be superior intelligence and an unusually strong personality. Special training that makes possible the development of the intellectual and personality potential that such handicapped children possess, is now available to a limited number of children in some locations.

In adolescence and adulthood, visual and auditory abilities are important factors in the selection of vocation, mate, and the type of home, social, and community life. As age advances, sight and hearing usually become impaired. Generally, however, properly prescribed glasses and hearing aids make it possible for the individual to function fairly well throughout the later years.

Intellectual Equipment

The individual's capacity for intellectual development is dependent upon the efficiency of his whole body, particularly of his nervous system, and most particularly of the upper portion of the brain, the *cerebrum*. Relatively inefficient organs of the body other than the cerebrum do not rule out the possibility of highly efficient cerebral activity. However, the individual with an efficiently functioning body is most likely to develop high efficiency of intellect, provided he has the potential and the motivation, because it is by means of his other organs that he develops his contacts with the world around him, as well as the ideas in his own self.

About 1880, psychologists began to attempt to measure innate intelligence or intellectual potential. They agreed to consider the intelligence which most people exhibited on their tests, at any given age, as "average." Various kinds of tests were devised and administered to large numbers of children. The score on certain of these tests was taken to indicate the *mental age* of the individual. Based on the Stanford-Binet test, the following formula:

$$\frac{\text{Mental age (M.A.)} \times 100}{\text{Chronological age (C.A.)}} = \text{Intelligence quotient (I.Q.)}$$

has been used extensively as an admittedly rough measurement of intelligence. An example may clarify the use of this formula. If a child 6 years and 8 months (80 months) of age attains a test score which the psychologist has come to expect of most children of 8 years and 4 months (100 months), the child is said to have a mental age of 8 years and 4 months. Substituting these figures, the formula reads:

$$\frac{100 \times 100}{80} = 125$$

an I.Q. considerably above average for the population.

As we have said, this sort of measurement is understood to be approximate rather than absolute. Psychologists are constantly working to improve their tests, to include in them only tasks that are demanded of one in actual living, in order that the score may indicate more precisely what the individual's hereditary capabilities are under any circumstances of the external environment.

Obviously, most people are born with normal nervous systems and average intellectual ability. Since the quality of the brain, like that of any other organ, is dependent to a certain extent upon the genes received at conception, it follows that innate intelligence is inherited also.

The I.Q. of the children in a family tends to be like that of the parents, their I.Q. usually varying from not more than a few points above or below either parental I.Q.

The following simplified table gives an idea of the degrees of intelligence of the native-born white population of the United States, as indicated by scores on the Stanford-Binet test:

I.Q.	CLASSIFICATION
140 and above	Very superior
120–139	Superior
110–119	High average
90–109	Average
80– 89	Low average
70– 79	Borderline defective
69 and below	Mentally defective

Generally speaking, individuals who as children score at the high levels remain superior in intellectual ability and vocational success as they go through life.[214] In one group of such children which was followed from childhood into middle adulthood,[214] 86 per cent of the boys were at mid-life engaged in professional or semiprofessional work, or in higher categories in business. Even as early as 45 years of age, 4 per cent of them were included in *Who's Who in America*. This latter, highly gifted group included individuals from all the ethnic elements in the area covered by the study, namely, Mongolians, Negroes, and Caucasians. They came from various kinds of homes, but the majority were the children of parents in professional and upper socioeconomic levels.

While children with high I.Q.'s seldom if ever come from parents with below-average I.Q.'s, children who make low scores on I.Q. tests may appear in families of all levels of intelligence. Low mentality may be inherited, caused by circumstances that are congenital (induced during prenatal life or at birth), or it may be caused by postnatal accidents, infections, or physiological aberrations.

The term *feeble-minded* is applied generally to individuals whose greatest mental development does not exceed the level considered normal for a twelve-year-old child, no matter how long they live or what training they receive. Individuals whose mental age never exceeds that of the normal twelve-year-old child but is not below that of the normal seven-year-old are referred to as *morons;* those whose mental age is between that of a normal seven-year-old and that of a two- to three-year-old are termed *imbeciles;* and those who never exceed what is expected of normal two- to three-year-olds are termed *idiots.* Some individuals with below-average mentality are among the useful members of society in that they are able to help perform the necessary but uncomplicated work of society and are happy doing it. They are those who lack the ability for formal intellectual education beyond elementary school, but who can be taught simple, noncompetitive tasks. They are thus able to care for themselves and for their families.

The level of mentality and of creative ability affects the developmental pattern of the personality, hence, the total life of the individual. The child who is especially talented in music, for example, may willingly put in long hours of practice. His life and personality develop quite differently from that of the boy whose baseball bat and glove lean against the piano while he concedes to his parents a half hour of practice. Likewise, the life of a person talented in abstract mathematics but lacking in mechanical aptitude differs from that of one who lacks mathematical ability but who enjoys working with tools. There are, of course, people who possess both mathematical and mechanical aptitude and those who lack both. We may argue that all human beings have a right to equal opportunity to develop their talents, but it is obvious that they are not created equal in respect to those talents.

THE CHILDHOOD FAMILY

The First and Most Important Postnatal Environment

The childhood family is a primary factor in growth and development because it provides the first social-cultural environment of the individual. Even if the child is adopted or living in an institution, the parents or substitute parents who care for him provide the early environment for the emergence and modification of his inherited potentialities. In infancy, the family is the child's whole world. In every contact between parent and child there is what psychologists call communication. Through this communication, the infant either learns to be at ease with his world, or to be uncertain and anxious about what may happen to him in it. Quite as important as adequate physical care are the attitudes and feelings of those who administer this care. The baby soon responds to tender, loving care or to parental resentment at his intrusion into the household. The unconscious sense of security or insecurity thus established affects his physical and psychological growth throughout his life.

The Parents or Substitute Parents

Parental attitudes and ability to provide a favorable environment for growth depend upon many factors. The most important of these is the parents' own family background—how their parents felt about them and dealt with them, what their parents considered of fundamental or superficial importance, and the values their parents held and passed on.

The coming of a child has a profound effect on the lives of his parents, changing the distribution of their daily activities, their hours of rest, their social life, their financial responsibilities, and their relations with each other. Wide variations exist among parents in the motives and feelings which they bring to parenthood. Even during pregnancy, parents-to-be begin to respond to the coming individual. Although women in pregnancy show psychological tendencies and traits that are characteristic of them prior to pregnancy, the experience itself intensifies and modifies these traits. One woman may feel an inner fulfillment, another only an unwanted interruption to her way of life. One man may feel a flow of importance and welcome the increased responsibility, another may resent the added burden.

A Child Development Study made at Harvard University [185] showed that although most of the mothers studied welcomed pregnancies, particularly if it was a first child, not all were happy about the fact of pregnancy. Many parents find a pregnancy under way when they had hoped to avoid one. If the parents are married when the pregnancy occurs, and if they are financially able to look ahead to the rearing of a child, the pregnancy, even though at first unwelcome, is usually accepted and when the baby arrives he is warmly received. In periods of economic prosperity the birth rate rises. This may be because parents feel that they can rear children comfortably. In periods of economic depression the birth rates drops, partly because the marriage rate drops and partly because pregnancies are avoided. There may be still other factors that affect the number of conceptions in such periods.

Once the child is born some parents accept him for what he is and encourage his unfolding personality. Other parents unconsciously have children to continue the family name, to fulfill some sense of duty, or for prestige. They may attempt to gratify their own unfulfilled ambitions through him. Some parents are adoring parents, some are kind and matter-of-fact, others are annoyed at the inconvenience the child imposes by his presence. Some parents move into the daily routine care of the children with self-confidence, joy, and efficiency; others are awkward and unskilled, anxious and unsure of their abilities as parents. If a child is being reared in an institution he may receive insufficient affection or tender care, and less personal attention than a child in a family home.

Parents set the prevailing emotional atmosphere of the family home. Children reflect this atmosphere and tend to adopt the emotional patterns which surround them. For example, humor is contagious in the family, as are gaiety, concern for others, and many other desirable personal traits and outlooks. The reverse of these may prevail. Value concepts are also passed on in families; they are "caught" rather than "taught." Students often state that they were never conscious of being taught honesty, responsibility, or dependability. They are likely to say, "I don't remember my parents specifically pointing out these traits—they just lived them and expected me to do so too." This is not to imply that talks about honor or responsibility are futile. They are helpful, especially in the later childhood period when abstract ideas are forming and when generalizations are being made. Talking, however, may be futile if it is done by parents or by other people who do not practice what they preach.

Each Parent Influences Each Child

Just how a given child among several children reflects the traits and attitudes of his parents or the people with whom he lives, depends upon a number of factors. Among these are whether the trait is characteristic of the male or of the female parent, and whether the child is a boy or a girl. Although children of either sex are responsive to both parents, there are circumstances in which the boy is more responsive to the mother and the girl to the father, and vice versa.

Physical care of the infant has, in our culture, until recently been done almost entirely by the mother or by some other woman, such as a nurse. However, fathers are sharing increasingly in the care of infants and young children, and most fathers enjoy this. The child thus cared for has the experience of close relationship with both parents (people of both sexes) in the earliest and most formative part of his life.

During the early childhood period the child becomes conscious not only of self but also of maleness or femaleness. He begins both consciously and unconsciously to model himself after the parent of the same sex. Customarily, both mother and father encourage manly traits in the son and womanly traits in the daughter. Each child is influenced in the formation of his or her sex role, however, mainly by the parent who sets the pattern for behavior by members of this sex. Psychoanalysts believe that during the early childhood period the little boy, in his awareness of his sex, becomes jealous of his father and unconsciously wishes to have his mother to himself. Conversely, the little girl becomes jealous of her mother in relation to her father. Opinions differ as to how intense or how universal is this so-called *Oedipus complex* * (the *Elektra complex* is the feminine

* Named from the Greek play in which Oedipus falls in love with his mother, not knowing she is his mother.

equivalent). There is speculation that with the increasing physical care by fathers of both boys and girls in the infancy period, this aspect of psychological development may be somewhat modified.

During later childhood, boys and girls give a good deal of time and attention to their playmates, yet remain close to both parents. In puberty and adolescence, emancipation from the family is in process, but as sexual awareness is sharpened by biological maturation, both the boy and the girl frequently experience a close attachment to the parent of the opposite sex. Since the girl usually goes through this process earlier than the boy, she is likely to be especially close to her father around 13 to 14 years of age, and the boy to his mother a year or so later than this. The young adolescent is deciding who and what he is as a person. He or she selects a model from among real or imaginary adults to serve as a pattern. Although this model is often some movie or TV personality, it may be the parent of the same sex. In this case, the parent again has an especially strong influence upon the development of the child. The early adolescent's model for himself may be an older sibling (brother or sister) of the same sex. Siblings who are three or more years older sometimes exert upon their younger siblings an influence comparable to that of parents.

Children do not choose their parents; neither, unless the child is adopted, do the parents choose their children. As children appear, bearing hereditary characteristics as they do, they may prove to be like or unlike the father or the mother. For this reason a given child may be especially favored or rejected. A boy, for example, may be favored by his father because of close similarity between them, or he may be rejected because the father sees in him traits he rejects in himself. So it may be for the girl and her mother. The girl who closely resembles her mother may be especially loved or rejected by her father because he especially loves or has come to dislike the mother. So, for comparable reasons, the boy who closely resembles his father may be especially loved or rejected by his mother. Rejections are probably more often unconscious than conscious, so that a parent may tend to be more severe with one child and more affectionate with another, yet would be unable to explain why this is so.

One of the difficult tasks of parenthood is the acceptance of each child for what he is. One study [119] of 60 "planned for" children who had developed serious behavior problems showed that, although they were planned for and therefore were welcome, in each case the parents had planned, not for *a* child, but for a particular type of child.

As a result, they were unable to adjust to the child who arrived because he did not fit their plans. The resulting emotional confusion for the child was thought to be the precipitating factor in the development of behavior problems. Evidently, if a child is to develop his optimum potential, he needs to be accepted and cherished for what he is: big or little, quick or slow, handsome or plain.

Even though they cherish all their children, at least as far as they know how to do so, almost every parent recognizes that he feels closer to one or another of the children than to the others. The mother may feel closest to the oldest son and the father to the oldest daughter, or both to the youngest child, or to an in-between child, than to the other children. Whether or not this results in favoritism depends upon the ability of the parents to control the impulse to express special affection for the preferred child.

Family Fulfillment of Basic Needs

Every individual has needs which are basic to his growth and development. Some of these are the physical needs for food, warmth, and protection from danger. Other needs are psychological, such as the need to be cherished and understood, the need to feel useful and important to someone, and the need to develop and express innate abilities.

Satisfaction of all these needs is important if the individual is to survive and prosper. Unless the physical needs in childhood are fulfilled at least reasonably well, the individual does not live to grow up. If the psychological needs are not fulfilled to at least a minimum degree, the infant, child, or adult does not prosper physically. Tensions interfere with his acceptance and utilization of food, with circulation, waste removal, and other bodily functions. Neither does he prosper in intellectual, emotional, or personal-social growth. Reasonable satisfaction of physical and psychological needs promotes optimal growth and development. Frustration of needs to any serious degree is reflected in all areas of growth and development. The manner in which the family provides for these needs during infancy, childhood, and adolescence influences both the pattern and rate of development in all areas.

The Best Kind of Love

Prior to the 1920's, the death rate of babies in foundling homes in the United States was considerably higher than that of babies in their own homes. In many such institutions, babies were known to receive adequate food and other material necessities but little personal attention. When the practice of giving personal attention began, by the nurse holding each baby close to her warm body, patting him gently and talking quietly to him as he took his bottle, for instance, a noticeable decline in the death rate occurred. Current studies [19, 164] show a close correlation between affectionate, accepting behavior by the parent and general well-being in the baby.

The need for affection is not a necessity for babies only; it is a basic need of everyone at every age. The toddler needs affection, as can be seen in the way he follows his mother around the house, reaching up to her, leaning against her, crying when she leaves him. The nursery school or kindergarten child may run gaily away from his mother to join his playmates, but after a time grows anxious to see her again. The child of school age puts on an appearance of nonchalance and is angry if his mother kisses him in the presence of his pals, but he misses it if she fails to tuck him into bed at night. The adolescent puts on a great show of independence and even transfers some of his need for affection and approval from adults to his peers, but is still genuinely dependent upon his parents for affection and approval. The adult expects to find love and mutual dependence in marriage; the widow or widower is lost for a time, after a happy marriage, without the accustomed love and support of the mate. Adults may cherish and be cherished by their children in a relationship satisfying to both. Occasionally this relationship is too close, and the parent or child—or both—may find it difficult to adjust to the child's growing need for independence in his childhood, adolescence, and even occasionally on into his adulthood.

A child who knows that he is cherished proceeds with assurance and is desirably aggressive; his growth in all areas tends to prosper. The unloved child is likely to be either timid or undesirably aggressive. Too small to have friends he can depend on, he feels alone in a frightening world which he senses he cannot deal with. As he becomes older and more conscious of his loneliness, his infant anxiety becomes childish panic, and later on the adolescent's sullen distrust of or aggressiveness toward society. Since he cannot at any of these stages of growth win the affection and reassurance that he craves, he may exhibit a range of behavior all the way from anxious attempts to please parents and others to panicky or aggressive boasting and "showing off." His behavior often deepens parental annoyance with him and may result in further evidences of their rejection of him.

Thus a vicious circle is established in which matters become progressively worse; seriously delinquent or withdrawn behavior may be the result if he remains in these circumstances for too long a time.

Symptoms of maladjustment occasionally appear in well-loved children whose parents do not express their affection in terms that children can understand. Ann was such a child. At six, she was puny and excessively shy. She lacked initiative with school work and in all personal contacts. She was becoming increasingly quiet and sullen. Her parents, of New England background, had married late and both continued to teach school after Ann was born. Ann was their only child. She was the most important person in their lives, but they were afraid of overindulging her. As a result, they carefully pointed out her faults to her but were slow to praise her. They seldom kissed or hugged her or gave her any form of physical affection. They loved her deeply—but she did not know this. The people at the clinic to which the parents were referred explained to them the child's needs and suggested that they express their love in ways the child could understand. Fortunately, the parents understood quickly, and began to treat Ann differently. The effect on Ann was soon evident. Within a few days, she seemed less anxious and was sleeping and eating better. Within a few weeks, she sometimes hummed and skipped as she went about her home chores. Within six months she had gained weight and was a happy youngster. Ann's case illustrates the fact that children need not only to be loved, but to know that they are loved.

On the other hand, overindulgence may make a child a victim of his own whims. Children intuitively tend to look upon adults as people wiser and more experienced than they are. They need help in achieving a balance between what they want and what is good for them, and in directing their energies toward accomplishment which is not possible without sustained effort. If their every wish is granted from infancy on, children learn to expect that they have only to wish in order to have their wishes fulfilled. If they never have to struggle to recover a fallen toy or to feed or dress themselves, they never learn the thrill that comes from effort expended with satisfying results. If they never have to wait for the fulfillment of a desire or never learn to choose among their many desires, they arrive at a stage where they do not know what they want.

Overindulgence sometimes obscures rejection of the child by a parent. The parent indulges the child in a conscious or unconscious attempt to compensate for the fact that he actually rejects him. Eddie was in such a situation. At five years of age, his mother brought him to a clinic because of severe temper tantrums. He had been increasingly unmanageable since he was two years old. After seeing mother and child together for a few minutes, it was evident to the clinic personnel that Eddie had never received any constructive discipline and that his every whim was being catered to. He proved to be an illegitimate child whose maternal grandparents had insisted that his mother rear him, but who never permitted her to forget the mistake that had produced him or how much care she owed him for bringing him into the world without a father. The mother was constantly fighting her sense of guilt and unconsciously wishing that he had never been born. Only by indulging him could she feel that she was making up to her parents, to him, and to her own conscience for her mistake. The child, in these circumstances, was fighting for security in a rejecting home.

Fortunately, there are many families in which the members are concerned to see that the needs and reasonable wishes of each are fulfilled. Each finds satisfaction in finding ways to give enjoyment to the others. If the children have done a good job, the parents in such a family compliment the children on doing their chores well. An older child helps a younger one to learn to throw a ball or to do his homework. A child who has learned how to make coffee safely makes it on Saturday morning and brings a cup to each parent in bed. In such an atmosphere, even the youngest child catches the idea, learns to contribute his share of the family's work, and finds excitement and satisfaction in planning surprises for the others. Children in such families derive benefit from learning to give of themselves while they are receiving from their elders. This is one way of learning what is probably the best kind of love.

The Best Kind of Discipline

Everyone needs discipline (rules of conduct) in order to adjust his needs and desires to those of others, and in order to keep the affection and approval of people around him. Throughout life, self-discipline is necessary for safety, for reasonable conformity to social norms of acceptable behavior, for taking responsibility, for maintaining self-control, and for deferring immediate satisfactions in favor of long-time goals.

In childhood, discipline serves two functions: first, to control actions of the child occurring at the moment, and second, to establish standards that will become an integral part of the child, thus modifying his subsequent behavior. Discipline is necessary to emotional security. Without clear standards by which the child can orient his behavior and control his impulses, he feels confused and insecure.[8] The absence of such standards places too great a burden on his limited degree of self-control and understanding. When his family is completely permissive, the child is afraid of the consequences of his own uninhibited behavior, and of the ensuing retribution and guilt.

Most people think of discipline as some sort of force that makes them do things that they would not do naturally, or as punishment for having done something they should not have done. However, a certain amount of discipline is innate in the healthy body at birth and throughout life. The healthy nervous system sends nerve impulses along the nerves smoothly, causing healthy muscles to maintain good tone and to contract and relax as needed. The healthy heart beats regularly, and the healthy breathing apparatus develops a regular rhythmical activity. These and other bodily activities speed up or slow down as needed, thus enabling the body to adapt to environmental changes. If these activities do not occur in a disciplined manner, the person experiences trouble or discomfort of some kind or another.

The baby's daily schedule itself is a form of discipline, because it helps him to adapt his inner physical needs gradually to some regularity, which in time fits him into the family schedule.[18] Discipline for the young child is largely a process of helping him to fit into the family, and to learn that others are members of the household also. As he grows older, discipline helps him fit into his expanding world, to stick to a job until it is well done, to practice skills until he performs them as well as his talent permits, and to eliminate nonproductive behavior. No artist, for example, develops his potential talent without many hours of disciplined practice. If he perfects his skills, critics refer to him as a highly disciplined artist. Likewise, the scientist could not unravel the complexities of problems in his field of study without rigorous self-control and the capacity to work with intense concentration for long periods of time.

Self-discipline means not doing many things that one may feel like doing, if doing them would interfere with one's future well-being or with the needs and rights of others. It means doing many things one would prefer not to do, if doing these things contributes to the fulfillment of the needs and rights of others, or to one's own future well-being.

Discipline Can Free the Individual

Discipline of the right sort frees the individual; it defines boundaries beyond which society has found danger to exist. The following illustration may show how wise restriction may operate. Some years ago, when progressive education was feeling its way, a psychologist in a nursery school decided that the play-yard should not be enclosed, and that the children should, on their own initiative, learn to keep inside the yard. He ordered the fence removed. This nursery school was in a large city, and its small yard was on a busy street. On the first fenceless day, the children, sensing the danger of the street, played less freely than usual. On succeeding days, they played only around the sandbox in the corner nearest the building, and did not play active games that required skipping and running about the yard. This behavior went on for a week, at the end of which the nursery school director requested that the fence be replaced during the week end. On the Monday following, the children fanned out all over the fenced-in yard and engaged in all kinds of active play, possibly without even noticing that the fence was there, but sensing the security that it gave them. Rather than restricting them, the fence had freed them. It marked the line of danger, and by merely being there prevented them from going where they might have been injured.

So it is, by and large, with the rules and laws of social convention. Social conventions incorporate the experience of generations in areas of behavior that are fraught with danger both to the individual and to society itself. It is not only nursery-school children who appreciate the freedom and security that come from knowing clearly defined lines of danger; adolescents appreciate lines of restriction, too, even though they may do a great deal of complaining about them. Most thoughtful adults, looking back on their childhood, feel a sense of gratitude for the discipline that helped them acquire whatever measure they have of self-control, of consideration for others, and of ability to take responsibility.

Family Patterns of Discipline Differ

Some parents see in their relationships with their children only the necessity to make them happy as each day goes by, not recognizing that this treatment may deprive the children of the strength that comes from wise restriction, and that it is likely to give them a false idea of what to expect from life outside the home. Such parents permit the child to select his activities as nearly as they can make it possible for him to do so. They give him a minimum of guidance, and may even consider guidance as domination of the child's personality. They lean over backwards to get the child to express his ideas, to say what he wants to say, in order to encourage his "self-expression." They state their own ideas as little as possible in order not to "indoctrinate" him. They praise his every effort in order to give him "self-confidence." They avoid correcting him or calling his errors to his attention so as not to give him "an inferiority complex." Parents who behave this way fail to realize that children need help in knowing what is good for them, and that only when children are sure that their parents will protect them and will see that they do what is good for them, can they feel genuinely secure.

On the other hand, some parents dominate the child's every move and even attempt to control his thoughts. They feel they know better than any child could what is good for him all the time. They give the child no opportunity to indicate what kind of individual he is, what ideas he could have if allowed to express them, what interests and talents he could develop if he were allowed to experiment in areas of his own interest. In such instances, parental expectations are usually high, and punishments for failures or for deviations from parental orders are severe. The child tends to react to such a situation in one of two or three ways. Either he is cowed into submission, afraid to think or act on his own, robbed of initiative and without sparkle of any kind, or he may rebel, fighting aboveboard or undercover for the right to be himself, hating his parents and the authority they represent, setting himself against even reasonable authority of all kinds for the rest of his life. Occasionally, a child discovers that such parents can be "managed." Some children do this by their charm; others do it by guile such as exaggerated deference or flattery. A few do it by "tattling" on their siblings, thus seeming to be "helping" the parents. Obviously, none of these reactions can be sound bases for optimal personality development.

In some homes one parent proceeds permissively, the other by domination. There is a good deal of evidence [149, 185] that, unfortunate as is either of the previously described patterns of family discipline, the most destructive pattern is the one in which two parents operate in the same home, one at one extreme, the other at the opposite extreme in discipline. Studies [19] show that it is not necessary for the two parents to pursue the same methods of discipline if they support each other in general aims and in specific permissions or denial of permissions. However, it is highly desirable for them to agree that, even if they differ they will support each other in specific instances. It is destructive for the child to discover that he can play one parent against the other, thus being able to do what he wants rather than do what is good for him. This agreement is also highly desirable for parents and teachers, who must work in some sort of harmony—or at least of mutual understanding—if the child is to develop soundly.

However, some differences of approach between parents in the home and between parents and teachers can be constructive because these differences serve as preparation for later life. As the child moves through school, for example, teachers will differ in methods of handling children. In adulthood, as the individual enters employment, there will be major differences in methods of approach to employees. In marriage, there will be two partners who are the products of different childhood disciplines. Capacity to adjust to differing personalities and to different patterns of human relations is a useful asset throughout life.

Types of Discipline

Many psychologists [9, 91, 185] believe that concepts and controls are established most effectively when discipline consists of reinforcements (*rewards*) as well as inhibitions (*punishments*) for behavior. Both encouragement and restraint are needed. To be helpful to the child's mental and emotional growth, both rewards and punishments need to be deserved and understood by the child. If either reward or punishment is given when not deserved, the child is confused and misled. A question may arise here as to what is meant by "deserved." Generally speaking, reward or punishment is deserved if the child, who has had the opportunity to learn from previous experience what is desirable behavior, has either performed that behavior better than might have been reasonably expected, or has failed to perform it as well as might be expected.

Punishment should not grow out of antagonism, but out of understanding and justice. Rewards and punishments need to fit the child and the situation both in type and in severity. Rewards and punishments that are excessive may do actual physical or emotional harm and almost certainly confuse the child's evaluation of himself and others. Rewards from a person whom the child knows from experience has his welfare at heart contribute to the child's legitimate self-esteem; punishments from such a person give rise to a mild anxiety to keep the approval of that person, which is effective in developing desirable adjustments in behavior.[9, 77]

Most children recognize the right of the parents to impose controls and do not question the legitimacy of disciplinary measures. The Survey Research Center of the University of Michigan [208, 209] found that of over a thousand eleven- to eighteen-year-old girls studied, the majority thought it legitimate and necessary for parents to make and enforce rules and agreed with the rules their particular parents made. Adolescent boys were also found to agree that clear-cut guide lines for behavior set up by parents were necessary and desirable.

Severity does not, as a rule, teach a child to do a task as well as he would do it with encouragement. No child, for example, can be taught to use the toilet, or any other activity involving muscle control, as effectively under strict and grim disciplinary methods as he can by encouragement and gentle persuasion.[185] Scolding a child who stutters only makes him stutter more.[10, 94] Beating a child physically may fail to stop his undesirable behavior, and even if it does succeed in changing the offending behavior it may, as we say, "break his will" by shattering his self-esteem.

Some parents use physical discipline because they have not discovered better ways of handling a child. One mother, for example, left alone to rear her son, said, "I does my best by him; I beats him all the time." As a result, the boy was bewildered and discouraged, but since he did not fear his mother or feel that he quite deserved all he got in the way of punishment, he had not developed a feeling of inadequacy. Somehow, through other things that she did for him, he seemed to sense that she was doing the best she knew to help him. Kanner [104] says that occasional spanking, yelling, and mismanagement leave no abiding ill-effects upon a child who feels that his parents "like him, and think he's all right." Some children deliberately invite physical punishment if they have no better way of getting parental attention, as in the case of one boy who continued behavior which got him severe whippings from his father simply because it was the only way he had of getting any attention from him.

The most frequently used punishment in the middle and upper socioeconomic groups in the United States is deprivation of privileges. This is effective as soon as the child is old enough to grasp simple cause-and-effect relationships. It works best when the privilege denied has some relevance to the offense committed. Many parents use a "natural consequences of the act" technique. For example, if the child refuses to eat his dinner, he gets no more food until the next meal; if he hits another child, and the child hits him back, this is the expected result. This latter type of punishment breaks down, however, when the child fails to make his bed or straighten his room and is left to live in it as it is. Since he does not have the parent's sensitivity to the untidiness, it fails to punish him.

Increasing numbers of parents try to use reasoning as a way of helping children to do the desired thing. Before three or four years of age, reasoning is unlikely to be effective. In simple form, it may be effective at about three or four, and becomes increasingly effective as the child's intelligence develops. In the opinion of most specialists, reasoning is the most effective method with normal adolescents and adults. Consistency in discipline helps the child to know what to expect and what the consequences of misbehavior are likely to be. Consistency breaks down as a principle when it becomes stereotyped to the point that the child can calculate in advance whether or not misbehavior will be worth the consequences.

Praise for accomplishment is effective in helping children to want to improve behavior and skills. Parental approval is a potent instrument in discipline. However, praise needs to be used judiciously, not just when the parent happens to feel in a pleasant mood, but when the child has done something really well. Otherwise the child can establish no reasonable standard by which he can measure his achievements.

Prevention of misbehavior is better than cure. A well-run home sets up situations which meet the needs of the children. It enables them to be occupied constructively but leaves plenty of free time and opportunity for "blowing off steam," and for cultivating individual interests. Schedules reasonably conceived and adhered to help the various members of the family live and work together smoothly and efficiently. The parents decide everything for infants. As the

children grow, family meetings give everyone opportunities to consider both the parents' and the children's points of view and to arrive
at a feasible working set-up for changing family life.

Thus we see a gradual growth from the complete and necessary
parental domination of the individual's life in infancy, giving way to
greater participation by the child, and later by the adolescent, in the
running of his own life. If this transition from complete dependency
in infancy to reasonable independence in adulthood is effected, the
individual becomes adult in his ability to manage his own affairs and
to take some responsibility for others. From the foregoing discussion,
we can recognize the basic reason for discipline: to free the individual so that he is fairly comfortable in controlling his own behavior,
with a minimum of external restrictions.

Both Affection and Discipline Are Essential

In summary, we can see that both affection and discipline are
essential if growth is to be optimal. Affection, which is often called
love, is not real affection or love unless it includes discipline. Love,
to be effective, must express itself partly in sound discipline if the
child is to prosper. Discipline, on the other hand, is ineffective
unless it operates against a background of love. Erikson,[49] p. 223,
says: "Firmness must protect him [the child] against the potential
anarchy of his as yet untrained sense of discrimination, his ability
to hold or to let go with discrimination. As his environment encourages him to 'stand on his own feet,' it must protect him against
meaningless and arbitrary experiences." Thus, the best home is
neither parent-dominated nor child-centered, but one in which
parents and children live together as a balanced unit that is continually changing as parents and children grow in maturity.

FAMILY STRUCTURE

The Usual Family

The family is usually made up of a father, a mother, and one or
more children. Sometimes grandparents or other relatives, perhaps
roomers, household help, or other people live in the same home.
How the members of the family get along with each other, the
amount of quiet for rest and school work, of space for daily routines

and individual activities all depend upon not only who is in the home but also upon how many people there are in relation to the available space, and how they cooperate in its use. Many variations of the usual family pattern of two parents and children exist; each has its influence upon child growth and development and upon the quality of life in the home for each family member. Let us consider some of these variations.

One-Parent Families

We have pointed out that the usual family contains a father and a mother. However, a number of situations exist in which only one parent, in some cases a father, in others a mother, is present. It is not unusual for one parent, particularly the father, to be absent for long periods of time, because of the requirements of his work, or because of military service. Either the mother or the father may be absent from the home for extended periods because of illness, tuberculosis or emotional illness, for example.

In some cases, death takes a parent in the early years of family life. Generally, if it is the father, the widowed mother manages to keep her family together with the help of relatives or social agencies. A widowed father may strive to do likewise, although it is somewhat less likely that he will be successful.

In cases of illegitimacy, if the child is kept by a parent rather than placed in an institution or for adoption, it is obviously almost always the mother who makes the home. While there are attempts to indoctrinate society to think in terms of this situation as an "illegitimate family," the more common reference is to the "illegitimate child," who is handicapped in his relations with his fellows whenever the facts of his birth are known.

Voluntary separation of parents for reasons other than business, military service, or illness brings about what are essentially one-parent families. Usually, when parents separate, the children remain with their mother, although sometimes they remain with the father; in some cases, they are switched from one to the other more or less alternately. There are other cases where some of the children live with the mother and the others live with the father.

Next to the death of a parent, divorce most definitely results in one-parent families. In families where a divorce has occurred, the disposition of the children varies as in voluntarily separated families.

In rare cases, children are adopted by single women. Generally speaking, however, adoption agencies place children only in homes where a husband and wife are present, and give reasonable evidence of being likely to remain together as a cooperating married couple.

Obviously, great differences exist in families in each of the categories described above. Most men and women who have reared children agree that a man and a woman sincerely interested in their marriage and the welfare of their children are best able to provide the optimal conditions for the rearing of future citizens. If they are right, it is also obvious that the mother alone or the father alone operates under a considerable handicap in rearing children. As we pointed out earlier, the child learns his or her sex role chiefly by living with parents of both sexes. With no firsthand experience with a parent, particularly of the opposite sex, the child may develop an unrealistic idea of that sex. There is also the possibility that the child may rationalize that everything that he does not like about his home and his life is the way it is because the one parent is absent. If that parent were present, he thinks, all would be well in his life.

Although we have no need for further generalizations about one-parent families, we may make a few observations about them. It is true that death is not easy for young children to comprehend, but it is definite and the deceased parent never comes back. Absence of a parent because of death is probably easier on a child than absence for any other reason. When a parent is absent for reasons of work, war, or illness, the child has to adjust not only to the parent's leaving and absence, but also to his or her return. Studies of father relations with war-born children [202] indicate that the adjustment of both the child and the parent upon the return of the latter is often difficult. When a parent is absent because of voluntary separation or divorce, the child has to adjust not only to the parent's leaving (if he is old enough to know about it), but also has to wrestle with the questions of why the absent parent left and why the parent does not return. If the parent does return at times, the child has to adjust to the return and probably to the leaving again. The child of divorced parents may consciously or subconsciously believe himself to be the cause of the divorce, that the parents, one or the other or both, were dissatisfied with him, and as a result could not continue to live together. If this is true, it is damaging to the child's self-esteem. How each parent regards the other is revealed to a minor or major degree in every contact of either parent with each child, if not by direct comment, then by the countless unconscious phrases or tones of voice in which the mother refers to the father or the father to the mother. If either is bitter, the child may be affected by the tone of voice in which the mother refers to men in general, or the father to women in general. When parents have not been happy together, it is easy for each of them to try to justify his own position and to tear down the position of the other. If each parent, or one of them, tears down the dignity and prestige of the other, the child is torn by competing loyalties, is not free to love an adult of each sex or to pattern himself after the parent of the same sex as himself.

Some rare people, even though their marriage is unsuccessful, manage to foster the child's feelings of love and respect for the parent who is not present. The child thus is free to love and to be loyal to the absent parent. In this way, if the children are with the mother, the growing girl can love her father and learn to like and trust boys and men; the boy can love and admire his father, and thus be free to proceed through the normal stages of molding himself in a masculine pattern. If the children live with such a father, the converse may also be true.

Unhappy Families

Let us look at the home in which the parents are not separated or divorced but, although unhappy, are staying together "for the sake of the children," or because their religion, cultural background, or economic situation does not permit them to get a divorce. If they stay together they may or may not manage to maintain a reasonably normal home atmosphere. Conscientious parents may do this fairly successfully, if they are courteous and considerate of each other, and if they think about and are successful in working as a team in discipline and in planning for the children. Of course, if they are successful at doing this, they may find that they are a happily married couple after all!

Most unhappy parents, however, are not very successful at being courteous and considerate. The antagonism between them lies close to the surface and explodes at intervals. They may even fight openly for the loyalty of the children. From the psychological point of view, this is destructive for the children, causing anxiety which interferes with school work and with interpersonal relationships outside of the home. In the long run, prolonged anxiety and competing loyalties or hatreds prove to be destructive to personality growth.

For children of unhappy marriages, the question often arises whether they are better off when the parents separate and they live with one parent, or whether their living in a family with both a male and a female parent is better for them even though the man and woman are not happy. Individual situations differ, of course, and circumstances cause what is best for the child to be different from case to case. If children live with only one parent, their life is likely to be more peaceful but less realistic as far as their future is concerned. They may develop a distrust of marriage and either avoid it, or marry, expecting and finding trouble.

If they live with two quarreling parents, their life will certainly not be peaceful, but they will be learning what at least one real man and one real woman are like. As a result of this experience they may also distrust marriage, although they may have more realistic ideas of what human beings are like and so be somewhat better prepared for living with a mate. One general statement may be made safely: divorce does not solve problems but only changes them.

Remarriages

Remarriages are those that are not first marriages. Remarriage usually means the taking on of another spouse following the death of a spouse or following divorce. In some cases, it refers to the taking back of the spouse from whom one has previously been divorced. In the latter case, if the two people concerned have done some growing up following the traumatic experience that almost always accompanies divorce, they may be able to live more congenially and therefore make a more suitable home for their children. Not all men and women profit in this way from their experiences, and the second attempt may not be successful either.

In the other kinds of remarriage, the presence of the stepparent and possibly of stepsiblings and half-siblings creates situations different from those found in the usual home. As one previously married wife told her previously married husband, "It's been an awful day. Your children and my children have been beating up our children."

In some cases, stepparents feel and show preference for their own children over their stepchildren. Some adults, however, take on the responsibilities of remarriage with love and compassion, and the result is happy homes in which all the children grow up as healthily and happily as in the usual home. Many students will recall the story of Abraham Lincoln and his stepmother as an example of a home in this kind of remarriage.

However, even when the situation is an ideal one from the point of view of equally shared affection and privileges, the younger children may not realize that the older children are stepsiblings or half-siblings. Parents sometimes assume that each child is fully aware of his situation. Growing children tend to forget, and may unconsciously wish to forget that beloved older siblings had another parent and are not full brothers or sisters. In later childhood, but particularly in adolescence, developing awareness of the facts may come as a shock, with temporarily disturbing effects.

Families with Adopted Children

Families with adopted children differ in various ways. Some parents have only one child, an adopted one; others have more than one child, but all adopted. Some parents with children of their own adopt others and it is not unusual for couples who have adopted a child because they believed they could not have one of their own, to achieve one or more pregnancies after the adoption.

People adopt children for a variety of reasons, not all of them altruistic. Some adopt because they sense that their marriages are in danger and they believe the cliché that "children hold marriages together." Others adopt children for personal prestige, because all the other couples in their social set have children. There are other reasons, some acceptable and others not.

Reputable adoption agencies are careful to find out what the motives are, when a couple applies for a child. They refuse to "place" children when the reasons are those mentioned above or similar ones, because it is obvious that such adults have a great deal of "unfinished business" themselves, which will either prevent them from giving as freely of themselves as competent parents must or possibly will cause them to overindulge the child. Sound agencies place a child with a couple only after thorough investigation of their motives, their moral and economic standing in the community, and to a reasonable extent, the permanence of their marriage.

Children who are adopted by couples who can satisfy this kind of investigation are fortunate. In one sense, they are even more fortunate than children who are born to couples, in that they are selected as nearly as possible for the characteristics that the parents would have hoped for in their own child, keeping in mind their own heredity. For example, a couple who are fair skinned with fair hair and blue eyes and with average I.Q.'s would usually not be given a dark child with either a very superior or a low I.Q., but a fair child with an average I.Q. Parents with superior I.Q.'s themselves would be given a child with a superior I.Q. and so on.

If adopted children do not learn of their adoption early in childhood, the knowledge may prove to be a damaging shock to their sensibilities—when it does come. Wise parents begin to talk to their adopted children while they are still babies or very young children about where they came from and how glad they are to have them specially picked out for them. If there are other children in the family, they too need to know about the adoption. Furthermore, the parents must see to it that their own children know they are also satisfactory, even though they were not specially selected. Actually all the children, adopted and otherwise, gain in self-esteem and their sense of security more through the kindly, matter-of-fact manner in which things are done for all of them, and by the reasonable chores expected of them, rather than by what particular things are said.

Adopted children can be reassured when they ask, as most children do, where they came from. The answer is not that they grew inside the body of the person they know as their mother, but that this mother and father wanted a baby like him and were lucky enough to find him. Questions about his "own" parents inevitably arise, as the child grows older and thinks about such things. Adoption agencies do not often provide this knowledge in detail; if this is the case, the parents can honestly answer that they do not know. If the answer is known, it may under favorable circumstances be given the child. If the child is developing normally and his relationships with his adopted parents are comfortable, he can accept the facts of his situation along with all the other knowledge that he and all children have to acquire about living.

Family Size

People who grow up in one- or two-child families often envy those who grow up in larger families, feeling that large families have more fun together (Fig. 2–2), sharing work and daily living in a companionable, live-and-let-live atmosphere. Some people in large families envy those smaller families in which each child has a room of his own and the "peace and quiet" thus made possible. Some are envious, too, of the fact that in the small family no one has to wear "hand-me-down" clothes, or go through life with his identity buried as "one of those numerous Joneses."

Large families who have income ample to cover basic necessities and some extras, along with educational opportunities, are perhaps most to be envied. They seem to have endless fun, there is always

Fig. 2–2. Some large families have fun together.

available someone to talk to when things go wrong, and mutual support to be counted on, especially in old age when age-peers are dying off. Some people, in fact, feel that one of the chief advantages of belonging to a large family is that old age is less likely to be a period when, as infirmity advances, one is both lonely and uncared for.

Whether a large family with limited financial resources is advantageous to character development, or is a handicap to it, depends upon the discipline and atmosphere of the particular family and, to some degree, upon the type of neighborhood in which it lives. If parental attitudes and strengths are such that each child can be welcomed and each older child can help in family and household routines, sometimes even in the provision of added income, the family is likely to provide a sound sense of responsibility and a wealth of affection. If, however, the large family is loosely held together, or not held together, by the parents, and especially if they live in an overcrowded home located in a neighborhood where the quality of family life tends to be poor, below-average physical and emotional health and even delinquency are possible results. They may come about as by-products of the crowded living conditions, of no space in which to have one's own possessions, to rest, to be alone for thought or for school work, to pursue a hobby, or to bring a boy or girl friend in. They may come also from the example set by some of the neighbors.

Small families may mean loneliness not only in old age but in childhood, too. They enhance for the parents the temptation to indulge the one or two children in the home, and to resist the young adolescent's attempts to shift the focus of his interests to outside the home. Small families increase the likelihood of pressure by parents upon young adults to marry someone close to home, in professions unlikely to require a change in the standard of living, and to choose a residence near to the parental home. In the later years of the parents' lives, small families are likely to place a heavy burden of responsibility for financial aid and companionship on each of the offspring.

The Child's Position in the Family

The fact that one is the oldest boy or the oldest girl in the family may lead to special favoritism by the mother or the father, as the case may be. The fact of being the *oldest child*, regardless of sex, is of some significance to growth and development. As the first child, he is the one on whom parents practice the art of parenthood. With the second and later children, parents have the feeling of "having been through" most of the phases of behavior which characterize the various growth periods. They know that the baby will not break when they bathe him, that a moderate amount of crying will do no harm, that temperatures can soar and return rapidly to normal. They realize that the run-about period will pass, that negativism and temper tantrums need not go on forever, that each early adolescent will seem a stranger for a time but will most probably again come back into the family circle as he establishes his freedom to be a person in his own right. These things they had to learn through the first child who, because they were often over-anxious, may have had to adjust to unskillful methods of handling or dealing with him.

Each child after the oldest will, from the beginning, share the parental affection and attention with one or more other children; the eldest will have had his parents to himself for a time before he has had to share them. Depending upon how smoothly this transition and the introduction of the next child is handled, this will either be a painful emotional experience or an incident easily adjusted to in the life of the first child. The case of a child whom we shall call Tripper illustrates how the arrival of a new baby can be a happy and constructive rather than a painful experience for a first child.

Tripper was two years and two months old when his mother told him that some day soon he was going to visit Grandma and Grandpa. Two weeks later she told him he was going to visit Grandma today, and that she and Daddy were going to have a new baby for him to see when he came home again. He was fond of his grandparents, so went willingly. While away from home, he "talked" on the telephone with his mother, and his father came to see him frequently. Tripper was always glad to be in touch with them but did not ask to go home. His father told him that he had a new brother whom he would see when he came home. He was mildly interested, being thoroughly happy where he was.

After Tripper had been home for about two weeks, his mother described the situation to the grandmother as follows: "Tripper and his new brother are making out very well. Tripper helps to hold the baby's bottle (as we see in Fig. 2–3). He helps tuck the baby into bed before coming downstairs for his usual romp with his father. He greets his brother happily in the morning and wants to help bathe him. He remarks about the baby's features, saying that he has eyes, a nose, and ears, but why doesn't he have any teeth. We got Tripper a new sand box so that he wouldn't feel neglected—but so far, I don't know which he likes better, the baby or the sand box."

These parents have handled the arrival of a new baby wisely. Tripper's father had always taken some time to play with him, and for some months the little boy had "helped" him with chores around the house and yard. Tripper had been accustomed from birth to having his parents leave him for short periods with someone else. He did not have to "yield a throne" to his younger brother because he had never occupied one. He had never been "king of the household" but rather was a welcome third member of a family that had been two until he got there. In such an atmosphere, turning a three- into a four-member family is a matter of expansion rather than of replacement, each individual from the beginning having been planned for and valued for himself.

As other children come into the family, the first-born is likely to take some responsibility for them with consequent strengthening of his own personality. *Who's Who in America* contains a higher pro-

Fig. 2–3. Helping to feed baby brother.

portion of first-born children than is in the general population. Many of them are oldest children whose fathers died when they were young, leaving them partly responsible for the care of younger siblings. Occasionally an oldest child is given too much responsibility too soon, with the result that his own physical and psychological growth suffers. He may become over-fatigued during his adolescent years and develop some physical difficulty as a consequence. Or he may stop school early in order to provide adequate income or education for younger siblings. In some large families a passing on of responsibility for helping with the education of the next younger sibling relieves the oldest of the responsibility for helping to educate more than one. In such cases the youngest child becomes the only one who carries no comparable burden, although in some families he is expected to assume a larger share of the eventual care of the parents if and when they need care.

A study made at Harvard University [186] shows that mothers are more often delighted with their first pregnancy than with later ones. This might be thought of as an indication that, boy or girl, the oldest child has an especially favored affectional environment. This same study found, however, that once the first child is born and is followed by other children, mothers were no more affectionate toward the first than to the other children. On the whole, the second and ensuing children were significantly less welcome than the first or other preceding children only when children came too frequently for the mother's health or for the economic condition of the family. In these cases, the difficulties of caring for two or more small children at once tended to make the mother less enthusiastic while carrying the coming child and somewhat less able to give him time, attention, and affection after he was born.

Much has been written about the first child's greater dependency upon the mother and about her inability to free him as he grows. The study mentioned above found that part of the first child's difficulty in adjusting to a second child was a reflection of his mother's difficulty in releasing him. Some parents, of course, have difficulty in accepting even a first child into their marriage.

Involved in these adjustments, such as the one between husband and wife upon the arrival of the first child, and that between the mother and first child upon the arrival of the second child, is a philosophy about what love can do, and how much it can encompass. Jealousy is based upon a feeling that love given to someone else must necessarily be taken away from someone. However, mature love grows with the need for it. Two parents who have developed an adult love for each other have love for their children, love that contains an awareness of the essential need for discipline of themselves and the children.

Studies in the 1930's often set aside *middle children* in the family for special comment. Contemporary studies, however, reveal little indication that middle children develop any special characteristics that mark them off from other children. A study of one group of middle children as compared to others showed that they had fewer unhappy marriages than children in the other categories.[36]

There is some indication that the *youngest child* in a family may suffer some handicap, but only if he is overindulged by his parents and older siblings. He may be regarded by his mother as her last opportunity to hold an infant in her arms, to nurse and be all-important to somebody. Her temptation, if this is the case, is to keep this all-satisfying possession of another person as long as possible. Older siblings, especially if they are several years older, may find satisfaction in indulging a youngest child. In families where the parents have the welfare of all at heart, they and their older children recognize the right of the youngest to grow up to be independent, and permit him to do so.

Traditionally, *only children* have been thought of as overindulged and as both vocationally and socially handicapped. Studies show that this is not always true. As in the case of oldest children, the proportion of only children in *Who's Who in America* is also higher than the proportion of their numbers in the population. Families with only one child may give that child superior educational and other advantages. A number of studies [10, 19] of "only" and "not-only" children show that more of the "only" than the "not-only" children in the groups studied were rated as personally well-adjusted, and about the same number of each category were listed as problem children. Many parents are aware of the danger of overindulging the only child and are successful in not doing so.

The *only boy* among girls or the *only girl* among boys may have experiences which tend to single them out, usually as especially desired and loved children. These may be experiences which handicap the child, or they may be experiences which demand too much of him, particularly in fulfilling the expectations of his parents.

The Harvard study mentioned above revealed that in families which already have children, if a first baby girl followed all boys, her advent was especially pleasing to 68 per cent of the mothers; if a first baby boy followed all girls, his advent was especially pleasing to 73 per cent of the mothers. It can be assumed that the arrival of the first boy or first girl produces some reaction in the mother which would have an effect upon the experiences of that particular child.

A member of a family of both boys and girls has, as a rule, some advantages over a member of a family of girls only, or of boys only, or an only child. These advantages reveal themselves particularly at adolescence, when dating begins. They tend to affect the type of mate the individual chooses and the manner in which adjustment is made to the mate. The chief advantage is that the member of a family of boys and girls knows something of what to expect of members of the opposite sex of his own generation. Unless the boy has a sister he may come to think of girls as beings set apart, as angels, perhaps, or as "gold-diggers"—in any case, not as real humans with some good and some bad traits, as boys and men have. Conversely, the girl who has never lived day-by-day with a brother may regard boys as gods or wolves but not as real human beings with lovable and difficult qualities, as girls and women have. Brothers and sisters tend to discover in each other the fact that people are people, regardless of sex. When, therefore, the sexual feelings of adolescence pull the individual toward the opposite sex, the judgments involved in wise selection of dates and mates may be more realistic in the individual who grew up with siblings of the opposite sex.

SUGGESTIONS FOR FURTHER DISCUSSION

1. In your library, seek information on defective sight and hearing, how it affects psychological development, and on what is being done about the training of children with one or both of these defects.

2. Discuss Olson's (References for Further Study) material on the respective roles of home and school in child development.

3. Discuss how you think handling a child by bribes, threats, and cajolery may affect his present behavior and future personality.

4. Discuss Shaffer and Shoben's (References for Further Study) "Home Influences on Personality" as it corroborates or refutes material in this chapter.

5. Call to mind a family with only one child now ten years or older, and another family with several children ranging in age up to the age of the first family child. Compare the life each of the two same-age children leads. Do you see personality effects of the family size and position in the family of each? If so, what are they?

REFERENCES FOR FURTHER STUDY

DENNIS, W. *Readings in Child Psychology*. Englewood Cliffs, N.J.: Prentice-Hall, Inc., 1951. Selection IX–1, the form of the family and child behavior; 2, child care in Samoa; 3, social class and color differences in child rearing.

DULANEY, D. E., JR. (ed.). *Contributions to Modern Psychology*. New York: Oxford University Press, 1958. Selections: 30, anxiety and learning; 33, traditional family ideology and its relation to personality; 35, permissive child rearing and adult role behavior.

OLSON, W. C. *Child Development*. (2d ed.). Boston: D. C. Heath & Co., 1959. Ch. 9, the child in the home and the community.

SEARS, R. R., MACCOBY, E. E., and LEVIN, H. *Patterns of Child Rearing*. Evanston, Ill.: Row, Peterson & Co., 1957. A Harvard University study on how 379 mothers actually are bringing up their children. Summaries of chapters give essential findings in the various areas of child rearing.

SEIDMAN, J. M. *The Child: A Book of Readings*. New York: Holt, Rinehart & Winston, Inc., 1958. Selections: 14, personality development in the family; 15, the child's perception of the parent; 16, the assertive behavior of children as related to parent behavior; 47, Maslow's theory of human motivation.

SHAFFER, L. F., and SHOBEN, E. J. *The Psychology of Adjustment*. Boston: Houghton Mifflin Co., 1956. Ch. 13, pp. 401–406, how personality is learned; pp. 431–447, family structure; home influences on personality.

THORPE, L. P., and CRUZE, W. W. *Developmental Psychology*. New York: The Ronald Press Co., 1956. Ch. 7, home and community relationships. This affords a good transition from Ch. 2 to Ch. 3 in this book.

For film suggestions see Film Supplement, in the Appendix.

CHAPTER 3

Secondary Influences on Development and Behavior

In Chapter 2, we discussed factors which have a primary influence on development. Human beings, however, are extremely complicated. They are what they are and they do what they do as the result of the interaction of many factors, some of which begin to shape the body and future personality during prenatal life, infancy, and early childhood. Of these, heredity and the influence of the parental family, for example, continue to be influential throughout childhood and adolescence and even as adulthood progresses into middle and old age. In addition to such primary influences, a number of other factors affect development in somewhat less fundamental ways, yet are influential in shaping the developing personality as the years pass. These may be thought of as secondary influences. They include such factors as housing, cultural mores, schools, other community agencies, and mass media.

HOUSING

Members of the human species, like those of most other species of animals, have a basic need for shelter from the elements and for a certain amount of privacy for the family group. Their methods of providing shelter and privacy vary with the conditions under which they live. Such conditions include the topography of the country, the climate, the possible construction materials and their availability (to be had for the taking, or for exchange), the amount of processing which the materials need, the availability of labor, availability of space, and the traditional customs of the particular society. This subject of man's provision of shelter and privacy is an interesting part of social anthropology. In this book, however, we shall limit our discussion largely to the more developed countries of the world, where the means for providing shelter and privacy are referred to as housing.

Standards for Adequate Housing

Sociologists find various standards desirable for adequate family housing. Their lists differ, but all lists include proof against weather; adequate light, heat, and water supply; and space for individual privacy, for the preparation and maintenance of family needs such as food and clothing, for family gatherings for meals, and for rest, recreation, and hobbies. Attention is called to the fact that the average preschool child spends 80 per cent, the average woman 60 per cent, and the average man 40 per cent of their time in their homes.[16]

Sociologists also point out that family dwellings need to be adapted for the different periods of family life. In the early period of marriage, for example, often only the husband and wife live in the home before the children are born. Then follow the ten to fifteen years, more or less, when the house is occupied by parents with infants and toddlers and their cribs, playpens, and toys, and later with school-aged children and their activities. Then come the years of peak activity when the parents are busy socially, and adolescent children not only crowd the house with their friends but also need more privacy. This is a period when aging grandparents may come to live with the family. Finally come the later years, when the children have gone, the grandparents have died, and the parents are alone again.

As it affects psychological development, housing is understood not only as the structure in which the individual lives, but also the relationship of the house to structures surrounding it and to the neighborhood as a whole (Fig. 3–1). The structure may be a trailer that the family moves from one camp to another, a unit in a row of attached houses, an apartment in a large building, a house on a half-acre lot, and so on. Individual and family development is affected by the structure in which the family lives, and by the conditions around it, the density and quality of the surrounding population, means of transportation and communication, the availability and

quality of shopping facilities, medical, dental, and other health facilities, places of worship, schools, fire and police protection, fuel,
water, and power supply, refuse disposal, the distance from the
breadwinner's place of employment, outside space for recreation,
and other such factors.

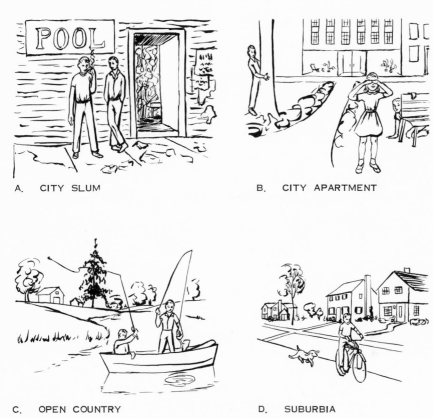

A. CITY SLUM   B. CITY APARTMENT

C. OPEN COUNTRY   D. SUBURBIA

Fig. 3–1. Environments in which children are growing up.

Families differ, of course, in their preferences for housing, and in
their economic ability to provide it. Let us look first at the housing of
people who are financially able to choose what they prefer. Since it
is usually the parents who select the housing, children are restricted
in choice to the parental home and its surroundings, at least for their
early years. To some extent, children tend to be comfortable in the
kind of home to which they were born. But this is not always the
case, especially as they get older.

Many young couples begin their married life in apartments either
in apartment buildings, in large old homes, or over garages which

have been converted into apartments. Such dwellings often provide comfortable living quarters with adequate space, lighting, heat, and water supply; some provide telephone, garage, and laundry facilities. Often such dwellings are near to places of employment, parks, stores, medical facilities, places of worship, and to theaters and other forms of entertainment. Many childless couples and couples with one or two children find such housing adequate and to their taste. They enjoy the social groups that they select, but they also enjoy the relative anonymity which city life offers. Some may not know other families who live on the same floor near them; others make friends with some of their close neighbors, especially if they have children. In some of the newer housing developments in large cities, where some units are in multiple unit buildings and others are single, families build social relationships much like those previously characteristic only of small towns.

Suburban life appeals to some families, especially some of those who have more than two children. These people like a view wider than is possible in most cities, they like to grow some of their own flowers and vegetables and to tend their lawns. Suburban life in many respects is not very different from city life, since it now has most of the advantages previously available only in cities. The disadvantages of suburban life for some people are the greater difficulty in preserving anonymity and privacy and the greater distances which the breadwinner has to travel to work.

Rural life probably brings people closer to nature than any other kind of life. If the family actually lives on a farm, or at the seashore, children may grow up with more understanding of the lives of species other than their own. If they develop a sense of kinship with the earth and sky, with plants and with other animals, they may be less easily thrown off balance by the troubles common to most human lives. By no means do all rural people develop such a sense, however, nor are all city dwellers devoid of it. People who live in the country in these days of easy and rapid transportation frequently complain of their lack of privacy. They seem to suffer a good deal from uninvited visitors.

Substandard Housing

Those areas in which housing is substandard in its provision for the health and safety of the inhabitants are called *slums*. Slums are usually crowded, not only in the number of people per unit of ground space, but also in the number of occupants per room. In the more populous parts of the world, a concentration of over a thousand people per acre is not unusual. In such areas, there is a high incidence of physical and emotional illnesses, high accident rates especially among children, and high rates of delinquency and serious crime. Partly because of crowding and partly because of poverty and the lack of facilities for adequate living, family life in slums, although it is often bound by affection and loyalty, is a constant struggle for mere existence. When several families share a few rooms, no one has privacy for personal care and certainly no quiet for reflection and thought. In many parts of the world today, children are sleeping four or five crosswise in one bed and that bed in a room that must also be used by adults. Such children cannot get adequate rest, where even the light is not extinguished until the last adult leaves the room or lies down somewhere to sleep. Preparation of school work in such quarters is obviously impossible. In spite of or possibly because of the conditions in such areas, the birth rate is high, so that the crowded conditions constantly worsen.

The extent of such substandard living conditions may perhaps be best grasped by a few figures. In the early 1950's, of a total of over 20 million urban dwellings in the United States alone, over 1 million had running water and one flush toilet and no private bath; over 1½ million had running water but no flush toilet or bath; and over 1 million had no running water, no toilet, and no bath.

The dwellings in which such conditions exist line streets crowded with traffic and are close to substandard stores, taverns, and places of amusement. Fire and police protection and refuse collection are often inadequate. Although some effort is being made to correct such conditions, they are increasing in number in many areas of the world as the birth rate continues to soar. Obviously, whatever the hereditary potential of the people born to such conditions, individual development is handicapped from the start.

Frequent Moving Versus "Roots"

Relatively few couples today spend all their lives in the same dwelling. As we have mentioned earlier, many young couples begin their married lives in apartments of one kind or another, others begin in the home of one set of parents, others in trailers, and so on. If the husband's employment is steady and his job is satisfactory, after one or two children come, the family often moves to a house which they either rent, buy, or build. Some families make several such moves to larger homes, as their income increases. After the children leave the home, some couples go to an apartment again.

Modern living, however, in many cases makes it seem desirable for the breadwinner either to change jobs or to accept changes in employment, both of which require him to move to other locations. Military, government, business, and many other skilled or professional careers make moving home and family almost imperative or, at least, the most practical thing to do. Students in colleges today often report that their families have moved from one to six times during their short lifetimes.

As a result of this common practice of moving, fewer families today put down "roots" in any particular community. They are less likely than were their ancestors to develop sentimental attachments to a particular home or community, part of the country, or even to any country. They are seeing more of the world today, its geography, climate, and native customs. They are hearing more dialects and languages spoken, many are learning to speak more than one language, and many are finding that they can live equally comfortably under different kinds of circumstances.

The things that have been said above may well be considered among the values of moving. The disadvantages of moving may point out the values of putting down "roots." Some people find it difficult to teach children respect for property when they frequently move from one place to another. Many children do not see parents working together to build a basement playroom or to develop a perennial flower garden, for instance, so that woodwork, walls, flower beds, and so on have no lasting value for them. Children who move from school to school may have no affection for any particular school and less time and opportunity to use judgment in making friends. One disadvantage of moving during late childhood lies in the increased difficulty of making the transition from the elementary school attitude toward the opposite sex to the adolescent dating attitude. Such youngsters have not had the opportunity of seeing members of the opposite sex grow from people toward whom they felt emotionally neutral into young people who are attractive and possibly exciting to them, and to realize how much young people change in growing up.

We have been referring to people who can, to some extent, choose whether they will move or not. One large class of people, in various parts of the world, is made up of migrant workers who must move from one place to another, as work runs out where they happen to be. It has been estimated that in the United States alone in 1958, over 600,000 children belonged to migrant families. The parents do temporary work such as harvesting perishable crops of fruit, vegetables, hay, and grain, or other seasonal work that must be done quickly. Most migrant workers live in substandard, temporary dwellings, a good many of which are on wheels. The children may never get uninterrupted terms of schooling, adequate medical and dental care, or even adequate nourishment.

Buying Power

What has been said about housing in these paragraphs obviously reflects the buying power of the family. Most families live either in as good homes as they can afford financially or in as good homes as they are permitted to occupy, depending upon zoning and other regulations of the community. If people belong to the race and faiths, for instance, that are considered most desirable in a community, they may choose desirable housing. If, on the other hand, they are not permitted to rent, buy, or build in certain locations because of their race, faith, or some other characteristic, they may have to put up with undesirable housing. Some people, so discriminated against, put large amounts of money into cars or other vehicles, and spend considerable amounts of time on the move, since they are more likely to be free to go where they choose than to live where they choose.

It is true, of course, that for psychological reasons such as "keeping up with the Joneses," some families live in more elaborate homes than they can really afford. They manage to meet rent or mortgage payments while their income is high, but if their income decreases, they may have to move to less expensive housing. Great numbers of families in all the more populous countries live on relatively low incomes, even in times of economic prosperity. They differ in their ability to manage on what they have, some thrifty families keeping up a strong family life and providing adequate care for their members on an income which is insufficient for other families of similar size, who either have never learned to manage or who do not care to. The latter are often partially dependent upon public assistance.

It is only in recent years that people past 65 years of age have made up a large segment of the population. While some of these elderly people are financially able to provide adequate housing for themselves, some are not. This latter group consists partly, of course, of some who either were unable to earn, or who were improvident during their lives. It also consists of many who had no opportunity during their most productive years to build up sufficient social security or other pension and insurance benefits to take care of their needs in later years. Some of these are either on public assistance or are eking out a minimal existence on their small incomes, which do not have the buying power that they once might have had. Various business and charitable organizations are now aiming at providing adequate housing for aging people that is within either their own incomes or within the funds allocated by taxes and charity for this purpose.[109]

CULTURAL MORES

Almost every individual is born, grows up, and continues to live in a society of other individuals. The habits, manners, beliefs, and values that a group of people have developed and which the members consider "right" are known as *cultural mores*. The term "mores" is the plural form of the Latin noun *mos*, meaning "manner." The mores are sometimes thought of as the manners and morals of a culture. Obviously, every individual is born into a situation characterized by a certain set of mores. He learns those of whatever culture he grows up in, and they are influential in molding his personality, including his ideas of right and wrong.

Mores Affect Development

Various sets of cultural mores occur in any given locality. For example, people in the southern United States have cultural practices different from those of people who live in the northern states. At the same time, various religious groups are present in both the northern and southern states. Regardless of his social group and of whether he lives in the North or the South, a Roman Catholic, for example, will learn from infancy not to eat meat on Fridays. Cultural mores are also independent of biological heredity. If a Mongolian child, for example, were reared in Japan, he would probably learn to eat with chopsticks; if he were reared in France he would probably learn to eat with a knife, fork, and spoon. This absence of dependence upon heredity holds with language also. If a native of Ethiopia is reared in Ethiopia, he learns the native language, but if he were reared in England, he would speak English with an English accent. If an Eskimo child grows up in his native environment, he learns to manage snowshoes and a kayak. If he were reared farther south, however, he would learn to manage a car and possibly a motorboat.

The mores also differ from one socioeconomic group to another. Child-rearing practices vary, for example, from one such group to another. Middle-class parents in the United States are on the whole more strict about toilet training, more ambitious for their children, and more inclined to push them to and even beyond their innate capabilities than are parents of lower socioeconomic groups.

Sex roles, generally speaking, are more clearly defined in the lower than in the middle and higher socioeconomic groups. The original roles of man, the provider, and woman, the preparer, are more nearly adhered to in the lower income groups. Fathers in these groups tend to do less housework than do those of the middle-class groups. If the women in the lower income groups work outside the home, they tend to work as waitresses, maids, or as factory workers.

If women in the middle socioeconomic classes work, they usually enter such professions as teaching, nursing, clerical and secretarial work, and various levels of sales work. Even though many married women work outside the home, concern has been expressed as to why relatively few women who have received college education continue after marriage to do so.[29] Most of them marry and have children. The costs of competent child care, housework, laundry, and so on, some of which the woman would do if she were not employed outside, are high. In the United States, married men may not deduct these costs as business expenses when computing their income tax. As a result, in many cases, it is not financially profitable for the mother of a family to work outside. Nor do all husbands find the additional home responsibilities that they must share worth the slight additional income provided by the wife.

Within each so-called class in any culture, however, wide individual differences exist in family standards. The family itself is more influential in the development of its members than are the social or economic levels to which the family belongs. Given a reasonable level of subsistence, how people look at life and what they value are more influential in their development than is the actual income level. Some individuals rebel against the restrictions or expectations of the cultural group of which they find themselves a part, but the majority strive to do what is expected of them.

Changing Mores

As a result of the impact of scientific developments in communication, transportation, medicine, and public health, and of more opportunity for recreation, during the last century, customs are changing in many localities of the world. For example, when more people lived in rural areas, and more families produced their own shelter, food, and clothing, family life was close because all of the members were dependent upon each other for satisfaction of their basic needs. One of the sources of struggle experienced by nearly all individuals at some time in their lives and by many people repeatedly, is the difference between their childhood mores and the mores of the culture at a later time or in another place. The speed and efficiency of modern means of transportation and communication that have been developed since World War II have made of the planet one community. Relatively sudden exposure to widely different ideas and customs is bringing about problems that are creating a wide gulf between the generations. This necessitates adjustments of viewpoints and habits. Young people born to foreign-born parents who had immigrated into countries such as the Americas and Australia during the last century and the beginning of the twentieth century found it almost impossible to live so that they were approved both by their parents and by their peers. Their problems, however, were relatively simple compared with some of the changes that people are making in their own living today. It may be that it is easier to change one's own ways to suit the culture than it is to attempt to suit two cultures at the same time, as children of immigrants have to. Recent developments in many parts of the world seem to indicate that this is true. In Japan, for example, since World War II, the people themselves are changing their outlook and ways of doing things. Their emperor is no longer considered divine, and they are regulating their excessive birth rate by approved, medically sound means.[168]

The speed and ease with which such changes are being accomplished not only by individuals but also by nations indicate that although cultural mores are handed down from generation to generation, different cultural patterns, particularly when they are practical, can be adopted readily both by individuals and by groups. Generally speaking, tradition itself is being progressively less accepted as a sound reason for complying with cultural mores. As a result, customs in many areas of living, such as diet, dress, education, religion, relations between the sexes, family size, techniques of family limitation, and the roles of the sexes in family life are changing rapidly.

SCHOOLS AS TRANSMITTERS OF THE CULTURE

History of Schools

"Schools" as we understand them today are a relatively recent invention. The term comes from the Greek *scholē* meaning "leisure, that in which leisure is employed, discussion, philosophy, a place where spare time is employed, a school." Obviously, the meaning of the word as well as its spelling has undergone change. Today, the school is considered as a preparation for life. As in the past, the family is today the chief transmitter of the culture from one generation to the next. Religious groups have always played a role in the indoctrination of the young in their own mores and beliefs. Schools are generally thought of as responsible to the oncoming generations for the transmission of the formal subjects of human knowledge.

Formal Education Required by Law

It was not until 1739 that compulsory free secular education was, by law, instituted in any part of the world. Table 3–1 lists a few countries and the dates in which they passed laws (at least on paper) requiring compulsory attendance of all fit children in schools of

Table 3–1

Places and Dates of Compulsory Free Education

Denmark	1739
Prussia	1763
United States (Pennsylvania only)	1834
Sweden	1852
France	1882
Norway	1889
England	1891
Spain	1909
Russia	1918
Italy	1922

elementary education. In the most populous countries of the world, particularly those in Asia, there is no compulsory academic education as we understand it. In the United States, attendance is now compulsory by law in almost all the states, but the age for leaving school varies, being 18 in five states, 17 in three, 15 in two, and 16 in all other states.

If a child's attendance is irregular and he is found to have no physical, mental, or emotional disorder which unfits him for school, he is considered a truant. Authorized persons investigate the reasons for his nonattendance. If truancy continues, he is placed, in most states, under the supervision of Juvenile Court, and his parents may be prosecuted for contributory delinquency. Table 3–2 indicates the effectiveness of the compulsory attendance law.

Table 3–2

School Enrollment in the United States in 1950 and 1957
Per Cent of Total Population of Each Age

Age, in Years	1950	1957
5	51.7	60.2
6	97.0	97.4
7– 9	98.9	99.5
10–13	98.6	99.5
14–17	83.3	89.5[*]
18–19	29.4	34.9
20–24	9.0	14.0
25–29	3.0	5.5
30–34	0.9	1.8

[*] School-leaving age in many states is 16 years or completion of the eighth grade. (National Education Assoc. Research Bull., Vol. 36, No. 1, Washington, D.C., Feb., 1958.)

Currently in Russia, attendance in school is compulsory for all fit children between the ages of 7 and 14 years. The Soviets hoped to have a 10-year program for children from 7 to 17 or 18 years of age available throughout the U.S.S.R. by 1960.

In many countries of the world where education is compulsory, the laws cannot be enforced because population growth is exceeding the ability (or the willingness in some cases) of the people to provide buildings, salaries, books, and other necessities. Even in the United States, classroom space is inadequate, so that in some relatively prosperous districts children are attending school in shifts. In 1960, nearly a million children were on half-day sessions. Even in some of the more adequate schools, certain teachers are referred to as "floating teachers" because there are not enough rooms for each to have a "home room."

It is important to note that in countries where school attendance has been made compulsory, even if for only a few years, the school is the only agency other than the family which, by law, deals with all children who are physically, emotionally, and mentally fit. This means that all individuals in these countries, regardless of their heredity and parental family, are taught along similar lines. It also means that the leisure of children is occupied to a large extent as the people who make the laws have seen fit. This, of course, does not always coincide with the desires of the children or even of all of the parents.

Formal Education Beyond Legal Requirements

Many of the countries that require education at the lower levels make publicly supported education available beyond the required level. In Russia, for example, after Grade VII where compulsory education for all ceases, three kinds of continuing education are made possible by the state: vocational, semiprofessional, and senior secondary. The first two are usually terminal in the formal education of the individual, having prepared him for productive living, whereas the secondary school is chiefly concerned with preparing students for still higher levels of education. Students who complete secondary schooling may take competitive examinations for admission to one of a number of schools, namely, agricultural, socioeconomic, teacher-training, or engineering institutes; medical schools; or schools of other fields of specialization. Courses in these schools vary in length from 4 to 6 years. Carefully selected graduates of these courses of study may go on at public expense for 2 or 3 years of postgraduate study.

In the United States, both federal and state governments have made provision for continuing education at public expense, following completion of the compulsory 10 to 12 years of education. In most cases, the parents or the students are responsible for living expenses, although some scholarships and fellowships provide for these also. Many other countries provide scholarships and fellowships, and these are usually assigned to students who have proved their ability on a competitive basis either through special examinations or by virtue of their past accomplishments. Almost all countries, whether they have compulsory education or not, have some forms of publicly or privately supported education.

What Is Transmitted

Even the most primitive tribes concern themselves to some extent with the employment of the leisure of the young. They have bodies of information which they consider essential and which they transmit to the young by various methods of instruction outside the family. Their examinations are, in some cases, administered in the form of *puberty rites,* involving physical and social tests which the members of the particular culture feel should be mastered by approximately the age at which biological puberty occurs.

As the body of knowledge that any culture requires becomes more complex, the means for transmitting it also become more complex and diversified. It has become obvious that no person, no matter how hard or how long he labors, can master even any one field of knowledge. It follows, then, that each culture must select from its body of knowledge that which it considers essential for the young to learn. This selected knowledge constitutes a *curriculum,* or course of study.

The simplest curriculum familiar to most of us is the "three R's," reading, 'riting, and 'rithmetic. These are *tool subjects,* and in many countries some degree of skill in their use is about all the culture hopes to achieve. When we consider the amount of illiteracy in some parts of the world we can well say that if a country succeeds in teaching all its people to use the tool subjects, it has a right to be proud. Accurate figures on illiteracy are hard to find. The term usually means inability to read and write one's native language at a very simple level. A UNESCO study reported in 1957 that 45 per cent of the world's adult population of over 700 million adults are illiterate. The report included the fact that over 200 million children of school age were without any school facilities whatsoever.

For many parts of Africa, Asia, and the Pacific islands, only rough guesses concerning literacy can be made. The lowest illiteracy rates are found in western Europe and North America. England and the Scandinavian countries claim the lowest rates, so that for them illiteracy is almost non-existent. In the U.S.S.R., the rate dropped from 70 per cent in 1920 to less than 10 per cent in 1950. In 1959, the

United States found 2.5 per cent of its people to be illiterate,[197] but the rate varies from about 1.0 per cent in the western North Central States to about 9.0 per cent in the eastern South Central States. Non-white illiteracy has been reduced from 30.4 per cent in 1910 to 10.2 per cent in 1952. Immigration laws passed in the early 1920's brought about a reduction in illiteracy in immigrants arriving in the United States from 25.5 per cent between 1900 and 1909 to 0.2 per cent in 1958.[197]

To the degree that the masses of its people master the tool subjects, a country moves forward as a whole into the study of history, language, the arts, philosophy, and most recently, science. When the people can read, printed media such as books, magazines, and newspapers became powerful means of transmitting information and also of molding ideas and opinions.

Most cultures recognize the need for training young people to serve as leaders. Nations and other cultural groups select individuals to receive special training for this purpose. Disagreement arises, of course, as to what shall be taught, how it shall be taught, and how the money to finance education shall be raised and distributed. In Russia, for example, the educational system is based upon the needs of the state and so is characterized by authoritarianism. In the United States, in contrast, the system is based upon democracy, and its goal is the development of each individual along the lines of his own aptitudes and his own best interests.

National governments today are spending huge sums of money upon various phases of education: acquisition of land; building of classrooms, laboratories, and offices; subsidizing studies of curricula, test construction, and methods of teacher training; salaries for administrators, teachers, and maintenance workers. Education is considered so important by the federal government of the United States that in World War II an Armed Forces Educational Policies Committee was set up. This committee, made up of Armed Forces Information and Education personnel and prominent lay educators, is still active. Its business is to see that continuing formal education is available to young men and women while they are on active duty in the armed forces. It is also responsible for making available formal education for the children of armed forces personnel who are assigned overseas and whose families are with them. As a result, excellent schools have been established at overseas bases, and adequate libraries are maintained for the use of both the adults and their children. Each state in the United States has its own department of education which is charged with providing for the state's own particular needs, and the federal government has its own department which is charged with the responsibility of studying and providing leadership for the improvement of conditions and quality of formal education within the nation generally.

Teachers

The need for classroom space, books, and so on has been mentioned. Studies of the effects of formal education upon people, however, indicate that the most influential single factor in a person's school life is the teacher. The teacher affects the young person's confidence in himself, his habits of study, and his general disposition. When the school is organized (as many are in the lower grades) so that children are with the same teacher throughout the school day, and day after day for nine months or so, that particular teacher is with the child, in an obviously influential position, more than any other person, including the child's mother. The effect may be beneficial to the child (and to the teacher) or it may be detrimental, depending upon the personalities of the teacher and the child. Parents find that the emotional quality of their relationship with their children during any school year depends considerably upon the children's relationship with their teachers. Teachers are influential in the upper grades, and in college also, but generally less so because the student meets a number of different teachers in the course of any day.

Home and School Cooperation

Since the parental family and the teachers are so influential in the development of children, it seems reasonable that the home and school would do well to understand each other in order to cooperate and reach their common goal as effectively as possible. Historically, however, such cooperation has not been practiced widely. In the early days of schools, as we think of them, most of the parents were uneducated and even ignorant. As a result, it probably did not occur to the educated men who began the schools to consider the parents as interested or competent to decide anything about the schools. This was especially true in Europe, and associations that include both parents and school people have developed in England and France, for example, only in the last twenty-five years.

The history of parent-teacher associations in the United States is different from that of Europe. The parents, from the beginning and throughout the nineteenth century, took a more active interest in the education of their children than did parents, on the whole, in Europe. The first association of parents concerned with child welfare in the schools was the National Congress of Mothers founded in 1897. In 1924, this became the National Congress of Parents and Teachers. Today, it has a membership of over one million with branches in almost all of the states. Its program stresses the desirability of contact between the school and the parents, particularly between the parents and the teachers, discussions of school problems of all kinds, and recently, child study. In many communities, Parent-Teacher Associations recognize specific needs which the school budget cannot cover. As a result, they engineer fund-raising campaigns of various kinds which are often highly successful. Some groups study school legislation and exert considerable pressure toward getting what they deem desirable legislation passed.

In some communities, PTSA's (Parent-Teacher-Student-Associations) are being established. The student body elects representatives to the governing board, and they serve as a voice for the student body on issues where the parents and teachers desire student opinion. The student representatives serve on committees and act as liaison people between the students and their elders. In doing so, they may learn to evaluate education better than they would in any other way.

Formal Education Is Everybody's Business

Understanding and financing formal education today is the business of the literate citizenry of all nations. As the world's population increases, the problems of education become increasingly difficult. Children can learn intellectually only when they are receiving sufficient food and adequate shelter and clothing. These basic needs are not being supplied for millions in various parts of the world. The problem at times seems to be more than the literate people of the world can manage. Production and distribution of sufficient food, adequate housing, medical care, and public health measures all hinge on the success of the efforts of educated and productive people.

Can they succeed? The education of young people costs money. Where is the money to come from? In the United States it has to come from the people who pay taxes and make voluntary contributions. How well are they doing? Although in 1955, a sum of 14 billion dollars, distributed as Fig. 3–2 shows, was spent on formal education in the United States, that amount proved inadequate to provide sufficient classrooms, books, and other needs and to pay the

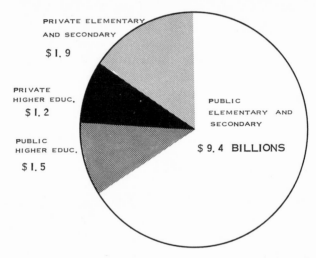

Fig. 3–2. Expenditures for formal education in the United States in 1955.

salaries of the needed school personnel. The numbers of students are increasing at such a rate that even in communities where new schools are being built, the buildings are often inadequate before the school is opened for use, with the result that half-day schooling for some of the grades has to be instituted from the opening of the school. Other problems enter the picture. In some areas, children have to be transported from considerable distances to the school buildings. This necessitates the use of buses, which require competent drivers and good roads.

One of the most difficult and continuing questions is, What is the most productive employment of leisure for all the different kinds of children? Another is, What of the culture is most important to transmit? If we decide that not all children can profit from receiving the same kind of education, how shall we differentiate among them? If we can do so, what shall we teach the different groups? Obviously, it takes an educated citizenry to grasp the problems in the first place and even to begin to work out solutions.

OTHER COMMUNITY AGENCIES

Institutions of Worship

Historically, religious institutions have played an influential part in the psychological development of individuals. The congregations affiliated with churches, synagogues, and other places of worship probably rank next to the home in influencing the personal development of the individual. Although children spend only a few hours under religious supervision as compared with the hours spent in academic school, their development may be strongly influenced by those few hours, especially if the family shares and supports the ideas and attitudes that the child is learning from the religious institution. If the child attends an academic school that is run by the same religious group, the religious training is likely to be reinforced. Children may thus learn that the mores of their religious group are the only "right" ones, and as a result run into difficulties when they mingle with people who have learned the mores of other religious groups.

As the world becomes progressively nearer to being a single community, the different kinds of religious groups take on a greater significance because their members come in contact with each other more than was once true. Currently the major faiths of the world are nine: Christian, Jewish, Moslem, Zoroastrian, Shinto, Taoist, Confucian, Buddhist, and Hindu. In the United States alone, in 1960, there existed 84 separately organized religious groups, each of which had at least 50,000 members. Many groups with smaller membership are also in existence.

Most religious bodies do not limit their activities to spiritual training, but also concern themselves with the social and political lives of their members. When, for example, a family moves into a new neighborhood, religious organizations welcome them, offering them not only a new religious home but a means of making new friends. Religious groups, while teaching their members to obey present laws, encourage them to go through proper channels to change laws which are not in agreement with their particular mores. Examples of this are laws permitting or requiring sampling of blood for premarital tests, inoculation against infectious diseases, information about birth control by mechanical and chemical means, and laws limiting marriage to monogamy.

Religious organizations, on the whole, recognize that the traditional methods of teaching and preaching need constant revision. Fluency in repeating catechisms and intellectual knowledge of statements of values do not guarantee that life will be lived accordingly. Many religious groups, while still teaching the history and mores of their faith, are using new devices for making the mores meaningful to children. Children act out the stories, discuss what they mean in their everyday living, and report ways in which their own behavior changes as a result of what they have learned. One can hope that they learn something of tenderness for other human beings in so doing. In adapted forms, these devices are also applied to sermons and adult group activity. Practical, up-to-date illustrations are used. Groups present case studies and later discuss them. Elderly people meet and discuss means of continuing usefulness in living, and continuing spiritual growth in preparation for death. The hope is that all this is done, not on a brittle, intellectual level, but on a level of feeling as well as understanding.

Libraries, Museums, and Other Educational Aids

Human beings have developed other facilities that contribute to their psychological development. Many communities, even small ones, maintain public libraries, and some have collections of recorded music and reproductions of paintings. Traveling book-and-record mobiles are popular today. The breadth and depth of the collections depends, in most cases, upon the education and insight of committees charged with the responsibility of choosing the items to be purchased. Most communities of any size have buildings for their collections which have quiet rooms for study of literary and artistic works and for listening to recordings of music, foreign languages, and dramatic works.

Many of the larger cities of the world have museums of art and science. Some have planetariums, zoological and botanical gardens, symphony orchestras, and opera companies. In many cases, exhibits and courses are especially designed for children and adults of various age levels.

Many communities have public and private camping facilities, where families may share outdoor experiences. Agencies provide camping facilities for children whose parents cannot provide for private camps. Some children benefit greatly from camp experience. The benefit, of course, depends upon the particular child, the kind of camp, the people who manage the camping activities, and the length of the child's stay. Some camps are planned for the use of elderly people only. In the United States, the state and national parks offer rest, recreation, and enjoyment for city and suburban dwellers and a means to acquaint themselves with their country as it was originally. In some of these parks, however, there is danger of overpopulation by tourists during the summer months, to the point that the condition of the parks is endangered.

Protective Agencies

By protective agencies, we mean agencies whose business it is to protect the health, life, and property of human beings. Governments of most countries have instituted medical and public health agencies whose chief concern is preventive measures. Through the work of such agencies, child health, prenatal, infant, and school-age treatments are carried on. Mothers receive care prenatally, and infants and children are vaccinated against smallpox and inoculated against such diseases as diphtheria, whooping cough, tetanus (lockjaw), and more recently poliomyelitis. Diagnostic clinics or mobile units detect such diseases as tuberculosis and syphilis, and sanatoria and other treatment clinics are set up for their cure.

Governments have also enacted laws dealing with the purity of water, foods, and drugs, with anti-narcotic legislation, and with sewage and waste disposal. Both private and public hospitals and clinics provide care for people of all ages including the senile and mentally and emotionally ill.

Even though, in many parts of the world, public health measures are still far from adequate for all individuals, lives are being prolonged and the birth rate is rising to the point that the actual numbers of living people are interfering with the maintenance of health measures for all. As a result, both private and public clinics are being established for the purpose of informing people about methods of family limitation. Some of these have been remarkably effective. Also in line with family limitation, heredity counseling services are being established in various parts of the world in order to assist potential parents in evaluating their hereditary constitution.

As Pope Pius XII stated in *L'Osservatore Romano* (September, 1953),[167] "Certainly it is right, in the greater number of cases it is a duty, to point out to those whose heredity is beyond doubt very defective the burden they are about to impose upon themselves, upon their marriage partner, and upon their offspring." We add here the necessity of considering the burden upon society as a whole.

Most communities of the world have organized some kind of protection against natural calamities such as floods, earthquakes, hurricanes, fire, and so on, and against man-made disasters such as fire, theft, and bodily harm. In smaller communities, fire protection is usually managed by volunteer organizations, but police protection is usually publicly supported. In larger communities, both fire and police departments are publicly supported.

Corrective Agencies

We use the term "corrective agencies" to include those whose business is the detection and treatment of individuals who have committed offenses against society, or who have broken rules established by society. Offenses are fewer where there are few restrictions upon personal freedom, but wherever people live in groups, some restrictions upon conduct develop, and the more crowded people are, the greater the number of restrictions and the greater the likelihood of their being broken.

The rules of society are not broken by any one class of society only. Since there are many more individuals in the lower socioeconomic strata than in the middle and upper strata, there are more offenses committed by people in the lower groups. However, people of all groups commit offenses, and need early detection and correction if possible.

It is estimated that approximately 50 per cent of criminals begin to commit criminal offenses before they are 21 years of age. Obviously, the importance of early detection and correction cannot be overestimated. While it cannot be proved, it is believed that the majority of potential criminals could become useful citizens if they are discovered and dealt with wisely while young. Children's courts in the more enlightened countries of the world have changed greatly since the day of Charles Dickens. Generally speaking, judges of modern children's courts proceed only after they have heard the reports of psychologists, physicians, and social workers, all of whom have investigated the background and present condition of the individual offender.

In some cases, the family of the young person is found to be in trouble of an emotional or financial nature, and to need help as much as does the individual. In some such cases, the offender is placed back in the care of his own family, which is also supervised. In other cases, the young offender is placed with specially selected foster parents, and in some cases is sent to a corrective institution. Some of these institutions are publicly supported, and others are privately supported.

In spite of all care, there will probably always be some men and women who will not or cannot live within the laws of their society. Because of this, the public must maintain permanent institutions for their incarceration. The old sentiments of revenge and punishment are giving way to efforts to understand why people commit offenses and if possible to remove the underlying causes. If overcrowding is one of the causes, for instance, it is within our power to control the numbers of people living in a given area. If unstable family life has produced an unfavorable environment for growing children, we can attempt to educate young men and women for competent parenthood better than we have been doing.

MASS MEDIA

Mass media are the various kinds of information and entertainment that reach people of all socioeconomic classes without their having to struggle to receive them. Such media change with scientific developments. Today's chief mass media in many parts of the world are newspapers, magazines, motion pictures, radio, television, and advertising in trolleys and buses, in billboards along the highways, in messages and pictures on commercial vehicles and on all sorts of containers of foods that people buy. There is little doubt that these media influence psychological development. Just what the effects are and how strong they are are matters for consideration. It is reasonable to assume that the extent and quality of their influence depend upon the amount and intensity of the exposure and upon the content and manner of presentation. The mass media all rely to some extent upon people's understanding of printed or spoken language. Since this is the case, they may be motivating factors in increasing vocabulary as well as in actually teaching new ideas that are carried by words.

Newspapers

The earliest modern newspapers were printed in western European countries in the early part of the seventeenth century, but today newspapers of some kind are produced all over the world. They are defined collectively as more-or-less continuous publications mainly concerned with reporting, illustrating, and commenting upon current events. In the United States, for instance, they vary all the way from mimeographed sheets prepared at intervals by school children about their school affairs to highly complex dailies such as *The New York Times,* whose community is the world. Some newspapers are controlled by specific political, religious, and ethnic groups; and others, as does *The New York Times,* strive to be free of any such influence and to print "All the News That's Fit to Print." Obviously, some judgment is exercised in the selection of the content of any publication.

Publication is a costly enterprise, and all kinds of means are employed to cover costs. These differ from one publication to another. Some depend on advertising to a large extent to defray costs. Many carry comics, special features, and contests of one kind or another to stimulate sales. Thus they appeal to different kinds of readers, and the different kinds of readers exert a strong influence upon the continuing character and content of the newspapers. From the very beginning of continuous newspapers, the public greed for sensational news has been obvious. Even as early as 1605, an English publisher established the success of his weekly paper by reporting on two dramatic murder trials in Yorkshire. Today, sensational journalism is definitely flourishing, but so also are newspapers that are more realistically balanced. What newspapers children read depends largely upon what are taken by the family. Adults read what they have been accustomed to reading since childhood, but they are also free to choose what they read, thereby influencing what is published and the manner of presentation.

Magazines or Periodicals

These terms usually refer to publications that appear at weekly, monthly, or at longer intervals. A study of periodicals read by the people of a culture provides some measure of the level of the average educated intelligence of the time. Like newspapers, modern periodicals began their development in the seventeenth century. Periodical literature has gone through various phases with varying goals during the past three centuries. Today the output of periodical literature is varied and vast. Some of it is serious and scholarly work. The rest is business enterprise with popular approval its chief goal.

Children's magazines were a development of the late nineteenth century, and in all of the more developed countries of the world today, children and their parents are wooed by a confusing variety. High on the list of the children's choices are the "comic" magazines. Since these depend heavily upon illustrations to communicate their message, they have been criticized by some as having a retarding influence upon reading development. They have also been held by some critics to contain excessive amounts of physical violence, luridly portrayed. Some investigators, however, have pointed out that comics are not all of low quality in content and presentation. Some comics, in fact, use a wider vocabulary than is presented in tests of vocabulary standardized for the seventh grade in American schools. As far as content is concerned, the range is as wide as that in any other form of publication.

When parents select magazines for children, they usually select those with what they consider "educational" or of "good citizen" content. Sometimes children enjoy these, and frequently they use them in connection with their school work. Interesting choices of reading material show up in families, in spite of parental selection for certain age groups. One family, for instance, has discovered that among other things the husband reads *The Ladies' Home Journal* to keep up with women, the wife reads *Esquire* to keep up with men, and the children read *Parents' Magazine* to keep up with their parents.

Whether or not individuals read, and what they read, seems to be determined by the late teens.[65] Gesell, who followed many children from birth through adolescence in the Yale University Laboratory for Child Study, found that those who are avid readers in their teens have been so since the age of seven, and that children who read little read slightly more in their teens than they did earlier. Exceptions occur, of course, when only slightly interested readers are inspired by a teacher or by some circumstance in the later teens. Some of these people become confirmed readers for life. Children who enter senior high school still uninterested in reading seldom change. It is not unusual in the United States for individuals to be graduated from college without ever having done any serious reading beyond what they had to do to pass their courses.

Radio Programs

Radio broadcasting for popular consumption began about 1920. It may be defined as the systematic diffusion by radio of music, lectures, drama, humor, news, speeches, ceremonies, sports events, and other matter that can be appreciated audibly by individuals or groups with appropriate receiving apparatus. As the cost of the receiving apparatus came within the reach of the people, radio programs became extremely popular and began to affect the level of information of the listeners.

As with other media, offerings especially for children soon developed, and those who worried about and studied the effect of lurid comics on children also worried about the blood-and-thunder radio programs, which seemed even more real because of the sound effects. Many children liked the programs, and many parents were only too happy to have the children occupied.

There is no questioning the fact that people of all ages learn of areas of human activity by way of radio that they would never have known existed without it. In addition, they are made aware of happenings the world over almost as soon as the event occurs, and in many cases concurrently with the event. Politicians, businessmen, educators, and anybody who has anything at all to do with the steering of human affairs have had to become more alert as a result of the popularity of radio.

Motion Pictures and Television Programs

While motion pictures antedate television programs as mass media by some 50 years, their effect on psychological development is somewhat the same. Both endeavor to transmit emotional stimuli and experience to the viewer by recreating events in spoken language, plastic and graphic arts, drama, and music, and in some cases, presenting events "live." As a result, the senses of sight and hearing are directly stimulated, and so effectively in many cases that the senses of smell, taste, touch, and balance are indirectly stimulated also.

While most people enjoy having their own senses stimulated to a certain extent, the effectiveness of movies and television in this area causes some concern about how much the senses of the young are being stimulated. This is especially true of television, since as they say, "it comes right into the family living room." There is also concern about the effect of excessive viewing on eyesight, on muscular and skeletal development, and upon sleep. Educators have been somewhat concerned about the hours given to viewing which might have been better spent on homework.

In the decade since television first became available to most people, changes have taken place in attitudes toward it and in the attitudes of the television industry toward itself. Its influence on the ideas and attitudes of people is unquestionably profound. People not only hear about things happening now, but they see heads of states, for instance, at meetings at which they are deciding the fate of millions. They hear and see great theatrical, symphonic, and operatic performances, thrilling sports events, awe-inspiring national and religious pageantry, documentary programs on problems of food supply, population, labor, production, and so on; that is, if they want to. Of course, they may also view all kinds of entertainment, western movies, detective stories, light musicals, humorous shows, and so on. No matter what they view, they are hearing words, seeing sights, and getting or fostering ideas, for better or for worse, which they might otherwise never have known about.

For some children, television has replaced their interest in non-television movies, comics, and radio.[134] Although at first it interfered with other recreational interests such as scouting, dancing, music, dramatics and athletics, its interference with these interests is now minimal.[27] When television was new, parents reported that it strained children's eyes, caused them to lose sleep, and to be nervous. Currently, however, children get about as much sleep as the average child did before TV and seem to have no more nervous difficulties than before.[230]

The National Society for the Prevention of Blindness states that televiewing does not affect sight adversely if simple rules for viewing are followed, as shown in Fig. 3–3: Namely, at some distance from the TV, with eyes on a level with the screen, with some light in the room, and with breaks from constant viewing. The novelty of television has worn off, to some extent, among older children. Young children have been born into a world where television is firmly established. In general, parents and teachers today as well as the children are taking television and motion pictures as part of our contemporary design of living. Educational institutions are making more and more effective use of both media as visual aids to learning.

NOT THIS.....................BUT.................THIS

NOT THIS.....................BUT.................THIS

NOT THIS.....................BUT.................THIS

Fig. 3–3. Best conditions for viewing TV.

The motion picture theaters have suffered considerably from the competition that television has given them. As a result, the quality of pictures may be improving. The situation has also given an impetus to drive-in theaters, where young couples particularly like to go, if not to see the picture, to have some place for privacy. Television, unless a family has a number of sets, has not taken the place of the movies for providing privacy which, in the United States at least, is difficult for young people to find elsewhere.

Advertising

Advertising is the process of disseminating information for commercial purposes; in other words, to influence people to buy what one has to sell. It is a very old procedure, and it has always made use of available mass media. Originally, people advertised their wares only by the spoken word. Today advertisers make use of all of the mass media mentioned and in so doing have made advertising a mass medium itself, according to our definition. Little children today know the names of different kinds of beer, women's undergarments, and models of cars; they have ideas about how steel and aluminum are processed; and they have concepts about the molecular structure of petroleum products. Their information may or may not be accurate, but they know, at least, that every kind of beer cannot be the finest ever made. They soon learn from experience that they cannot expect products to live up to all the claims of the advertisers.

SUGGESTIONS FOR FURTHER DISCUSSION

1. Read some of the references below on child rearing in other cultures. Read, also, from the other references for information on our cultural practices. Contrast the practices you know best with the ones you find in the reading, for effectiveness in preparing children for the lives they will probably lead as adults.

2. Discuss the effect of city apartment versus small town living on body development, play interests, intellectual development, and social life.

3. Find out when your home community last voted on a school bond issue. What was the outcome of the election? Why do you think the vote came out as it did?

4. Visit a Juvenile Court if one is available. Find out, if you can, what factors are associated most often with the lives of the children brought in for delinquency, as distinguished from children not in trouble with the law. Visit also, if possible, an agency for the care of dependent and defective children. Learn what you can about some of the children under its care. Discuss anything that you think is contributing to the normality of their development.

5. Discuss the quality of radio and TV programs in your community. What effect do you think these media have on the children?

6. Have you had, or do you know anyone who has had an experience with closed-circuit TV teaching in regular courses? What do you think were its advantages? Its disadvantages?

7. Look through current new developments in newspapers, magazines, and books, for material on educational films, radio, and TV in your community or elsewhere. Discuss your information in class.

REFERENCES FOR FURTHER STUDY

BENEDICT, R. *Patterns of Culture.* Rev. ed. Boston: Houghton Mifflin Co., 1948.
Ch. 3, an anthropologist discusses how culture affects human development.

DENNIS, W. *Readings in Child Psychology.* Englewood Cliffs, N.J.: Prentice-Hall,
Inc., 1951. Ch. 9, Selection 4, effects of social climate; Ch. 10, Selection 2, success
and failure in the classroom; Selection 3, teachers and behavior problems.

DEWEY, R., and HUMBER, W. J. *The Development of Human Behavior.* New York:
The Macmillan Co., 1951. Ch. 5, environment: geographic and social heritage;
rural-sacred and urban-secular continuum; universals, specialties, alternatives, and
individual peculiarities. Illustrations.

LANE, H., and BEAUCHAMP, M. *Understanding Human Development.* Englewood
Cliffs, N.J.: Prentice-Hall, Inc., 1959. Ch. 5, the cultural origins of the individual:
common attributes of people in all cultures; each individual's culture unique to
him; dominant themes of American culture; cultural roadblocks to full development; teacher's role in cultural differences.

OLSON, W. C. *Child Development.* (2d ed.). Boston: D. C. Heath & Co., 1959. Ch.
11, the teacher in individual and group relationships; Ch. 12, development through
curriculum and methods in the school; Ch. 13, child development in the organization and administration of schools.

SANDERS, I. T. *The Community.* New York: The Ronald Press Co., 1958. Ch. 1, the
community as a place; Ch. 2, the people; Ch. 3, the community as a job and service
center; Ch. 8, the community as an area of integration. These serve as a background for the understanding of what the community is and does in development.

SEARS, R. R., MACCOBY, E. E., and LEVIN, H. *Patterns of Child Rearing.* Evanston,
Ill.: Row, Peterson & Co., 1957. Ch. 12, socio-economic level, education, and age
of mother: effects on child-rearing practices.

SEIDMAN, J. M. *The Adolescent: A Book of Readings.* New York: Holt, Rinehart &
Winston, Inc., 1953. Pp. 2–15, adolescence the Hopi way.

SEIDMAN, J. M. *The Child: A Book of Readings.* New York: Holt, Rinehart & Winston,
Inc., 1958. Selection 13, childhood the Hopi way; Selection 17, finger paints as a
function of class differences in child-training practices; Selection 39, why do children watch T.V.? Selection 45, development of the ideal self in New Zealand and
American children.

SHAFFER, L. F., and SHOBEN, E. J. *The Psychology of Adjustment.* Boston: Houghton
Mifflin Co., 1956. Ch. 13, pp. 407–430, culture and personality; social class and
personality.

WHITING, W. M., and CHILD, I. L. *Child Training and Personality.* New Haven: Yale
University Press, 1958. Ch. 4, variations in child training practices.

For film suggestions see Film Supplement, in the Appendix.

CHAPTER 4

Prenatal Life and Infancy

PRENATAL BEHAVIOR

It is difficult if not impossible to learn exactly what behavior the human being is capable of before birth if it remains within the uterus for the full term of about 266 days. Pregnant women speak of feeling "life" or "quickening" usually some time during the fifth month following conception. These sensations within the uterus result from movements of the fetus (the name by which the embryo is known after nine weeks). By means of the stethoscope, the heartbeat also can usually be detected during the fifth month of life.

While it is true that we can know little of what is actually going on within the uterus, extremely prematurely delivered embryos and fetuses provide glimpses of behavior that we may assume unborn fetuses of similar ages would be capable of, also.[85] From these embryos and fetuses, it has been learned that if the maintenance system set up within the mother's uterus is adequate, development goes on rapidly within the first nine weeks of life and growth occurs still more rapidly in the subsequent weeks. Figure 4–1 shows the development of body form and size during the first four months of prenatal life. By the end of the ninth week, the embryo is obviously human. The neck muscles are beginning to hold the head erect, the nose is flat, the eyes are wide apart, the ears are low on the head, the trunk is evenly rounded, the limbs are nicely molded, the fingers and toes are well formed with the nailfolds apparent, the tail has regressed inward, and the embryo has attained the fetal state.

The fetal period, the time between the ninth week after conception and the day of birth is devoted to growth and refinement of the body. During its life within the uterus, the embryo (later, the fetus) is suspended in the amniotic fluid, attached only by its umbilical cord. The fluid, which acts as a shock absorber, protects it from the pressures and jolts of the mother's body. Fetal wax secreted by the

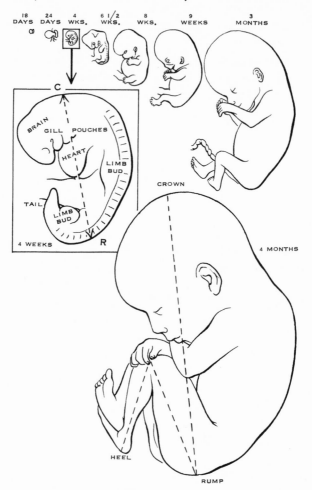

Fig. 4–1. The prenatal development of body size and form.

skin glands prevents the body from adhering to the enveloping membranes. The fetus is therefore free to change its position as soon as its internal organs are sufficiently developed to permit it to move.

Embryonic and fetal behavior in the form of movements begin as soon as the organs reach the necessary stage of development. The earliest movement is *autogenic,* that is, originating in the organ itself. The initial heartbeat is an example of autogenic activity, beginning about the twenty-fifth day after conception, before the heart has any connection with the nervous system.

Neurogenic activity in an organ results from its receiving nerve impulses from the spinal cord by way of motor nerves, the endings of which have penetrated the tissues of the organ. Endings of the motor nerves reach some of the muscles in the sixth prenatal week.

By the middle of the seventh prenatal week, some *reflexogenic* activity is possible. Reflexogenic activity is dependent upon the

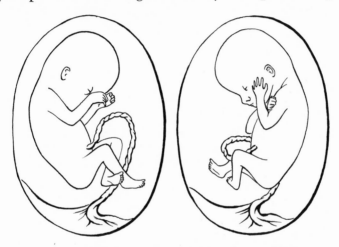

Fig. 4–2. Wormlike twisting of the twelve-week fetus.

development of nerve cells in connection with either the brain or spinal cord, and their sequential activity constitutes a reflex arc.

The earliest reflexogenic movement that has been noted in extremely prematurely delivered embryos is the sidewise bending of the neck in response to light stroking of the face. This may occur as early as the middle of the seventh week. By the middle of the eleventh week, not only the neck, but first the upper and then the lower trunk bends sidewise and may also straighten from the typical C-shaped posture shown in Fig. 4–1. In fetuses a little older, the hips turn. All these movements, following each other in sequence, produce (as Fig. 4–2 shows) an over-all, wormlike twisting. Movement occurs in a head-to-rump direction. This anterior-posterior sequence is maintained throughout both physical development and behavior.

From this time forward, arm and leg movements develop and become increasingly stronger. Movements of facial muscles and of fingers and toes become possible. By the nineteenth week contractions of chest and diaphragm muscles occur as "practice motions," as it were, for breathing to begin. No fetus born earlier than twenty-three and a half weeks after conception has ever been observed to breath, even temporarily. The earliest independent breathing observed under such conditions has been at about twenty-seven weeks after conception. During the later months of prenatal development, most fetuses become progressively more active so that their mothers have no doubt about their being alive.

The unborn fetus usually has alternating periods of activity and quiescence. It is likely to be active when the mother is still, and quiescent when she is active. Obviously the baby is already used to some "rocking and cuddling," as it were, before birth, so it is understandable that some rocking and cuddling is desirable after birth. When the chemical and physical changes that initiate the birth process occur, the fetus settles into one of a number of positions, the most usual of which is the one shown in Fig. 4–3, the so-called crown presentation. Table 4–1 provides a reference that shows the degree of development throughout the prenatal period.

All of the intrauterine movements we have described are involuntary; that is, they are reflexogenic, probably in response to stimuli such as increasing pressure of the uterine walls and changing internal chemistry. At no time during prenatal development nor for a short time after normal full-term birth, does the baby give evidences of voluntary behavior, that is, behavior controlled by the cerebral cortex of the brain. Because of this fact, in some instances of brain defect, postnatal behavior does not reveal the results of the defect for some weeks or even months.

THE NEWBORN INFANT

General Characteristics

Since most of the readers of this book will become parents, we shall give a few descriptions of newborn infants taken from their parents' notes, made on the day following the births. The names are fictitious:

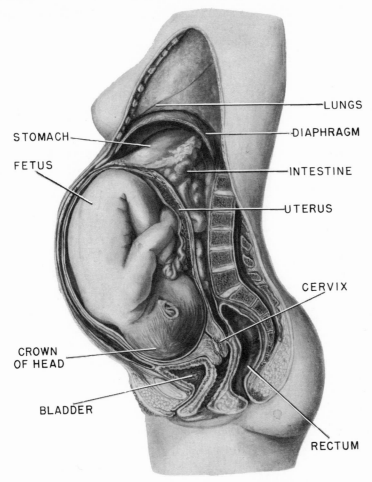

STOMACH

FETUS

LUNGS

DIAPHRAGM

INTESTINE

UTERUS

CERVIX

CROWN
OF HEAD

BLADDER

RECTUM

Fig. 4–3. A pregnancy in the ninth lunar month, showing a crown presentation. (Courtesy, Maternity Center Association, New York.)

INFANT NO. 1. MARK GERALD McINDOE

Born:	Friday, January 22, 1960 at 6:11 P.M. Expected January 30
Birth weight:	6 lbs. 15 oz., in delivery room
	6 lbs. 11 oz., in nursery, 2 hours later (must have urinated, had a bowel movement, and lost mucus, or all three)
Birth length:	20 inches
Circumference of head:	14 inches
Eye color:	Dark blue
Skin:	Red and wrinkled

Table 4—1

A Reference Table of Embryonic and Fetal Development

Age in Weeks	Crown-Rump Size in Inches	Body Form	Skin and Appendages	Mouth	Alimentary System	Breathing Apparatus	Urinary System
2.5	1/16	Flat embryonic disc	Single layer of cells		Continuous with yolk-sac		Embryonic bladder present
3.5	3/32	Cylindrical	Single layer of cells	A definite pit Membrane ruptures	Pharynx broad and flat Intestine present Bud of liver present	Groove in pharynx "Gill clefts" forming	First kidney present
4	3/16	Body flexed into C-shape Limb buds present	Single layer of cells	Jaws and tongue beginning	Pharynx, esophagus, stomach, intestine, liver, gall bladder, pancreas begun	Trachea and paired lung buds present Larynx a slit	First kidney degenerated Second kidney flourishing Third kidney begins
5	3/8	Nasal pits present Tail prominent	Epidermis two cells thick	Jaws developing	All above developing Intestine loops Cecum begun	Bronchial buds forming	Second kidney reaches limit Ureters begin
6	1/2	Head dominates Limbs recognizable Face forming	Milk (nipple) lines indicated	Lips and gums forming Salivary gland buds	Stomach changes position Intestine elongating Rectum indicated	Bronchi subdividing	Urethra forming

Week	Size						
7	3/4	Face and neck form; Digits beginning; Back straightens; Tail regressing	Mammary glands forming	Right and left palate folds forming	Stomach in final shape and position; Anus opens	Lung "lobes" indicated; Larynx developing; Nasal conchae appear	Third kidney developing; Urethra opens
8	15/16	Body evenly rotund; Fetal form attained	Continuing development	Continuing development	Intestinal villi forming; Liver very large	Lungs gland-like; Nostrils plugged	Continuing development interrelated with genitalia
10	1 5/8	Head erect; Limbs molded	Nail folds show; Epidermis thickens; Facial hair follicles forming	Palate folds fusing	Continuing development	Nasal passages forming	Kidneys secreting urine; Bladder develops
12	2 1/4	External genitalia (sex) distinguishable	Epidermis 3 cells thick; Dermis distinct	Milk tooth buds form; Palate fused	Bile secreted; Muscle in intestine	Conchae formed; Lungs acquire definite shape	Bladder becoming muscular
16	4 5/16	Face human; Body growing faster than head	Body hair, sweat, and sebaceous glands appearing	Hard and soft palates differentiated	Stomach and intestinal glands forming; Feces collecting	Nasal sinuses developing	Kidneys attain more typical shape
20–40 (5–10 months)	6 1/4–13 3/4	Fetus lean, wrinkled, red (5, 6, and 7 months); Fat collecting, body rounding (8–10 months)	Fetal wax present; Nails developed; Hair shed between 7 and 10 months	Permanent tooth buds form	Canal parts all developed	Faucial and pharyngeal tonsils typical; nostrils open	Kidney tubules form until birth, then cease

Table 4-1
A Reference Table of Embryonic and Fetal Development (Cont'd)

Age in Weeks	Circulatory System	Skeletal System	Muscular System	Sense Organs	Nervous System	Endocrines	Reproductive System
2.5	Blood islands in yolk-sac Cardiac plate present	Notochordal plate present			Neural groove		
3.5	Blood cells and vessels present Heart formed and beat begins	Notochord a rod	Mesenchyme segmenting	Optic and auditory plates present	Neural groove closing	Thyroid indicated in pharynx	
4	Chief arteries and veins formed Heart 2-chambered	Primitive vertebrae mass about notochord	40 pairs of mesenchymal segments present	Middle ear beginning Optic and auditory apparatus developing Olfactory plates arise	Neural tube closed Primary brain and paired nerves formed	Hypophysis begins	
5	Vessels extending Heart septa forming Spleen begins	Condensation of mesenchyme in positions of future bones	Primitive muscle masses in head, trunk, and limbs	Eyes and ears developing Olfactory pits form	5 brain vesicles Cerebrum bulging Nerves extending		Genital ridges present
6	Blood cells forming in liver Heart acquires its definite external form	First cartilage First indications of skull bones	Segmentation gone Premuscle masses coalescing	Eyes at 160°	Brain bending as result of growth Nerves extending Meninges forming	Thymus forms Parathyroids forming	Sexless gonads developing

7	Vessels, heart, and spleen developing	Cartilage formation more general	Muscles assuming final shape and positions	Continuing development	Cerebral hemispheres enlarging	Further development Suprarenals begin	Testes and ovaries distinguishable
8	Lymph sacs present	First ossification centers	Fetus capable of movement	Eyes converging External, middle, internal ears formed Taste-buds forming	Cerebral cortex and olfactory lobes differentiated	Continuing development	Ducts of the opposite sex degenerating
10	Lymphatic system developing	Continuing cartilage and bone formation	Lower trunk muscles developing	Iris, ciliary body and lacrimal glands forming	Spinal cord attains its internal structure		Uterus, sperm ducts, prostate Seminal vesicles
12	Blood cells forming in bone marrow Vessels become muscular	Notochord degenerating Upper bones well outlined	Smooth muscle in viscera	Retinal layers forming	Brain attains definitive shape Nerves developing	Pancreatic tissue forming	Testes in position for descent Vagina formed
16	Blood cells form in spleen Heart muscle developing	Most bones outlined Joints forming	Fetal movements can be detected through maternal body wall	Eye, ear, nose approaching final form General receptors forming	Cerebrum covers other brain parts Cerebellum developing	Thyroid attains typical shape	
20–40 (5–10 months)	Blood cells forming more in marrow and less in liver Some fetal blood vessels close (10)	Some ossification	Lower trunk muscles take typical form	All sense organs partially developed All functioning at birth except ear	Continuing development	Continuing development	Testes descend between 7 and 9 months

Infant No. 1. Mark Gerald McIndoe (*Cont'd*)

Hair: Brown and straight, 2 inches long at back
Eyebrows: None
Eyelashes: Short and light colored
Sex: Definitely male, testes in scrotum
Peculiarities: Second and third toes on each foot partially joined
Remarks: Cried at birth; skin covered with "peach fuzz"; very active
                     immediately after birth; instrument mark on side of head;
                     footprints look flat; several horizontal wrinkles across fore-
                     head

Infant No. 2. Gwen Ursula Pragliola

Born: Saturday, January 30, 1960 at 2:23 a.m. Expected January 27
Weight: 7 lbs. 4 oz.
Length: 19 inches
Eyes: Blue
Hair: Very little anywhere, very light peach fuzz all over
Skin: Pink
Eyebrows and
  eyelashes: Almost none
Peculiarities: Small wart on top of head; small toe on right foot lies on top
                     of next toe; dimple in left cheek
Remarks: Cried very little; long pointed fingernails, and she began im-
                     mediately to scratch herself with them (not intentionally, of
                     course)

Infant No. 3. Andrew Kane Klawansky

Born: February 15, 1960, at 5:23 a.m. Expected March 12
Weight: 7 lbs. 7 oz. (so not premature in development)
Length: 20 ⅘ inches
Hair: Dark brown, curly
Eyes: Dark blue
Skin: Red, not very wrinkled
Sex: Male, rather small genitals, needs circumcising
Peculiarities: None, except long thin arms and legs
Remarks: Sneezed as he was being born and for quite a while afterwards;
                     cried between sneezes; kicked a lot

It is obvious from these three typical descriptions that considerable variation occurs in time of birth, weight, proportions, general
appearance, and behavior of normal infants. The infant is a complete stranger to his parents, and the parents in these cases recorded
the facts as they were told to them, and also things that they them-

selves noticed. The professional obstetrician, pediatrician, and psychologist would note some other characteristics in addition. Some of these are discussed in the following paragraphs.

Reflexes

It will be recalled that all the systems of the infant's body begin to develop early in prenatal life and that he (or she) has been making facial grimaces, swallowing, making chest movements that will be used in breathing, grasping, kicking, punching, and squirming in response to stimuli within his own body and in his cramped environment for some months. These movements are all reflexogenic or, as they are more frequently called, *reflex actions.*

If the infant is to live outside the mother's body, the first and most important reflex action that must occur is breathing. Until birth, the infant has been completely immersed in amniotic fluid and his lungs have never expanded. But if he is normal, all his organs are ready to work when he comes in contact with air. The contact with the air itself, an unaccustomed medium of a different temperature, may stimulate some of the necessary nerve impulses. It is believed, however, that the accumulation of carbon dioxide in the infant's blood, as the placenta loosens, stimulates a nerve center in the lower brain to send nerve impulses, by way of nerve fibers, to the *diaphragm* (the sheet of muscle that forms the floor of the chest cavity) and to the chest muscles. The nerve impulses cause the diaphragm to contract and lower, thereby increasing the size of the chest cavity. Air then passes into the lungs, inflating them until they fill at least a good portion of the chest cavity. The carbon dioxide content of the blood decreases, and the diaphragm relaxes and helps to push out the inhaled air. As carbon dioxide then increases in the blood, the diaphragm and chest muscles contract again, and rhythmical breathing has begun. Sneezing, coughing, and yawning are all reflex actions that can occur as soon as breathing is established.

It has been noted that, soon after birth, the normally developing infant performs certain definite responses to stimuli received at definite locations of the body. Figure 4–4A, B, shows one of these responses, the *Babinski reflex,* the fanning apart of the toes following a gentle stroking of the sole of the foot. This response indicates that nerve endings in the skin of the sole of the foot are capable of responding by physicochemical change to the slight pressure of the stroking. Their response initiates the same kind of change, which is the *nerve impulse,* along nerve fibers in the legs in the direction of the spinal cord. These impulses stimulate other endings of neurons

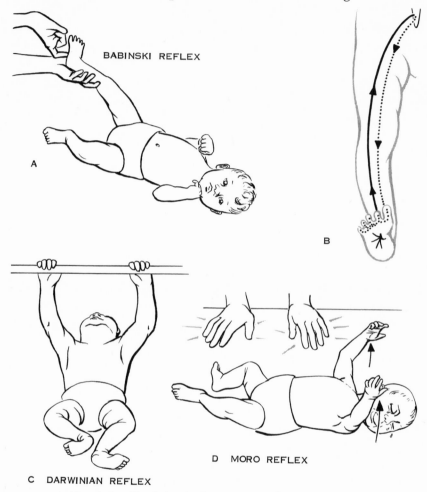

BABINSKI REFLEX

A

B

C   DARWINIAN REFLEX

D   MORO REFLEX

Fig. 4–4.   The Babinski, Darwinian, and Moro reflexes.

in the cord, which, in turn, initiate changes in the motor nerves which begin in the cord and terminate in the muscles attached to the toes. As a result, the toes fan apart in less time than it takes to read this explanation.

Figure 4–4C shows the *Darwinian* or "grasp" *reflex,* which occurs when nerve endings in the palms of the hands are stimulated by contact with something firm. Apparently nerve impulses arriving in the spinal cord stimulate association neurons and motor nerves that end in the muscles of the palms and the fingers, although not in those of the thumbs. Most infants grasp with such strength that they can be lifted up by a rod in their grasp.

When a newborn baby is placed flat on his back on a firm, flat surface, he throws out his arms and legs, then brings them—particularly his arms—forward, in a movement resembling an embrace. Figure 4–4D shows this *Moro* or "startle" *reflex*. Crying usually accompanies it. Apparently the response to stimulation of nerve endings in the skin of the infant's back initiates the stimulation of sensory fibers to the spinal cord, association neurons in the cord, and motor nerves going to all parts of the body, resulting in these mass spontaneous movements. The Babinski, Darwinian, and Moro reflexes are all to be expected as a follow-up of what is known of fetal behavior and neurology.[85] All three cease to occur during the early months of postnatal life.

Other reflexes that the infant performs at birth or soon after remain throughout life, some with modifications. Sucking depends upon important reflex movements, since it is by this method that the infant gets most of his nourishment for some time. The initial stimulus for sucking is somewhat different from what some mothers expect. If the infant's lips are touched, the response may be a firm closing of the mouth. If, however, the lower cheek is stroked gently, the lips are likely to begin to purse and relax rhythmically, which are the movements necessary for sucking. Once the infant begins to suck in food satisfactorily, the cheek-stroking becomes unnecessary. Apparently the stimulus for the lips to purse and relax results from stimulation of the sensory nerves of the lower cheeks rather than from those of the lips. This stimulation happens naturally when the mother puts the child to her own breast. Swallowing is a reflex action that occurs as a result of stimulation by liquids in the mouth, either saliva itself or food mixed with saliva. Hiccupping, which results from the spasmodic contraction of the diaphragm and windpipe, is common in babies. Defecation, or colon elimination, and urination occur as purely reflex activities soon after birth and for months thereafter. Apparently pressure of the contents of the lower intestine or the urinary bladder respectively stimulates nerve endings in their walls. Nerve impulses pass to the spinal cord, stimulating association neurons in the cord and along motor nerves which end in the intestine or the bladder, causing them to contract and force their contents out of the body.

A number of other reflexes occur following birth. The infant blinks his eyelids, and in doing so squeezes his tear glands and so keeps the surface of the eyes moist. His irises contract and relax in response to light, changing the size of the pupils, thus regulating the amount of light that enters the eyeballs. The infant also turns his head from side to side, kicks and squirms, and cries in response to discomfort of any kind.

Equipment for Development of Physical Skills

As we have seen, babies have already begun to develop physical skills before they are born. While the fetus is being nourished and protected by the mother's body, physical skills such as grasping, kicking, and twisting may develop even though some fetal systems—the circulatory system, for example—may be defective. At the time of leaving the mother's body, however, the baby's systems—the skin, the nervous, digestive, breathing, circulatory, excretory, skeletal, muscular, and endocrine systems—all must be functional, at least to a degree, if the physical skills that are necessary for normal living are to continue to develop. It is for this reason that the obstetrician or pediatrician is interested in the infant's performance of the expected reflex actions, in the regularity and quality of his heartbeat, in the condition of his glands such as the thymus and testes, and in his general health and bodily development.

Some defects, such as openings in the walls of the heart or undescended testes, may be eliminated naturally after birth; in other cases, treatment, possibly by surgery, may be necessary. In the great majority of babies, however, the basic equipment is sufficiently well-developed so that coordination and effective physical skills may develop satisfactorily.

Equipment for Development of Vocal Skills

Vocal skills develop through the regulation of the passage of air through the breathing apparatus and the mouth. Since the breathing apparatus is not in contact with air before the birth process is under way, no use of the vocal organs can be made before delivery is occurring. If the breathing apparatus is ready to function on contact with air, however, as is the case in most babies, sounds may be made even before the baby is completely delivered. Much has been written about the significance of the "birth cry." To the mother, it means simply but wonderfully that her child is alive. To the obstetrician, it indicates that the baby's breathing apparatus is performing the necessary exchange of gases between his body and the air, and it also permits him to see if the roof of the mouth, the tongue, and other mouth parts are developed normally.

Babies' cries at birth differ with the strength and development of the baby and with the length and difficulty of the labor to which the baby has been exposed. Usually, the cry of the newborn sounds something like "la, la, la," each "la" accompanying an exhalation of breath. The cries can be vehement if the baby is strong. In order to cry, equally strong inhalations have to be performed. These inhalations help to inflate the lungs, and so assist in the exchange of carbon dioxide from the body for oxygen from the inhaled air. At birth, all sounds that the baby makes are entirely random and reflexogenic in nature.

Equipment for Development of Intellect

Intellect is the power of perceiving, thinking, understanding, and of relating of concepts. It is in the potential development of intellect that the human species differs most markedly from all other species of animals. Upon what, then, does intellect depend? Obviously upon the functioning of the whole body, since all systems are interdependent. However, if the other systems are normal, it is upon the efficiency of the nervous system and the sense organs that the development of intellect is chiefly dependent.

At birth, the nervous system: the brain, spinal cord, cranial and spinal nerves, and autonomic branches, is present and functioning to some extent. Compared with the functioning of the circulatory and breathing systems, however, parts of the nervous system are functioning in a very immature manner at birth. The autonomic branches, those which regulate movements of the internal organs such as the digestive tract and the blood vessels, are functioning most efficiently of all. The cranial and spinal nerves, the spinal cord, and the lower portions of the brain are also functioning efficiently, as we have seen in our discussion of reflexes. It is the *cerebrum*, the uppermost part of the brain, the efficiency of which is necessary for perception, thought, and understanding, that is the part of the nervous system least well developed at birth. All the basic cerebral structures are present at birth and are continuing the development already well begun in fetal life. Their efficiency, however, will depend partly upon their degree of maturity and partly upon the effects of the external environment in postnatal life.

The external environment has its effects on the developing nervous system chiefly through the sense organs. The sense organs are, for the most part, highly specialized structures connected with the brain by fine extensions of nervous tissue, the *nerves*. The endings of these nerves, the *receptors*, are affected chemically and physically by specific conditions which we call *stimuli*. The stimuli induce physicochemical changes (*nerve impulses*) progressively along the nerves toward the brain, where changes in the cells result in various kinds of awareness which are called *sensations*.

It is difficult to learn exactly what sensations the typical newborn infant is capable of developing. It is known that chemical activity in the neurons of the cerebral cortex is necessary for the development of sensations, and that infants respond to some stimuli which produce sensations in adults. But we cannot be sure that the infant's response is a response to a sensation or merely a reflexogenic activity resulting from stimulation of nerves entering the brain stem, or in some cases, the spinal cord, and in turn of nerves leaving it.

All of the sense organs are fairly well developed structurally long before birth, but we do not know in all cases when the nerves that connect the sense organs with the brain begin to carry nerve impulses. The newborn infant gives no signs of recognition of anything. All his responses are either movements to or away from the stimulus, sometimes accompanied by crying and sometimes not.

It is unlikely that the newborn infant hears any sounds, because his middle ear cavities, at birth, are blocked with gelatinous tissue. This prevents the movements of the mechanisms (the eardrums and the bones of the middle ears) that are essential for conducting sound waves to the inner ears. Response to sounds usually does not occur until a few days after birth, when the ear cavities have cleared, and even then ordinary household sounds, such as the voices of the family and radio or TV, elicit no response. Sudden, loud noises, however, elicit mass movements, crying, and acceleration of breathing and pulse rates. The newborn has no sense of balance.

The human baby, unlike many other mammals at birth, has unfused eyelids and the eyes are open when the infant is not sleeping. The retina, the inner coat of the eyeball, contains the light-sensitive nerve endings, the "rods and cones." These are differentiated during the seventh month of prenatal life, and infants seem to be sensitive to light at birth. Intense light causes contraction of the irises (making the pupils smaller), the closing of the eyelids, and a general startled body reaction usually accompanied by crying. Continuous steady light seems to inhibit body activity; and infants tend to be more active in dim light than in either moderate light or in darkness. Whether or not the lens of the newborn changes in thickness is not known. The muscles which move the eyeballs in their sockets are weak and uncoordinated at birth, so it is not unusual for the infant to be temporarily "cross-eyed" or "wall-eyed."

Compared with the sensitivity of adults, the infant's gustatory sensitivity (the sense of taste) seems poorly developed. The tongue is well supplied with taste buds, but it is difficult to know how sensitive the nerve endings are and to what stimuli they are sensitive. Most young infants readily suck in semisweet solutions such as mother's milk, but sometimes reject salty, bitter, and sour solutions by refusing to suck and by crying.

Little is known with certainty about the olfactory sense (the sense of smell) at birth. By eight months of prenatal life, the olfactory structures are completed. Certain rather pungent substances such as vinegar, lemon, turpentine, and ammonia bring about more facial movements than does ordinary air, but these responses may result from stimulation of nerve endings in the mucous membranes other than those of the olfactory nerves, and thus are not proof of actual olfactory sensations developed in the cortex of the brain.

The sensations dependent upon stimulation of nerve endings in the skin seem to be the best developed at birth. Variation exists among infants, but most respond to warmth against their body by reduced movement often followed by peaceful sleep. Most infants cry, kick, and wave violently when exposed to cold. Even very young infants shiver when their bodies are bared to cool air. Again, of course, we cannot know whether these responses follow actual sensation, or whether they are purely reflexogenic. Most infants respond to gentle pressures and pats (cuddling) with quietness and what seems to adults to be comfort, and they cry in response to the quality of touch that may result from a parent's uncertainty about handling an infant. It would be helpful, of course, if young and inexperienced parents could know what sensations their baby actually experiences. Without that knowledge, even on the part of professionals in child development, it is probably fortunate that most parents interpret the child's reactions as how they themselves would feel under similar circumstances. Most parents soon develop confidence in handling their babies, so that their own movements become more relaxed.

Equipment for Development of Personality

Personality is usually thought of as the way each particular individual tends to behave, or as the behavior which distinguishes and characterizes an individual. It is a complex of biological and social reactions, which are determined partly by the hereditary nature of the physical systems and partly by the effect of the environment upon the functioning of the systems and of the body as a whole. Obviously, the personality of the newborn infant is not developed, but since the equipment for the development of motor and language skills, intellect, and emotions is present, it follows that this is also the equipment for the development of personality.

Each child is born with his own potential. Which traits of that potential develop and which do not, and to what degree any of them develop are matters of concern to all members of society. Society holds the parents most responsible for what happens to the child's potential in his early years, but even at birth, society intervenes in various ways. For example, most cultures require the newborn to be named and registered, and many require certain medical procedures such as use of 1 per cent silver nitrate solution in the eyes as a precaution against venereal infection.

At birth the human being has already undergone a tremendous amount of structural development. All his body systems are there, and birth is a graduation to a new environment which will push him and pull him, develop him and check him, and bring him to his adulthood as a unique person, the exact like of whom has never before lived.

Premature Infants

We have described the behavior of infants who are born well enough developed to live outside the mother's body without any particular kinds of care other than that expected of such immature beings. In the early part of this chapter, we described the behavior of embryos and fetuses delivered too early in their development to continue to live. Births of this type are referred to as *spontaneous abortions* or "miscarriages." When infants are born after seven months (rarely after six and a half months), they have a chance of living if they are sufficiently well developed and sufficiently well cared for. Approximately seven to ten per cent of all live births are premature.

Premature infants usually need careful regulation of temperature and moisture, and special feeding at short intervals. They are kept in incubators as long as they need this special kind of environment. Prematurity is a matter of degree of development rather than merely one of time spent in developing, and babies are usually designated as premature if they weigh less than 5½ pounds, regardless of their time of birth. The incidence of prematurity varies with the culture, the rate in the United States, for example, being higher in the lower socioeconomic groups than in the middle and upper groups.

The premature infant's chances for life depend upon a number of factors. In general, the nearer his weight is to normal birth weight, the better are his chances. His development is likely to differ somewhat from that of the infant of normal birth weight. Neurological defects and defects in vision occur more frequently in premature than they do in other infants.

The general characteristics are, as would be expected, somewhat different from those of infants of normal birth weight and development. In addition to difference in size, premature infants are relatively inactive, their breathing rate is irregular, and their cries are feeble. The head is relatively large with prominent eyes, and the abdomen protrudes. Male genitalia are small, and umbilical hernia (protrusion of the intestine under the skin at the navel) is common. The skin is thinner, more wrinkled, and of a deeper red than in the normal newborn. The nails are soft and the lanugo (fetal) hair is prominent over most of the body. Fat under the skin is scanty; hence the wrinkles in the skin. Body temperature is below normal. The blood vessels are extremely fragile, so that the infants bleed easily and require very careful handling. Their sucking and swallowing reflexes are particularly weak.

Mortality is still high in the first month of life for premature infants. It is estimated from hospital records alone that between 12 and 20 per cent die. More than half of these die in the first 24 hours after delivery. The chances for life and normal development increase with each day of survival.

If these babies survive and prove to be healthy, on the whole they seem to get along well. Gesell,[63] who has made intensive studies of premature infants as compared to normal full-term infants, says that the healthy premature baby does not have any advantage or precocity in development because of his head start. Neither does he suffer any appreciable setback. He follows the regular, orderly, and predictable sequence of growth which characterizes full-term infants. He proceeds along the path of physical and intellectual growth much as do other babies if allowance is made for his prematurity, meaning if his age is counted from conception rather than from birth. For example, a baby born two months premature (seven months after conception), should at six months of postnatal age be judged on developmental scales for full-term babies aged four months. By two years of postnatal age, the premature is little different from other two-year-olds.

There are details, however, in which the healthy infant who was born prematurely is likely to differ from the typical full-term infant, even when allowance is made for adjusted age. Prematurely born infants develop somewhat more slowly in motor controls, in speech, and in the development of relationships with other people. These are areas in which development may be slightly slower because of possible neurological weaknesses. It has been speculated, however, that the premature baby is likely to suffer these handicaps because of the over-protective attitude by his parents who for understandable reasons find it difficult not to be overprotective. Whether this is a reason for the slowness of development is still not fully confirmed by research. In sensory reactions, interestingly enough, prematures seem on the whole to be more alert than full-term infants. They hear less intense sounds, and react to less obvious things-to-be-seen than do average babies.[63] This doubtless explains why they have a tendency to react more easily to stimuli in the environment, hence, to be poorer sleepers, to become more easily fatigued, more irritable, and to have more nervous habits such as excessive thumb-sucking.

In summary, premature born babies have a higher mortality rate, and have more defects than do non-prematures. If, however, they survive and prove to be healthy, they grow physically and intellectually about as well as full-term children, but they seem not to make social and emotional adjustments quite as easily.

PHYSICAL ROUTINES DURING INFANCY

General Considerations

In Chapter 2, we discussed the fact that the parents are a primary influence on the baby's physical and psychological development. Since most of the contacts between parents and the baby stem from his routine needs, it is obvious that the character of the physical routines influences the child's development during his early postnatal life.

Sometimes young parents-to-be express concern about their ability to be good parents. Relatives and acquaintances respond to this concern in different ways. Some say in a sort of a threatening manner, "Don't worry! The baby will show you!" Others, more kindly disposed but less realistic, say, "Parenthood—motherhood anyway—comes naturally. You'll know what to do for your baby when you get him!"

Neither of these statements is true in all cases, especially among civilized people. By the time civilized people become parents, the culture in which they have been living for years may have confused them about the down-to-earth facts of human living. Their esthetic senses, for instance, have been trained to the point that they may overemphasize the appearance of the baby, his clothing, furniture, and so on. Normal odors may be displeasing to them, many women secretly feel that exposing the breasts for nursing is indecent, and some find nursing painful. Parents also have been subjected to all kinds of contradictory statements as they have been growing up. They have heard, "Do not play with the baby," "Cuddle the baby," "Feed the baby only on schedule," "Feed when the baby is hungry, not when the clock says so," "Constipation is dangerous," and "Constipation is not harmful." No wonder inexperienced men and women question their adequacy for parenthood!

The experience of having grown up in a family with a man and a woman who have been comfortable as a married couple and as parents, plus a basic knowledge of what a baby is, are two of the most valuable assets for adequate parenthood. Not everybody has had the first, and it is beyond one's power to acquire it. But all parents can acquire the second by a reasonable amount of study supplemented with sympathetic imagination.

If people understand that the new baby is about 7 pounds of normally developed and integrated organs, coordinated in their activities by a marvelously intricate nervous system, they have a good start. When the doctor tells them, "It's a boy," or "It's a girl," and "He (or she) is all right," they know that they have something to be grateful for right there. Most parents do not care what sex the baby has, they do not even notice that he is not beautiful, esthetically speaking, and they do not wonder what his potential intelligence will be. They are just glad that after the long months of pregnancy, he or she is a new human being structurally and functionally all right for his age.

It is reasonable to believe that this feeling of gratitude is the beginning of true parental love, and parental love guided by intelligent use of knowledge is as good a basis for the adequate management of a child and his environment as there is. Good pediatricians are guided by a concern to use their knowledge on a broad and deep scale, and the availability of such a physician for advice and treatment for the child, when needed, is the kind of reassuring tower of strength that even the most competent parents need.

As we have seen, just how much a young baby actually senses is questionable. His reflexes are highly efficient, however, so that by his crying when his body needs adjustment, he is well able to furnish attentive parents with clues to his needs. The manner in which these needs are cared for is as important as their fulfillment, since physical effects, and psychological effects, as well, are derived from fulfillment.

The baby "knows" practically nothing at birth; he may even have to be stimulated on the cheek to suck. He has recently come from a stable environment which was dark, warm, wet, soundproofed, and often in motion, into the outside world, which is sometimes light and sometimes dark, cooler, drier, often noisy, and sometimes still. Until his birth, he has never breathed; since birth, he has had to inhale and exhale air rhythmically. Before birth, he has never been in need of food because he had been supplied by way of his umbilical cord; since birth, he has had to learn to suck for food. He had never felt clothing; since birth, he has had to get accustomed to being wrapped up and laid on something firm. Before birth, his wastes had been flowing away continuously; he now has to get accustomed to their emerging from his body and to someone removing them and cleansing his body. Before birth, his sense organs had little stimulation; afterwards, many kinds of stimuli, varying degrees of light, moving objects, sound waves, chemical substances in food and air, textures of clothing, pressures of hands, of bath water, the bathinette, the crib, and varying temperatures, all begin to stimulate his sense organs.

Infants are not all alike, any more than adults are. They all have digestive tracts, but some have relatively strong mouth parts that enable them to suck well; others are weaker and suck poorly. Stomachs are not all of the same capacity; some infants can take in 6 ounces of food, and others can take in more or less, as the case may be. As a result, some need feeding more frequently than others. Nervous stimulation in the intestines differs among infants, so that some infants have colic, and others do not. Some tend to be constipated, and others tend to have loose bowel movements. As a result of these differences, infants "feel" differently early in life.

All infants have nervous systems and sense organs, but some infants are more sensitive to stimuli than others. Some are more sensitive to certain stimuli and less sensitive to others, and vice versa. Some have skins which become irritated more easily than others, so that one baby can stand soap, and another may not be able to. All infants have urinary bladders, but these differ in capacity and sensitivity to contents.

It is obvious that every infant is a unique individual whose parents can get acquainted with him and can adjust their own routines to him only after he is born. It is from the way in which they fulfil his needs as well as the degree to which they fulfil them that the infant begins to learn what the world is like. If, in his early life, the world seems good to him, he can, as he grows up, gradually accept facts about it that are not so good. If, in his infancy, the world seems to him cruel and untrustworthy, it may be very difficult for him, in later years, to accept the idea that anything or anybody in the world can be good and worthy of his trust. Children differ in this respect also, some being able to throw off the effects of early childhood as they gain in self-respect and self-confidence, others not being able to gain sufficiently in self-respect. It is helpful to parents to realize that the infant apparently lacks the mental capacity to detect the attitudes of the parents to him. He is sensitive not to the attitudes themselves but to the effects of the attitudes upon their methods of fulfilling his needs. Parental uncertainty, per se, has little or no effect; it is what the parent does and how she or he does it that has the effect.

The Need for Food

None of the complicated processes of growth and development occurs without the presence of adequate nutrients in the food. The infant at birth is equipped to take food in liquid form only. The substances produced by the mammary glands in the mother's body are his natural foods. True milk does not appear in the mother's breasts until some time between 48 and 96 hours after the baby's delivery. Prior to that time, even during the last few months of pregnancy in some cases, the breasts produce an alkaline, yellow secretion called *colostrum*. Colostrum contains more protein, vitamin A, and minerals, and less carbohydrate and fat than does true breast milk. It also contains chemical substances which have an antibiotic effect. It is mildly laxative, and the ideal first food for the infant to take by mouth.

If the baby is born at home or in a hospital where he is kept in a bassinet beside the mother's bed (the "rooming-in method"), the natural thing for most mothers to do is to offer the breast whenever the baby cries for no apparent reason other than hunger. The baby's early and relatively weak sucking stimulates the mother's entire body by way of her autonomic nervous system and also prepares her nipples for later, more vigorous sucking. When *lactation* (production of true milk) begins, the breasts often become full and firm. The mother derives relief from the baby's sucking. If mother and infant are together, she is likely to offer the breast whenever he seems to be willing to suck. Because the feeding gives mutual satisfaction and comfort to both mother and infant, they tend to work out a more or less flexible schedule to their mutual advantage. Home birth or rooming-in in a hospital is conducive of this achievement.

In many parts of the world today, however, babies are born in hospitals which operate on the group nursery rather than the rooming-in plan. Because the babies are brought to their mothers on schedule and left with them for only a certain number of minutes, during which time, some may not be hungry or sufficiently awake to suck well, some mothers and babies are unable to work out a satisfactory breast-feeding arrangement. If this is the case, the baby cries after he is returned to the nursery, and he is given a bottle of a prepared formula. The formula satisfies his need for food and he sleeps. As a result, he is likely to be sleepy or not hungry when he is next taken to his mother. Because he does not suck well, her glands soon respond by producing less milk. In addition, the baby finds it easier to get milk from the rubber nipple than from his mother's. As a result, in many cases, by the time mother and infant leave the hospital, both have found breast feeding unsatisfactory, and the baby thereafter is fed from the bottle.

A number of other factors enter into the feeding of infants. For example, the way in which an infant is to be fed is determined not only by hospital procedures but also by the ideas, feelings, and interrelationships of the wife, husband, baby, and the other siblings, and their relationships with their environment. Some husbands and wives do not favor breast feeding for various reasons, such as the emotional nature of the wife, or because of other factors in their particular way of living. Some physicians feel that the wife's physical or emotional health, in relation to the demands of home and perhaps outside work, is such that it is wise for her to feed her baby artificially.

In times past, if mother's milk was not available, babies died. Among the wealthier people in many cultures, it was customary for "wet nurses" to feed the babies, while the mother's milk production ceased from lack of stimulation of the breasts. Formerly, some hospitals maintained what was called a Registry for Mothers' Milk, to which mothers who had milk to spare donated or sold it. It was used to feed babies whose mothers could not provide their own milk for them.

Today, artificial formulas are so numerous and well tested that it is not difficult, in most cases, to find one that suits an infant who is not being breast fed. In actual practice, it seems to be not so much a matter of the kind of feeding the infant receives as the manner in which he is given it. The adult—mother, father, or nurse—can hold the baby close to the warm body and feed him from a bottle in almost the same position as if he were feeding from the breast. The baby seems to be sensitive to the warmth and gentle pressures and pattings of being held, and to the sound of the adult's voice, while he is getting adequate nourishment and sufficient sucking experience at the same time. Each individual case may be managed differently, however, and the details of procedure vary according to the type of situation and persons concerned.

Generally speaking, both the baby and the one who feeds him seem to benefit if, over a period of some months, the baby is held while feeding. The baby not only continues to benefit from the warmth and contact with the feeder's body and arms, but also learns to know the one who feeds him (Fig. 4–5). Thus his intellect and

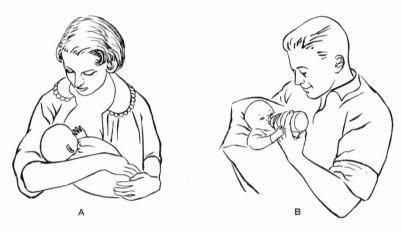

A   B

Fig. 4–5. The baby feels warmth and comfort and learns to know the one who feeds him.

personality begin to grow as he makes contact with another human being. The benefit of the close association is, of course, not all to the infant. The one who feeds the baby gains personally in the satisfaction that comes with contributing to the fulfillment of another's basic needs. Many busy mothers find nursing pleasant partly because it gives them time to sit down and rest.

As the months pass, and the infant gets stronger, he may seem to prefer not to be picked up to be fed. If he is happy, he may take the bottle comfortably in the sitting position without being held. When to hold and when not to hold the baby is one thing among many other things that the ones who care for a particular baby learn from him as he gives clues, provided they are sufficiently sensitive and interested to notice them.

All that a baby actually must have in the way of food to survive physically during the early months of life is sufficient mother's milk or properly balanced formula. However, in the interests of widening his experiences by way of all his sense organs, introduction of different kinds, textures, colors, flavors, and consistencies of foods as early as practical is desirable. Infants differ as to when they can begin to accept new foods and new ways of taking in foods. As early as the third month, many learn to take by spoon semisolid foods such as prepared cereals, strained fruit, and mashed egg yolk mixed with milk. Very small amounts are practical at first, and the quantity may be increased as the baby indicates he wants more. Infants differ in their likes and dislikes. One child may eat with obvious pleasure a mixture of strained pumpkin, tomato, and green beans; another will spit that mixture out, but seem to relish strained beef and liver soup. When the teeth begin to erupt at about six months of age, the baby begins to enjoy chewing many kinds of things, dry toast, crisp bacon, and in some cultures, uncooked bacon rind.

If the one who does the feeding has time, the process is interesting. It is enlightening to see what an infant can do in the way of learning to take food from a cup or a spoon, and to see his preferences and his dislikes. It is exciting to hear a tooth clink against a spoon for the first time, and the feeder and the infant can enjoy communicating with each other during the feeding process.

Weaning, which is generally understood to mean the cessation of eating by way of a nipple, is best done gradually. Infants seem to need a good deal of the experience of sucking even after they are able to eat from spoon and cup. As in many other things, they usually give the clue as to when they are ready to give up the nipple. When weaning is done sufficiently gradually, most infants give up the nipple by 18 months of age, although some still want it until later than that. It is not unusual for a child to have weaned himself and then to want his bottle back if another baby comes. If he is permitted to have it again, and the relationship between him and the new baby works out satisfactorily, he usually gives it up again shortly. Cultures differ greatly in the time and method of weaning.

Infants generally begin to want to feed themselves with their fingers or spoon before many months pass. They need the experience of doing so. During the second year of life, many children eat less than they did during the latter part of the first year. This is normal because growth rates reduce naturally, and the child needs less food. If those in charge of feeding the child accept the decreased appetite as something to be expected, and make no issue of it, feeding problems are unlikely to develop. The child's appetite increases when his needs increase. Most two-year-olds eat nearly all the foods the other members of the family eat. They need to have meat and other resistant foods broken up into pieces that they can manage. If the mealtime is pleasant, they tend to learn to use eating utensils in the same manner that their elders use them.

The Need for Sleep

All human beings need sleep; that is, recurring periods of normal unconsciousness. The more complete the lack of consciousness, the deeper we say the sleep is. Most newborn babies sleep a great deal. Many sleep from one feeding until the next. Babies differ in respect to sleep. Some sleep more of the time than others do. Some sleep more deeply than others do, and so are wakened less easily. As the baby gets older, he needs less sleep, and begins to have wakeful periods. Some have their wakeful periods early in the day, others in the afternoon, some in the evening, and some at night. The baby's wakeful time may be changed somewhat by changing his feeding, bathing, and other routines.

Many newborn babies seem to sleep most comfortably in the position that they were in most of their time in the uterus; others sleep comfortably on their backs with their legs drawn up, their hands to one side, and their arms bent at the elbows (Fig. 4–6). As time passes, and the baby gets stronger, he changes his position more during his sleep, but many children revert to the "fetal" position during sleep for months and even years.

Generally speaking, if the home has enough rooms, it is desirable for the baby not to sleep in his parents' room. Most mothers are extremely sensitive to a baby's cry, but as long as the baby sleeps where he can be heard, it is better for him to start sleeping away from his parents so that the habit does not have to be broken later on, when he is aware of where he sleeps. The baby is being better prepared for his future life if the parent goes to his room when he needs help rather than having the baby (when he is able) get into the habit of going to the parents' room. Sometimes siblings manage to sleep well and actually enjoy each other's company in the same

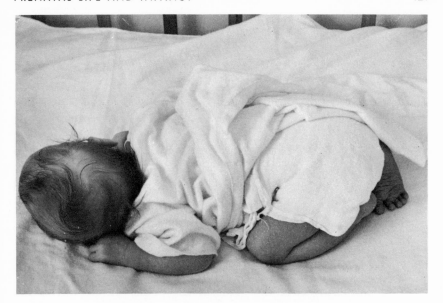

A

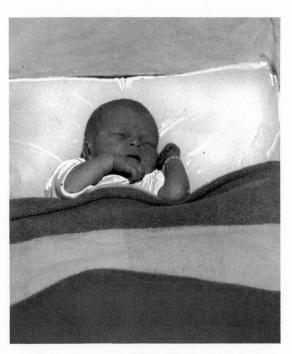

B

Fig. 4–6. Typical sleeping positions of the newborn.

room, at least, in their early years. Just as with feeding, cultures differ greatly in their customs connected with sleeping arrangements.

The Need for Bodily Comfort

In addition to being fed and being permitted to sleep comfortably, infants have certain other simple needs. Having come from an environment where the temperature was fairly constant, they need a more equable temperature than do older children. Gradually their bodies adapt to a wider range of temperature, and they soon enjoy bright, warm sunshine outdoors. Between their first and second birthdays, if they are comfortably clothed, most babies begin to like to play with snow, if they live in climates where there is snow.

Infants also need to be kept reasonably clean. Many pediatricians recommend circumcision of boys in the first two weeks of life, especially if the opening in the foreskin is too small to permit it to be moved back easily over the glans of the penis. If the boy is not circumcised, lint and secretions may accumulate under the foreskin and cause irritation.

Very young infants need little if any bathing. Pediatricians often recommend that the skin be wiped with a damp sterile cloth or with a bland oil. Secretions may be gently removed from the eyes, ears, nostrils, and mouth, and the genitalia need to be kept clean. Secretions and lint cause irritation if allowed to accumulate between the labia in baby girls. As infants grow and move around more, they enjoy their bath. Confident handling in a comfortable container of warm water is pleasant to most infants.

Since most human beings live in parts of the world where the climate is not always comfortable, some kind of clothing becomes necessary. Babies need only sufficient clothing to enable them to maintain a fairly constant temperature, and to contain urine and feces. They have no interest in what they are clothed and wrapped in, but adults have. As a result, babies' clothing and furnishings easily become matters of adult prestige.

As babies grow and develop, they exercise their bodies, and freedom to do so is essential to their continuing development. The problem of those who care for a baby is one of making sufficient freedom available while at the same time keeping it safe from bodily harm and protecting the property of others. As in all areas of child rearing, cultures vary tremendously in customs connected with cleanliness and clothing. Cross-cultural studies in these areas are enlightening to the student of child development.[227]

PHYSICAL GROWTH

Growth in Size

We have said that the average newborn infant weighs 7 to 7½ pounds and measures about 19 inches in length. Boys on the whole are slightly longer and slightly heavier than girls. In most families, the first-born baby usually weighs less at birth than subsequent siblings. According to Dr. Alan Guttmacher[72] of Johns Hopkins University, the smallest babies, weighing 6½ pounds or less, are likely to be born to teen-aged Chinese peasant women; the largest babies, weighing 7½ pounds or more, are likely to be born to white women of the upper socioeconomic classes, 35 years or more of age, and after bearing 10 or 11 children previously. Negro babies are usually intermediate, weighing between 6½ and 7½ pounds. Generally speaking, privileged socioeconomic classes have heavier babies than do less privileged classes.

If the physical routines of infants are favorable and if the infants are in good general health at birth, they usually lose 7 to 8 per cent of their birth weight and then begin to gain. Birth weight is usually regained by about 10 days after birth. They may be expected to double their birth weight between the fourth and fifth months, and to triple it by the end of their first year.

Infants grow rapidly in length also. By 3 months, as Fig. 4–7 shows, the typical infant gains 20 per cent of his birth length; by 12 months, 50 per cent; and by 2 years, 75 per cent. Girls usually attain half of their adult height by between 1½ and 2 years of age, and boys between 2 and 2½ years. Changes in body proportions from 2 months of prenatal life to 2 years of postnatal life are as spectacular as are over-all weight and height changes, as Fig. 4–8 shows. After birth, the legs grow more rapidly than does the trunk.

Individual Differences

Around each of the averages mentioned, there is a wide range of normality. Heredity as well as prenatal and postnatal environment affect both the degree and rate of growth. Heredity, of course, is a matter that is settled at conception, but the genes develop their full

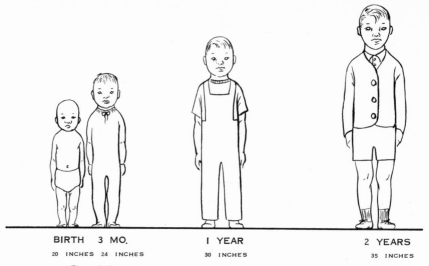

BIRTH   3 MO.   I YEAR   2 YEARS
20 INCHES 24 INCHES   30 INCHES   35 INCHES

Fig. 4–7.   Increase in height from birth until two years.

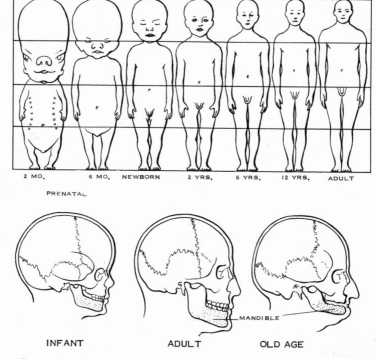

2 MO.   6 MO.   NEWBORN   2 YRS.   6 YRS.   12 YRS.   ADULT

PRENATAL

INFANT   ADULT   OLD AGE

Fig. 4–8.   Changes in body proportion between two months of prenatal life and adulthood.

potentialities for height, weight, and body proportions only in the most favorable environment. Prenatal environment involves the health, habits, and nutrition of the mother; postnatal environment involves the physical routines that we have discussed. If the infant receives the necessary constituents of the diet and if his emotional environment is also satisfactory, he grows as his genes dictate, fast or more slowly, long and slender, or short and stocky, as the case may be. On the other hand, if these needs are not supplied, his growth may be affected. If, for instance, he lacks sufficient vitamin D, he may develop *rickets* (*rachitis*), the essential feature of which is defective bone development. Not as evident to the eye but quite as real is the effect of insufficient kindly attention. We quote the 1959 *Handbook of Pediatrics* [194] as follows: "If the infant is deprived of the security and affection necessary to produce a sense of trust, he may respond with immobility, unresponsiveness, and indifferent appetite." Indifferent appetite alone may affect bone development. The emotional state may affect exercise and posture, which in turn affect the shape of the developing bones. On the whole, height is less affected by environmental forces than is weight, which may fluctuate from time to time as a result of illness or changes in diet, exercise, and rest.

THE DEVELOPMENT OF MOTOR SKILLS

The infant, as we have seen, is born sufficiently well developed to carry on his internal physical and chemical processes and also to make random, uncoordinated movements by means of his skeletal muscles. All of the skilled movements that he will master in his lifetime develop from these random movements; that is, all the movements of hands, eyes, of the organs involved with speech and facial expression, and all the total body movements that will result in the individual's degree of poise and grace at rest and in motion.

The mastery of motor skills begins to develop in infancy from two factors: (1) continuing *growth* and *maturation* of body tissues, and (2) the infant's *learning* to control muscle contractions, through which he gradually eliminates wasteful, unproductive movements while retaining the strengthening, useful and satisfying movements through practice.

The development of motor control follows definite patterns. From mass movements, specific movements emerge; generally, large muscles are controlled before smaller ones. The development of total body control, as Fig. 4–9 indicates, proceeds from head down the trunk (cephalocaudal direction), and from the trunk to hands and feet (proximodistal direction).

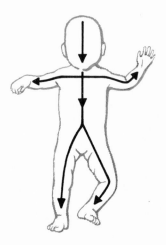

Fig. 4–9. Direction of development of motor controls.

Achievement of Erect Posture

One of the traits that distinguishes the human from most other mammalian species is erect posture. However, human infants have to mature sufficiently before they can achieve this trait. Achievement of erect posture is an interesting example of cephalocaudal development, as the accompanying figures show (Fig. 4–10, A–G).

At birth, when the baby is laid in the prone (face down) position (Fig. 4–10A), he is able to lift his head briefly. When laid in the supine (face up) position (Fig. 4–10B), he can turn his head from one side to the other and bend his trunk slightly in the worm-like movement he had developed before birth, but he cannot lift any part of his trunk.

By about 3 months after birth, when lying in a supine position, the trunk is likely to be straight rather than twisted, as it was earlier. When in the prone position (Fig. 4–10C), the infant lifts his head and chest and directs his gaze in various directions.

At 4 months, the infant can be pulled into a sitting position, as in Fig. 4–10D. The head lags a little at this time. By 5 months, the head lag disappears when the infant is pulled into this position. At about this time, the infant can roll his body from the supine to the prone position.

Between 6 and 7 months, the infant sits briefly when placed in a sitting position, and then topples over. By about 7 months, when placed in the prone position, he can pivot his body around a point, thus describing a circle.

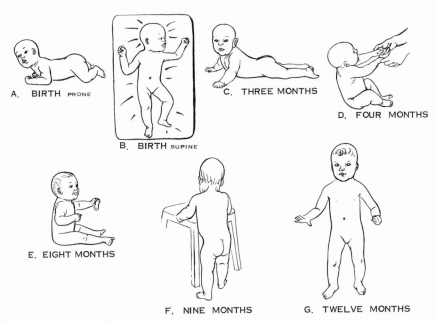

A. BIRTH PRONE

B. BIRTH SUPINE

C. THREE MONTHS

D. FOUR MONTHS

E. EIGHT MONTHS

F. NINE MONTHS

G. TWELVE MONTHS

Fig. 4–10. Achievement of erect posture.

By 8 months, most infants can sit without support and play with a toy at the same time (Fig. 4–10E). Most 9-months-old infants creep * on hands and knees (or some modification of that position), and most can pull themselves into a standing position at this age (Fig. 4–10F). Their legs are still very short in proportion to the trunk, and the buttocks are small in proportion to the shoulders.

* The words used to describe infant locomotion may be confusing because they differ with cultures. Generally speaking, "crawl" is used in England to designate any kind of locomotion in which all four limbs are used. In the United States, "creep" is more generally used for four-limb locomotion. Some people, however, use both "crawl" and "creep" and distinguish between them as follows: "crawling" referring to locomotion with the trunk touching the floor and being moved along by the pulling and swimming-like movements of the limbs; "creeping" referring to locomotion when the trunk is raised off the floor and moved by the hands and knees. The two kinds of movements indicate increasing strength and control of the trunk muscles, with "crawling" preceding "creeping." [87]

By 12 months, most infants have developed sufficient neural, skeletal, and muscular structures and controls to be able to stand alone (as in Fig. 4–10G) for brief periods. For many months thereafter they easily and frequently fall into the quadruped position, but by one year of postnatal life they have at least begun to perfect the human attribute of erect posture.

Learning To Walk

The accomplishment of locomotion in the erect position is a complicated process involving strength, coordination, and psychological factors. After an infant pulls himself into the standing position, it usually is not long before he begins to "cruise" along his playpen railing, or around whatever he pulled himself up by. He does what his muscles and nervous system permit him to do. The exercise that his body gets from doing what he is ready to do stimulates further development and coordination.

By 11 months of age, most infants will walk with both of their hands held. Most evince delight at their prowess and give evidence of a developing sense of satisfaction with their accomplishment, especially if adults express encouragement.

By 12 months of age, most of them are ready to walk with only one hand held. Their balance is poor, and they often stumble, hanging on to the one hand with great strength. If accidents such as painful falls or illnesses do not affect their attitude toward walking, most infants begin to walk alone between 12 and 15 months. Some begin earlier, and some equally healthy children do not begin until later. In two or three months after they begin to walk, most infants begin to run awkwardly.

Obviously, adequate nutrition and general normal development are necessary for successful walking. Heavy infants have more trouble coordinating their bodies, and when they fall, they may feel more pain. Children who are encouraged to walk before their bodies are ready may become fearful and so delay their muscular and nervous development. Infants generally walk alone when their bodies are ready for them to do so. Some overprotective adults interfere with normal walking when the infant is ready. Their interference may have undesirable results in the form of irritability or fearfulness on the part of the infant.

Learning To Use the Eye Muscles

The three pairs of muscles that move each eyeball in its socket, and the internal muscles that regulate the size of the pupils, are sufficiently developed before birth to begin practice movements. Most newborn infants open their eyes for brief periods. Their pupils contract in response to light within the first few days after birth. Many infants seem to be mildly responsive to light in the first few weeks of postnatal life, in that their eyes follow a shining object back and forth.

By two months of age, most infants can focus both eyes at the same time upon an object for short periods. Deviation of one eye or the other is common until 6 months of age, after which periodic instability is common until 18 months of age. As is true of any system, the muscles and nerves supplying the eyes and controlling eye movements have to develop to a state of readiness before they can begin to function efficiently. Once they arrive at the necessary state of development, the infant practices their use and thereby further stimulates their development.

If, after about 18 months of age, the two eyes fail to maintain parallel coordination, the child becomes cross-eyed if one or both eyes turn toward the nose, or wall-eyed if one or both eyes turn toward the side of the face. In cases where one eye only turns, the image received in the brain from that eye tends to be suppressed, with consequent lessening of vision from that eye. As a result, the child begins to depend upon the other eye only. Surgical correction or correction by exercise sometimes brings good results.[194]

Learning To Use the Hands

Earlier in this chapter we discussed the Darwinian reflex, which involves the palm of the hand and the four fingers, with the thumb only slightly involved. This characteristic involuntary grasp begins to weaken in the first month after birth. By about 2 months of age, if objects such as toys or fingers are placed within the infant's hand, either left or right, he voluntarily holds on to them. By 4 months, he moves whatever he is holding toward his mouth. By about 5 months, he reaches out with whichever hand is closer to the object that he wants. By 7 months, he can transfer an object from one hand to the other, and can bang the table or the floor with the object in his hand. Soon after this age, he can handle an object in each hand at the same time, although he still has little use of the thumb.

Thumb-finger opposition is gradually achieved by about 8 months of age. Gesell [61] has said that the infant takes hold of his world with his eyes before he can take hold of it with his hands. Figure 4–11, A–D shows the development of hand skill in infancy. Figure 4–11A

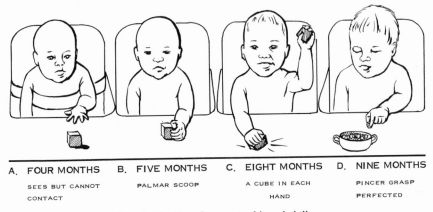

A. FOUR MONTHS	B. FIVE MONTHS	C. EIGHT MONTHS	D. NINE MONTHS
SEES BUT CANNOT CONTACT	PALMAR SCOOP	A CUBE IN EACH HAND	PINCER GRASP PERFECTED

Fig. 4–11. Development of hand skills.

shows a child 4 months of age who sees but cannot make skilled contact with an object. His eyes are focused on the cube; he waves his hands but cannot make anything but an accidental contact with it.

Figure 4–11B shows a child 5 months old with eyes focused on the cube and one hand scooping it from the side with his palm and four fingers. By 8 months of age, as Fig. 4–11C shows, the child has been able to pick up a cube in each hand, and his thumbs are taking part in holding on to the cubes. By 9 months of age, the child has perfected a "pincer" grasp. In Fig. 4–11D, he is picking up a sugar pellet about the size of an aspirin tablet, with dainty movements of the thumb and forefinger.

Most infants show no preference in using their hands during the first year of life. They shift from using one to the other, depending largely on the proximity of the hand to what is wanted. Shifting continues in the second year, but most infants begin to show preference for the use of one hand or the other during the second year. Opinions differ as to whether a slightly left-handed child should be influenced to use his right hand or not. Some believe that the child should be permitted to find and develop his own preference; [19] others believe that "handedness" should be trained.[81] Actually, left-handedness is not as much of a handicap as it once was, when everything was made and done for right-handed people. Today many tools, appliances, classroom chairs, and other furnishings are made for left-handed as well as for right-handed people.

During the second year of life, children enjoy scribbling with crayons and pencils. They try to imitate simple marks made by adults. Children who still use bottles may like to hold their own bottles. They are able to hold spoons and cups and to feed themselves with some spilling and mess. Often, the spoon turns upside down before its contents are deposited in the mouth, and sometimes the spoon hits beside the mouth rather than in it. These manual skills all improve with practice, and most infants are anxious to practice.

Learning To Use the Mechanism for Speech

Just as muscular skills develop from the random movements that the infant executes at birth, so skills connected with language and social communication develop from the sounds that the infant begins to make early in life. All the sounds that the human being makes by way of his vocal apparatus are made by regulating the amount of force of the air as it passes over the vocal cords in the larynx. Most of the sounds are made as the air is exhaled. Figure 4–12 shows the vocal mechanism in action. In order for air to pass in and out of the body, the muscles of the chest, throat, and head must function in a coordinated manner. Jaws, tongue, and lips all operate in regulating the kind of sounds that are emitted with the exhaled air.

If the newborn breathes satisfactorily, he can force air out vigorously and so cry noisily. This is purely a reflex activity. The noise he makes is likely to sound like "la, la, la" because his tongue hits the roof of his mouth with each exhalation. As he develops, the "la" sound changes to "wa" or "ya" because the jaw and lip muscles begin to affect the sound by their contractions.

During the early months of life, the infant learns by experience that his crying is followed by feeding or some treatment that makes him less uncomfortable. When he is very young, he is asleep whenever he is comfortable, but gradually he begins to remain awake when nothing is disturbing him. In these wakeful periods, he begins to move his mouth parts and so make sounds other than those made in crying, such as coos, babbles, gurgles, and grunts. Babies sometimes seem to be listening to their own hiccups.

By 4 months of age, the normal infant laughs aloud. By 5 months, he squeals, and by 9 months he has added "da-da" and "ma-ma" and other vowel sounds to his repertory. By 12 months, he may have

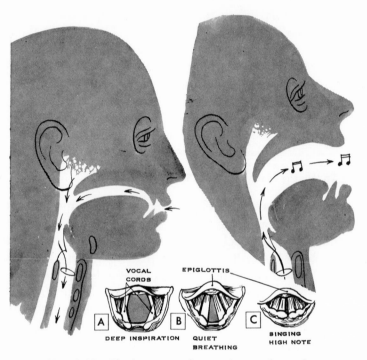

Fig. 4–12. The human mechanism for vocal sounds.

added 3 to 6 words. These may be parts of names such as "Pa" for a sister Patty, or "bye-bye" or "ta-ta" for "good-by." Many families help the baby to associate his sounds, "da-da" or "pa-pa" with his father, and "ma-ma" with his mother. Parental approval, expressed by their smiles, kind words, and caresses, is highly satisfying to the baby. His feeling of satisfaction connected with his achievement of certain words results in his retaining those words or syllables and in his dropping other less rewarding syllables such as "la-la" and "ug-ug."

Very frequently, babies of 12 to 15 months of age not only have their few words mastered, but also develop what has been called "expressive jargon," a sequence of sounds with a rhythm and inflection, closely approximating the language of the culture which they will eventually speak.

This stage in the development of language occurs at about the time when a great deal of the child's energy is being used in accomplishing upright locomotion. For some children, this is a period when so much attention is given to walking and learning to run that language development falls into the background. Usually, when walking and running skills are achieved, progress in language development is resumed.

Learning To Control the Elimination of Body Wastes

All cultures require children to learn some habits connected with the elimination of their body wastes, although they differ in their expectations and methods. Achievement of control in this area, like all others, depends upon the readiness of the organs concerned. The organs concerned in waste elimination are the lower part of the *large intestine* and the *anal sphincter* (circular muscle around the posterior opening of the alimentary canal) and the *urinary bladder* and the *urethral sphincter* (circular muscle around the lower opening of the bladder). Voluntary control of these sphincter muscles occurs only when nerve impulses from the intestine and bladder reach the forebrain and result in sensations of fullness, and when the sphincters can be held in a state of contraction. As we have seen, development occurs in a cephalocaudal sequence. As a result of their location, voluntary control of the sphincters is somewhat delayed.

Infants seem to be aware of fullness in the lower intestine for some months before they are aware of bladder fullness. As a result, control of bowel elimination is likely to be achieved earlier than is control of urination. Even as early as 6 months of age and from then on, some babies become quiet and look preoccupied as they sit still and cease to play with their toys. If at these times they are picked up pleasantly and, without fuss, sat on a pot or toilet, they may defecate. If the infant is aware that his achievement meets with approval, he soon learns to associate the sensation of fullness with a certain place and a feeling of satisfaction if he controls his anal sphincter ("holds back") until he is in the "right place" for defecation.

In most infants, awareness of urinary bladder fullness does not occur until near the middle of their second year. The child does not know that his bladder was full until he feels it emptying. Gradually he associates certain sensations with bladder fullness, and it is not until then that he can begin to inform anyone that he needs to empty his bladder. With approval that comes with waiting and urinating in an accepted place, he begins to increase his control, at least while he is awake. Most children do not achieve dryness while sleeping until some time after their second birthday.

Table 4–2 provides an over-all picture of postnatal development at the various stages of life. Students may find it helpful to refer to Table 4–1 (pages 98 ff.) and Table 4–2 as they study the various periods of life in the following chapters.

THE DEVELOPMENT OF EMOTIONS

Early Generalized Emotion

In the early part of the twentieth century, psychologists believed that newborn infants were capable of three kinds of emotion: fear, love, and anger.[224] If they were dropped or exposed to sudden, loud noise, their behavior was interpreted to express fear; if they were stroked or patted, they were believed to express love; and if their movements were restricted, their behavior was interpreted to express anger.

Increased knowledge of the neurological and muscular development of the infant at birth, together with more objective observation, has led to the current view that the newborn infant is capable only of *generalized* and *undifferentiated excitement* in response to the stimuli that his environment provides. As his life proceeds, these responses are sorted out, as it were, those that are productive of satisfaction in specific situations being retained, and those that are unproductive of satisfaction being eliminated. It will be noted that this principle in the development of specific emotional responses is similar to that shown in the development of motor skills from random, uncoordinated movements, and in the development of language skills from the meaningless sounds of early life.

The genes that are received by way of the egg and the sperm at conception dictate the prenatal development of the systems of the body. In so doing, they also predispose certain parts of the body to be sensitive to certain stimuli after birth, the skin to soft touch, and the muscles to restriction of movement, for example. The genes also predispose certain parts of the body to respond in certain ways to certain stimuli. For example, the baby whose muscular movements are restrained uses his breathing and vocal apparatus to scream.

Development of Specific Emotions

As in all cases, environment begins to modify hereditary behavior in early infancy, and in a few months, the early generalized responses to the environment begin to differentiate. By 6 months of age, most infants are able to express their *distress, delight, fear, disgust,* and *anger* in ways that adults can easily interpret. Since we tend to forget that all behavior, including emotion, is expressed by way of the systems of the body, it may be well to describe briefly how these five emotions are usually expressed. Distress, fear, and anger are all expressed by crying, that is, by the vigorous use of the breathing and vocal apparatus, but they are differentiated from each other by muscular movements of the other parts of the body as well as by the kind of crying. The cry of distress, such as from hunger or general bodily discomfort, is monotonous. If the distress is not alleviated, the cry rises in pitch, and if distress continues unalleviated, the cry gives way to low moans as the infant becomes exhausted. In distress, the body is mildly active. The cry of anger is a longer, more piercing cry. The infant sucks in deep breaths between cries and may "hold his breath." If he does, his face becomes purpled. If he loses consciousness, he immediately begins to breathe again. In anger, the infant beats the air or clothing with his hands and feet more vigorously than in distress. The cry of fear is sharp and high-pitched, and the infant tries to move his body in the direction away from the cause of his fear, such as a dog, for example.

The baby is likely to express disgust, in connection with feeding, for example, and tries to get away from the cause of his disgust. If the nipple disgusts him, he pushes it out of his mouth. He spits out food that displeases him. In a few months he uses his hands to push disgusting things away. If he does not succeed, disgust gives way to anger, and he begins to express himself in screaming, waving, and kicking.

The infant expresses delight as vigorously as he expresses unpleasant emotions. By 6 weeks of age or soon after, he smiles, and if encouraged, laughs aloud, beats the air with his hands palms down, kicks, and uses all the muscles in his body. He responds gaily to

Table 4–2

A Reference Table of Postnatal Development

Age	Stage	Height	Weight	Proportions and Posture	Skin
0	Newborn	18"–21"	6–8 lbs.	Head large: ¼ of total body length; limbs especially legs short; thorax large; pelvis small	Smooth, delicate, and downy
0–2 yrs.	Infancy	27"–32"	Birth weight triples in first year 27–29 lbs. by 2 yrs.	Trunk and limbs lengthening faster than head. Lower face growing faster than skull; erect posture acquired	Smooth, delicate, and downy
2–6 yrs.	Early childhood	32"–44"	Slow gain 40–42 lbs. by 6 yrs.	Preceding tendencies continuing; baby fat disappearing toward 6 years	Becoming less delicate and downy
6–12 yrs.	Late childhood	Great variation; girls tending to be taller than boys	Slow gain 80± lbs. by 12 yrs.	Fat continuing to decrease; body becomes more and more "gangling"	Becoming less delicate and downy
12–16 yrs.	Early adolescence	Great variation; boys tend to gain on girls; spurt usual	Male 120± female 100–110± by 16 years	Growth spurt; limbs elongate; boys' shoulders broaden; girls' pelvis and bust develop	Pores enlarge; glands more active; acne frequent
16–21 yrs.	Late adolescence	Male 67"± female 64"±	Male 140± female 120±	Continued growth and figure development, but slowing down	Acne tends to decrease, then cease entirely; glands stabilize
21–45 yrs.	Early adulthood	Male 67"± female 64"±	Male female Great variation 130–250 100–175	Fully developed and fully functional Head ⅛ total body length Trunk ⅜ total body length Legs ½ total body length	Wrinkling begins in most mobile parts: face, neck, hands, and genitalia
45–65 yrs.	Middle adulthood	Male 67"± female 64"± Tendency to begin to decrease	Tendency to increase in both sexes; somewhat more in female	Cartilage begins shrinkage, causing postural changes	Wrinkling increases; pigmentation increasing
65 yrs.	Late adulthood	Decreasing	Tendency to decrease	Shrinkage continues; posture continues to change in many	Wrinkling increases and deepens; pigmentation increases

Age	Hair	Teeth	Alimentary Tract	Breathing Apparatus	Voice
0	None — considerable; very fine; often not typical of later hair; usually comes out	None usually erupted	Stomach empty every 3–4 hours; equipped for liquid diet only	Fully functional *34–45 inhalations per minute; low susceptibility to infection	Crying sounds only
0–2 yrs.	Good growth of more typical color and texture	4–15 mos.: 8 incisors 12–18 mos.: 4 molars 18–24 mos.: 4 canines 16 temporary teeth	2 wks. to 3 mos.: colic common; 3–6 mos.: first solid food; 5–12 mos.: 3 meals a day, very hungry, usually "grown-up" diet by 2 yrs.	25–35 inhalations per minute; some susceptibility to infection	Range of sounds increases through cries, grunts, gurgles, babbling, and imitative word formation
2–6 yrs.	Often begins to darken	24–36 mos.: 4 molars By 3 yrs. 20 temporary teeth. Tooth loss begins between 5 and 6	Less interest in food; general diet	20–30 inhalations per minute; greatly increased susceptibility to infection	Range increases; sexes similar
6–12 yrs.	Often continues to darken; pubic and axillary hair may begin	4 six-year molars, 8 incisors, 8 premolars, 4 canines, 4 twelve-year molars, 28 permanent teeth	Often little interest in food; food dislikes Some have big appetite	18–25 inhalations per minute; susceptibility to infection lessening	Range increases slowly; sexes still similar
12–16 yrs.	Facial and body hair develops in both sexes; head hair tends to coarsen and darken	4 "wisdom" teeth between 18–21 years (Sometimes missing) 32 teeth (full dentition)	Sudden increased interest in food common Digestion excellent	16–20 inhalations per minute; susceptibility to infection stabilizing	Vocal cords elongate more in male than in female, resulting in "breaking" of boy's voice
16–21 yrs.	All hair tends to coarsen and to darken somewhat; mature texture achieved	Full dentition, lacking care, tooth loss may begin here (or earlier)	Appetite stabilizing Digestion excellent	16–20 inhalations per minute; susceptibility to infection stabilizing	Vocal cords continue to elongate but more slowly; male voice pitched lower

* averages at rest

Table 4–2

A Reference Table of Postnatal Development (Cont'd)

Age	Hair	Teeth	Alimentary Tract	Breathing Apparatus	Voice
21–45 yrs.	Darkening continues; graying begins in some; head hair loss begins in many men towards later years	Full dentition; wearing off of enamel begins to be apparent; tendency to darken	Competence of digestion closely related to manner of living	16–20 inhalations per minute; susceptibility to infection stabilizing	Voice mature
45–65 yrs.	Graying and thinning common in both sexes; balding common in men; facial hair becomes common in women	Full dentition; wearing off of enamel begins to be apparent; tendency to darken	Somewhat less food needed, especially in women during and after menopause	16–20 inhalations per minute; susceptibility to infection stabilizing	Voice mature
65 yrs.	Graying and thinning of head hair continue; coarse facial hair increases in women	Some teeth may persist; often complete loss of teeth	Competence of digestion closely related to previous patterns of living	Inhalation rate increases; pulmonary and bronchial susceptibility to infection increases	Muscles of pharynx and larynx begin to lose tonus; voices of males become higher pitched; male and female voices become similar

Age	Circulatory System	Urinary System	Skeleton	Muscles
0	Fully functional; *heartbeat 130± per minute; *blood pressure low—40± mm.	Kidneys fully functional; no control of bladder; urine voided 20± times daily	270 ossifications present; much cartilage present; soft spots in skull; only 2 ankle bones begun; no wrist bones begun	Skeletal muscle poorly defined and uncoordinated; smooth and cardiac muscle better developed than striated; sphincters weak
0–2 yrs.	Rate of heartbeat decreases; 125–90 by 2 years; blood pressure 80± mm.	Bladder grows gradually; urine voided every 2 hrs. ±; a few dry at night by 2 years; sensation of fullness begins	Soft spots closed by 1 yr.; facial bones grow more than cranial bones; limb bones elongate slowly; 4 ankle bones begun	Development steady; coordination developing; sitting—7 to 9 months; standing—8 to 11 months; walking—11 to 18 months; sphincters strengthening

*averages at rest

Age	Heartbeat / Blood pressure	Bladder / Kidney	Skeleton	Muscle
2–6 yrs.	Heartbeat 105–85 per minute by 6 years; blood pressure 85± mm.	Sensation of bladder fullness develops; control increasing; usually complete by 6 years	Spinal curvatures developing; bridge of nose forming; some fusions occurring as in skull; all 7 ankle bones begun	Steady development; coordination increasing; running, jumping, climbing possible; sphincters usually controlled
6–12 yrs.	Heartbeat 100–70 per minute; blood pressure 105± mm.	Bladder control complete; a few still lack control during sleep	Slow cranial and facial growth; limb bones elongating; eighth wrist bone forms	Continuing physical development and perfection of muscular skills; strength increasing
12–16 yrs.	Heartbeat 100–70 per minute; blood pressure 110–120 mm.	Bladder control complete	Limb bones elongate markedly, especially in boys; 350 ossifications present; fusions occurring	Growth and strength of striated muscles increase rapidly especially in boys; smooth and cardiac muscle function well
16–21 yrs.	Heartbeat 100–70 per minute; blood pressure 120± mm.	Bladder control complete	Limb bones elongate more slowly; fusions continuing; cartilage mature by 20 years	Continued but slower growth of striated muscle; smooth and cardiac at optimum
21–45 yrs.	Heartbeat 90–60 per minute; blood pressure 120–140 mm.	Bladder control complete	Skeleton complete; 206 ossifications after fusions are completed; spinal curvatures mature	Continued but slower growth of striated muscle; smooth and cardiac at optimum. Striated muscle reaches maximum strength at 30 years
45–65 yrs.	Heartbeat 90–60 per minute; blood pressure 130–142 mm.	Bladder control complete Kidney function dependent upon health of circulatory tissues	Calcification and shrinkage of cartilage begins about 40 years; joints become less flexible	Striated muscle increases in bulk until 50 years±; begins decline in bulk after 50. Smooth muscle efficient
65 yrs.	Heartbeat rate increases slightly; valve function impaired, blood pressure increases in many; arterial walls tend to harden	Kidney function dependent upon health of circulatory tissues Bladder control impaired in some	Joints continue to stiffen; bones become brittle; spinal curvatures change in many	Smooth muscle retains efficiency the longest; cardiac undergoes changes; striated weaken as they become more fibrous and shrink

Table 4-2

A Reference Table of Postnatal Development (Con'd)

Age	Nervous System	Sense Organs	Reproductive System	Endocrines
0	Connections with vital organs functional; many "hook-ups" incomplete; cerebral cortex incomplete; autonomic structures best developed	All partially functional, except cochlea; can distinguish between light & dark; can taste, smell, feel with little discrimination	Both sexes have all structures in an immature state; possibly some six hormones produced; tactile sensations present	All (except corpus luteum and placenta) functioning to a degree
0–2 yrs.	Continuing development and "hook-ups" throughout life. Alteration and loss of neurons occurs throughout life	Coordinate eyes at 3 mos.±; can hear by 1 week; all senses continue development; sense of equilibrium weak	Slow growth of systems	All (except corpus luteum and placenta) functioning to a degree
2–6 yrs.	Continuing development and "hook-ups" throughout life. Alteration and loss of neurons occurs throughout life	All senses developing; equilibrium improves rapidly after 3 years. Most are farsighted at 6	Slow growth of systems	All (except corpus luteum and placenta) functioning to a degree
6–12 yrs.	Continuing development and "hook-ups" throughout life. Alteration and loss of neurons occurs throughout life	All senses functioning well; discrimination and judgment developing; hearing acuity levels off at 10 years±	Slow growth of systems	Hypophysis begins gonadotrophic hormone production at about 9 yrs. in girls and 10 yrs. in boys

Age	Nervous System	Senses	Reproductive	Glands
12–16 yrs.	Continuing development and "hook-ups" throughout life. Alteration and loss of neurons occurs throughout life	All senses functioning well; discrimination and judgment developing. Taste preferences change throughout life	Female: Ovulation and menstruation begin 11–14 yrs. Growth of systems more rapid. Male: Semen production begins 12–15 years	All glands (except placenta) functioning
16–21 yrs.	Full power achieved; new "hook-ups" continue to come into function	Highest visual acuity at 20 yrs. ±	Growth of systems more rapid. Both become fully functional: female by early 20s; male by late teens	All glands (except placenta) functioning. If conception occurs corpus luteum persists and placenta forms; all glands function
21–45 yrs.	Full power achieved; new "hook-ups" continue to come into function	Slow decline in visual acuity	Both fully functional. Female: Menopause may begin before 45. Male: Prostate changes common after 40 yrs.	If conception occurs corpus luteum persists and placenta forms; all glands function
45–65 yrs.	Circulation impairment impairs function; some forgetfulness; slower learning	Visual acuity declines rapidly; bifocals become necessary; hearing acuity declines after 60 yrs.	Female: Menopause usual 45–55 yrs.; ovulation and menstruation cease; sterile, may be potent. Male: Some decline in sexual activity; still fertile and potent	Female: Hypophysis reduces FSH; ovarian hormones reduce. Male: Not well investigated yet
65 yrs.	Memory of recent events tends to weaken; judgment and reason retained in some; weakened or lost in some. Autonomic activity retained longest	Visual, hearing, taste, and equilibrium acuity all decline. Senses of smell and touch last the longest	Some remain potent; uterus, etc. shrink. Some of both sexes become impotent. Some retain fertility and potency	Decreasing production of all hormones

changes in orientation if he is in the hands of someone in whom he has confidence, and laughs when he is tickled. If kept in a pleasant state of excitement until he becomes fatigued, his behavior changes to that of distress.

By 12 months of age, delight differentiates into *elation* and *affection*,[20] elation being expressed somewhat as we have described delight, affection including cuddling up to the object of the emotion, the mother, or a pet dog, for example. By 18 months, *jealousy* may be apparent. If the parent is paying attention to a new baby or a pet, for instance, from 18 months on, the child may attempt to push himself between the object of his affection and the one who is receiving attention. By 2 years of age, all of the emotions mentioned become more clearly differentiated. The young child, however, still slips easily and quickly from one emotional state to another.

PERSONAL-SOCIAL DEVELOPMENT

Newborn infants and very young infants are often referred to as "skin-limited" in that they are concerned only with what goes on inside and on their skins. While they are completely dependent upon other people for the fulfillment of all their needs, they give nothing in return. Any pleasures that the parent or nurse derives from taking care of them results not from the infant but from the adult's mature satisfaction in being able to fulfill another's needs.

Nevertheless, the newborn infant is a social being-in-the-making because his material being, in which his personal and social ties with other people will be established as his life proceeds, is already present. The infant, even before his birth, has profoundly affected the lives of his parents, and after his birth, the effects of his presence on their lives is extremely specific for 24 hours a day. As has already been pointed out, his degree of confidence in the world gets its beginning in the early months of life in connection with his physical routines. By 4 months he knows his mother and possibly his father (or whoever takes care of him), and his behavior begins to shape itself in ways that win him approval from the people who care for him. As the months proceed, he comes to know his siblings, other people who enter the home, and people whom he sees fairly frequently in stores, the nursery, or in his parents' place of worship. Between his first and second year, he may learn to recognize neighbor children, although he is not well enough developed to play with them. By 2 years of age, he differentiates between people who show that they approve of him and people who do not show approval, but the infant cannot tell whether they actually do or do not like him.

DEVELOPMENT OF INTELLECT

In terms of the various levels of the central nervous system (the spinal cord and brain), the young infant lives a vegetative existence which depends largely upon the functioning of the spinal cord and the lower levels of the brain. In the first few months, however, the various muscle groups and the sense organs begin to send and receive nerve impulses to and from the forebrain. As soon as such connections are made, behavior becomes more "cerebral," more aware, and more subject to voluntary control.

As we have pointed out, the infant is aware of practically nothing at birth, all his behavior being reflex in nature. As the months pass, however, his senses become more acute, and he gains skill in the management of his body. The world about becomes clearer. He recognizes objects in his room, and in the world outside, trees, birds, other people, cars, and so on catch his eye and ear. As soon as he can move himself around, he begins to explore. He tries everything for taste, feel, and smell. He learns about his own dimensions and about his different bodily parts and how they feel. His intellectual and emotional growth proceeds or is crippled, depending upon the way in which the results of his explorations are handled. Just as an infant may become fearful of walking if protected too much against trying and falling, so also he may become fearful or confused by the disapproving responses of his parents to his "getting into things" that they prize, or to his discovering pleasant sensations in his own body, for example.

Infants use the "scientific method" in its purest sense; that is, they observe, they test by means of all their senses, they notice the responses of other people to their testing, they collect their data, and they begin to form their hypotheses. By 2 years of age, while they still lack skill in the use of language, they understand words and have the beginnings of ideas about what in their worlds leads to satisfactions and what does not. By the end of the infancy period they are on their way, physically, emotionally, socially, and intellectually.

SUGGESTIONS FOR FURTHER DISCUSSION

1. From your baby-sitting or other experiences with babies, recall incidents which illustrate points in this chapter. Be prepared to report these to the class.

2. Having studied this chapter and readings, observe an infant to discover what you can now see and interpret from his activities that you did not see before.

3. Observe some infants whose age you do not know and try to judge age from behavior. Check your answer by finding out the child's age.

4. Read some of the original studies listed under "References for Further Study." Discuss these in class.

REFERENCES FOR FURTHER STUDY

DEWEY, R., and HUMBER, W. J. *The Development of Human Behavior.* New York: The Macmillan Co., 1951. Ch. 9, infancy and the pre-school years; trends in infant training practices; the socialization process; development of selfhood and personality. Case studies.

LANE, H., and BEAUCHAMP, M. *Understanding Human Development.* Englewood Cliffs, N.J.: Prentice-Hall, Inc., 1959. Ch. 8, the pre-memory age; prenatal life; the baby.

MARTIN, P. C., and VINCENT, E. L. *Human Biological Development.* New York: The Ronald Press Co., 1960. Ch. 4, effects of emotions and attitudes on digestion and nutrition begin in infancy. Ch. 5, elimination of solid wastes in postnatal life.

WHITING, J. W. M., and CHILD, I. L. *Child Training and Personality.* New Haven: Yale University Press, 1953. This study examines norms and range of variation in child-training practices in infancy in a world-wide sample of 75 societies, and places United States practices in broad perspective.

For film suggestions see Film Supplement, in the Appendix.

CHAPTER 5

Early Childhood

The Period of Early Childhood

Early childhood is usually considered as the stage between 2 and 6 years of age. In countries where most children attend school, it is often referred to as the preschool period. The age boundaries of the period are only approximations because children differ in their rate of development. Unless we state otherwise, we shall be discussing average children, who comprise the middle two-thirds of the distribution of development.

The period of early childhood is one of transition. In the early part of the period, the child is still somewhat of a baby. During his sixth year, however, he shows some of the body proportions, interests, activities, and intellectual abilities of the child that he will be throughout the later period of his childhood.

GROWTH AND CONTROL OF THE BODY

Gains in Height and Weight

In early childhood, as Table 4–2 shows, height and weight increase more slowly than they did in infancy, and more rapidly than they will in the period of later childhood. In one study,[207] eighty per cent of a group of 2-year-old, healthy, white boys measured from 33.1 to 35.9 inches in height, a variation among them of 2.8 inches (Fig. 5–1). Twenty per cent of them were taller or shorter than this range. Eighty per cent of the same boys, when 5 years of age, measured between 40.8 and 45.2 inches in height, a variation among them of 4.4 inches. The variation among them increased considerably in 3 years, as the effects of their heredity interacting with

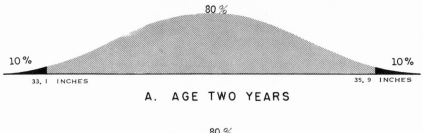

80 %

10 %   10 %

33. 1   INCHES   35. 9   INCHES

A.   AGE TWO YEARS

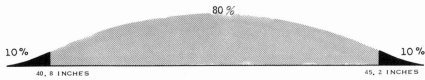

80 %

10 %   10 %

40. 8 INCHES   45. 2 INCHES

B.   AGE FIVE YEARS

Fig. 5–1. Variation in height in boys at two and at five years of age.

their environment began to show. Girls show comparable differences, but, as at birth, they are somewhat shorter than boys. As
Fig. 5–2 shows, girls achieve 60 per cent of their adult height by

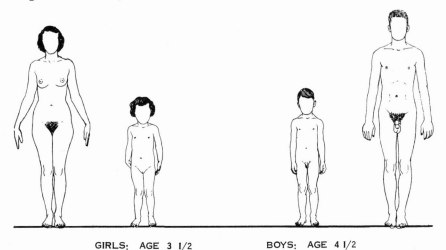

GIRLS: AGE 3 1/2   BOYS: AGE 4 1/2

Fig. 5–2. Age at which 60 per cent of adult height is achieved.

3½ years of age, while boys achieve 60 per cent of their adult stature
by 4½ years of age.[195] Thus, although girls, generally speaking,
remain shorter than boys throughout the period of their early childhood, they progress toward their mature height more rapidly than
do boys.

Individual children of both sexes vary considerably from the average. If, however, their nutrition and other factors of their environment are satisfactory, they are probably growing at a rate determined by their hereditary constitution.

Children 2 years of age weigh about one-fifth of what will be their weight at 18, and at 5 years of age weigh about one-third of that weight. As in height, girls advance more rapidly toward their adult weight than do boys. Variation in weight among individual children is present at each age and stage of growth.

Changes in Body Proportions

During the period of early childhood, body proportions also change, and the child ceases to look like a baby. At 2 years of age, he is still infant-like in his leg-to-trunk and face-to-skull proportions. His lips tend to be full and his cheeks are still padded with baby fat. His legs are shorter than his trunk, as Fig. 5–3 shows; as a result, he can play "all the ducks go swimming in the water." To play this game he squats with legs alongside his trunk, knees near his shoul-

Fig. 5–3. Changes in body proportions in early childhood: 2, 4, and 6 years.

ders, and he waddles in a remarkable imitation of a duck. In most children, about halfway through the third year, proportions change so that the "duck" game loses its appeal. The legs gain in length faster than the trunk does, so that when the child squats, he sits over his heels and can no longer waddle with ease. Between 2½ and 6 years of age, the legs and trunk continue to elongate, the legs faster than the trunk, so that by the end of early childhood the legs are about as long as the trunk. The head increases in size more slowly than the trunk, and the lower facial parts grow faster than does the cranium, so that instead of the eyes being placed about midway between the top of the head and the chin as in babyhood, by 6 years of age they are about two-thirds up from the chin. Similarly, the ears seem to "move up."

Growth of the Body Systems

If we start at the left of Table 4–2, pp. 136 ff., at the 2–6 year level, we can see as we move to the right across the table the changes which take place during the period of early childhood. In addition to the changes in height, weight, and body proportions already referred to, changes are occurring in all the organs and systems of the body. The skin, for instance, becomes less downy and delicate. As the epidermis thickens, the child's body can withstand somewhat rougher mechanical and chemical treatment than it could in babyhood. In many children, more pigment begins to form in the skin and hair. The hair grows longer, and is straight, wavy, or kinky, depending upon the genes which the parents have contributed and the treatment that they are subjecting it to, such as curling and cutting.

Four more molars usually erupt between 14 and 36 months of age, bringing the number of temporary teeth to 20. Although the child is able to eat all kinds and textures of food, he is likely to become less interested in food than he was in babyhood. Most children begin to lose some of their temporary teeth in their sixth year, and the first teeth of the permanent dentition erupt soon after their predecessors are lost.

The breathing apparatus grows as the child grows, and the rate of breathing decreases to between 30 and 20 inhalations per minute. Children in the period of early childhood have little or no immunity against communicable disease organisms, and are usually highly susceptible to infections of the breathing apparatus such as colds, measles, diphtheria, and poliomyelitis. Because in many countries, children begin group schooling between 4 and 6 years of age, at this time they come in contact with a great variety of organisms against which they may lack immunity.

The heart and circulatory vessels continue development, and the rate of heartbeat decreases from about 105 beats per minute at 2 years of age to about 85 at 6 years of age. Blood-vessel walls are thin in many parts of the body, and bleeding from bumps and from the nose following colds is not unusual. On the whole, however, the circulatory system is adequate for the vigorous physical play which is usual at this age.

By 2 years of age, most children are conscious of fullness of the urinary bladder. They are likely to be able to control the emptying of the bladder while awake, and by 3 or 4 years of age most of them remain dry while sleeping. Continued lack of control after 4 or 5 years of age is often called *enuresis,* and is more common in boys than in girls. In some cases, enuresis is associated with emotional disturbances; in other cases, with deep sleep, structural or physiological defects, or with infections. In attempts to end enuresis, it is advisable to ascertain a child's physical condition before attempting to reorient such psychological factors as family relationships.

The skeleton not only grows but changes in its constitution. Ossification (bone-producing) centers in the bones are very active; cartilage is being resorbed and replaced by bone. Spaces between bones decrease, so that parts of the body are less flexible than they were in babyhood. The normal curvatures of the spine are developing. Fusions between bones of the skull are continuing: the bridge of the nose is forming, all 7 bones in each ankle begin to form, and the wrist bones continue to form. Adequate nutrition and active play during the period from birth to 7 years of age are essential to good bone development.

The musculature and the nervous system continue to grow and develop. Alteration and growth of neurons goes on throughout the period and new "hookups" come into existence. As a result, the child understands his sensations better and is progressively better able to interpret them to other people and to ask questions about his environment.

All the sense organs are operating efficiently in early childhood, in some cases reaching their greatest acuity. Most children see, hear, smell, taste, and feel with discrimination, and have an increasingly effective sense of balance. Most of them are "farsighted" at about the age of 6 years, and become more "nearsighted" during the next few years.

The reproductive systems in both boys and girls grow very slowly during early childhood. The genitalia are distinct, but the systems are non-functional as far as the formation of mature sex cells is concerned. All of the endocrine glands present at this time are active, and hypo- or hyperactivity is relatively rare in normal children of this age period.

Progress in Control of Large Muscles

At 2 years of age, most children walk up and down stairs alone; that is, they hold on to a rail or put one hand against the wall, and go up or come down one step at a time, putting both feet on the same step before progressing to the next one. In walking and running, they still have some trouble coordinating the movements of their growing trunk and limb muscles. In addition, because they are still perfecting their sense of balance, they often collide with objects instead of steering themselves or their toys around them. These collisions occur especially when the children are in a hurry or are preoccupied with something other than locomotion itself. Their nervous controls are not yet sufficiently automatic to be depended upon for quick adjustments. Two-year-olds also like to jump from one or two steps and over low objects.

Three-year-olds often begin to walk up and down stairs in a more grown-up fashion; that is, alternating their feet, having only one foot on a step at a time. They can also pedal a tricycle. By 3½ years, they can balance on one foot for brief periods. By this age, they have sufficiently mastered the muscles that are used in walking and running to permit them to concentrate on other activities that involve these skills, as Fig. 5–4 shows.

By 4 years of age, control of the large muscles is automatic enough to permit freedom to play ball, climb, ride a scooter, jump from a height of 4 or 5 steps, walk a 12-inch plank down a fairly steep incline, roller skate (Fig. 5–5), and perform other such tests of coordination and balance. Any kind of apparatus that provides bars, ladders and swings, challenges children of around this age to climb, hang by the hands, or by the knees, and do other comparable stunts.

Fig. 5–4. Age three can run in pairs.

Once a physical skill is under reasonably good control, children tend to "embroider" it by adding variations to it. Most 5-year-olds have reached their peak of walking skill, for instance, and they embroider this skill by moving suddenly in any direction, by adapting movements to obstacles of various heights and depths, and by skirting objects. Their movements are often actually graceful. The speed and ease with which they learn new skills depend on a number of factors, their hereditary structure and aptitudes, their physical and emotional health, their level of intelligence, and the conditions under which they are permitted to learn and practice. They need adequate, safe space with challenging objects or equipment and definite limits, and playmates of equal or greater skill than themselves.

Progress in the Control of Small Muscles

Mastery of the smaller muscles of the body used in such everyday tasks as dressing, eating, bathing, and picking up one's possessions comes more slowly than does mastery of the large muscles. The proximodistal principle of development is exemplified here: it takes longer for the child to learn to manipulate the muscles of the fingers than those of the arms, and he learns to manipulate his toes later than

Fig. 5–5. Age four can learn to roller skate.

his fingers. If his hands are normal, he probably never will learn to master his toe muscles as well as his finger muscles. Some children, however, handicapped in the use of their hands by crippling defects or diseases, learn to be skillful with their toes, so that they learn to use spoons, scissors, crayons, and so on with dexterity.

Many 2-year-olds can direct a spoon full of non-liquid food into their mouths without spilling. Sometimes they miss and hit around the mouth. Figure 5–6 shows a 2-year-old preferring to pick his food up with his fingers. By 3 years of age, many children feed themselves with a small fork or spoon with only occasional spilling. When spilling occurs, they can wipe up the spilled food. If they are provided with low chairs and tables, they can carry their own plates and bowls of food to the table and remove them when finished.

Fig. 5–6. Finger feeding at two years of age. (Courtesy, Merrill-Palmer Institute, Detroit.)

By 5 years of age, most children can butter their own bread, pour liquids from a pitcher, and if their meat is cut up, they can feed themselves fairly efficiently. They can learn that it is best not to try to eat and talk at the same time, and they can begin to learn consideration for other people at meal time by learning to chew with closed lips and by avoiding reaching and unnecessary spilling. In other words, they begin to learn practical table manners.

Two-year-olds can take off their own shoes and socks. If other garments are unfastened, they enjoy removing them. Between 2 and

3 years of age, children can turn water and gas fixtures on, so they need considerable supervision and teaching where and when not to do such things. They like to try to bathe themselves, and often resist getting out of the water and being dressed.

By 3½ years, most children can undo buttons, although they may have difficulty getting buttons into buttonholes. By 4 years they have improved in this skill, and can wash their hands and face efficiently, brush their teeth fairly well, and lace their shoes, although they may not be able to tie the laces. If sufficiently large loops of tape are sewn on clothing, they can hang garments up on hooks that are within their reach. During their fifth and sixth years, most children can manage their out-of-door clothing, such as snowsuits and waterproof footgear, and this is a necessary skill before they start formal schooling.

If practical facilities for waste elimination are provided, such as "potty chairs" or small seats that can be attached to adult plumbing fixtures and a box or something to step up on, most children of 2 years of age begin to want to manage their own affairs in this area. As we have pointed out earlier, their sensations, or possibly their reactions to their sensations, are not reliable for some years. But if the family atmosphere is conducive to it, they tend to want to establish their independence. As a result, if the mother (or other attendant) enjoys their successes with them and does not make an issue of their failures, they begin to tell in some way when they need to eliminate wastes so that they get the necessary help with clothing and cleaning themselves after eliminating. Obviously, it is helpful to them if their clothing is the kind that is easily removed and replaced, and if soft toilet paper and running water are available. Incidentally, they need to be taught how to wipe after bowel elimination so as to avoid infections of the vagina or urethra. It is easy for them to learn to wipe to the right or left of the anus rather than forward. This is especially true of girls, since microorganisms that live harmlessly in the intestine can grow and cause trouble in other areas. By six years of age or earlier, most children are capable of taking care of these needs. As has been mentioned, some children are bothered with lack of bladder control, while asleep, for some years.

The finer muscle skills needed for reading, writing, and drawing develop gradually during early childhood. Both the external and the internal muscles of the eyes have been practicing their movements since before birth, and between the ages of 2 and 6 years, children usually perfect these movements. As a result, and since the lenses are very elastic in this period, they can focus quickly on objects at varying distances, and can move both eyes coordinately up and down and from left to right and right to left. From even earlier than 2 years of age, many children like books, first durable rag books and later paper books. With skillful fingers, they turn pages; with their increasingly skillful eye movements, they focus on pictures, large letters, and so on. They point to marks or colors that interest them, and with developing skill in the use of their speech muscles, make various sounds and try to imitate what an older person says in his interpretation of what the child points to. This exercise is excellent practice for reading, although most children cannot concentrate for sufficiently long periods to read fluently before 6 or 7 years of age.

Skill in the use of hand and finger muscles develops with the handling of such things as crayons, pencils, scissors, modeling clay, finger paint, and large needles with yarn or cotton and marked paper or cloth. Two-year-olds enjoy holding a pencil in a tight grip and scribbling. At 2 to 2½ years, they make vertical lines and, as we see in Fig. 5–7, this takes concentration. Horizontal lines follow, and then diagonal lines. The ability to copy a circle has developed in most late 3-year-olds, and the majority of 4-year-olds can copy a square in one trial out of three. Many children like to play with tools such as hammers and wrenches, with cooking utensils, and clothes-pins. Some toy manufacturers have recognized children's potential abilities, and make toys that are excellent for developing skills. Not all children develop these small muscle controls at the same age. Many normal children, for example, are too busy with large muscle play out-of-doors to allow themselves to develop skills involving the small muscles. Such children leave small muscle skills until later.

The Matter of Handedness

As we pointed out earlier, hand preference usually develops during the second year. Conclusions drawn from studies of handedness are conflicting. Some psychological studies [81] indicate that the choice is largely determined by the culture. Other studies [15, 217] indicate that the preference is more the result of the child's heredity. Clinically, it appears that some children who show a strong preference for using the left hand and who are continually forced to use the

Fig. 5–7. Vertical lines at two years eight months of age require concentration.

right hand present various kinds of nervous behavior which disappear when the children are permitted to use the left hand. Our own conclusion is that most children may be encouraged mildly but not forced to use the right hand. The matter is relevant in this chapter because habitual use of one hand more than the other begins during the period of early childhood and usually lasts throughout life.

Young children need frequent rest periods and changes in muscular activity. As indefatigable as children often seem to be, their muscles and nerves tire quickly. They can sit building with blocks or cutting with scissors, for instance, for only relatively brief periods before they become restless, at which time they need to be free to get around and exercise their larger muscles. Their developing bodies demand frequent changes in activity interspersed with periods of quiet rest or sleep.

Patterns of Living Established in Early Childhood

By 6 years of age, children have made important beginnings in the establishment of certain patterns of behavior in their physical lives. Either they have developed some regularity in their physical habits, or they have developed irregularity in these habits. For instance, if they live in a culture where schooling is required of all children, they need habits of sleep that permit them to rise sufficiently early in the morning to wash and dress, to eat an adequate breakfast, to eliminate wastes, and to get to school on time. In school, they need to be able to remove outdoor clothing and place it where it belongs, to speak plainly, to greet others, to follow directions, and to concentrate for appropriate periods on the job to be accomplished. They need to be able to sit still and keep quiet for certain periods, and to share the attention of an adult with others.

If bowel action has become regular by 6 years of age, the child may not be bothered with that during school time. However, most children's digestive tracts are not completely reliable, and so they have to be able to tell the teacher of their needs and to take care of both bowel and bladder elimination by themselves. They need to have learned to cover their faces when they cough or sneeze, and to be able to wipe their noses. It is during these early years that people begin to develop habits which either render them regular throughout their lives or else make of them chronic sufferers from constipation or other uncomfortable physical conditions.

THE DEVELOPMENT OF EMOTIONS

Emotions Become More Specific

It will be recalled that the newborn infant is capable of only generalized and undifferentiated excitement in response to stimuli, and that by 2 years of age, children respond to various situations with such specific emotions as elation, affection, distress, fear, disgust, anger, and jealousy. In the period of early childhood, this process of differentiation continues, emotions becoming increasingly specific for certain stimuli, and showing finer gradations of intensity. For example, the child becomes capable of expressing indifference, mild interest, strong interest, enthusiasm, or such intense joy that he cannot keep still but jumps up and down shouting "Yippee!" or some other satisfying vocalization. In feelings of affection toward people, animals, or toys he expresses indifference, shy approval, moderate affection, or he can be warm and enthusiastic even to the point of roughness. With things or situations that are displeasing to him, he can show mild irritability, annoyance, anger, or rage which he may express by physical attack on the object of his displeasure. In fear-provoking situations, he shows uneasiness, mild anxiety, strong anxiety, or in extreme cases, panic, which he may express in screaming and running away or in hiding behind an adult.

As children live through these early years, they react to different stimuli. In infancy, they react only to stimuli which directly affect their sense organs. As they grow older, however, they begin to remember situations and sensations associated with them. As a result, they begin to anticipate sensations. For example, a child may receive his first hypodermic shot with little or no emotion. If the needle does not stimulate pain nerve endings he probably will be only curious at the giving of a future shot. If, however, pain nerve endings are stimulated he may associate the mental picture of the situation, including the needle, the word "shot," and the sensation of pain, so that he may develop anxiety or even fear concerning future shots. In the same way, through specific experiences, he may learn to anticipate pleasure. In other words, he begins to be able to experience emotions in response to the stimuli of remembered situations or to symbols of things and situations. Children are likely to forget the actual situations that originally stimulated their emotions, but they continue to respond to the stimuli. It is in this way that what seem to be groundless emotional habits, some desirable and some undesirable, develop and persist throughout life. For example, a child may feel comfortable and happy with a person who often wears a certain color. Throughout his life, he may "like" that color without being conscious of the reason. Similarly, a baby may be frightened by a kitten, and go through life with a dislike or even a fear of anything "furry," without remembering the initial incident but responding to the symbol, "furriness."

The Expression of Emotion Changes

In infancy, the expression of emotion is direct and uninhibited. The period from 2 to 6 years of age is normally one in which children make progress in controlling their emotional behavior. Even by 2 years of age, responses to minor discomfort such as mild hunger are less vigorous than they were in infancy. By 2½ years, most children react violently to interference with their activities or with their toys and other possessions, but six months later, their reactions are likely to be less vigorous.[62] Two-year-olds are likely to hit, poke, bite, or kick other children; by 5 years of age, most children have given up some of these activities. What they do, of course, in the way of aggressive behavior depends to a large extent upon the culture in which they are growing up.[227] In most cultures, by their sixth year, children have learned that hitting is disapproved generally, but permissible in self-defense.[19]

At 2 or 3 years of age, many children indulge in vigorous temper tantrums—kicking, stamping, rolling on the floor, and screaming—if they cannot have something they want or are not permitted to do something that they want to do. Most 5- and 6-year-olds pretty well give up this kind of reaction as they learn more rewarding ways of behaving. Children suffering from excessive frustration, or from fear, shame, guilt, or other sources of conflict, may continue relatively unproductive behavior such as temper tantrums.[10]

Children between 2 and 4 years of age usually express fear by getting away physically from the object of their fear. As they learn to talk, however, they begin to express their fears in language. It is often difficult for adults to comprehend what the child fears, because he does not yet have the skill in language or the understanding of his feelings necessary to communicate effectively. A child who fears darkness may not say that he does; instead, after his mother has put him to bed, he may keep calling for "a drink" or something that makes no sense to the mother. By 6 years of age, most children can communicate what some of their fears are, and have begun to develop the courage to face some of the things they fear. The development of courage is greatly influenced by the behavior of parents and other people with whom the child comes in contact. For example, if the noise of thunder frightens a child, his mother can help him to lose his fear if she holds him in her arms and they look out of the window together at the lightning and the rain. Her reassuring voice, telling him that the rain makes the grass grow and the thunder is the noise made by the pretty lightning helps him to understand and possibly even to enjoy the storm.

Jealousy is a common emotion in early childhood. At the beginning of this period, children are likely to express it by direct attack.

A 2-year-old may squeeze a baby brother in order to hurt him, to get even with him, as it were. Because most parents make it clear that they disapprove of this kind of behavior, most children who feel jealousy cease to express their feelings directly, but continue to express it in indirect ways, some of which seem so unrelated to the object of the jealousy that parents may be unaware of the child's actual feelings. Jealousy is a withering sort of emotion. It prevents the child from being as happy and out-going as he might be.

Affection in early childhood is less the feeling of sheer comfort it was in infancy and more a feeling directed toward others. Whereas the infant can express his feeling only by smiling and cuddling up to the person making him comfortable, the young child takes initiative in affectionate behavior by climbing up on an adult's lap, putting arms around an adult's neck, and running to an adult's outstretched arms to be picked up and hugged, hugging in return. Some 4-year-olds occasionally pat and hug younger children, sometimes too vigorously for the younger child's comfort. Five-year-olds tend to become more reserved in their display of affection, depending more on words to express their feelings.[62]

Most children express humor. If permitted to, they have a lot of fun. Children in the period between 2 and 6 years of age find occurrences funny that do not seem at all funny to adults. For example, if they themselves, or someone else, slip and fall on the ice, they are likely to laugh. They can share more desirable humor with people older than they are too. Two-year-olds, for instance, have their own funny tricks such as bending forward and viewing the upside-down world from between their legs. If anything strikes children funny, most of them tend to laugh vigorously.

Sympathy, or the ability to feel something of what another person feels in a particular situation, begins to develop during the period of early childhood. The 2½-year-old may attempt to quiet a crying baby sister or brother by tucking his own favorite toy into the crib beside the baby. This kind of action seems to adults to indicate the older child's feeling for the younger one's distress. It may really express something quite different, his annoyance at the baby's crying, for instance. Three-year-olds seem to express more curiosity than sympathy toward another child's injury. If a child falls and blood flows freely from his wounded knee, the 3-year-old may stare and say "Does it hurt?" or "Look at him bleed!" A 4-year-old in such a situation is more likely to do something about it, such as helping the hurt child to his feet or running for help.[155] If the 4-year-old is the cause of the injury, he may try to help or he may ignore the situation. Whatever he does indicates increasing insight into his own behavior in relation to the unhappiness of another person. Five-year-olds sometimes step into a situation to defend a younger child or to protect a pet, thus demonstrating further growth in emotional development.

Children in early childhood still slip quickly and easily from one emotional state to another. Their moods are transient, and their emotional behavior is often baffling to observers. As the early years pass, however, the normal child gains in emotional stability, giving up some of the behavior that causes him and other people trouble, and refining behavior that brings him satisfaction. He reacts more reasonably to appropriate stimuli, and his reactions are more appropriate to the circumstances.

Factors Influencing Emotional Development

Emotional development, like everything else in the human being, is dependent upon the *hereditary constitution* of the child as it is affected by the child's environment. The young child is an organism, the quality of whose systems is initially determined by the genes he received from his parents at conception. The rate and degree of *maturation* of his bodily systems, such as his nervous system, his sense organs, and his endocrine system are to some extent also determined by his genes. As his systems mature the child becomes capable of differing types and degrees of reactions. During his daily life he has many different experiences under many kinds of circumstances. His experiences are accompanied by more or less intense emotional reactions, either on his part or on the part of someone who is with him at the time of the experience. We mentioned this kind of thing earlier in connection with a child's liking a particular color or disliking "furriness." These latter reactions are considered *conditioned emotional reactions.* In other words, the child, as the result of multiple simultaneous stimulation, has experienced two or more sensations simultaneously as nerve impulses arrive in his cerebrum. In the examples used, he associates comfort with the visual sensation of the color and fright with the tactile sensation of the fur. These associations result in liking and fearing, which in these instances are conditioned responses.

General physical condition influences the speed and intensity of emotional reactions. Children who are free from organic disease and infections, and who are rested and well-nourished, tend to respond quickly and to be active, out-going, and gay. Children who are not in good health or who are tired or hungry tend to be either listless or irritable, restless, and weepy. In a study conducted in one nursery school,[71] 50 per cent of all of the temper tantrums for the day occurred within the 30 minutes before the midday meal.

Immediate emotional reactions are affected by the *general emotional "set"* of the individual at the time. "Set" has been defined as the readiness or tendency to respond in a particular way.[196] General emotional set is at least partially a product of the factors already discussed: hereditary constitution, maturation, conditioning, and physical condition. It is the individual's basic inner feelings at any given time. Psychologists, however, are not as yet in complete agreement as to what determines an individual's basic emotional set. For example, the psychoanalytic school [55, 86] teaches that an important part of the basic set of each individual stems from certain universal fears, namely, fear of punishment, physical injury, loss of maternal love, and father's competition for mother's love. The psychoanalytic theory holds that anxieties arise from these fears in early childhood, and if the child is to be free to develop his emotional self, these fears must be resolved in the early years. If they are not resolved, the child's emotional development is restricted, and he either withdraws from others or becomes excessively aggressive toward others.

The studies of other psychologists [9] lead them to disagree with the concept that such fears are universal in young children. Some studies [129] indicate that such basic emotional sets as the tendency to be domineering, general disobedience, and the tendency to make excessive demands on others occur more frequently in children who have been overindulged; and that basic sets such as excessive compliance with authority, timidity, and withdrawal from peers occur more frequently in children who have been dominated and overprotected. These undesirable basic emotional sets are believed by these investigators to result, not from universal fears but from *parental practices* in child-rearing, which in turn result from certain parental attitudes.[10, 186] It is possible, of course, that some parental practices inspire fears.

One basic set which profoundly affects emotional development is that related to sex. Although very little growth occurs in the sex organs themselves during early childhood, sex is nevertheless present at birth and throughout this period. Infants of both sexes are responsive to gentle touches or soft rubbing of clothing in the genital area. Internal conditions such as filling the stomach by sucking and fullness of the bowel or bladder are sometimes accompanied by erection of the penis in infant boys. In the period of early childhood, many children of both sexes learn to stimulate their genitalia with pleasurable results. By the third and fourth years, many children become interested in the more social aspects of sex, the differences between their parents, and their brothers and sisters and playmates.

All human societies control sexual behavior in young children to some degree, although they vary greatly in method and degree. In some cultures, for example, mothers stroke their babies' genitalia to soothe them; in United States cultures, this practice is not common. In some cultures, self-stimulation of the genitalia is considered a natural part of growing up, while in the United States it is generally discouraged to the point that parents may not admit or may not even have recognized that their children have practiced it.[186]

Very young children begin to ask questions about where babies come from, why they differ from their brothers and sisters, and whether they will ever come to resemble their mother or father. A study of 379 New England mothers of 5-year-old children [186] showed that the mothers all attempted to control sexual behavior by various methods, among which were preventing stimulation, changing stimulation (diversion), avoiding accurate terms relating to waste elimination, and controlling the amount and kind of information given. Results of these methods on continuing emotional set are unavailable at this time.

An interesting study in this area would be to discover the goals of a group of mothers in rearing children. We suppose that these goals, if any, are not well thought-out by many parents. It would also be of interest to find out if and how methods of dealing with the control of sex differ with parental goals. We propose that one goal might well be "to rear my sons to be future husbands and my daughters to be future wives." If those were their goals, the parents might realize how important is a comfortable set in regard to sex in marriage, and as a result, regulate their methods of control accordingly.

The matter of basic emotional set is influential in determining behavior throughout life. In early childhood, it has much to do with the child's learning useful routines. If he likes to eat, for instance, he will probably learn mealtime regularity with ease. If he likes bed-time, he will learn easily to be regular in his habits of sleep and rest. If he enjoys eliminating his body wastes, he is likely to develop regularity in that area. Conversely, if his emotional set in these and other areas is unpleasant, it is more difficult to establish useful routines which can free him for other activities.

PERSONAL-SOCIAL DEVELOPMENT

It used to be believed that an individual's personality traits were decided by the time he was 5 or 6 years of age. Modern psychologists, while recognizing that the experiences of these early years are influential in personality development, are in fair agreement that changes are possible throughout later childhood and adolescence and even on into mature adult life. If this were not so, public support of corrective agencies, described briefly in Chapter 3, would not be worth while.

Awareness of Self

As we pointed out in Chapter 4, the infant's and the young child's awareness of self is "skin-limited," not going much beyond himself. In the period of early childhood, self-awareness continues to develop, and the form that it takes during these years constitutes one of the most influential bases of personality development in the future.

The growth of self-awareness is a difficult one for investigators to study. The young child lacks the language necessary to communicate his ideas. His judgment of various relationships, spatial, social, and so on, is still in the early stages of development. As a result, much has to be inferred from what the child says and does about himself and his surroundings.

Children have to learn their own dimensions, which are changing, but gradually enough in the period of early childhood so as not to disturb them. Children learn these dimensions in various ways. They learn where their bodies end and their surroundings begin through the use of their senses. For example, a child creeps and crawls around under furniture, stands up and bumps his head; in that way, he learns where he stops and the table begins. He may hit a wooden peg with his hand and find that his hand hurts; then he may hit the peg with a hammer and find that his hand does not hurt. Self-aware-

ness develops as the child continues to differentiate between himself
and his surroundings. Gradually he builds a concept of himself as a
living being among non-living things, and among other living beings,
and becomes aware of his strengths and his vulnerabilities.[204]

Another step in self-awareness is the child's discovery that he is
somewhat like other living beings. Most children probably find first
that they are similar to adult human beings, their parents for example, and then other children. They recognize similar characteristics,
hair on heads, smooth skins on cheeks, clothing on bodies, and shoes
on feet. They learn that other children eat, bathe, move around as
they do, and, possibly, get hurt as they do. If they come in contact
with birds, fish, dogs, cats, horses, and so on, they note some similarities between themselves and the animals, and some differences.

Another step is the discovery that human beings come in different
sizes, from big parents to babies even smaller than they themselves
are. Along with this discovery comes another, that there are two
kinds of big ones and two kinds of little ones, which the child gradually learns are called by different terms, man and woman, father
and mother, boy and girl, brother and sister, and so on, depending
on the language of his culture. This awareness leads him to put
himself into certain categories. He learns, for instance, that he is a
boy, a son, and possibly a brother.

He becomes interested in the anatomical differences between boys
and girls and fathers and mothers. Even if he is permitted to learn
the differences in his own home, he wants to know if they hold for
other people also, and children are likely to try to find out. He may
find out that a girl playmate has no penis, or that the penis of Billy,
who lives next door, is not like his, because his has been circumcised and Billy's has not. If he has sufficient language skill and
the emotional set necessary for asking questions, he may be able to
get understandable explanations and go on with his development of
self-awareness. If not, he continues to think about and to seek
answers to his questions in other ways.

Along with the similarities that the child recognizes between children and adults, he recognizes the differences that exist between
them also. To children, adults seem to be all-powerful and all-
knowing. The recognition of the difference in power and knowledge
may be a source of anxiety to the child. "Will I ever get to be an
adult?" and "If I do, what will I have to do to get there?" may be
vaguely formed questions in his mind.

Even when the young child has become fairly clear about his own identity, he still may have difficulty in being aware of himself and other people simultaneously. For example, a 4-year-old, when asked how many brothers he has, answered, "Two—John and Bill." Asked how many brothers John has, he answered, "One—Bill," failing to include himself among John's brothers. When asked to draw a picture of his family, he is likely to omit himself. Somewhat later in this period, however, awareness of self will have increased considerably. For example, 5-year-old Jane, on being shown a picture of her parents' wedding party, asked "Where was I?"

Paralleling the development of self-awareness is the growing awareness of certain dangers such as kidnapping, the possibility of being hit by cars, of falling and getting hurt, and so on. Four- and 5-year-olds often express anxiety about getting hurt.[204] Children, when wounded enough to lose blood, get panicky, probably not so much from pain as from fear of bleeding to death, about which they have heard people talking.

The first actual awareness of the possibility of death usually comes around 4 or 5 years of age. Parents find death difficult to explain, especially if the concept is repugnant to them. Some parents feel that the death of pets, such as fish, birds, dogs, or cats, serves a real function in helping children to accept death as the natural end of living things, including other people and themselves.

Relationships with Adults

With this growing awareness of himself as an individual, comes the child's need for establishing his individuality in the awareness of the people who surround him. People who live with children become aware of the "Me do" of the 2-year-old, the "No" and "I won't" of the 2½- to 3-year-old, and the physical violence of the 3- to 4-year-old when he becomes frustrated at continued interference with his wishes. All these and other forms of behavior are the ways in which the child makes known his needs for increasing independence to think, decide, and act as an individual. It is important to his continuing development that he be permitted to exercise his powers. Some parents unwittingly stifle initiative because it is easier and faster for them to do things for the child than to permit him to do them for himself, but the independence that the young child is developing is the precursor of that which he will need to make adult decisions and to be a competent citizen.

If he is to grow to adulthood, however, the young child has to have a certain amount of protection from danger. He has to learn what the dangers of his environment are, that hot things burn, for instance, that falls from heights may hurt him, that dogs may bite, and that moving traffic may injure him. In some cases, experience may be his best teacher, but experience in moving traffic, for instance, may annihilate him then and there.

Obviously, *discipline* is an essential part of staying alive and growing up. Probably the most difficult job in child-rearing is deciding how best to handle situations in order to develop an adult, competent to be a marriage partner, a parent, and a citizen who can share the burdens of his society. Discipline of the right kind during the early childhood period is probably of more strategic importance in the development of attitudes toward self and of sound relations with others than is discipline during any other period. During this early childhood period, constructive discipline lays the foundation for strength of personality during all the ensuing periods of life. Although we have discussed discipline in Chapter 2 as part of the parent-child relation, we would like to discuss it here in a new sense, namely, as "experience that strengthens."

Let us think back to the fertilized egg, the beginning of every human life. In order for growth toward a functional human being to occur, the pairs of chromosomes in that cell must behave in an orderly manner, so that when the cell divides, two cells form, each containing the same hereditary components. This is the process of *mitosis.* Such orderly mitotic divisions go on by the hundreds in the development of an embryo, and in a matter of only a few weeks, as Table 4–1 (pages 98 ff.) shows, certain of these cells begin to specialize as they enter into the formation of essential organs. This is the most basic kind of discipline: an "experience" of the cells, tissues, and organs that strengthens the developing body for continuing growth.

Let us see what happens when cells behave in an undisciplined manner. Figure 5–8 shows two results of undisciplined cell division following human conception. Cells that behave in an undisciplined manner are the delinquents in the society of cells that constitutes the body. Either they fail to do their jobs completely, as in Fig. 5–8A, where they failed to form a body; or they fail to do their jobs properly, as in Fig. 5–8B, where they failed to form organs. A body, like a community, can carry a limited number of undisciplined units as parasites, but when the number of undisciplined units becomes too great for the body to support them, death of the body occurs, just as excessive delinquency may wreck a community.

To get back to the discipline of children in the period of early childhood. Their cells and organs are sufficiently well disciplined to date, or they would not have lived as healthy individuals to this age.

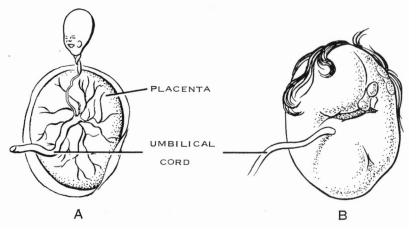

Fig. 5–8. Results of "undisciplined" cell behavior: (A) human fetus without a body; (B) formless human embryo. (After Arey.)

In order to continue to develop in a healthy fashion, their bodies and their personalities, which are their systems in operation, must be trained in order to become strong enough to meet the demands of life as they continue to grow.

This point of view in regard to child rearing certainly will not provide adults with any comfortable list of do's and don'ts for discipline, but it may help the adult to select a type of discipline in a particular situation. It may or may not work, but it will at least not leave the adult with a feeling of guilt. Children differ in their hereditary make-up and in their rate of maturation. A kindly word will prevent one child from getting too near the hot stove, and a tap on the fingers may work better with another. As we have seen, children learn by way of their senses. The mother's voice saying "No, no" in connection with the warmth of the stove may be effective in teaching one child; those stimuli may fail with the second child, while the tactile sensation of the tap on the fingers in connection with the warmth of the stove may work. In other words, discipline is not a matter of being for or against physical contacts such as tapping fingers or pulling a child from a busy street; rather, it is one of stimulating the child's senses in ways that have useful meanings to him at the time. As the years pass between the ages of 2 and 6, the child responds differently to different kinds of stimuli, and what may work at 6 might not have been appropriate at 2, and vice versa.

As Table 4–2 (pages 136 ff.) shows, children between 2 and 6 years of age are highly susceptible to infections, particularly those which enter the body by way of the breathing apparatus. As a result of advances in medical research, communities in many parts of the world now immunize children during infancy or early childhood against diseases such as smallpox, whooping cough, diphtheria, tetanus, and poliomyelitis. Children who are healthy are relatively unconscious of their physical bodies as long as they feel well. This, of course, is a wholesome way for them to be. Parental overprotection against injury and infections can result in anxiety on the part of some children, which interferes with their emotional and social development. While it seems reasonable to protect them from infections which they might lack the strength to combat in their early years, some physicians recommend exposure to certain infections such as rubella (three-day or German measles) for which there is no artificial immunity to date, and which may cause serious complications if it occurs early in pregnancy.

Children in this age period have to learn how to stay alive and unharmed, and they also have to learn about ownership of property: "what is mine and what is thine." This comes more easily for some children than for others, but none are born with the knowledge. They all have to learn how to get along with other people.

Relationships with Other Children

The relationships of 2- to 6-year-old children depend to some extent upon whether or not they are members of a family of children, whether there are possibilities for mothers and their children to spend time together, and whether or not they go first to a nursery school and later to a kindergarten.

Regardless of the child's position in the family, 2-year-old relationships are characterized by the child's immaturity in language, in his muscular skills, and in his awareness of others. If children of this age are brought together, they tend to disregard each other, proceeding to play some distance apart. If they are playing more closely together, each occupies himself with his own business and is oblivious of the other unless they both want the same object or their play interferes with their freedom. For example, if two 2-year-olds play in the same sandbox, one may accidentally throw sand on the other and so annoy him, or they may both want the same shovel. If they do not interfere with each other, they tend to exchange ideas only as one sees or imitates the other. One may say, "See—big hole!" The other may say, "See mine." This kind of relationship is called *parallel play;* it is the first step in sharing. In this relationship, each child stays with an idea longer and makes more variations of it than he would if playing alone. Each child stimulates the other to try new ideas.

Between parallel play and the relatively organized gang or cooperative play of later childhood, intermediate types of relationships develop which are sometimes called *shifting-group* or *associative play.* One or two children begin a game of grocery store, for instance, by shifting blocks and boxes around a space to make the store. A third child joins in, volunteering to make shelves for canned goods, or to make mud pies to sell. Meanwhile, the first child may have become tired of the strain of cooperating and go off to play on a swing for a change. Two other children may have joined the group by this time, either replacing the first child or acting as customers. So the game goes on, so loosely organized that no special role has to be taken by any particular person. Hence, no child needs to stay longer than his brief attention span or his quick fatigue makes comfortable. Four- and 5-year-olds enjoy these loosely knit games, in which they are preparing for the more highly organized activities of later childhood.

Children of different ages sometimes play together well for short periods, although often the younger one irritates the older one by his inability to appreciate his achievements or by his lack of certain skills. Figure 5–9 shows a 6-, a 4-, and a 2-year-old together very temporarily to have a picture taken. The two younger ones are enjoying trying to tickle each other, while the 6-year-old looks on with an attitude of resignation that seems almost adult. The 6-year-old is much more aware of the feelings of the adult photographer than are the 4- and the 2-year-old. Children progress in personal-social development with other people as they do in other areas; that is, through the interaction of their maturing physical systems and their

Fig. 5–9. A six-, a four-, and a two-year-old get together, "waiting" to have a picture taken.

experiences. Table 5–1 shows the shift from solitary, to parallel, to associative, to cooperative play that is typical as maturing and learning proceed in early childhood.

Table 5–1

Type of Play at Ages Two, Three, and Four Years

Ages	Solitary	Parallel	Associative	Cooperative
2	About 25%	About 50%	About 20%	About 5%
3	About 15%	About 30%	About 30%	About 25%
4	About 10%	About 30%	About 32%	About 28%

NOTE: Percentages are of total play time by the child.
SOURCE: From data presented by M. L. Parten, "Leadership Among Preschool Children," *J. Abnorm. and Soc. Psychol.*, 1933, 27, 430–442.

INTELLECTUAL DEVELOPMENT

Intellect, the power of understanding, or the development of intelligence, begins in infancy. In the preceding chapter, we pointed out the infant's use of the "scientific method," by which he learns through his senses and begins to generalize about himself and his surroundings. Between the ages of 2 and 6 years, children make immense strides in intellectual development. Their curiosity is high, their senses are keen, and they are not overwhelmed with duties to be performed.

Language

The development of intellect and language are so closely related that vocabulary is used as one index of the development of intelligence. Generally speaking, children of superior intelligence speak earlier than those of average intelligence, and children of average intelligence speak earlier than do those of subnormal intelligence.[144] However, for a number of reasons, such as deafness, defective mechanisms necessary for speech, reliance upon older siblings, or emotional conditions of various kinds, children of average or even superior intelligence may be slow in talking. We shall discuss the pattern of development which characterizes average, normal children.

Truly expressive speech usually begins during the second year of life. Children understand words before they actually use them. The words that the child understands but does not use constitute his *passive* vocabulary, while those that he both understands and uses constitute his *active* vocabulary. As a rule, girls are ahead of boys in the acquisition and use of language. From about 2 years of age in girls and 2½ in boys, on the average, active vocabulary increases by 500 to 600 words each year during early childhood. As Gesell,[64] in discussing the 4-year-old, puts it, "Indeed within his limits, he [the child] becomes an entertaining raconteur, whereas 4 years earlier he was unable to articulate a single word."

Articulation, or utterance of clearly formulated sounds, is an important task of early childhood. The quality of the child's articulation depends upon a number of factors: among them are degree of maturation of the nerves and muscles of the speech mechanism, level of native intelligence, quality of hearing, and the quality of the articulation of those people whom the child hears speaking. Children pronounce vowels before consonants. Normal 3-year-olds pronounce correctly two-thirds of the single consonants and somewhat more than one-half of the blended consonants; by 5 years of age, they pronounce most sounds correctly.[221]

Stuttering, compulsive repetition of certain syllables, and *stammering,* complete blocking of some speech at times, are now considered to be almost always emotional in origin.[194] Some stuttering is not surprising in children 2½ to 3½ years of age, since at this age emotional tension arises from the acquisition of numerous skills and of the desire to do many things simultaneously. Children have more passive vocabulary than they can make active quickly enough for people to listen to them. Three or four times as many boys as girls stutter for a time around this age.[146] This difficulty with speech is often transient if the child is not made excessively aware of it. Understanding on the part of adults, and their ability to help the child to relax, usually prevent more serious speech impairments from developing and lasting. When the child enters into more formal group living such as school, the ability to make himself understood with ease becomes important to his continuing social and intellectual development.

The uses of language are numerous. Probably the first use is to *make wants known.* Even in infancy, the child makes known his needs for food, attention, being made comfortable, and for objects beyond his reach by making sounds which become more intelligible to adults as the months pass.

Almost as soon as the child can put two words together, he begins to *ask for information,* his desire often being for the names of objects. His "What dat?" results in a rapid increase in his noun vocabulary. This desire is soon followed by the desire to know the uses of objects. His "What dat for?" increases his verb vocabulary. Early childhood is the great age for questions, as adults who live with children well know, and it is through his questions and how they are answered that the child's intellect develops. We have mentioned his learning of nouns and verbs. By 2 years of age, most children use some pronouns, "me" chiefly. By 3 years, they use some prepositions, adverbs, adjectives, conjunctions, and interjections, not being aware that they are doing so, of course. For example, they say "Where you go?", "Nice doggy," "Me and Tom," and "Ouch!"

By 4 years of age, many children use language for *narration.* They enjoy telling of events that have occurred, and often spin elaborate imaginary tales. In connection with narration, much of the language of 2- to 6-year-olds is used for *social intercourse.* They want other people to pay attention to them, and talking is one way to get attention. If adults respect them and understand their needs, they can learn much about their children. By listening to them at this age, they build a firm foundation for their interpersonal contacts with them for years to come. Parents often wonder with concern why their adolescent children do not tell them of their affairs or ask their advice. They may have been "too busy" or "not interested" in listening to those children when they were 2 to 6 years of age.

As children are listened to, they may also learn to listen to others, thereby developing an interest in the affairs of other people as well as in their own. This is the beginning of pleasant and rewarding conversation, an art which is relatively rare in modern life. As we may have seen in this brief discussion, language serves as a thermometer of the child's emotions and also as a means for expressing his thoughts and ideas.

Concept Formation

Intelligence is sometimes defined as that endowment of the human being through which he learns about himself and his surroundings and by which he deals with them more or less effectively. It develops through the child's organization of his cerebral impressions which result, as Fig. 5–10, A–F shows, from the stimulation of

A   B

Fig. 5–10. Avenues to the mind: (A) sight, (B) hearing, (C) touch,

C

D

E

F

(D) smell, (E) taste, and (F) freedom to explore.

his sense organs by factors in his internal and external environment. Until sensations have meaning to the child, his reactions to them are unintelligent. To begin with, his judgments of himself and his environment are not accurate, and he has to learn to judge accurately such properties as size, shape, distance, chemical nature, and so on.

Differences between the intelligent (bright) and the unintelligent (dull) child are discernible in the speed and in the accuracy with which they sense conditions, with which they interpret their sensations, and with which they react to them. There may well be differences between their initial sensations, but knowledge of those differences is almost impossible for the investigator to acquire. As a result, intelligence tests are based largely upon speed and accuracy of interpretation and reaction. Obviously, a totally deaf or a totally blind child is denied certain sensations. Some of these children, however, such as Helen Keller was, because of superior endowment and expert training, are able to utilize their other senses to such a degree that they exhibit even superior intelligence.

One of the tasks of the period of early childhood is the formation of reasonably accurate concepts of the physical and social world. A child is said to have formed a concept when he recognizes that various objects, events, or ideas belong to a class and when he responds similarly to all members of that class. For example, a child has formed a concept of "dogs" when he calls a great Dane, a collie, and a boxer all "doggie!" He recognizes them all as dogs (the class) and responds by calling them all "doggie." Concepts, as we see, are preceded by sensations; in the example used, by visual and probably by auditory, olfactory, and tactile sensations also.

Sensations are not sufficient, however; they must be followed by *perception.* Perception is the experience of *meaningfulness.* For example, the visual image of the dog does not at first mean "dog" to the young child. By further experience and the help of other people, he learns to perceive "dog." Likewise, the auditory sensation of the dog's bark does not at first mean "dog" to the child, nor does the olfactory or the tactile sensation mean "dog." Gradually, or possibly suddenly, the several sensations together mean "dog," and the child perceives. His perceptions then combine to form the concept of "dog."

Some authors [204] refer to "the naming of things perceived" as the first level of concept formation. We recognize that the child is forming concepts when he accurately names such classes as "baby," "man," "apple," "trunk," "light," "fire," and so on. Through his active exploration, he observes, smells, tastes, listens, feels, manipulates, and names not only objects but the *attributes of objects* such as their size ("big," "little"), shape ("round," "square"), color ("red," "blue," "green," "yellow," "black," "white"), texture ("rough," "smooth"), weight ("heavy," "light"), degree of pleasingness to him ("nice," "nasty"), distance ("here," "over there"), and so on.

"Educational" toys and school experiences affect the development of concepts in children, but it is the impulses resulting from the children's physical maturation that motivate them to seek experiences by which they can develop their growing capacities. In other words, they "play." Play is the young child's school, whether it takes place in a building special for that purpose or not. Given freedom in the average household, children happily learn many useful concepts by stacking kitchen utensils according to size and shape, fitting lids on pans, sorting and matching materials of different textures from the ragbag, stringing buttons of various colors and shapes, measuring sand and mud and molding pies in the backyard, and so on.

In their play, children also gain concepts of themselves and other people. Two-year-olds try to squeeze through spaces which are too narrow for their bodies; a 3-year-old may sit on a doll's-house chair and break it by his weight, and a 4-year-old may try to lift a coil of garden hose as he has seen his father do.

Becoming able to remember objects that are not present and to judge a present object by a remembered one is important in the development of concepts.[10] For example, a 4-year-old may say to another child, "Your coat is red; I have a coat like that, but it's blue."

The concepts of *time* and *space* are difficult for young children to acquire. To the 3-year-old in nursery school for the first day, for example, "Mother will come for you this afternoon," has no meaning. He is more likely to understand if he is told, "She will come after we play and then have lunch." [18] The 4-year-old understands, "Daddy will be home late this afternoon," but he is puzzled by "yesterday," "tomorrow," and "last week." [204] Five-year-olds understand these terms, but not "last spring" or "next year." They have only a vague concept of the days of the week,[3] and have difficulty understanding the term "noon." Accurate judgment of passing time is complicated by the psychological state of the child at the moment. Time pleasantly spent seems shorter than time spent disagreeably. The child's lack of judgment of passing time is one of the reasons why "dawdling" is characteristic of young children.

The concept of space depends upon many variables. It depends upon appreciation of the degree of permanence of objects in any given location, as for example, a car that moves or is parked, or a cake of ice that gets smaller and eventually disappears; upon the ability to recognize one's own movements and the movements of other people or objects; upon the ability to unify information from the various senses, such as the sight of a train and the sound of its whistle; and the ability to judge the spatial relations of remembered objects.

The beginnings of all these abilities have usually been achieved by 2 years of age.[10] Rapid improvement occurs in all of them between the ages of 2 and 6 years but judgment of distance, particularly of moving objects, is so unreliable at 6 years of age that children still require some help in crossing busy streets. Many cities employ women and older pupil volunteers to help young children at intersections. Most 5-year-olds find their way to and from school or the neighborhood store without getting lost.

Thinking and Reasoning

Thinking is a type of mental activity. It involves the passage of nerve impulses along the neurons of the cerebral cortex and from neurons to other neurons, with or without the concurrent arrival of impulses from the sense organs. Perception and thinking are closely related, thinking being impossible without sensation followed by perception, with memory intervening between perception and the unifying of perceptions. For example, the child cannot *think* "dog" until after he has sensed and perceived "dog."

Children first solve their problems by simple manipulation of tangible objects, as when the 2-year-old pulls the tablecloth toward him to reach a dish he wants. Increasingly between 2 and 6 years of age, they react to problems by thinking about them either in addition to or instead of manipulating them.[6] The child's knowledge, his muscular, sensory, and language skills, and his social behavior develop; his thinking is the result of what he remembers. When he associates his memories with his problems at hand he draws conclusions about his problems, and is said to be reasoning.[178]

The child's thinking and reasoning is limited by his immature level of ability to proceed from, and to deduce from, what he knows,[10] by the egocentricity of his interests,[166] and by his lack of factual information. For example, the mother of a 4-year-old has said, "Take your boots off outside the door!" After a winter of obedience, spring comes, and the boy dashes in with his rubbers on. When the mother scolds him, he answers, "You said boots." A 3½-year-old, looking out of the window, murmurs, "Trees move. Wind blows. Trees moving make the wind blow." A precocious 4-year-old says to her 18-month-old sister, "You be the baby and I'll be the mama," pauses, then says, "No, I'll be the baby-sitter." Her mother, a well-paid professional writer, asks, "Why baby-sitter, and not mama?" The child answers, "'cause the baby-sitter makes more money." In these examples, the children related previously acquired concepts to current situations. The first child failed to generalize rubber footgear, the second confused cause and effect, and the third lacked a relevant fact.

An understanding of the reasoning prowess of young children has practical implications. Until about 1900, adults supposed that reasoning ability did not develop until around 12 years of age, and that younger children were able only to memorize facts, imitate adults, and obey or resist commands. These beliefs resulted in the approach to children's training being one of "Adults know what's best" and "You are too young to understand." Hence discipline was arbitrary, education was a matter of memorization, and children were taught "to be seen and not heard." Since 1900, understanding of the child's capacity to think and to reason has increased. As a result, some of the changes in patterns of child-rearing have been revolutionary, possibly in isolated cases, excessively so. In most literate countries today, as children grow in their ability to generalize and associate ideas, they are given opportunities to explore and to decide certain things for themselves, with gradually decreasing dependence upon adult supervision.

Imagination

We have seen that as the young child accumulates knowledge and forms concepts, he has many incomplete and many false impressions. His mind is active, however, and his thoughts range over wide areas of association with a freedom that a knowledge of facts will eventually restrict. This kind of mental activity is *imagination*. In young childhood, it can be enjoyed in the world of wishes with minimal regard for the world of reality.

The 2-year-old, for example, identifies himself with a parent, and plays with his doll in so faithful an imitation of the way in which that parent has treated him that the parent observing may realize some of his own feelings and behavior toward his child. The 3-year-old plays Mickey Mouse with realistic movements and noises. The 4-year-old builds a car with his blocks and drives down an imaginary street with appropriate sounds and actions. To the 2-to-5-year-old child, dreams are real events taking place;[204] things wished for and found in imagination are often confused with real happenings and defended as such.[19] As a result, children may be punished for lying, which only adds to their confusion about the real and the imaginary world and about parental love and understanding.

Imaginative play and speech provide children with a way to clarify the roles of adults and children in life situations. One study[137] found that 2½-year-olds used on the average 2 or more imaginative situations per hour during their play; 3½-year-olds used 10 or more; and that 9 to 26 per cent of the remarks made by 4-year-olds were imaginative.

Imagination opens new possibilities for creative expression through dramatic play and also through the use of blocks, clay, crayons, and paints. Most of what the child does in the early part of this period is manipulative, and results are purely accidental. However, some 2-year-olds show considerable satisfaction in imagining some object out of the lump of clay they have manipulated, and 4-year-olds can create the likeness of an object intentionally. After age 4, the ability to create from an idea develops rapidly, as Fig. 5–11, A–B shows. In A, a 4-year and three-month-old child drew a human figure lacking hair, ears, legs, with a disproportionate head and trunk. In B, 3 months later, the same child drew a human figure with hair, legs, handbag, head and trunk in better proportion, and a background tree.

Young children often create for themselves *imaginary companions*, especially at about 4 or 5 years of age.[204] This is true of some children who lack playmates, but some who have playmates create imaginary ones who in some cases only fill otherwise idle time, or who are supposed to impress real companions. They probably fill certain psychological needs, such as someone to blame instead of oneself, and sometimes endure for months.

B

A

Fig. 5–11. Increase in drawing skills: (A) drawing by a child four years and three months; (B) drawing by the same child three months later. Note in (A) the lack of legs and the disproportion between arms and trunk; in (B) the details of hair, handbag, background tree, the continued lack of feet, neck, and palms of hands, as well as the disproportion between fingers and arms, and between tree height and height of girl.

Parents sometimes become concerned about these imaginary companions, especially when they are asked to set places at table for them, and so on. If they accept the companion with a sense of kindly humor, the child is helped to keep the matter of real and unreal clearly in mind, and the companion is sooner or later forgotten.

Some imaginative activity is helpful, and some is detrimental to normal development. Such activity is desirable if it develops abilities and if it clarifies ideas which later can be developed constructively. Such imagination precedes all inventions, works of art, scientific discoveries, and new ways of doing things. Imagination is considered detrimental if it carries the child so far away from the reasonable demands of his life that he becomes unable to meet them and continue his development toward adulthood.

Conscience

As a child learns what he is able or unable to do physically and intellectually, he also learns what he is permitted or not permitted to do personally and socially. Three kinds of control of behavior are discernible in child-rearing practices.[186] The first is the control that comes from outside the child, often by way of the mother, as when she takes father's cigarettes away from the child. The second kind of control is that based on his fear of punishment or expectation of reward. This kind of control is still dependent on some other person. The third kind of control of behavior comes from the child's acceptance of standards other than his own. It seems as though he agrees within himself to accept and to adapt to what external forces have been trying to teach him. The time comes when it no longer pays him to do certain things because of the inner discomfort that doing them causes him. This third kind of control we call *conscience*.

Ability to accept blame for actions displeasing to adults is still in a developing state during early childhood as the following episode illustrates: a grandmother, whose 3- and 4-year-old granddaughters were visiting her found crayon marks on their bedroom wall.

"Who did this?" she asked.

"Not me," said the 3-year-old.

After a pause, the 4-year-old said, "I think I saw me do it."

Gradually the child learns to like himself when he has been "good," and to be dissatisfied and unhappy with himself when he has been "bad." Thus he begins to develop a conscience and to feel guilty when he does not live according to what he has learned is considered "good" behavior. Feelings of guilt do not inevitably result in desirable behavior; they may produce just the opposite. For example, a child may begin to feel that he is too "bad" for other children to play with, and so tend to withdraw from normal social contacts. Obviously, what parents and others teach children concerning acceptable and unacceptable behavior has great influence on their ability to continue to develop into mature adults. It is clear that children, with their limited knowledge, need help in reasoning out what is acceptable and unacceptable behavior and why it is so.[186] With adult help in this area, they can also learn that what is inappropriate behavior at one age level may become appropriate at a later age, and vice versa.

SUGGESTIONS FOR FURTHER DISCUSSION

1. If possible, observe some two- to five-year-old child. Report to the class the child's age and your observations about his: (a) muscular development, (b) language development, and (c) personal-social development. Compare his development in each of these areas with that of the average child of his age.

2. Based upon this chapter and the references below, make recommendations for helping young children who appear to be having difficulty in learning to: (a) talk clearly and at a normal level of vocabulary, (b) get along with other children, (c) establish expected-for-age independence, and (d) develop concepts appropriate to their age.

3. What are reasons other than those discussed in the text for temper tantrums in young childhood? What suggestions do you have for helping children of this growth period to overcome temper tantrums?

4. What are some of the explanations beyond those in the text for delays in control of waste elimination? What can be done to help children in this area?

5. Formulate desirable answers for the following questions of young children: (a) Where do babies come from? (b) What is the difference between boys and girls? (c) After Grandfather's death: Where is Grandpa? What happened to him?

6. Have some one read from Baldwin's chapter on "Self-Control" (see References for Further Study) and report to the class for discussion on: (a) causes of frustration, (b) methods of achieving self-control, and (c) consequences of insufficient self-control.

REFERENCES FOR FURTHER STUDY

BALDWIN, A. L. *Behavior and Development in Childhood.* New York: Holt, Rinehart & Winston, Inc., 1955. Ch. 10, self-control in childhood.

DANIEL, R. S. *Contemporary Readings in General Psychology.* Boston: Houghton Mifflin Co., 1959. Selection 34, a day in the life of a "three."

DENNIS, W. *Readings in Child Psychology.* Englewood Cliffs, N.J.: Prentice-Hall, Inc., 1951. Selection IV-1, learning and maturation in preschool children; Selection IV-2, neural maturation as exemplified by the achievement of bladder control; Selection VI-2, the constancy of mental test performance during the preschool period; Selection VIII-6, personality organization in children; Selection X-6, children's social adjustment in the nursery school.

HARTLEY, R. E., and GOLDENSON, R. M. *The Complete Book of Children's Play.* New York: The Thomas Crowell Co., 1957. Pp. 1–38.

LANE, H., and BEAUCHAMP, M. *Understanding Human Development.* Englewood Cliffs, N.J.: Prentice-Hall, Inc., 1959. Ch. 9, the preschool years.

MUNN, N. L. *The Evolution and Growth of Human Behavior.* Boston: Houghton Mifflin Co., 1955. Ch. 11, symbolic processes in children: memory, imagery, imagination, ideation, conception, generalization, abstraction, thinking, and reasoning; gives excellent background for our discussion of development of intellect. Ch. 12, gives the same kind of background for development of language.

SEARS, R. R., MACCOBY, E. E., and LEVIN, H. *Patterns of Child Rearing.* Evanston, Ill.: Row, Peterson & Co., 1957. Ch. 10, the development of conscience.

SEIDMAN, J. M. *The Child: A Book of Readings.* New York: Holt, Rinehart & Winston, Inc., 1958. Selection: factors in aggressive behavior of preschool children.

SMITH, K. U., and SMITH, W. M. *The Behavior of Man.* New York: Holt, Rinehart, & Winston, Inc., 1957. A good discussion of "Set." P. 493.

For film suggestions see Film Supplement, in the Appendix.

CHAPTER 6

Later Childhood

Introduction

Later childhood includes the period from 6 years of age to puberty. Puberty occurs at widely variable ages in different children, but on the average, occurs at about 13 or 14 years of age. In this chapter, we shall discuss children from 6 through 12 years of age.

In countries where schooling is compulsory, this period is often known as the elementary school period. It is characterized by the tendency of children to associate in groups or "gangs." Adjustment to school and to gang activities is serious business to children throughout these years. Development and behavior during this period are complex and often contradictory. One film on the early part of this period is called *Sociable Six to Noisy Nine* (see Film Supplement, in the Appendix), but Gesell [63] refers to the 6-year-old as "difficult, aggressive, explosive, demanding," and says that his behavior is "fresh, nasty, insulting, impudent, bratty, rude, and argumentative." Granted that the latter list of adjectives is somewhat repetitive, the contradiction between "sociable" and Gesell's list is indicative of the fact that the 6-year-old presents various facets to observers, and both satisfaction and distress to his parents.

Similar contradictory descriptive adjectives also are applicable to children at each year from 6 through 12, since children in later childhood are characteristically integrated in one area of growth while in transition and conflict in other areas. Behavior varies from year to year and differs somewhat between the sexes. Generally speaking, boys get into more trouble with adults than girls do, but both boys and girls are annoying and lovable in turn, and each one struggles to establish individuality, not only as a person but as a boy or a girl.

The period is one of continuing preparation for future life, one in which ideas and behavior can be tried out without too serious consequences if they turn out to be mistakes. Adults tend to remember the period in their own lives as a time of considerable freedom, pleasure, and excitement, with its problems, however, such as schoolwork, home chores, and getting along with peers and adults.

PHYSICAL GROWTH AND DEVELOPMENT

Growth of the Body

Reference to Table 4–2 (pages 136 ff.), at the 6–12 year level, shows the general trend of physical development during this period. Increases in height and weight continue at a slow rate, as in early childhood. Body proportions change gradually toward the longer-legged body typical of the 12-year-old. Facial proportions approach the adult ratio of face to skull. The skeleton continues to ossify, becoming less cartilaginous in proportion to bone. The eighth wrist bone usually forms toward the end of this period. The skin remains smooth but becomes less delicate. The hair often begins to darken.

The loss of the temporary teeth continues, the first teeth being replaced by "permanent" teeth. By 12 years of age, most children have 8 incisors, 4 canines, 8 premolars, 4 six-year molars, and 4 twelve-year molars, a total of 28 of their second set of teeth. Tooth decay and tooth loss occur in most children unless they have adequate dental care. Heredity is known to play a part in tooth formation, dominant genes being responsible for the complete absence of some teeth, for absence of enamel, and for defective dentine. Without doubt, tooth decay is influenced by environmental factors such as diet, cleanliness, and lack of dental care, but the inherited chemical quality of the teeth seems to result from the possession of certain genes.[228]

Children between 6 and 12 years often have little interest in food, although some eat well, and some develop strong likes and dislikes. As the breathing apparatus continues to grow, inhalations reduce in number from 25 to 18 per minute. Susceptibility to infections is still high, but begins to decrease as the years pass. The voices of the two sexes are still similar in range and quality. The rate of heartbeat remains about the same as in early childhood, but blood pressure increases somewhat. The heart and blood vessels grow in proportion to each other, so that vigorous activity is normally possible without undue fatigue.

Bladder and bowel control is complete in most children of this period, although some still lack bladder control during deep sleep. Enuresis in children causes parents, in cultures like those of the United States, so much emotional concern that it is difficult to get accurate statistics on its occurrence. Physicians report that it is more common than is generally believed, and that in many cases it results from unusually deep sleep rather than from other more serious emotional problems. Since enuresis is also troublesome to the child, medical treatment that can regulate the depth of sleep or whatever the trouble is, is highly desirable.[225]

Muscular development continues during these years. Cardiac and visceral muscles tend to work well. Skeletal muscles grow with the skeleton and become stronger with exercise. The vigorous physical play of children in this period increases their muscular skill and coordination. The body is in a formative state throughout these years, and postural habits that will characterize the individual throughout his life are likely to be established in this period.[19] Excessive exercise resulting in fatigue, insufficient exercise, and poorly coordinated positions for reading and other forms of study, may adversely effect body development.

The nervous system grows with the body. During these years, the brain attains almost its adult weight. Neurons continue to grow, so new associations may continue to develop. Physiologically, nerve impulses make new connections between neurons, and thus the child is able to continue to learn.

Normally, all the sense organs function well during these years. Increasingly accurate discrimination and judgment develop in connection with sensations. Hearing acuity levels off at about 10 years of age. Where schooling is customary, defects in vision and hearing show up frequently in this period.[163]

The reproductive systems, including the external genitalia, grow slowly. The endocrine glands normally secrete hormones effectively, and the anterior lobe of the hypophysis (pituitary gland) begins to produce gonadotrophic hormones in girls at about 9 years of age and in boys about a year later, on the average. Figure 6–1 shows the endocrine glands as they are located in the body, and Tables 4–2 and

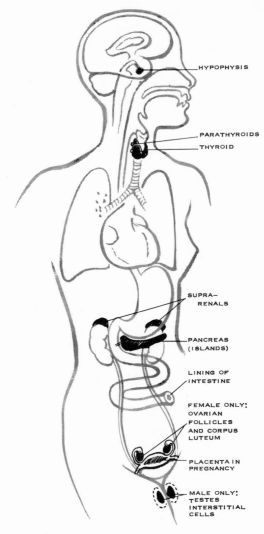

Fig. 6–1. Locations of the endocrine glands.

6–1 give an over-all view of endocrine functions throughout life. We shall have reason to refer to these tables in subsequent chapters in this book.

Handedness

Handedness, either right or left, is usually well established by 6 or 7 years of age. Some children are ambidextrous, using both hands equally well, or they use one hand for certain skills and the other for different skills. For example, some throw a ball with the left hand, and hit right-handedly or vice versa. If strongly left-handed children are forced to do things right-handedly, some of them suffer confusion and delay in accomplishing efficient hand skills such as writing and forming numbers. Some write words such as "was" as "saw" and even write phrases backwards.[163]

General Health

The general health of children between 6 and 12 years of age may be poorer than it was in early childhood. By about 6 years of age, most children begin to come in contact with other people in relatively close group situations such as play, school, and church, so that they are likely to encounter pathogenic microorganisms against which they have little or no immunity. The numerous adjustments in living which they have to make about this age, to school, getting accustomed to new schedules, and so on, may be so fatiguing as to lower their resistance to organisms. As a result, children of this age period are highly susceptible to such diseases as tuberculosis, scarlet fever, diphtheria, whooping cough, poliomyelitis, measles, smallpox, chickenpox, and mumps, and to the numerous varieties of colds, influenza, and pneumonia.

In countries where preventive medicine and public health measures are adequate, no single one of these diseases accounts for more than 2 or 3 per cent of deaths in later childhood. This is not true of some of the more populous countries of the world, however. In the United States, accidents are the leading cause of death in this period, accounting for about one-third of all later childhood deaths. Accidents include fire, drowning, electrocution, and traffic fatalities.

Headaches, upset stomachs, and constipation are not unusual between 6 and 12 years, in many children. Some never have any of these troubles, but other children, as soon as they are free to spend a little money, tend to spend it on soft drinks and candy which may interfere with digestion, resulting in stomach upsets and headaches. They may be too busy with their affairs to respond to their sensations of fullness in the lower intestine, and so permit themselves to become constipated. Headaches sometimes result from eyestrain or various emotional strains connected with their lives, which in this period are complicated by all kinds of frustrations and conflicts among desires.

Table 6–1

Summary of Endocrine Functions in Relation to Growth and Behavior

Name of Gland	Parts of Gland	Hormones	Functions	Effect of Deficiency	Effect of Excess
Hypophysis (Pituitary)	Anterior Lobe	Growth (somatotrophic) hormone	Regulation of general growth	Dwarfism	Gigantism
		Gonadotrophins 1. Follicle stimulating hormone, FSH	Stimulates ovarian follicles and sperm formation	Atrophy of gonads	Unknown
		2. Luteinizing hormone, LH	Production of eggs and corpus luteum	Infertility	Unknown
		3. Luteotrophic hormone, LTH	Stimulates corpus luteum and mammary glands	Miscarriage of embryo	Unknown
		Thyrotrophin, TSH	Stimulates the thyroid	Atrophy of thyroid	Enlargement of thyroid
		Adrenocorticotrophic hormone, ACTH	Stimulates the suprarenal cortex	Atrophy of suprarenal cortex	Unknown
	Posterior Lobe	Vasopressin (Pitressin)	Affects water content of tissues; increases blood pressure	Excessive urine formation	Unknown
		Oxytocin (Pitocin)	Stimulates uterine longitudinal muscle contraction	Slow labor	Unknown
Thyroid		Thyroxin	Regulates general metabolism	Cretinism in children Myxedema in adults Lowered metabolic rates	Exophthalmic goiter Increased metabolic rate

Gland	Hormone	Function		
Parathyroids	Parathyrin (Parathormone)	Regulates calcium metabolism	Excessive excitability of the nervous system	Softening of bones
Pancreatic Islands (Islands or Islets of Langerhans)	Insulin	Control of carbohydrate metabolism	Diabetes mellitus (liver loses glycogen, sugar excreted, weakness)	Hunger and weakness
Cells of the Intestinal Epithelium	Secretin	Activates the pancreas to secrete pancreatic juice	Unknown	Unknown
	Cholecystokinin	Contraction of the gall bladder, releasing bile	Unknown	Unknown
Suprarenals (Adrenals)	Cortex: Cortin 1. Cortisone 2. Androgens 3. Estrogens	Maintains 1. water and other chemical balance in tissue fluids 2. carbohydrate balance in tissues 3. health of connective tissue 4. resistance to stress Assists in sexual development	Addison's disease, a fatal wasting condition	Masculinizes boys and women
	Medulla: Norepinephrine (Noradrenalin)	Uncertain	Unknown	Unknown
	Epinephrine (Adrenalin(e), Adrenin(e))	Reinforces the sympathetic nervous system; in so doing integrates body to meet emergencies	Unknown	High blood pressure; impaired metabolism

Table 6–1

Summary of Endocrine Functions in Relation to Growth and Behavior (Cont'd)

Name of Gland	Parts of Gland	Hormones	Functions	Effect of Deficiency	Effect of Excess
Ovarian Structures	Graafian Follicles	Estrogen (Estrin)	Initiates development of female secondary sexual characteristics; stimulates reproductive organs to develop	Retardation of sexual development	Unknown
	Corpus luteum	Progesterone (Progestin)	Completes the development of the uterus in preparation for pregnancy and maintains uterus for first few months of pregnancy	Miscarriage of the early embryo	Unknown
Cells in the Testes	Interstitial cells; possibly tubule cells	Testosterone (Androgen)	Initiates development of male secondary sexual characteristics; stimulates reproductive organs to develop	Retardation of sexual development	Questionable
Placenta	Embryonic portions	Placental Gonadotrophin	Suppresses the production of gonadotrophin by the hypophysis, thereby preventing further ovulation	Unknown	Unknown
		Estrogen	Seems to counteract the effect of LTH upon the mammary glands, preventing milk formation	Unknown	Unknown
		Progesterone	Takes over function of corpus luteum progesterone as it diminishes	Miscarriage of fetus	Unknown

Gradations of robustness and of quality of the physical body exist in various individuals, and because these factors affect the child's feelings and interest in food, exercise, and play, they also affect general health and development. The Midcentury White House Conference on Children and Youth [146] concluded that probably few children in the United States are at an optimal level of health in every respect, but that there are relatively few who are totally unable to live satisfactory lives. Wide variations occur with respect to physical abilities and disabilities, and these variations are combined with an equally wide range of intellectual and personal-social capacities.

It is not unusual for children to suffer some months or even years of relative physical inactivity because of illness, such as asthma and heart defects, or because of crippling accidents. If such children can learn substitute skills that will bring other children to them, they often develop socially and intellectually. If they get well enough physically, they may find it relatively easy to win acceptance from groups of their own age. If they are overprotected or overindulged during their illness, they may have difficulties in getting back in the swim, both socially and physically.

Physical Routines

As we have seen, physical routines in early childhood are largely supervised by the parents. By 6 years of age, children begin to spend a good many hours of each day away from their homes. In the early grades in school, they are away for 3 or 4 hours at a time, and by the time they are 8 or 9, most children are away for the whole day, including the noon meal. Children of this period tend to belong to clubs or groups that play games or carry on activities outside the home, so that the typical child sleeps, bathes, dresses, and eats about two meals a day at home, in addition to doing school work and home chores. During the time when he is not under the supervision of the home or the school he is learning to look out for himself.

It is now that the discipline which began in infancy begins to take effect. If the child learned in infancy and early childhood that certain routines of eating, sleeping, waste elimination, and being active or at rest made him comfortable, he may continue along the same lines even when on his own. Undoubtedly he will change, as a result of his own physical changes and of meeting other people and seeing what they do. If, however, habits that result in efficiency and comfort get "built in," as it were, in the nervous system as the child grows, his physical, emotional, and mental health is likely to be of better quality than if less efficient habits are established. Studies [171] show that children in trouble with the law often come from homes where there is little regularity in getting up, eating, cleaning the home, going to bed, and other daily routines. While it is quite true that all children from such homes do not get into trouble with the law, there is sufficient evidence to show that, generally speaking, children are helped rather than hindered by a certain amount of order in their lives.

Boys and girls learn personal routines about equally well, although girls tend to assume routine responsibilities in the care of the home somewhat earlier than boys do.[223] If space and facilities for storing things, shelves, cupboards, and so on, are provided, children of both sexes can learn to be reasonably orderly. During these years, however, their periodic forgetfulness and procrastination about routines cause considerable conflict between them and their parents, teachers, and other adults.[65]

Physical Skills

Cne of the developmental tasks of later childhood is perfecting some physical skills and learning new ones that are necessary for satisfactory performance in games, in home chores, and in school work. Such skills are conducive to the child's whole physical, emotional, social, and intellectual development.

Most of the physical skills used in free play, such as skating, bicycle riding, ball playing, and so on, are learned partially through trial and error, helped along by suggestions from playmates who have more skill or more experience. Parents and teachers often help children to give up non-productive motions, and in that way they increase their skills. Not all adults are helpful. If the relationship between father and son, for instance, becomes an unhappy one because the boy does not learn as rapidly as his father thinks he should, the boy may develop a distaste for that kind of skill, whether it is swimming, playing ball, or something else.

Those who train children in skills involving the large muscles often utilize the following steps: they give the children a general acquaintance with the equipment, materials, and surroundings used in the sport; a few simple demonstrations of what is to be done, with

a minimum of verbal instructions; and encouragement to begin trying to follow the directions. As the children practice, pointers as to
how to improve are often helpful.[170]

Some communities promote competitive sports for children of this
age period, particularly for boys. There is considerable debate in the
fields of pediatrics and child development as to the advisability of
competitive sports such as football and baseball for children in this
period of their lives. While most youngsters are certainly strong
enough to play rough games which can end when they themselves
have had enough, it is possible that the physical and emotional strain
of performing for the team, and for the sponsor of the team, until the
game is won or lost, may be excessive for some children.

Most of the physical skills needed for the performance of home
chores are learned partly by imitating the parents or older siblings
or by being taught by them. Most 6-year-olds are able to rake leaves,
sweep or shovel snow, dispose of trash, and help to keep the house
tidy. When children grow tall enough, they can push the lawn
mower, help with washing the car, and push the grocery cart around
the supermarket.

Skill in the use of the smaller muscles is necessary for some games
such as Chinese checkers, for household chores such as sewing on
buttons, tightening screws, ironing clothes, and washing dishes, and
for school work such as drawing, cutting, pasting, and especially
writing. Products of these activities at 6 or 7 years of age are crudely
executed, as a rule. Figure 6–2 is a drawing of a horse and rider by
a 6½-year-old boy. Some girls between 6 and 12 years of age learn
to wash and iron, knit, sew, and mend competently; in some countries, they are expected to bring the family clothing to mend in
school time. Some 8- to 12-year-old boys make usable objects from
metal or wood, and some children's hand skills permit them to play
musical instruments and to use the typewriter.

Skill in controlling the muscles of the eyes is sufficiently well
developed for most 6- and 7-year-olds to read if the print is fairly
large and the lines of print are not too close. By 10 to 12 years of age,
most children can read newspapers and other average-sized print for
extended periods without eyestrain, if they have adequate light and
physical comfort.

Handwriting demands skill in the use of both the eye and hand
muscles. Most children like to imitate printed letters first, and to
begin to tie them together later. Children of this age period often

develop legible but not very fast handwriting. Generally speaking, so many demands are made of them that they lack the time for the practice that is necessary to develop handwriting that is both legible and fast.

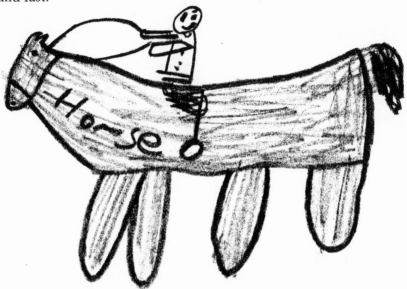

Fig. 6–2. Drawing of horse and rider by a boy aged six and one-half years.

EMOTIONAL DEVELOPMENT

Increasing Specificity of Emotion

Children in later childhood can learn increasing control over the expression of their emotions, and can increase their ability to delay their reactions and to behave appropriately for the situation. They develop the ability to feel an increasing range of emotions. Different and more subtle stimuli arouse different emotional patterns. For example, the child learns to be less afraid of some of the things he has · hitherto feared, such as thunder and darkness, and to be more afraid of getting low grades and of not being liked by others. He becomes more understanding and tolerant of some things, and less so of others. For instance, he may be less bothered by his younger siblings, but more irritated with his own lack of skill. Things that previously fascinated him begin to bore him, while new things arouse his enthusiasm. He feels differently toward some of the experiences with which he is familiar, such as going to bed and getting up, and he is developing positive or negative emotions toward experiences which are new to him, such as learning multiplication tables and using public transportation alone.

Sensitivity and Altruism

As the child's perceptions and judgments increase, his ability to recognize and react to finer and subtler stimuli grows. Thus he becomes more aware of facial expressions, tones of voice, gestures, and other results of the feelings of others. He also becomes increasingly able to submerge self-interest in favor of concern about other beings, and thus becomes somewhat altruistic. An 8-year-old feels concern, for instance, if the spirits of his canary seem droopy, and he will bathe and massage a dog's lame leg. He will protect a small child from a bully. He may hope that his action is noticed, and if so he hopes to be praised for it. Ten-year-olds begin to sense satisfaction resulting from being kind and helpful. Twelve-year-olds, who have been exposed to ideas involving gentleness and charity, at home and in contacts outside the home, may experience sufficient satisfaction in practicing these principles to want to continue living them.

If growing children experience parental dissatisfaction and condemnation of the destructive emotions of anger and fear, they may learn not only to inhibit the cruder ways of expressing them, but also to feel patience and courage and to express those emotions instead. Not all children, unfortunately, have such constructive experiences at home or in their outside contacts, and not all who do have them react altruistically.

Humor

"Humor is the sense within us which sets up a kindly contemplation of the incongruities of life." * The sense of humor, if cultivated, develops rapidly during later childhood. Not only do children find actions funny, but their development of ideas and language also makes verbal humor possible. Children between 6 and 10 years of age enjoy making puns, phrases, and statements with double meanings, "pig Latin," and other variations on words. Some 8- to 12-year-olds have a seemingly inexhaustible supply of riddles and jokes with which they sometimes amuse others and never fail to amuse them-

* Stephen Leacock, *Encyclopaedia Britannica* (1947), Volume II, p. 883.

selves. They find practical jokes riotously funny.[65] The jokes may be cruel, but they usually lose their punch if they result in injury to the victims.

Humor, at this age as at later ages, is sometimes used to help control feelings. The child discovers that a laugh can release feelings that might otherwise result in tears, anger, or embarrassment. Children "kid" each other out of dour moods. They sometimes warp humor into sarcasm or ridicule as a weapon against somebody else, but fail to take it with good grace when it is directed at themselves.

It is believed by some psychologists [128] that the capacity to laugh mirthfully is a measure of one's adjustment to his environment. Sex and aggression * are frequent themes in humor and this is understandable because they are the sources of many of the anxieties in human beings which develop in later childhood. According to Freud,[55] humor is pleasurable because it permits the temporary gratification of some hidden or forbidden wish and at the same time reduces the anxiety that normally inhibits the fulfillment of the wish. If these ideas are true, children's humor can develop, as they themselves achieve emotional, social, and intellectual development.

Emotional Stress

Although later childhood is, in general, a period of good emotional health, some children experience considerable emotional stress. Common sources of this stress are adjustment to school, to the peer group, and to the expectations and demands of parents. These all begin early in the period under discussion. An additional source of stress develops throughout the period, becoming increasingly strong as the years pass. This source is the child's growing sensitivity toward the reactions of other people to him; in other words, Do they like him?

Most children want very much to be accepted both by their peers and by adults. They take seriously their jobs of succeeding at school, with their peers, and with adults such as parents and teachers. Some of them pretend that they don't care, but their pretense is usually a defense mechanism. Whatever their successes or failures were

---

* Used in this context, the term *sex* may be defined as "the condition of maleness and femaleness in a species and the activities that result from the condition," and *aggression* may be defined as "the bold and energetic pursuit of one's goals, sometimes positive and sometimes negative to the welfare of the individual and others."

through early childhood, in later childhood they sense that they are being tested by the whole world.

If they do well in one or more areas and not so well in another, they may feel fairly comfortable. If parents are pleased with their success in their peer group and accept it as a worthy substitute for success in school, for instance, they may feel fine. But if a father wanted a football player and gets a physically frail scholar for a son, or if he wanted a scholar and gets a son who is good only at sports, success in his aptitude brings little emotional satisfaction to the child. Emotional stress resulting from situations like these may show physically in lack of appetite for food, digestive upsets, restless sleep, fatigue, and heightened susceptibility to infections.[19] It may also show in forms of nervous behavior such as enuresis, nail biting, excessive masturbation (self-stimulation of the genitals), or irritability.[163] Stress may reveal itself in personality traits such as cruelty to animals or to smaller children; critical attitudes toward others; preoccupation with jokes about waste elimination, sex, and aggression; lying; stealing; running away; setting fires; and destruction of property. Any of these symptoms usually disappears if the cause of the stress can be alleviated. In some cases, parents need the help of an objective counselor in order to see what the causes of the stress are.

PERSONAL-SOCIAL DEVELOPMENT

Need for Increasing Independence

We have referred to the many-faceted personality of the 6-year-old. The succeeding years are ones during which the child can develop rapidly in independence of thought and action if his environment permits. As his circle of contacts widens and he feels increasing freedom from parental supervision, he meets the challenge of getting along with his peers largely by methods of trial-and-error. He is noisy and brash in his attempts to impress them and to reassure himself about his ability to take his place among them. He also puts out awkward bids for the attention of adults, often behaving in an unattractive manner because he has not yet learned better ways of winning approving attention. The 6-year-old's constant "Look at me," "See me," "Hey! Look what I'm doing" reveal his compelling need to be noticed and approved. If all goes well, by 8 or 10 years of age, he has learned more subtle ways of winning attention and approval from adults, but is still over-obvious in his bids for attention from his peers.[65] By 12 or 13 years of age, his approach to both adults and peers is smoother. Some children are even gracious, especially to adults whom they like or respect.

During later childhood, boys generally have less satisfactory relationships with their parents than girls do,[79] and boys are less satisfied with and more critical of parents than girls are. Studies of some 10- and 12-year-old children,[79, 208, 209] show, however, that the majority of the children studied were satisfied with the treatment that they were receiving at home and that they considered their parents' demands reasonable. These studies would indicate that at least the parents of these children understood the older child's need for increasing independence, and were being fairly successful in tapering off their supervision of their children's activities.

Self-Judgment

In emerging from the world of early childhood to that of later childhood, children have problems in judging their adequacies and their limitations. This judgment does not come easily. In trying to become independent they may attempt to take on responsibility for their own behavior before they are fully capable of doing so. Between the ages of 6 and 9, they tend to be excessively meticulous about how they perform tasks and over-anxious about succeeding in tasks new to them.[65] Part of this fussiness about standards of performance for themselves spills over into the critical attitudes that have been mentioned about the performances of others. With all of these involvements, however, children become increasingly able to judge their own achievements with some objectivity. For instance, they are sometimes heard to say, "I did that good," or "I sure messed that up!"

Parents, in their concern for the welfare of their children, sometimes nag them, with the result that the children hide their real feelings from them. One mother and father, for example, became disturbed at the increasing shyness of their 7-year-old son, who previously had been friendly. He would not even mumble "Hello" to any of their friends. Upon consultation with a counselor, it became evident to them that they had been excessively anxious for their son to be "popular" and have "nice manners." They had overcoached him because they were over-anxious to receive favorable comments about him. Their treatment had resulted in the boy's becoming acutely self-conscious in the presence of adults.

The Role of Peers in Development

An important factor in the development of the child's ability to establish himself apart from his parents is the effect his peers have upon him. He depends upon them not only for companionship but even more for support in his gradual acquisition of independence from his parents. For example, to gain independence, the child sometimes finds it necessary to disobey parental rules. Disobedience involves risking the loss of parental affection, and children find it easier to take this risk if they have the support of their peers. This support also sometimes gives them the courage to oppose the authority of the school officials.[199] From their peers, children also get ideas of what is expected by the parents of other children, and what these children do about what is expected of them. Thus children get views of the world through the eyes of their companions. They learn that other ideas exist in the world beyond their homes, and that there are other ways of doing things.

However, what children have learned throughout the years of infancy and early childhood exerts control over all their later thoughts and behavior. In their contacts with their peers, they often advance the ideas of their parents as if these ideas were their own. Sometimes they defend these ideas with vigor, and in so doing convince themselves that the ideas were their own. In some cases, they convince their peers of the "rightness" of the ideas they defend, and in some cases, become convinced of the "rightness" of the other fellow's ideas. In the latter event, they tend to feel somewhat uncomfortable, and only the support of the group makes the new idea tenable. Together, the members of the group give each other support of parental ideas on the one hand, or the strength to differ from them on the other. Children who are confident of the love and acceptance of their parents tend to be more able to risk identification with something outside of the family than are children who lack confidence in their place in the family.

Self-identification and other phases of personal growth are not absolutely dependent upon experiences with groups of peers.[65] Some children never have more than one or two friends of their own age.

By means of their own maturation and experiences with adults, they nevertheless manage to develop into comfortable, responsible citizens.

There are some phases of social development, however, that take place more effectively through gang experience than without it. The ability to give and take in social interchange is one of these. As one watches a group of 8- to 10-year-olds in action, one wonders how they can take what they do from each other. The blunt remarks, the crude approaches, and the physical assaults seem actually cruel. Some children cannot take them, or give them back. These usually drop out or are excluded from the group, thus missing some lessons in human relations. Most children, however, who are confident at home, can both give and take kindness and unkindness, and enjoy doing so.

Learning to accept criticism and to maintain poise in the face of it is good preparation for being an employee, in the future. Learning through other children's bluntness that people do not always agree with one or want to do the things one wants to do is good training for recognizing the more subtle signs by which people show disagreement or displeasure in adult life. Discovering that, in a temper, people may say things that they do not really mean may save many friendships and even marriages in later years.

If children in later childhood have numerous acquaintances of their own age, it is likely to be a period of somewhat organized team play in which they learn that not everyone can pitch, and that the team needs outfielders as well as a pitcher. Learning to be a competent member of a team is good training for teamwork in marriage, and for remunerative work later on. If one does not have what it takes to be a playing member of a team, one may learn that the batboy, waterboy, and business manager are also important to the functioning of the group. Learning to get along in a group made up of both people one likes and people one dislikes is priceless training for working and socializing smoothly with a variety of people in adult life. The gang is probably the best teacher of learning to live and let live.

Most children learn the kind of things described by the time they reach 12 years of age, but some do not until later—and some people never learn! A study of 14- to 16-year-old boys made by the University of Michigan in 1955 [208] revealed that many of the boys of that age range were still immature in their relations with their peers and in the criteria they had developed for judging friends.

Girls in their groups learn the same kinds of lessons as boys learn, usually with somewhat less physical violence but with equally vigorous verbal activity. If they are to be accepted socially by their peers, as they approach adolescence, both boys and girls have to learn to substitute milder tactics for the vigorous ones of later childhood, and to show more regard for the feelings of others.

Learning Sex Roles

Part of self-judgment is the understanding of one's sex role. Children learn from the culture in which they are growing up what the adult male role is and what the adult female role is. Adult patterns for the sex roles were clearer formerly than they are today, in many cultures. When the man was essentially and obviously the provider and the woman the preparer, it was a simpler matter for children to assume those roles.[9] Today, in many cultures, the providing and preparing roles are shared by the parents, mothers wear slacks and have their hair cut, and both men and women smoke and enjoy similar forms of recreation. Neither is the differentiation between the sexes in childhood as clear as it once was. Both boys and girls wear overalls in infancy and jeans and slacks during childhood, and they share many of the same activities, as Fig. 6–3 shows.

Nevertheless, the period between 6 and 12 years is normally somewhat homosexual, in the sense that boys prefer boys' companionship, and girls prefer girls', at least part of the time. As this preference develops, typically male and female activities develop also. Boys tend to like more rough-and-tumble games than girls do; they build models of planes, ships, and so on, and fly kites and model planes. Some like to work with carpenter's tools, others like experimenting with electricity and chemicals.

Girls, on the other hand, are more likely to enjoy jumping rope and rollerskating. Some make dolls' clothes which they wash, hang on lines, and iron with considerable care. Some like to cook. In some cases, where the boys have a shack or a "clubhouse" of some sort, girls think it would be nice to make curtains for it. Some boys go along with such feminine ideas, and others will have no such "nonsense." In schools where practical course work is available, boys usually choose print shop, carpentry, metal, or electrical shop; and girls usually choose cooking and sewing. In recent years, however, more and more boys have been asking to take cooking, and more girls take shop.

In connection with learning sex roles, children of this period normally have a good deal of interest in sex and the activities that sex involves.[19] They think about it and get together in groups to

Fig. 6–3. Today's boys and girls play together.

discuss it. Because parents in many cultures attempt to control sexual activities by avoiding accurate terms and restricting information about sex,[186] children may develop a greater desire for this information than they would if it were more freely given. At any rate, they are avid for information. If information has been freely given in the home, they ask their questions at home as well as outside, but if the home has been restrictive in the giving of information, they discuss their questions only outside. Partly because the sex organs are so intimately associated with those of waste elimination, and partly because mothers of young children tend to make the association for them, for instance, by telling children they are being "dirty" when they touch their genitals, children in later childhood deal considerably in jokes that have to do with sex and waste elimination. They get together and trade these jokes and laugh at them with gusto.[65] Among boys particularly, some group investigation and experimentation with the sex organs goes on. Girls are more likely to do their investigation in private. Some children of both sexes masturbate, although this is not as typical as it is in adolescence.[106, 107]

This curiosity about sex is part of the general curiosity children have about their world. While they wondered and probably asked in early childhood such questions as "Where do babies come from?", in later childhood they think more deeply about such matters. Typical questions are: "How do babies get out of their mothers' bodies?", "Why do some children look like their fathers?", "Why do we have fathers anyway?", "Why do only married people have babies?" If they have been getting information along the way they have little difficulty in understanding the essentials of human reproduction, but if they do not get information little by little, as they can absorb it, they become confused when many details come into their awareness in rapid succession. Some of them never do clear up their confusion, with resulting emotional discomfort.

By 12 years of age, boys begin to think of sexual affairs as less "dirty" than they did a year or two earlier.[65] If they get accurate information, they lose some of their relish for jokes about sex, and it takes its place as one of the natural functions which are essential to keeping the species going. Comfortable answers given in response to children's questions whenever they are asked provide a foundation for healthy attitudes and practices in the future.

Some Like To Be Alone

For various reasons, some children prefer to be alone a great deal and to spend their energy on doing things that can be done without companions. Some, like Wordsworth (to paraphrase his words), may like to bound over the mountains, by the sides of the deep rivers, and along the lonely streams wherever nature leads.* Some like to get their experiences vicariously through reading, and others like to do scientific experiments alone. There is nothing the matter with a child's wanting to do things alone, as long as he is developing physi-

* William Wordsworth, "Lines Composed a Few Miles Above Tintern Abbey."

cally and as long as he is able to be comfortable when he must spend time with other people.

Adventure

Children all need adventure, but how they get it depends partly upon their inherited constitution and partly upon their surroundings. Some of their adventure will be constructive and conducive to comfortable relations with other people, and some is likely to be destructive and not conducive to comfortable relations, as Fig. 6–4A and 6–4B show. Children may learn valuable lessons from getting into some mischief if they have sympathetic and constructive guidance, particularly at home.

INTELLECTUAL DEVELOPMENT

Adjustment to School

In countries where schooling is available and especially in those in which it is compulsory, schooling is the child's first job, as it were. Schooling tests the adequacy of his achievements, and he must attend, whether he wants to or not. In most families, children are subjected to considerable pressure to do well in school. Adjustment to school involves adjustment to a new situation which represents "a microcosm of human life: everything happens that happens later, but on a smaller scale." [200] During the elementary school years, children are expected to master the tool subjects: reading, writing, spelling, and arithmetic. If they master these tools, they learn other subjects more easily. If they do not, their academic "unfinished business" handicaps their future learning.

The degree of success in elementary school carries implications for success in future vocational and professional life, and for the range and type of people with whom the individual may associate in later life. It also affects habits, feelings, and attitudes associated with continuing physical, emotional, and mental health. For example, if a child accepts the requirements of his school job and habitually does his best with it, he is likely to derive satisfaction from doing his best in whatever job he tackles in the future. If he enjoys learning facts and ideas new to him, he is likely to keep an open mind as he goes through life.

B

A

Fig. 6–4.   (A) Constructive adventure.   (B) Destructive adventure.

As we have pointed out, adjustment to school is also personal-social adjustment, and in school competition the child sees himself in comparison with other children. He gains a new and more realistic conception of himself as he finds that in some skills he surpasses other children, and in some, they surpass him. The adjustment to school is so broad that, obviously, self-reliant living in early childhood is the best preparation for it.[205]

Attention and Memory

The child's ability to pay attention to a task increases through the years of later childhood. In the first few years of the period, however, his attention span is so brief and his attention is so easily diverted that serious concentration for more than brief periods is impossible. Most modern schools recognize this and so keep periods of study and recitation short and permit considerable bodily freedom through the first three grades. Periods are lengthened as the span of the children's attention elongates. In order to stimulate the development of longer and more concentrated attention, schools try to develop methods of presenting information in ways that will get and hold the children's interest.

Memory span increases during later childhood, to the degree that children can memorize tables of numbers, poems, and so on with comparative ease. They can do this without any comprehension of what they have memorized. The modern educational practice of pupil-pupil and pupil-teacher interchange is an attempt to assure that the child comprehends what he memorizes. As sometimes happens in human experimentation with ways of doing things, the pendulum may have swung too far in the direction away from memorization. Parents often ask why their children are not learning the poems and other literary passages they learned when they went to school. They feel that while they did not always understand what they memorized at the time, the drill was good, and more important than that, lines learned in childhood often run through their adult minds and have valuable meaning for them.

Some boys and girls who are in college today are handicapped by their later childhood failure to memorize such material as multiplication tables and the spelling of an adequate vocabulary. A memory trained to recall people's names, dates, location of streets, and so on is a real asset in adult life. The habit of remembering, like most other useful habits, is most easily and permanently developed during childhood.

Spoken Language

By the end of early childhood, the average child has acquired a vocabulary and the use of sentence structure in his native language that serves most of his needs for oral communication. In later childhood he is expected to increase his spoken vocabulary, to become able to communicate his ideas in written language, and to read and comprehend the written and printed ideas of others.

Children in later childhood like to talk. It is not uncommon for family conversation at mealtime to be dominated by one of the children. Sometimes parents have to keep the most vocal one quiet long enough to give the others a chance to say something, or to say something themselves. The youngsters talk about all kinds of things, specializing in their own prowess; in so doing, they practice their newly acquired vocabulary. In their peer groups, they also talk a great deal, often a number of them at the same time, seeming to be more interested in their own talking than in whether or not they are being listened to. Sex and aggression figure largely in their peer talk, as these topics do in their humor. It is difficult for students of child behavior to find out in detail just what the subject matter and vocabulary of peer group discussions is. If children and early adolescents can feel sure that their confidence will not be violated, they will sometimes report on these subjects from memory and current observation. From this source, and from recorded conversations, it has been learned that most first graders know and use some words relating to waste elimination but not many, if any, relating to sex. At about 9 years of age, they begin to learn some words relating to sex although they do not understand them all. By this time, they also know and use some words relating to aggression; swear words, for instance. Boys know and use more words relating to waste elimination, sex, and aggression than girls do, although some of the girls who have brothers close to their own age are about as proficient in this area as the boys are. The lists of words used differ somewhat with the culture (private school or public school, for instance), but there is considerable overlapping. In general, the lists include all the words that gave D. H. Lawrence trouble with the censors,[123] and many more in addition.

Reading

Before children can learn to read, they must have achieved what is known as *readiness to read.* Reading readiness depends upon a number of factors. Those which have been recognized to date are: a certain degree of maturation of the eyes and the nervous system, which renders the child able to pay attention to details; an ability to recognize differences in the formation of letters such as *m* and *n* and *b* and *d;* some knowledge of the meaning of words; a background of experience related to what is to be read; and a motivation to read.[163]

Most 6-year-old children have had experiences that lead toward readiness for reading, and apparently about three-fourths of the children who enter school have achieved the necessary degree of physical maturity of the eyes and nervous system to permit them to make reasonably satisfactory progress in reading in the first grade.[163] About one-fourth fail to do so in the first grade, and many of these never learn to read well. Children who make good progress early in the grades usually master the fundamentals of efficient reading by the fourth grade. They enjoy reading and so practice their skill. By the end of sixth grade, these children have achieved reasonably good speed and comprehension in both oral and silent reading, so that reading from then on is a tool by means of which other subjects are learned.

Reading interests change during the years of later childhood. Six-, 7-, and 8-year-olds like books about nature, fairy tales, and stories about children in other lands. At ages 9 and 10, interest in fairy tales declines, and differentiation in interests develops between the sexes. Boys become more interested in books of adventure, mystery, and popular science; girls become more interested in stories about girls, family situations, and some of the professions that are largely feminine, such as nursing. Girls, however, read more boys' books than boys read books that are written for girls.[232] Both sexes like comics.

Written Language

We have mentioned handwriting among the physical skills. In the elementary grades, children are expected to learn to form letters with speed and legibility, and are also expected to learn to express their ideas and knowledge by way of the written word. Writing becomes a tool in the learning of other subject matter. If children learn the principles of clear sentence structure and composition in the grades, they are equipped with a way of expressing themselves that stands them in good stead throughout their lives. Clarity of thinking is essential for good sentence formation, and some children need more help than others in thinking things out step by step, in the proper order, and writing them down accordingly.

Concepts of Time and Space

The older child is capable of retrospection and anticipation to a degree that was not possible in early childhood. Accordingly, history and geography enter the curriculum of most schools by the fourth grade. By 9 or 10 years of age, most children can think in terms of time through which they have not lived and of space with which they are not personally familiar. Seven-year-olds usually know the seasons in the correct sequence, 8-year-olds understand the date of the month. Some schools try with questionable success to teach 12-year-olds concepts such as the International Date Line and the Papal Line of Demarcation. Paleontologists have learned that children 13 years of age can rarely conceive of geological time, and so they show them fossils but do not expect them to understand how far in the past the animals and plants lived. Today's children talk and act as though they have relatively clear concepts of outer space and the position of the Earth among the other planets that revolve around our sun. In some ways, the 6- to 12-year-olds have an advantage over adult scientists in that they are not restricted in their imagination by troublesome factual data; therefore, they can roam at will in outer space.

Concept of Numbers

Beyond the ability to count objects up to 10 in number, 5-year-olds have little concept of numbers or of quantity.[166] They do not understand that the number of objects does not change if the objects are moved into different patterns, or are clustered into one large and several smaller groups, or that number does not depend upon the order in which objects are counted.[10] Between 6 and 10 years of age, these concepts are grasped rapidly. Children of this age also grasp such properties of number as the whole equals the sum of its parts. They show finer discrimination in handling quantitative differences, and develop a vocabulary for expressing quantities.[139]

Most 6-year-olds enjoy showing off their ability to recite number sequences up to 100 and beyond. Accurate counting of objects in large numbers is more difficult for them, but if the objects are arranged so that they can be followed easily with the eyes, with patience on their part and some encouragement from adults, 6-year-olds can do this also. A wide developmental difference exists between being able to talk about a number such as 5 or 100 and being able to comprehend that these numbers mean the sum of 5 or 100 single objects. An appreciation of "fiveness" is usually achieved by 6-year-olds; of "nineness" and "tenness" by 7-year-olds. From this age on, appreciation of increasingly large numbers makes beginnings of arithmetic possible in the second grade. At first, the combinations are restricted to under 10 additions, followed by subtractions. Simple multiplication and division follow in the third grade, along with "carrying" and "borrowing" in addition and subtraction. Long division, fractions, percentage, and reasoning problems follow in the fourth grade and up.

Important for progress in arithmetic is a sound "feeling" for numbers and number combinations. Some children learn from their play with blocks that $2 + 2 = 4$, that $3 + 1 = 4$, that $4 - 1 = 3$, and so on. Games like dominoes teach that blocks of numbers such as 2 twos make 4; 2 threes make 6; and so on. Family games that encourage counting and recognizing number combinations give practice in the handling of numbers under emotionally favorable conditions.

Numbers take on new and important meanings for children as they begin to use money. Most parents who can afford to do so give their children cash allowances at more or less regular intervals. These help children to appreciate numbers and also to learn to manage money. Studies [208, 209] show that two-thirds to three-fourths of the children in the middle and upper economic brackets in the United States receive allowances beginning at 6 or 7 years of age, and running through 13 or 14 years or longer. The amounts taper off as the children begin to earn money. Table 6–2 shows the distribution of amounts of allowances given to a nationwide sampling of Girl Scouts, aged 7 through 12 years.[210] Small earnings began in this group at 7 years of age; 66 per cent of the 7-year-olds and 80 per cent of the 10-year-olds earned some money, chiefly for doing home chores. Ten per cent of the 7-year-olds and 33 per cent of the 11-year-olds were earning money by helping to take care of smaller children outside of their own homes. Boys of these ages earned

Table 6–2

Amounts of Fixed Weekly Allowances Given by Parents to Girl Scouts,
Ages Seven Through Thirteen Years

Age	25–49¢	50–99¢	$1.00–$1.99	$2.00 or More	Amount Not Known
7	53%	21%	3%	12%	11%
9	41%	39%	16%	2%*	2%
11	15%	45%	31%	5%*	4%
13	3%	12%	46%	33%	6%

Figures based on University of Michigan Survey Research Center Study.[210]

* Reductions of $2.00-or-more amounts at ages nine and eleven were explained as withdrawals of larger amounts which had not been used wisely.

money by delivering newspapers, helping to take care of small children, and by doing other similar tasks.[208]

Thinking and Reasoning

Learning about numbers, time, and space are only some of the aspects of the increasing capacity for handling abstract ideas which typifies later childhood. Russell,[178] in a study of the intellectual development of older children and adolescents, concluded that their thinking includes four main groups of factors. These are (1) the materials of thinking: sensations, perceptions, memories, images, and concepts; (2) motives for thinking: feelings, needs, attitudes, habits of thought; (3) processes in thinking: selecting, eliminating, searching, manipulating, organizing; (4) abilities in thinking: habits, techniques, guides for improvement. All of these aspects of thinking are refinements of the processes achieved in early childhood.

At about 6 or 7 years of age, children begin to discuss such abstract concepts as honor and fairness. As they struggle to clarify the meanings of these terms, they do so at first in concrete details. It is not right, for example, to take another child's pencil, but school chalk does not belong to any one person so it is all right to take it. One should not hit a friend or tell tales on a friend, but it is "o.k." or even expected that one should do so to an enemy. Adults often further confuse children. "It is not right to hit people," they say, and yet a father may scold his son if he does not defend himself.

Equally confusing is the concept of truth. One of the problems in early childhood is to distinguish between imagined and real things or events. In later childhood, many apparent contradictions must be harmonized. For example, children are told to tell the truth. To them, truth means fact. But they must not tell the truth if doing so would prove socially tactless. So they must reconcile the differences between "bad" lies, "white" lies, truth one tells, and truth one does not tell.

Gradually, children begin to be able to think with fewer concrete symbols. The abandonment of the flesh-and-blood concept of Santa Claus may illustrate this. Many children, as early as 5 years of age, observe that they have seen Santa Claus inside a department store and again on the street corner outside, that Santa is bigger around than is the hole in the chimney, and that one Santa cannot possibly visit all the children in the world on the same night. Early in the period of later childhood they usually go along with the idea of Santa having helpers, and with the idea that "Daddy is Santa in our house." By 7 years of age, even though the parents may go to all sorts of trouble to preserve the idea of the flesh-and-blood Santa Claus, from various sources such as conversations in other homes, what they hear in school or church, what they see and hear on television, children begin to form the concept that Santa represents the spirit of Christmas. Along with this concept comes the idea that Christmas is the celebration of a birthday of someone who was born a long time ago who grew up to be a good, kind man. They cannot grasp the idea that the philosophy of the individual whose birth is celebrated is the foundation for one of the world's greatest religions, and many Christian groups do not formally induct children until they are in their early teens.

Children of this developmental period also struggle with such ideas as the possibility of life after death. The following conversation illustrates the idea of two children in this area.

Andy, aged 7, said to his brother Ralph, aged 10, "I don't believe in heaven 'cause I've seen skeletons." Here Andy reveals that he has gathered, from what people have told him, that people inhabit heaven in their physical bodies.

After a pause, Ralph answered, "Well, as I hear it, it's just your thoughts that go to heaven." Here Ralph reveals his concept of the human soul separated from the body.

After an interval in which Andy turned this idea over in his mind he said, "Well, then, I don't want to go to heaven, 'cause I don't want everybody knowing what my thoughts are."

At that, they changed the subject.

People of all ages differ widely in their ability to deal with abstract ideas. Inherent intelligence is one factor, but, assuming equal intelligence to be present, people still differ in their ability to reason in abstractions. Another factor in their ultimate ability seems to be the amount and kind of reasoning done in this period of later childhood. As in other areas, if practice in abstract thinking is done as early as the nervous system is mature enough to permit it, and a habit of abstract thinking is "built in" to the nervous system, the child may learn to enjoy it, just as he does any skill in which he is proficient. If the habit of abstract thinking does not develop as early as maturation permits, it may, of course, develop later. However, many individuals who fail to discover in childhood the satisfaction of using their intellectual ability, develop habits of passive receptivity to whatever is offered by the mass media or their peers, and are likely to continue these habits for life. Successful human living today demands the ability, inclination, and enjoyment of abstract thinking. One of the challenges to educators is to stimulate children to form the habits necessary to fulfil these demands.

Broadening of Interests

Accompanying intellectual development in later childhood is the broadening of the interests which children pursue with varying degrees of concentration. With longer attention span, multiplication of useful concepts, increased muscular skills, and freedom in the realm of ideas in print, children develop all kinds of new interests. Although they still devote considerable time to what looks like aimless play, watching television, "fooling around" with collections, or bicycle-riding nowhere in particular, they begin to like to see results in some areas of their activity. They enjoy their sense of accomplishment when, for instance, a model plane that they have made flies, when they can see their baseball skills improving, or when an experiment in chemistry works. Girls are thrilled, for example, when their cakes turn out well, or their pleated skirts look as if an expert had pressed them.

Some communities do things that expand horizons for the children by taking them on trips into the wider community, to dairy farms, for instance, or industrial plants, art and nature museums, concerts, different kinds of churches and synagogues, and observatories. These opportunities are helpful, because children cannot develop interest in areas with which they are unfamiliar. However, the possibility of over-scheduling their time exists. One nationwide study of pre-adolescent and adolescent girls [209] revealed that one-half of all girls in middle and upper class families were taking from one to five private lessons per week at something outside of regular schoolwork. A high percentage of boys and girls from 6 to 12 years of age [208, 209] belong to more or less formally organized groups which meet at regular intervals. When we add to these activities the time children spend in religious instruction outside of school hours, we find that many children between 8 and 12 years of age are scheduled for from 2 to 8 hours weekly in addition to their hours spent in school, and at homework required by the school.[146] Many children have regularly assigned duties connected with the maintenance of the home and its surroundings, and with the care of younger siblings. Children of this age period need time for solitude, also, in which they can read and dream about their interests (Figs. 6–5A, 6–5B).

Individual Differences in Intelligence

As we pointed out in Chapter 2, intellectual ability differs from individual to individual, ranging all the way from helpless idiocy to very superior. Tests attempt to identify those who are unfit for regular schooling, and those who can go only a certain distance in school. The definitely unfit are kept out of regular school, and those whose ability fits them for entrance but limits their advance are either permitted to go as far as they can with normal children, or, in some cases, are put in special classes for the intellectually less well-endowed. The majority of communities lack special facilities for mentally handicapped children, and such children tend to drop out of school as soon as the law permits. They are likely to be unoccupied, bored, and frustrated, and many of them become troublesome to society.[70] As the world's population increases, the numbers of these children grow larger also. Society has not yet learned how to cope with this problem.

In recent years, more and more attempts are being made to identify children who are endowed with superior intellectual ability and also to identify their special aptitudes. In some communities, these children are placed in special classes; more frequently, they are placed in regular classes with children of average ability and the school curriculum is arranged in such a way that they are not restricted to the pace or interests of the other pupils. In other com-

B

A

Fig. 6—5. (A) Time to read. (B) Time to dream.

munities, however, there is no provision for them to go ahead, or to broaden their interests. Unless these children have opportunities at home or opportunities to go to libraries, museums, and so on, they are likely to become lazy, restless, bored, and eventually trouble-some.[163] As a result, society does not benefit from their abilities as it might if they were helped to develop constructive habits in child-hood.

DEVELOPMENT OF VALUES

Basic Assumptions

Society assumes that each normal individual is capable of respon-sible behavior in accordance with the values that it considers essen-tial to satisfactory group living. We referred to values to some extent in our discussion of cultural mores in Chapter 3. A *value* has been defined as "(1) an abstract concept, often merely implicit, that defines what ends or means to an end are desirable; (2) a goal; (3) the degree of worth ascribed to an object or activity."[73]

Children are born lacking any sense of values; they develop them as they grow. The system of values which they eventually develop is dependent partly upon their inherent intelligence and partly upon their experiences in the culture or cultures in which they grow up. If they are sufficiently well-endowed intellectually, and if they grow up in a family of people who have a well-developed consciousness of being partially responsible for the welfare of society, they are likely to develop similar values. If, on the other hand, they lack sufficient intellectual ability or if they grow up among people who lack a sense of social responsibility, they are likely to develop dif-ferent values and their socializing process may be slow or always incomplete. Development of values involves continuing develop-ment of conscience.

Development of Conscience

We have seen that conscience begins to develop in early child-hood. In later childhood, conscience strengthens considerably in most children. By 6 years of age, it is the "still, small voice" inside them that makes them pass up enticing objects on variety store counters even while their mothers are occupied in other directions.

A small boy looks longingly at a toy car, for instance. He hesitates, picks it up, moves it back and forth, and reluctantly puts it back in its place on the counter.

However, he may put it in his pocket. Nearly all children between 6 and 10 years of age take one or two or more things that they understand clearly do not belong to them and which they have no right to take. If conscience is developing normally, however, they feel so uncomfortable that they have to do something to ease their feelings. The following incident illustrates this point. The first graders under their teacher's direction were arranging the furnishings of their classroom. In the moving around, a small wooden duck became unglued from a cabinet. Six-year-old Frances liked it and put it in her pocket. When they went to glue the duck back into place, no one could find it. It was time to go into the reading for the day, and the duck was temporarily forgotten. During the reading, the teacher noticed Frances' uneasiness. Toward the end of the period, the little girl burst forth with "I haven't got it! I haven't got it! I haven't got it in my pocket." She *did* have it in her pocket. Her agitation led to the "I haven't got it", and her conscience to the "I haven't got it in my pocket." The teacher, realizing the child's conscience was developing well enough to give her trouble, said, "Well, I'm glad we've found it. We'll glue it on when we have finished our reading."

We have mentioned children's confusion about the abstract concept of truth. However, aside from that difficulty, they tend during later childhood to do some compromising for reasons other than social tact. They may lie to impress others, to escape punishment, to excuse procrastination, to bolster themselves when they are afraid, or for revenge. Sometimes they lie because they cannot bear to disappoint parents, teachers, or friends. They may eventually find lying impractical, especially if they can't remember exactly how they lied; or they may be so uncomfortable, however painful the truth is, that it may be less painful than the plaguings of their conscience.

Although children are not born cheaters, for various reasons they sometimes learn to cheat in school or at games. Children in the early grades often "copy" their neighbors' work without realizing that they are doing something considered wrong. They are supposed to be getting certain information, the other child is writing it down, they do not know it, so they copy it. They have to be taught that this is not the best way to master the material. Likewise, on multiple-choice tests, a child knows that his teacher wants him to pick the correct answer. He reasons that if he checks them all, he can't miss. He has to be taught why this is not what is wanted. Normal children soon learn that this behavior is undesirable, and their consciences may remind them in future. If, however, pressure for good grades is too great, fear of parental displeasure over grades may be more painful than conscience, and the practice may become a habit.

Internalization of Values

Since conscience depends upon the child's acceptance of parental, or other standards of conduct as his own,[186] it is obvious that the internalization of standards for conduct may result in a wide range of values in the areas of honesty, aggression, sexual behavior, and so on.

Concerning honesty, studies have led to some generalizations about children.[65] Of 10-year-olds, Gesell says that they are more aware of what is "wrong," according to their culture, than of what is "right." They are opposed to cheating and have stern codes against dishonesty. Of 11-year-olds, he says that they are more aware of what is "right" than they were earlier, but they do not always do what is considered right. They are critical of unfairness, but do not treat truth as sacred. Of 12-year-olds, Gesell says that conscience is becoming a genuine guide, that stealing and cheating are under control, but that cheating at games may be a test of skill to see who can do it most successfully.

Generally speaking, cultures teach children to respect their consciences. As a result, if the values that the conscience accepts are reasonable and sound, conscience is helpful throughout life. On the other hand, if the values that the conscience accepts are not in accord with basic human nature, the conscience can be a real handicap in later life. This is particularly true in the areas of dependency, aggression, and sexual life.

In the area of dependency, for instance, in the United States, motherhood is considered more or less sacred, and society gives approval to customs that indicate respect for mothers. Among those are the celebration of Mother's Day with accompanying cards, gifts, and so on. In the elementary grades, children often are given assignments to make cards and gifts for Mother's Day. No such all-out respect is taught for women as wives. As a result, many young men grow up confused as to whom they owe their first allegiance, to their wives or to their mothers. They are also confused whether they may expect the greatest understanding of themselves, as adults, from their wives or from their mothers.

In the area of aggression, for another example, girls are customarily taught, although not so effectively in recent years as formerly, that "mother's place is in the home." As a result, many girls of superior intellectual ability who are encouraged intellectually as children, have twinges of conscience when they even think of taking some kind of a job, remunerative or otherwise, before their children have left home. In line with this teaching, boys used to be taught that it was a reflection upon a husband's power to provide for his family if his wife worked for money. Even today, in spite of the number of wives who are working, many husbands still suffer qualms of conscience as a result of the values they adopted as boys.

In the area of sexual life, values based on lack of information or on inaccurate information are accepted by the consciences of many people, while other sounder values are rejected. Parents, as has been pointed out, sometimes use inaccurate terms and restrict information, as means of controlling sexual activity in children. As a result of this treatment, girls especially may feel qualms of conscience when they even try to find out how their bodies are constructed and as a further result, suffer from a variety of fears for the rest of their lives. About sexual matters, parents say frequently, "My children know the difference between right and wrong" without having actually taught them anything in direct terms. This failure is largely due to the fact that they themselves are still confused, even though they are parents.

The many conflicts and complications in most cultures today make the development of a sense of sound values and a useful conscience a very difficult matter. It is understandable that children between 6 and 12 years of age should experience confusion during that period, but it is unfortunate (to put it mildly) that adults are not better equipped to help them eliminate some of their confusion as they move on toward adolescence.

SUGGESTIONS FOR FURTHER DISCUSSION

1. Have three members of the class observe a 6- to 8-year-old, an 8- to 10-year-old, and a 10- to 12-year-old. Have various other members of the class read case studies from Millard and Rothney's *The Elementary School Child* (below). Discuss, in the following areas, the developmental status of the chil-

dren covered: (a) Daily schedule—not what it should be, but what it actually is in the children observed, (b) physical growth, (c) motor (muscle) controls, (d) vocabulary and use of language, (e) time and space concepts, (f) general knowledge, (g) breadth of interests, (h) development of conscience, and (i) general emotional adjustment.

2. Observe a group of 6- to 12-year-olds at play. Note and report to the class on what you found in their organization of play. Who decided what they did? How many leaders were there? How many followers? What seemed to be the personal characteristics and the developmental stages of leaders versus followers? What kind of differences of opinion arose in the group? How were these settled?

3. Recall your own adjustment to school entrance. What situations did you find most difficult? Most satisfying? What did you find in the text and readings below to help you understand yourself as you were at age 6?

4. Recall the best teacher you ever had. What influence did he (she) have on your growth? Be specific.

5. What did you find in the readings below to supplement the text on the development of conscience, and why older children make the mistakes they do in respecting property right and in dealing with the truth? What can you add to this from your own personal experience?

6. Formulate answers to the questions older children ask about sex.

7. Make suggestions for: (a) Drawing out a quiet child, (b) helping a child who is having difficulty in keeping up with his school grade, (c) helping a group of 10- to 12-year-old boys who are destructive in their play, and (d) helping a crippled child to find companionship and social growth.

REFERENCES FOR FURTHER STUDY

DENNIS, W. *Readings in Child Psychology.* Englewood Cliffs, N.J.: Prentice-Hall, Inc., 1951. Selection X–2, success and failure in the classroom; Selection X–3, teachers and behavior problems; Selection X–4, when should children begin to read?

DEWEY, R., and HUMBER, W. J. *The Development of Human Behavior.* New York: The Macmillan Co., 1951. Ch. X, Childhood: physiological development, continuation of the socialization process, achievement of new status in neighborhood and school, personality development.

LANE, H., and BEAUCHAMP, M. *Understanding Human Development.* Englewood Cliffs, N.J.: Prentice-Hall, Inc., 1959. Chs. 10 and 11, the early and middle years of childhood; the physical thrust, the social thrust, the mental thrust.

MILLARD, C. V., and ROTHNEY, J. W. M. *The Elementary School Child: A Book of Cases.* New York: Holt, Rinehart & Winston, Inc., 1957. Excellent case studies.

OLSON, W. C. *Child Development* (2d ed.). Boston: D. C. Heath & Co., 1959. Ch. 10, pp. 311–328, the affective life of the child: fears and affective disturbances; nervous symptoms, habits, and overflow movements; frustration in the classroom; mechanisms of adjustments; projective methods.

SEIDMAN, J. M. *The Child: A Book of Readings.* New York: Holt, Rinehart & Winston, Inc., 1958. Selection 18, how well do elementary school teachers understand child behavior? Selection 33, concept formation in children of school age; Selection 38, children's play at different ages; Selection 65, preadolescents: what makes them tick?

For film suggestions see Film Supplement, in the Appendix.

CHAPTER 7

Puberty

General Considerations

In preceding chapters we have been following the development of children from their conception through the thirteenth year of their postnatal lives. In this and the next two chapters, we shall follow their development as they make the transition from childhood to early adulthood. The beginning of this transition period is called *puberty*. Puberty and the Latin term "pubertas," to which it is related, both refer to the fact that physical changes related to sex begin to be apparent at about this time in the child's life, and that these are external evidence of internal changes that have been taking place for some time.

Closely related to the physical changes are psychological changes, which come about partly as results of the physical changes and partly as results of the developing intellect, social experiences, and of the cultural setting in which the child is growing up. The psychological changes, which include changes in emotions, attitudes, and behavior, are quite as significant as the physical changes in the life of the individual and in his relations with other people.

We have seen that physical, emotional, personal-social, and intellectual growth during early life occur concurrently and continuously; that, at some stages, greater progress is made in some areas than in others; and that the pace in all areas varies from one stage to the next. The pace of physical growth, for example, is most rapid from conception to birth, remains rapid throughout infancy, and becomes less rapid in early and late childhood. At puberty, the pace increases rapidly and relatively suddenly, so that we recognize what is often called "the growth spurt" of puberty. Many of these rapid physical changes are obvious; others equally rapid are less obvious because they take place within the body.

PHYSICAL CHANGES

The physical changes of puberty are pervasive, and they are closely interrelated with the personal-social development of the individual during this and the adolescent developmental periods. What is happening to the body is clearly evident, often misunderstood (with serious consequences to behavior and personality development), and always a matter of intense interest to the individual in whose body they are occurring. Parents, educators, and others who live and work with pubescent and adolescent young people can understand and work with them successfully only if they understand the physical as well as the psychological changes occurring in these developmental periods. It is important both to the individual young person and to those who live and work with him to understand the wide individual differences in age at which these physical changes occur, and the effect that the timing of the changes as well as the changes themselves have upon the individual.

Height and Weight

Among the earliest signs of puberty is the obvious spurt in height. Psychological changes may precede, parallel, or follow this spurt; as a rule, they parallel or follow, rather than precede it.[71, 204] The age at which the growth spurt begins differs with the sexes and from individual to individual within each sex. Girls generally begin their rapid growth between 8 and 13½ years of age, boys between about 10 and 15 years.[193] Rapid growth usually continues for a year or two and then begins to taper off. Boys may gain from 5 to 12 inches during this period, some boys as much as 6 to 8 inches in one year. Girls grow almost as fast, but usually taper off sooner.

Rapid gains in weight often accompany gains in height. Some children gain weight noticeably just before the spurt in height begins; others gain weight fairly steadily throughout the spurt period, but their gain in weight in relation to their gain in height is so slow that they take on the "beanpole" look, seeming to be chiefly arms and legs. Some children, whose heredity is for a small body, grow so gradually that their height and weight gains are hardly noticeable.

In general, differences between the sexes and from individual to individual within each sex are clearly discernible, the girls not only coming to puberty earlier than the boys, but individuals within each sex varying considerably from the average for the sex. The sex differences are reflected in height gains to such an extent that, between 10½ and 14 years of age, the average girl is as much as three-quarters of an inch taller than the average boy of the same age. As Fig. 7–1

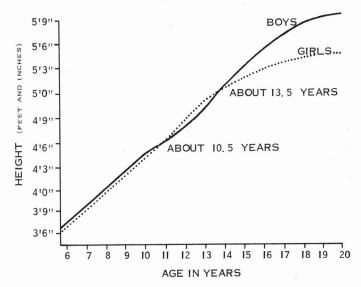

Fig. 7–1. Average height of boys and girls aged six through nineteen years. (After F. K. Shuttleworth.)

shows, males in the United States are, on the average, taller than females throughout most of the life span, but for a time which coincides with the junior high school years, girls are taller than boys. Although stature is largely a matter of heredity, if diet and general health are good, parents often have children who grow taller than they are.[228]

The Skeleton

As the skeleton grows toward maturity, the calcification of the bones progresses, and the long bones of the limbs grow rapidly for a year or two, resulting in the often startling increase in stature. New bones form, and some bone elements already present begin to fuse; so that the number of separate bones in the body changes.

About 350 separate bones are present during puberty, as opposed to about 270 at birth. New small bones appear particularly in the ankles and the wrists. Among the bones which appear in late childhood are the *sesamoid bones* in the tendons of the thumb joints. The appearance and degree of calcification of the wrist bones and of certain other bones as revealed by X rays have been found useful as an index of the degree of general physical maturation. A relationship exists, for example, between the development of the sesamoid bones of the thumbs in girls and the onset of the menstruation. The sesamoid bones have been found to develop about 2½ years prior to the onset of menstruation.[22] X-ray pictures of the skeleton reveal that, on the average, girls are about two years ahead of boys in skeletal development.[22]

Body Proportions

As would be expected, changes in body proportions also occur at puberty. The limbs grow more rapidly than the trunk, and hands and feet enlarge considerably. Most children, even though their muscles have become fairly well coordinated in later childhood, find that these temporary new proportions between parts of their bodies confuse them in their movements. They trip over their own feet, particularly in moments of social embarrassment and self-consciousness; they drop things; and they collide with stationary objects. As a result, puberty is sometimes called the awkward age.

Some girls and boys suffer acutely over their awkwardness, and as a result, become tense and more clumsy than ever. Others laugh it off. The attitude of adults toward it makes a great difference; nagging, for example, only makes them more nervous and awkward. If the awkwardness is a result of nothing but the changes in body proportions unaccompanied by emotional difficulties, it is soon outgrown. If, as a result of nagging, awkwardness becomes an emotional problem, it may last a long time, even becoming a lifelong habit.[50]

Considerable disproportion of facial features often occurs in puberty. The nose, particularly, seems to grow faster than the other features. Enlargement of the nose bothers some girls and boys greatly, and plastic surgery to improve the size and shape of the nose has become fairly popular among young people. Often during the years of adolescence, the features become better proportioned; if not, surgery may be helpful psychologically. Nose shape and size is definitely hereditary,[182] although some environmental factors such as blows from boxing may affect the shape.

The contours of the body change, the pelvis (hips) becoming broader in proportion to the rest of the body in most girls, the shoulders becoming broader than the pelvis in most boys. General body structure, however, is basically a matter of heredity. Girls tend to develop smaller waists than do boys. A girl in a family whose women typically have small pelvises is likely to have a small pelvis, unless genes from the paternal side have influenced her structure more than those from the maternal side of the family. The pelvises of some girls remain so small or so narrow that they are unable to deliver babies naturally, and have to be delivered by Cesarean operation.

Deposits of fat accumulate in some boys and girls before or during puberty, and disappear later on. Girls and boys in most cultures are unhappy about being fat, although in a few cultures large accumulations of fat in women are considered marks of beauty, and it is the slender ones who are unhappy.[183] *Obesity,* or abnormal fatness, is hereditary in some cases, and in others is the result of faulty diet or physiology. Faulty physiology may itself be hereditary, but medical science may be able to correct it, at least partially. Correction is certainly worth attempting, because obesity can not only grow out of psychological conditions, it can easily develop into a psychological as well as a physical problem. A vicious circle may develop in which a child who is unhappy about his appearance behaves badly, becomes still more unhappy, finds eating his greatest happiness, and becomes still more obese.

In most girls, the *mammary glands* in the breasts begin to develop between 10 and 13 years of age. The *areolae,* the darker areas surrounding the nipples, enlarge somewhat and become slightly puffy. For about the first year and a half after the changes show up, the breasts are conical in shape. In some boys, the mammary glands show slight enlargement at puberty, but this enlargement soon subsides.

Growth of Hair

As we have seen, the word puberty comes from the Latin noun, *pubes,* meaning "hair." The growth of hair in new locations on the body and of new texture and pigmentation is characteristic of the period under discussion. At about the same time that changes in the breasts occur, or soon after, hair begins to grow in the pubic region, at the base of the abdomen, in both sexes. It is at first soft and lightly pigmented, tending to become curly and darker as time goes on. Somewhat later, hair appears in the armpits (*axillae*) of both sexes.

Facial hair begins to develop in some boys as early as 13, and in others not until about 15 years of age. At first, it is fine and silky, but tends to become coarser and darker in color as time passes. Depending upon their heredity, boys may or may not develop luxurious hair growth on the body, legs, and arms. Hairiness seems to have little relation to virility, some boys becoming very hairy, others remaining comparatively hairless. The degree of hairiness varies to some extent with the ethnic group. In boys, the head hair line tends to recede at the temples with the onset of puberty.

Changes in the Voice

Changes in the voice accompany changes in the larynx and the elongation of the vocal cords. Greater changes occur in the larynx of boys than in that of girls, and as a result, deepening of the voice in boys is more noticeable than in girls. Prior to the growth spurt, brothers and sisters who are close in age sound alike even to their mothers. When boys of this age answer the telephone they are often irritated by being taken for their sisters.

When the voice change begins in a boy, it is often so rapid that he has difficulty in learning quick control of his elongating vocal cords. As a result, his voice is said to "break" at times, while he is singing or speaking. About 40 per cent of boys experience these voice breaks, while in the other 60 per cent either the change is sufficiently gradual or they learn control quickly enough to prevent noticeable difficulty with the voice.[136]

Changes in the Skin Glands

During puberty, changes occur in the sweat glands, particularly those of the armpits and in regions between the legs. The glands become more active, giving off more sweat than formerly. Since sweat is similar in composition to dilute urine, it is easy for boys and girls to develop an offensive body odor at this time. The *sebaceous* or oil glands that open into the hair follicles also become larger and more active, so that both the skin and the hair become more oily.

Partly as a result of these changes in the activity of the glands of the skin, disturbances in the health and appearance of the skin are common during puberty and for some time thereafter. About 50 per cent of both boys and girls begin to be bothered with blackheads and pimples when they enter puberty.[136] General physical health involving diet, exercise, rest, elimination of wastes, and cleanliness has some relation to the activity of the sebaceous and sweat glands, and it is the malfunction of these glands that causes most of the skin blemishes at this time.

If the openings of the pores and the hair follicles become plugged with secretions and dirt which adheres to the oil and sweat, the secretions continue to accumulate from below. These plugs become blackheads, chiefly because of chemical changes in the oil which cause it to darken in color. If the boy or girl squeezes the skin to remove the blackhead, bacteria gain access and find conditions suitable for their multiplication. White corpuscles escape from the tiny blood and lymph capillaries in the surrounding skin. Some of them kill bacteria, and some are killed in the battle. The result is inflammation, with the formation of pus (dead bacteria and dead white corpuscles) and a "pimple." If this condition becomes chronic and widespread, it is called *acne*. It is likely to occur chiefly on the face, shoulders, and chest where the skin glands are numerous and highly active.

Misconceptions about acne are common. Some people think that children with acne have "bad blood." Others feel acne is somehow related to venereal diseases, or to masturbation, or to other kinds of sexual activity. All of these ideas are completely false.[59] Another mistaken idea is that acne should be ignored, because it will be outgrown in time. If the causes as described have been understood, it is obvious that observing the general rules of good health may be helpful. Medical science may help too, since the hormonal basis of changing glandular activity is better understood than it was formerly, and more efficient healing agents are continually being found.

The Circulatory System

The heart and blood vessel ratio changes considerably in early life. In infancy, the heart is large in relation to the blood vessels. If we take 1 to represent the blood vessels, the ratio of the heart to the blood vessels in infancy is about 1.25:1. The heart pumps blood into relatively large blood vessels that traverse the small body and, as a result, blood pressure against the blood vessel walls is comparatively low. The ratio of heart to blood vessels gradually changes, so that at puberty the ratio is about 2.8:1. The larger heart pumps blood into relatively smaller blood vessels which traverse a larger body. Blood pressure rises accordingly.

During childhood and puberty there is little if any difference in blood pressure between the sexes. Pressure, measured when the heart is in a state of contraction (*systolic pressure*), increases in both sexes in puberty. Heart beat, measured by pulse rate, is about 100 to 70 beats per minute, slightly more rapid in girls than in boys.

The Breathing Apparatus

Sex differences in the breathing apparatus are negligible during childhood. At puberty, however, the lungs begin to grow more rapidly. Along with the greater skeletal growth and therefore chest capacity in boys, the lungs grow larger in boys than in girls. The rate of breathing which has been from 18 to 25 inhalations per minute at ages 6 to 10, in puberty drops to a rate from 16 to 20 per minute. Susceptibility to infections of the breathing passages begins to stabilize, so that although boys and girls still get colds and other infections, they are less severely affected than they were earlier.

The Digestive System

Until puberty, considerable variation in the shape of the stomach exists in different individuals. At puberty, the entire digestive tract enlarges along with the rest of the body. The empty stomach assumes a shape somewhat like the letter J in both sexes. When it is full, it broadens, particularly the stem of the J. In females, the stomach eventually is located lower in the abdomen than it is in males. Even after puberty, great variation exists among individuals in the size of the stomach, which accounts for the varying capacities for food from individual to individual.

Accompanying growth, food intake is likely to increase also. In order to provide the raw materials for growth, a diet that is well balanced in carbohydrates, fats, proteins, vitamins, minerals, and water is essential. The proteins and minerals are the essential materials for the building of additional protoplasm, into which some of the carbohydrates and fats go also, and the energy needed to do all this growing in addition to the other activities of this age is derived from the carbohydrates and fats.

The Muscles

In strength of skeletal muscle, boys surpass girls from infancy on. When muscular strength is measured by the strength of the grip, boys surpass girls by about 5 per cent of points registered on a dynamometer until about 14 years of age, when they surpass girls by 10 per cent. The difference increases during the adolescent years.[232] As a group, boys tend to outdistance girls in muscular activities which require strength and endurance, whereas girls tend to surpass boys in activities requiring balance, grace and fine muscle coordination. Strength of cardiac and visceral muscle is difficult to determine, and no clearcut differences at this age are apparent.

Secondary Sex Characteristics

Among the changes of puberty that have been discussed, we have mentioned some that differ with the sexes. These are often referred to as the *secondary sex characteristics*. We can summarize these secondary sex characteristics as follows:

Girls	Boys
Increase in height	Increase in height
Increase in weight	Increase in weight
Pelvis widens	Shoulders broaden
Breasts develop	Breasts fail to develop
Pubic and axillary hair	Pubic, axillary, face, and body hair
Head hairline remains	Head hair recedes at temples
Voice changes slightly	Voice changes markedly
Skin coarsens somewhat	Skin coarsens considerably
Lungs grow somewhat	Lungs grow considerably
Skeletal muscle grows somewhat	Skeletal muscle grows and strengthens markedly

Primary Sex Changes

Primary sex changes are those that occur in the primary sex organs, which are the organs directly concerned with the reproduction of the species. Changes in these organs differ with the sexes.

We began our discussion of the physical changes of puberty by saying that understanding of what is happening to the body in puberty, not only in structure and functioning but also in timing, is vital to the psychological well-being of the individual. This is true of knowledge about the total body, but it is especially true that an understanding of, acceptance of, and a normal feeling about the primary sex changes are vital to the developing individual's peace of mind, his ability to concentrate on work or play, his sense of self, and his relations to others. Since most young people and the adults who live and work with them know less than they would like to know about these changes, and since substantial numbers have had no opportunity to acquire accurate information about them, we are

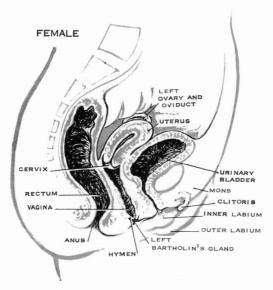

Fig. 7–2. Primary sex organs in the female.

presenting at some length the anatomy and physiology of the primary sex organs and the changes that occur in them during puberty.

IN GIRLS. The primary sex organs in girls are two *ovaries*, two *Fallopian tubes* or *oviducts*, one *uterus* or *womb*, one *vagina*, two *Bartholin's* or *lubricating glands*, and a *hymen* of variable size and thickness. The external genitalia include a pair of *inner* or *minor labia*, a pair of *outer* or *major labia*, a *clitoris* (a tiny, imperfectly formed penis), and the *mons veneris* (of Venus) or, after puberty, the *mons pubis* (hairy). Figure 7–2 shows these organs as they are located in relation to other abdominal organs.

At birth, the ovaries each contain a large number (estimates vary from 40,000 to 400,000) of cells (*oogonia*) that potentially might form eggs (*ova*). During childhood, as we have pointed out in earlier chapters, little growth occurs in the sex organs. In the ovaries, some oogonia shrivel and disappear while others develop. The oviducts, uterus, vagina, and external genitalia are small at birth, and they remain small during childhood. At about 9 years of age in most girls, it is believed, the anterior lobe of the hypophysis (see Chapter 6, p. 187) begins to secrete sufficient *gonadotrophic hormone* to stimulate the oogonia to further development. Some of them form *ovarian follicles* which themselves produce another kind of hormone, *estrogen* (female-affecting hormone). Estrogen diffuses into the blood vessels of the ovaries and is carried in the blood to the heart, which pumps blood containing estrogen to all the tissues of the body.

For some years, the amount of gonadotrophic hormone produced is insufficient to bring any of the ovarian follicles to maturity. They grow, producing estrogen, up to a certain point. These then degenerate, but in the meantime others have been growing. Meanwhile the estrogen in the blood has been affecting the whole body, resulting in the development of the secondary sex characteristics which we have already summarized, and also affecting the other primary sex organs.

Usually between 11 and 14 years of age, the lining of the vagina begins to thicken. The uterus begins to grow, and its lining (the *endometrium*) begins to get thicker. Within the endometrium, very numerous, small, twisted blood vessels and coiled mucous glands begin to develop. This condition of the endometrium is necessary for its reception of a fertilized egg, should one arrive in the uterus. At the age of puberty, of course, it is very unlikely that sperms will be present in the tract to fertilize an egg if one were expelled from the ovary. At about this time, the pubic hair begins to appear on the mons and the outer surfaces of the major labia.

If sufficient estrogen is being produced, one of the ovarian follicles may grow sufficiently to reach the surface of the ovary in which it is developing. If so, it may burst through the ovary wall and release a partially developed egg or ovum. If this happens, all the other follicles that were nearly as well developed begin to shrink and eventually disappear.

Whether the well-developed follicle bursts and releases its partially developed egg, or whether it shrinks within the ovary without expelling its contents, in approximately 14 days the endometrium breaks down, rupturing its tiny blood vessels and glands. The endometrial tissue plus the released blood and mucus leaves the body by way of the vagina, and the girl experiences the onset of her first *menstrual period*. (The onset of the first menstrual period is often referred to as the *menarche*, from the Latin *mensis*, "month" and the Greek *arche*, "beginning.") The flow lasts three or four days, more or less, depending upon the individual girl.

In the meantime, other follicles have been growing, producing and releasing estrogen into the blood. As a result, after the menstrual flow stops, the endometrium begins to build up again as before, until another follicle ruptures or shrivels as the case may be. Whereupon, in a matter of about two weeks, the menstrual flow appears again, and the young girl's rhythm is on its way to being established. If the period between the onset of one menstrual flow and the next is 28 days, ovulation will occur, or the nearly mature follicle will subside, approximately halfway between one menstrual period and the next. However, since the time between periods is not always 28 days, studies have shown that ovulation is more likely to occur 14 to 16 days *before* the onset of the next menstruation rather than 14 days *after* the last one.[203]

There is no pattern concerning which of the two ovaries functions in producing the follicle that brings about the endometrial changes. It is possible for the ovaries to alternate, one ovary one time and the other ovary the next, and so on, but it is just as likely that the right ovary may function time after time, then the left one for a time or two, and then the right, and so on. Both ovaries are actively producing follicles all the time, and the follicles are all active in producing estrogen.

In puberty, it is very likely that the girl will not have regular menstrual periods appearing every 28 days. Such regularity, in fact, is rare at any age, but the periods are likely to become more regular a few years after puberty occurs. Also, while we have indicated that if ovulation occurs, it is likely to happen 14 days *before* the onset of the next mentrual period, it should be understood that the time relationships may vary considerably from individual to individual and from one time to another in the same individual. Because it has been found that menstruation frequently occurs in young girls without the ovulation of a fertilizable egg, the term "adolescent sterility"[7] has become widely used. While the concept is statistically valid, incidents of pregnancy in girls soon after puberty are not rare.[203]

IN BOYS. The primary sex organs in boys are two *testes* or *testicles* composed of numerous *seminiferous tubules* embedded in *interstitial cells,* two *sperm ducts* (each consisting of three parts, the *epididymis,* the *vas deferens,* and the *ejaculatory duct*), two *seminal vesicles,* which are outgrowths from the sperm ducts, one *prostate gland* surrounding the *urethra* into which the ejaculatory ducts empty, two *bulbourethral (Cowper's) glands,* which also empty into the urethra just below the prostate gland, and the *urethra* itself.

The external genitalia consist of the *scrotum,* the sac that contains the testes and which hangs at the base of the abdomen in front of the legs, and the *penis* which contains the urethra. The *foreskin* or

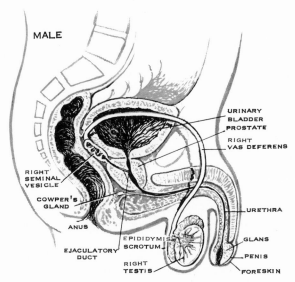

Fig. 7–3. Primary sex organs in the male.

prepuce, the loose skin at the end of the penis, surrounds the underlying head of the penis, often called the *glans.* It is this skin that is often circumcised a few days after birth, primarily for hygienic reasons, but also as a religious ritual in some faiths. Figure 7–3 shows these organs as they are located in relation to the surrounding organs.

During childhood, little growth occurs in the sex organs. At about 10 years of age in most boys, it is believed, the gonadotrophic hormone begins to be produced by the anterior lobe of the hypophysis in sufficient quantity to stimulate the testes to activity. As a result, the interstitial tissue of the testes produces male hormone, often called *testosterone,* which diffuses into the blood vessels of the testes and is carried by the blood to the heart, which pumps it (in the blood) to all the tissues of the body. It is testosterone which is at least partially responsible for the development of the male secondary sex characteristics which we have summarized earlier, and for the growth of the primary sex organs at this time.

Some time between 13 and 15 years of age in most boys, the glands associated with the reproductive system (the seminal vesicles, prostate gland, and bulbourethral glands) begin to secrete fluids. Following this activity, the seminiferous tubules of the testes begin to produce functional *spermatozoa,* usually called *sperms.* When these changes have occurred, the boy may ejaculate the *semen,* the fluids from the various glands, and sperms, from the testes. It may be ejaculated involuntarily during sleep, in what are often referred to as "wet dreams," "seminal emissions," or "nocturnal emissions" (although they are not always nocturnal), or it may be ejaculated voluntarily by masturbation. If not ejaculated from the body, some of the semen is absorbed by the surrounding tissues. There is no sure way to know just when a boy begins to produce sperms. Generally speaking, sperm production occurs at about the time of the appearance of pubic hair and of the first ejaculation.[107]

Endocrine Changes

Figure 6–1 (page 188) and Table 6–1 (pages 190 ff.) provided an over-all view of the location of the endocrine glands in the body, their activities, and the effects of their activities when they are known. In this chapter we shall summarize only the endocrine activities that relate directly to puberty. Obviously, endocrine activity is complicated physiology, and it must be understood that our knowledge of all the interrelations of the endocrine secretions is not yet complete.[218]

Figure 7–4 shows, in a highly simplified manner, the changes that take place in a typical girl and boy at puberty as results of endocrine activity. It will be noticed that the girl is a little taller than the boy. The growth hormone of the hypophysis, *somatotrophin,* is stimulating general growth in both girl and boy, particularly that of the long bones of the limbs, the pelvis of the girl, and the shoulders of the boy. The *gonadotrophins* are stimulating the ovaries and the mammary glands in the girl and the testes in the boy. As a result, the ovaries are producing estrogen which is stimulating the growth of the uterus and associated tubes, the axillary and pubic hair, and the glands of the skin, particularly those of the face. The testes are producing testosterone, which is stimulating the growth of the penis and the associated ducts and glands, the axillary, pubic, face, and body hair, the vocal cords, and the glands of the skin, particularly those of the face and neck. It should again be noted, in Table 6–1, that the suprarenal glands located above the kidneys produce both androgens (male-affecting hormones), and estrogens in both sexes, so that boys

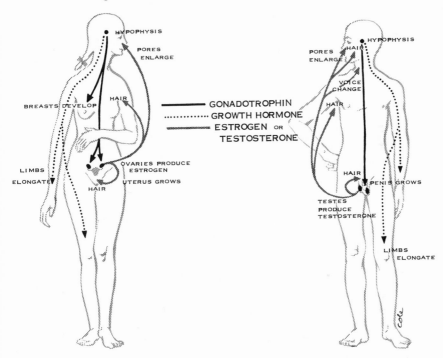

Fig. 7–4. Endocrine effects in puberty.

and girls are affected in their development by both male- and female-affecting hormones, in varying proportions.

Because her recurring menstrual periods are facts that a girl cannot possibly ignore, her attitude toward them plays a very significant part in her emotional life from menarche through menopause, when they cease altogether. An understanding of her basic reproductive physiology assists most girls in accepting what they might otherwise consider a very long-lasting, recurrent nuisance.

Not only girls but boys also are perplexed by the phenomena of female physiology. It is important to their future domestic harmony that both sexes understand as much as possible of the physiology that is intimately related with psychological states of both sexes in marriage. Because peace of mind is so desirable, we shall devote a few paragraphs to clarify what occurs in the female reproductive system as the girl grows into early adulthood.

The menstrual cycle is easier to understand if we follow it into adolescence. The hypophysis produces little if any gonadotrophins in infancy and early childhood. As a result, the breasts remain small, the ovaries contain oogonia in primary follicles, and the lining of the uterus is relatively thin and simple. In later childhood, at about 9 years of age, gonadotrophin production by the hypophysis begins to stimulate the growth of the ovarian follicles. The ovarian follicles produce estrogen, which stimulates the endometrium to thicken, and the blood capillaries and mucous glands to develop and coil in its substance.

The ovarian follicle enlarges but does not expel even a partially mature egg, and the endometrium, lacking the hormone necessary to maintain it, breaks down and forms the menstrual flow. Bleeding lasts 4 or 5 days. In the meantime, follicles in the ovaries are enlarging and producing estrogen. In response, the endometrium begins to thicken again (the *proliferative phase*). On about the fourteenth day following the onset of menstruation, one follicle may rupture, expelling a maturing egg. The ruptured follicle reorganizes, and its cellular contents form a *yellow body*, the *corpus luteum*.

The corpus luteum grows and produces a new hormone called *progesterone*. Progesterone diffuses into the small blood vessels of the ovary that surround the corpus luteum. It is carried by the blood to the heart, which pumps it to all the tissues of the body. The tissue that responds to it is the endometrium, which secretes a great deal of mucus for the next few days. If, however, the egg that was ovulated a few days earlier is not fertilized, the corpus luteum begins to shrivel, thereby reducing the amount of progesterone being diffused into the blood. On approximately the fourteenth day after the date of ovulation, the endometrium again breaks down and the second menstrual period begins.

This rhythmic activity: estrogen production, ovulation, corpus luteum formation, progesterone production, corpus luteum degeneration, menstruation, and estrogen production, goes on time after time, more or less regularly, unless an egg is joined by a sperm and fertilized. Most girls are aware of menstruation only. Some experience rhythmic feelings of elation and depression or fatigue that they think of as correlated with certain phases of the cycle. Others can detect little or no correlation between their psychological and physiological states. We shall leave the behavior following fertilization (*conception*) until a later chapter, since conception, as we have seen earlier, is unlikely although not impossible in puberty. It will be noted that two gonadotrophins, the follicle-stimulating hormone and the luteinizing hormone, have been active, and that estrogen and progesterone both affect breast development.

Individual Differences

The average age at which girls and boys enter puberty is less significant than the wide range of individual differences in the onset

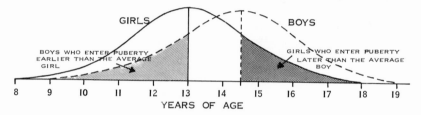

Fig. 7–5. Age of onset of puberty in the United States.

of puberty. Extensive studies [19] show that girls on the average reach puberty earlier than do boys on the average. Their ranges in age at onset, however, overlap. The normal range for girls is from 8 to 18 years of age; for boys, it is from 9 to 19 years. Among girls, about 1 in 250 to 300 begins to menstruate at one extreme or the other; for boys, about 1 in 300 develops pubic hair and has his first ejaculation at one extreme or the other. Figure 7–5, summarizing a number of studies, shows that between 85 and 90 per cent of girls experience the menarche between their eleventh and fifteenth birthdays, with the average around the thirteenth. A comparable percentage of the boys comes into puberty between the twelfth and sixteenth birthdays, with the average at about age 14½. On the average, girls are about a year and a half ahead of boys. However, as Fig. 7–5 shows, some girls enter puberty later than do the average boys, and some boys enter puberty earlier than the average girls.

Popular opinion has it that girls and boys growing up in hot climates enter puberty earlier than those who grow up in temperate and cold climates, but studies [193] indicate that this opinion is open to question. Table 7–1 indicates that age of menarche has little relation to climate, and that factors other than climate determine age of menarche.

Table 7–1
Average Age of First Menstruation (1937) *

Country	Age
United States	About 13.50 years
Canada	About 14.00 years
Central and South America	About 14.25 years
India (Calcutta)	About 14.25 years
Central Europe	About 14.25 years
Italy and Spain	About 14.50 years
Philippine Islands	About 15.10 years
China and Japan	About 15.35 years
N. Europe and Scotland	About 15.35 years

* Shuttleworth, F. K. *The Adolescent Period: A Graphic Atlas.* Evanston, Ill.: Monographs XIV (1). Society for Research in Child Development, Inc., 1951.

PSYCHOLOGICAL ASPECTS OF PUBERTY

What it means to enter puberty differs from individual to individual, depending upon a complex of psychobiological factors. We have discussed the biological factors that lead up to puberty, and how they operate when puberty begins. The psychological factors, however, are somewhat more difficult to study. Students often ask how psychologists can draw the conclusions that they do about certain aspects of human physical behavior in relation to certain psychological factors. Their questions are indications of good intellectual health, and this may be as good a time as any to describe briefly some of the methods employed in the study of human behavior.

Methods of Study

Psychologists study human behavior in a number of ways, depending upon such things as the type of problem, the availability of subjects, the equipment necessary, and the interests and aptitudes of the investigators themselves. Psychologists are human beings with certain adequacies and certain limitations, and they differ from one

to another. Sound knowledge about an area is most effectively accumulated when differently trained investigators direct their attention to the same problem, study it, draw their individual conclusions,
and then publish their conclusions. Other competent individuals
can then synthesize these conclusions into a body of integrated
knowledge, thereby revealing some gaps remaining in our knowledge.

We shall describe only three of the ways which psychologists and
others use in obtaining knowledge of human behavior. One is the
study of *single-case histories*. This method involves the acquisition
of as many facts as possible concerning an individual's life up to the
time of the occurrence of the situation which is under investigation.
Physicians, including psychiatrists, as well as psychologists, make
constant use of this method in attempting to diagnose and to pre-
scribe treatment for individuals under their care.

Another method is the *experimental method*. This involves the
study of a restricted segment of behavior about which the investigator has evolved a *hypothesis* as one possible explanation for the
particular behavior. A hypothesis has been called an "intelligent
hunch." It consists of the statement of a possible relationship between two events. For example, we might use the hypothesis we
mentioned earlier, that "the mean annual temperature of the region
in which girls grow up affects the age of onset of their puberty." The
experimental method depends upon the availability of a sufficiently
large sample of as nearly as possible identical individuals, and upon
the possibility of subjecting one or more groups of them to only one
variable condition. In the case of the hypothesis that we have set up,
this method would require a large number of girls (say 1,500) of the
same age, race, general health, and so on. These girls would be
divided into groups of 500 each, living at different latitudes in the
some longitude. One group would grow up in one latitude, say at
Coral Harbor in Hudson Bay (or in Trondheim, Norway), another
group in Pittsburgh, Pa. (or in Rome, Italy), and the other group in
Quito, Ecuador.

Even though we have exaggerated the distance necessary between
the latitudes, it would be so expensive and so difficult to test this
particular hypothesis experimentally, and there would still be so
many variables that could not be controlled, that the experimental
method for the study of this hypothesis can hardly be regarded as
feasible.

The other way of studying human behavior is the *correlational testing method.* In this method, the investigator looks, in a large number of individuals, for the condition that is thought possibly to be antecedent to another condition occurring later in the same individuals. He notes and records the presence or absence of the supposedly *antecedent condition* in each individual and also the presence or absence of the expected *consequent condition* in the same individual. If we use the same hypothesis as an example for testing by this method, the investigator would gather data on a large number, say 1,500 16-year-old girls. For each case, he would record the mean annual temperature (antecedent condition) of the region in which the girl grew up and the date of the onset of her first menstrual period (consequent condition). If his data show that most girls who grew up where the mean annual temperature is below 30° F., or above 60° F., did not menstruate until after their fifteenth birthdays, and most girls who grew up where the mean annual temperature is between 30° F. and 60° F., menstruated later than the other two groups, or if the group in the lowest (or highest) temperature menstruated earlier or later than the other two groups, the evidence would still support the hypothesis. But if about as many girls menstruated before and after their fifteenth birthday in all three groups, his evidence would weaken his hypothesis.

Data collected in the correlation testing method are carefully recorded and processed statistically to determine the *degree of significant relationship* between the supposedly antecedent and consequent conditions, and the relationship is then said to be of *no significance,* of *low,* or of *high significance* as the statistical treatment shows. Students who are interested in statistical methods of handling raw data such as these we have mentioned are referred to standard textbooks on that subject.[60]

It will be obvious to the questioning student that no one or two of all three of these methods are capable of giving a complete picture of human behavior in any area. These methods, and others that are continually being devised and refined, are helpful, however, in establishing the possible truth or error of commonly held notions. It is easy for human beings, in observing the behavior of themselves or other members of their own species, to accept and to hold attractive hypotheses as truths and to attempt to regulate their own and the behavior of others accordingly. We are on firmer ground if we keep our minds continually ready to accept new evidence based upon as careful study as is possible, so that we are ready to discard a hypothesis when carefully accumulated evidence reveals its weaknesses.

A considerable number of investigators have studied children chiefly by means of the single-case history and the correlational testing methods for evidence of antecedent and consequent conditions related to puberty.[95, 99, 112, 157]

Certain conditions, such as the age of onset of puberty, can be studied for correlation, or lack of it, with such possible antecedent conditions as heredity, birth weight, age of weaning, quality of diet during childhood, quality of general health during childhood, mean annual temperature or mean length of day of the region in which childhood was spent, and many other similar conditions. The age of onset of puberty may also be considered the antecedent condition, and its relation to certain hypothesized consequent conditions can be studied. In addition, all the characteristics of children which we have mentioned in preceding chapters can be studied as they occur in children around the time of the onset of puberty.

As children grow older, they become more difficult to study. We pointed out that, in early and later childhood, they become increasingly aware of their own identity and of their personal-social relationships with other people. An investigator can observe infants and children under normal conditions in early childhood without their being aware of him. This is not possible in later childhood and from then on throughout life, so that in interpreting data from studies it is essential that we remain aware that what we can see of human behavior may be somewhat in the same proportion to covert behavior as the visible part of the iceberg is to the submerged portion. This awareness need not deter us from further study, however, nor lessen our respectful and sympathetic interest in the evidence that is being uncovered.

General Psychological Condition

When children enter puberty, they experience psychological changes along with and often because of misunderstanding about the physiological and anatomical changes that are taking place in their bodies. Puberty may be regarded as a period in which the individual learns to cope with the changes accompanying sexual development and to adapt to the sudden changes in metabolism that are occurring, unknown to him. These changes affect the individual's emotional, personal-social, and intellectual development.

Emotional Characteristics

Most children, at about the time of puberty and for an indefinite time thereafter, experience relatively sudden changes of mood which surprise them as well as the people with whom they come in contact. They have been experiencing the comparative calm of later childhood, and the changes taking place in their bodies are understandably somewhat disturbing to their peace of mind. Just how disturbing these changes are seems to depend largely upon the cultural mores of the group to which a child belongs. It used to be considered that puberty inevitably brought turmoil with it. Studies of puberty in some cultures, however, have shed doubt on the inevitability of turmoil.

Whatever the degree of emotional turmoil in any given culture, it need not be all unpleasant. Puberty may be welcomed by some children, and not by others, depending among other things upon their preparation for its coming.[115, 203] Many students of human behavior feel strongly that parental attitudes toward sexual matters affect the direction of children's attitudes toward sex and adulthood in general.[19] They feel, also, that the kind and timing of learning about puberty affects the manner of acceptance of puberty.

For example, we have seen in the studies[186] of New England mothers that many children have been educated about sexual matters in unfortunate ways. Among these have been emphasis upon prevention of sexual stimulation and immediate diversion from it if it occurs, and hyperemotional reactions to the child's interest in his own waste products and sometimes to the whole situation of elimination. Such parent-induced feelings of shame or excitement, or both, in connection with the primary sexual and waste elimination organs can be expected to cause an intensified reaction to the appearance of pubic and axillary hair, the rapid growth of breasts and of genitalia, the appearance of the menstrual flow, or the first seminal emission. Children reared in this manner have had little opportunity to learn from their parents about these pubertal changes, or to appreciate that such changes would occur in them. Fortunately, in many parts of the world, parents' attitudes are changing. According to Kinsey,[106] parents in increasing numbers have come to realize the importance of the early education of their children about sexual matters. Children also learn from peers, older children, and various other sources. Kinsey [106] reported that of the 8,000 females in his 1953 study, not more than a few per cent—perhaps not more than 5 per cent—recalled that they had received anything more than the most incidental sort of information from their parents and their religious mentors.

"Sex education" is often restricted to the giving of a minimum of information to girls about menstruation and to both girls and boys about where babies come from.[115] Even today, in the most civilized countries of the world, it is possible for girls to have no knowledge of the coming of pubic hair, for instance, and for boys to have no knowledge of the meaning of seminal emissions, and for both sexes to lack knowledge of the occurrences natural to the opposite sex. It even more often happens that little if anything of the emotional nature of normal, functional sex is communicated to children either before or after puberty.

Let us look, from another point of view, at the relation to attitudes and feelings of adequate knowledge about physical changes. If during their lives, from infancy on, children have been taught that all parts of their bodies are equally important to their well-being, if their mothers have enjoyed bathing and toweling their bodies all over with no more haste about clothing one part than another, if little brothers and sisters have bathed together until they grew too big for comfort in the tub together, if they have seen their parents nude from time to time, if their mothers explained to both boys and girls about their own menstrual flow and how they take care of its absorption, and if parents have explained over the years to both sexes the changes that they can expect which will make them more like adults, if this is the way children have grown to the age of puberty, there will be a good chance that when the changes to puberty do begin the individual will react with understanding, acceptance, and readiness to grow into adulthood.

Regardless of the manner in which children have been prepared for puberty, they have to cope with its changes as they come. If the girl knows about the appearance of pubic hair, for example, when she detects her first silky hairs, she may feel that she is really growing up, and if growing up looks pleasant to her, she may even feel elated. If she does not know about pubic hair, she may feel terrified that something is "wrong with her." If she is prepared for her breasts to begin to develop she may enjoy telling her mother that she needs

a brassiere, and the two "women" may have a delightful time selecting one, even if it does turn out that only a #30AAA is needed. After
that, she may enjoy noting her need for increasingly larger sizes.

If she is prepared for her first menstrual period and has her equipment handy to protect her clothing and knows how to adjust it, she
may feel that she has really "arrived"; if she is not prepared, her only
association with bleeding will probably be with "being hurt." She
may become frightened about the source of the bleeding. If she
becomes frightened, her autonomic nervous system may cause her
uterine muscles to contract excessively, resulting in "menstrual
cramps." To add to her discomfort, she does not know what to do to
absorb the flow and to protect her clothing.

We are sorry that we must say more about the girl who is unprepared than about the girl who is prepared, but the troubles of life are
likely to get more attention than the joys. We do not need to go into
detail about the different reactions in prepared and unprepared girls
for growth in height and weight, skin changes, and so on, but the
same kinds of discussion about these subjects may stimulate our
thinking. While nothing quite as dramatic as menstruation occurs in
boys, some of their changes may be welcomed or not, as the case
may be. Since he cannot help knowing about facial hair in men, a
boy is less likely to be surprised by pubic, axillary, and other body
hair. Boys tend to be less modest than girls, so that they are likely
to have seen the genitalia of older boys and men. They are likely to
be aware of growth in height and of the changes in the skin that
come with puberty. They may or may not find the changes in voice
somewhat disconcerting, as we have mentioned.

It is difficult to learn how boys react to their first ejaculation of
seminal fluid. If they are prepared for it, they understand and may
say nothing about it, the amount of fluid being insufficient to cause
discomfort and usually drying very quickly. If they are not prepared,
they may be concerned or not, but tend to keep their feelings to
themselves, even when they may feel considerable anxiety.[232]

Although we know so little of how children actually feel about
their puberty, it is generally assumed their sharp changes in mood
are affected by their pleasant excitement at growing up, or by their
worries about what they only partly understand of the changes that
are taking place, and frequently by alternations between these
feelings.

Personal-Social Characteristics

The personal-social development of children at puberty is affected by their feelings. They are intensely aware of their physical appearance, especially as they feel it impresses other people.[152] They themselves tend to judge other people more by their obvious external traits than by inner less obvious traits of character. For example, muscular strength in boys and personal appearance for both sexes are more highly correlated with popularity than are intelligence or even social status.[96] Because of this attitude, girls and boys who have recently entered puberty, or are about to, are excessively concerned with their own appearance. One study [201] reports that over 30 per cent of the boys and over 40 per cent of the girls studied experienced major discomfort, because of the difficulty in accepting their physical characteristics. Small size, fatness, lack of muscular strength, and acne worried the boys; and large size, fatness, facial features, acne and small breasts worried the girls.

Because they worry about their height, girls and boys may behave in various unattractive ways. Some tall, big-boned girls, for example, because they want so badly to be cute and cuddly, dress in a fussy manner and snuggle up to people, not realizing that their behavior makes their appearance more noticeable. Other big girls, realizing their size, adopt severe dress and move in an athletic fashion that also emphasizes their size. Parents and teachers can be of great help to girls in accentuating the good points of height and in assisting them in selecting clothing that makes the best of their height. If they can learn to feel that people like their height, children are more likely to develop attractive posture and smooth muscular coordination.

Girls whose breasts are too small can wear some of the shaped brassieres which make their outer clothing fit better. It is a help to such girls if they realize that they do not have one problem that the girls with big breasts have: the problem of support against the pull of gravity. Small breasts have years in which to develop to increasingly more attractive size, while big breasts early in life must have constant support and exercise of the surrounding muscles to keep them in their place on the body. Good posture, the girls may realize, also improves the breast line.

Boys who are smaller than their peers or who are deficient in muscular strength may feel that they are at a disadvantage in the eyes of their peers and adults.[183] Again, the attitude of parents and teachers toward them has much to do with the boys' feelings. Their own special interests and talents or their courtesy may make up for other deficiencies.

Both girls and boys can be helped not to become excessively worried over acne and fatness if they know they have the best medical advice and treatment available, and are aware that if they follow reasonable disciplines in eating, resting, exercising, keeping clean, and eliminating wastes both conditions are likely to be transitory.

Most girls and boys are conscious of grooming, although for various reasons; at times, they may even take pains to be poorly groomed. The troublesome factors in their appearance may also be grounds for their seeming interest in lack of grooming. This is especially likely if, after trying to improve their personal appearance, they become discouraged. They may then begin to rationalize as follows:

"Looks are superficial. What counts is personality!"

"It's sissy to be fussy about looks!" and so on.

Actually, some studies [87] of this age period indicate that such traits as "neat and clean" are high on lists of traits associated with popularity. Girls tend to be more annoyed with untidiness than are boys. Girls are sufficiently concerned with hair dressing even when their clothing is extremely casual (blue jeans, for example) to spend an average of one to one and a half hours daily on its care. Boys also begin to spend considerable time washing their bodies where "it shows" and trying to groom their hair into styles that are popular. Grooming for both sexes is likely to include fads in hair styling, footgear, fit (or lack of fit) in clothing, clothing worn unfastened, and so on.

Concerns do not all stem from real or fancied defects in appearance. Sometimes the "too-good-looking" boy may receive favors and personal attentions that are the reactions of others to his looks, without regard for his qualities of intellect or character. If he is not aware of this, he can easily be fooled as to his own actual lasting worth; if he is aware, he has to learn to size up those who pay attention to him. The "too-attractive" girl may have some of the same problems. In addition, her parents may feel concern about the quality of her social relationships with boys who are older and more experienced than she is.

Another factor which influences personal-social relations of children in puberty and thereafter is the expectations of the culture in which they are growing up. In some cultures, the roles of adult males and females are much more clear-cut than in others. In cultures where the social structure is based on the biological nature of the two sexes, the roles of husband and wife, of provider and preparer, of father and mother, are easier for the growing children to understand and therefore to prepare themselves for, with the help and example of their parents.[143]

Some cultures still employ definite means of testing or of announcing children's readiness for the responsibilities of adulthood. The nature of such "puberty rites" depends a good deal upon what is emphasized in the particular culture, for example, the biological, social, or religious responsibilities. These are not mutually exclusive, but in pre- or semiliterate cultures, ceremonies usually have to do with the boy's readiness for warfare, the provision of food, and so on, and with the girl's readiness for housekeeping, wifehood, and motherhood.[143] In more literate cultures, the ceremonies tend to deal more frequently with religious or social responsibilities such as confirmation in the various faiths, and presentation to society in a formal way. Cultural inconsistencies are present in that children of 13 or 14 years of age are obviously insufficiently mature to take on adult responsibility, biological, social, or otherwise.

Intellectual Characteristics

We have already discussed intellectual activity as involving the activity of the neurons of the cerebral cortex, and have indicated that cerebral activity is often stimulated by impulses arriving from the sense organs. It is obvious from the discussion in this chapter that the new awareness of children in puberty must mean considerable cerebral activity on their part. Whether or not they have learned, before puberty, of the changes to be expected, they learn a great deal more as they experience these changes in themselves and see them taking place in their peers.

In cultures like most of those of the Western world, there is at present something of a denial of the differences between the sexes, and, as a result, some confusion regarding the male and female roles. In most countries where schooling is compulsory, it is compulsory for both sexes. To a considerable degree, intellectually, the

children are treated as if sex were nonexistent. They are taught
hygiene, but often with sexless books, charts and models. They all
learn the same subject matter presented in the same way. In most
countries, it is not until after puberty that they have any choice in
practical subject matter such as home economics or wood, metal, and
electrical shop.

With the great amount of energy that is going into growing and
changing, and with school subject matter being so far removed from
their most active interests, it is no wonder that children of this age
period typically exhibit boredom and listlessness in connection with
school work. It is not unusual for parents who have become accustomed to seeing high grades on their children's report cards to
receive severe jolts at their drop in grades.

When the work of children who have been doing reasonably well
in school becomes slipshod, they are likely to be accused of being
lazy. Actually, their bodies are working very hard indeed and it is
difficult for them to understand why their school work slips. This
confusion, in turn, makes them antagonistic to "nagging" teachers
and parents. As a result, their intellectual troubles are reflected in
their behavior, and they tend to be characterized as "antagonistic" to
any kind of authority.[87]

In previous chapters we have referred to the development of conscience, in our consideration of intellectual development. From what
has been said here of children in puberty, it is obviously difficult to
know what is really happening in the area of conscience. Because
children tend to be so "ornery" at this age, it is dangerous to put
stock in their verbalizations. We shall probably do best to assume,
here, that conscience is also in a state of upheaval at this stage. Since
this state continues into adolescence, we shall discuss it more fully
in subsequent chapters on adolescence.

Effects of Early and Late Onset of Puberty

We have discussed the effects of puberty in girls as a group and in
boys as a group. There are additional factors which affect the individuals, within each sex, who enter puberty either early or late, and
thus differ from the average individuals of their group. For any
given individual, the timing of puberty in relation to his chronological age, and to the expectation of his cultural group, may present
certain problems. Some studies indicate that early entrance into

puberty may, for the time being, carry some social advantages for boys but some social disadvantages for girls, whereas late entrance into puberty is less disadvantageous, for the time being, for girls than it is for boys.[95, 98, 99, 100]

The boy who enters puberty early is likely to be one of the few boys who are taller than the average in the sixth and seventh grades, for instance. Because of his height, he may be more in demand socially than the average boys. If he is well coordinated, he may also be prominent in athletics. Boys of this type are often leaders of their grades in junior high school, and may retain their leadership on into senior high school.[99] They have, as a result, a somewhat easier time socially than do average and late entrants into puberty. Since they are likely to be treated both by their peers and adults as being more mature than their fellows, they have less need to strive for status. As a result, they may be more attractive, more matter-of-fact, more relaxed, and more self-confident as Fig. 7–6 indicates, than other boys of comparable chronological age.

In contrast to the boys who enter puberty early are those who enter later than the average. These, while chronologically in the later teens, tend to be short and slight in build, less strong muscularly, and later in acquiring signs of masculinity that are most noticeable in locker-room situations at school or camp, such as body hair and developing genitalia. Their own attitude toward their lateness depends a good deal on the attitude of their parents toward them. If they have been assured by a physician in whom they and the family have confidence, that they are probably just later than the average, they may be able to accept their situation with a minimum of anxiety. If, on the other hand, their relations with their parents are such that they sense parental disappointment or excessive concern, and if they lack the reassurance of a competent physician, they may suffer acutely from anxiety lest they never will mature or that they are in some other way abnormal.

Boys who enter puberty late may exhibit many forms of relatively immature behavior for their age. This may be partly because adults tend to treat them as little boys.[99] Some of them seem to strive to get attention by more-than-average physical activity and talkativeness.

Thus it can be seen that late puberty is likely to be hard on boys, and that early puberty may be advantageous to boys. Time, however, tends to erase the differences in personality between the two groups, although one study [98] indicates that to some extent, some of the differences may remain. The study compared a group of eleven 33-year-old men who entered puberty early with a group of men of the same age who entered puberty late. The personality differences between the two groups of men were less marked than they had been

Fig. 7–6. The boy who enters puberty early may be the picture of self-confidence.

during their puberty and adolescence. Physical differences were negligible. However, according to the criteria in the tests used, those who entered puberty early were still making a better impression on others, were less impulsive and less flexible than the group who entered puberty late. Of the eleven who entered puberty early, four held important managerial positions, while none of the late group held comparable positions. The sample in this follow-up study is too small to be conclusive, and some of the characteristics of the 33-year-olds, such as "less flexibility" in the early group, are hard to explain on the basis of "greater relaxation" in puberty in the early group.

Girls who enter puberty early may experience some difficulties in personal-social relations.[116] If they begin to menstruate while they are in the fifth or sixth grades, for instance, they may feel somewhat out of touch with their peers, depending largely upon how comfortable they feel about the process of menstruating and taking care of the flow. Some girls feel that other people, especially boys, know by various and sundry signs when they are menstruating.

Along with the physical changes, psychological changes may make the girl aware of a new kind of interest in boys which she does not know how to express without seeming "fast." Her girl friends who have not yet entered puberty may seem silly and childish to her, or she may feel jealous of their freedom. The parents of girls who enter puberty early may become over-concerned about relationships with boys. As a result of these feelings, such girls may become lonely and disgruntled and withdraw into daydreams where everything is the way they would like to have it. Fortunately, the average-maturing girls begin to catch up with the early ones before long, and in most cases, the disadvantages of early puberty begin to disappear.

Girls who enter puberty later than the average may feel their peers moving past them, and as a result, experience some anxiety. Here again parental acceptance of the lateness and the reassurance of a competent physician work wonders. Culturally, the girls who are late are in a less distressing situation than are boys who are late, since in most cultures girls and women are not expected to prove their competence to the same extent that boys and men are. Muscular strength and aggressiveness are not particularly attractive in girls, so that deficiency in these areas is not so noticeable.

Body size is not as important in girls as in boys. In fact, petiteness may be an advantage. Lack of breast development may cause girls some anxiety, but judicious use of suitable clothing can make the lack unnoticeable. In most school and camp situations, girls are permitted somewhat more privacy in dressing and showering than are boys, and physical immaturity can pass with less notice in girls than in boys.

Girls who enter puberty late are less subject to parental anxiety about their social affairs than are girls who are early. They have time and experience on their side, in which they may attain some degree of social and intellectual maturity before they become much concerned by their physical drives.

Follow-up studies of girls [100] show even fewer and less enduring personality differences between early and late entrants into puberty. In girls, the differences tend to last during the years of early adolescence, and to diminish significantly during later adolescence as the girls develop toward adulthood.

SUGGESTIONS FOR FURTHER DISCUSSION

1. The May, 1957 edition of *Today's Health* contained an article which said that the robust growth of commercially supported children's competitive sports programs is "one of the most interesting and most unnatural social movements since the Children's Crusades." In the light of what you know about physical changes preceding and during puberty, and about the wide range of individual differences in rate and timing of physical development, what light can you throw on the word "unnatural," as used above?

2. Observe some ten- to fifteen-year-olds of both sexes. Where would you judge each of them to be in the continuum shown in Fig. 7–5? Do you notice in them any of the psychological or social reactions to growth status discussed in the text or in the readings below? Be specific.

3. Where did you yourself place in this continuum? What were your psychological and social reactions?

4. How would you prepare average-developing ten- to fourteen-year-olds of each sex for the advent of puberty? How would you detect signs of early puberty in girls? In boys? Of late development in each sex? How would you prepare the early developers in each sex? How would you enlighten and help the late developers in each sex?

5. Have various members of the class read selections from the readings below which answer questions not fully covered in the text, or which give different viewpoints from those given in the text. Discuss the answers and these differences.

REFERENCES FOR FURTHER STUDY

Crow, L. D., and Crow, A. *Adolescent Adjustment and Development*. New York: McGraw-Hill Book Co., Inc., 1956. Ch. 2, biological and cultural heritage: primitive, middle ages, and early modern times; modern complex society. Ch. 4, physical and physiological growth.

Dewey, R., and Humber, W. J. *The Development of Human Behavior*. New York: The Macmillan Co., 1951. Ch. 11, adolescence, pp. 291–297 (physiological development).

Garrett, H. E. *Statistics in Psychology and Education*. (3d ed.). New York: Longmans, Green & Co., 1947. A useful reference for an understanding of the statistical methods used in psychological experimentation.

JERSILD, A. T. *The Psychology of Adolescence.* New York: The Macmillan Co., 1957. Ch. 3, the changing body: the body image and self-evaluation; maturing and its psychological effects, especially of early and late maturing.

LANE, H., and BEAUCHAMP, M. *Understanding Human Development.* Englewood Cliffs, N.J.: Prentice-Hall, Inc., 1959. Ch. 12, early adolescence: puberty changes; adult and adolescent perceptions about adolescence.

MARTIN, P. C., and VINCENT, E. L. *Human Biological Development.* New York: The Ronald Press Co., 1960. Ch. 3, exterior of the body, pp. 96–98 (skin care). Discusses care of acne and general grooming in adolescence. Ch. 11, pp. 388–397 (the endocrine tissues of the gonads: male, female).

SEIDMAN, J. M. *The Adolescent: A Book of Readings.* New York: Holt, Rinehart & Winston, Inc., 1953. Selection 12, adolescent concerns with physique; Selection 13, physical maturing among boys as related to behavior.

For film suggestions see Film Supplement, in the Appendix.

CHAPTER 8

Early Adolescence

A PERIOD OF TRANSITION

Adolescence is the period of transition between childhood and adulthood. Puberty marks its beginning and, according to law, the twenty-first birthday marks its ending. From the physical viewpoint, nothing ends adolescence that is comparable to the dramatic changes which begin it, at puberty. Probably an even wider range of individual differences exists in the psychological achievement of adulthood, in the full sense of the word, than exists in the achievement of puberty. Setting the twenty-first birthday as the beginning of legal adulthood is a matter of convenience, and not in every case is it the time at which an individual comes into the possession of wisdom.

With full awareness of this wide range of individual differences in age at the beginning and ending of adolescence, we shall discuss it in two phases: a period of early adolescence from about 12 or 13 to 16 or 17 years of age, and a period of late adolescence which covers the years from 16 or 17 to the early 20's.

As we have seen, the hereditary constitution of the individual is affected by his environmental experiences throughout his prenatal life, infancy, early childhood, later childhood, and puberty. His experiences during adolescence continue to affect his physical traits, his habits, attitudes, and his personality in general. They determine in significant ways what he will be like, and how he will behave, as an adult.

General Characteristics

Much has been said about adolescence as a period of "storm and stress," about the "terrible teens," and so on. These epithets give the connotation that adolescents are unpleasant for people of other age levels to live with and even to contemplate. In some cultures such as cities in the United States, being a "teenager" is almost equivalent to being the scapegoat for much of what is wrong in the community. If incidents of vandalism occur, teenagers are likely to be suspected. In automobile accidents where the age of one of the drivers is listed as 17, that driver, in the minds of readers, is automatically assumed to be at fault, and so on.

On the other hand, poets and songwriters glorify the days of youth as the "golden days," the days "when all knowledge is delight," and so on. There are grounds for both of these attitudes toward adolescence, as we shall see as we direct our attention to the physical, emotional, personal-social, and intellectual development going on during the period. Not all adolescents are alike. Individual differences that were dimly apparent in childhood become more pronounced in the adolescent years. However, adolescence tends to be a period of turbulence, of ups and downs, of wanting responsibility and of wanting to avoid responsibility, of wanting to be grown up and of clinging to childhood. In other words, it is a period of *ambivalence*, which may be defined as bipolarity of feeling, a tendency to be drawn at the same time in opposite directions, a feeling of love and hate, of acceptance and rejection, of affirmation and denial of both people and ideas.

A TEST OF PREVIOUS GROWTH AND DEVELOPMENT

Adolescence, with all of its transitions, is a critical period in both the physical and the psychological aspects of development. It tests the strength and soundness of both body and personality as they have grown and developed up to this time.

Organ and Tissue Development

In the body, the organ and tissue structures change rapidly, but must be built on what has developed earlier. New cells by the thousands are added to many of the tissues that were begun before birth and which have been growing ever since. New muscle cells, new bone cells, new blood cells, new connective tissue cells, and new epithelial cells form in great numbers (Table 4–1, pages 98 ff.) In many tissues, old cells have been constantly dying while new cells have been forming. The endocrine system in puberty begins to produce some new hormones, and the balance among the hormones has changed in both sexes, in the female to a fairly definite rhythm. As a result, the reproductive systems have begun to develop from the childhood system toward the adult condition, usually becoming functional during the teens in both sexes.

In personality, old outlooks and habits are changing into new ones, but neurologically this must come about through additions to or redirection of existing neural patterns. Some of the contradictions of adolescent behavior and mood can, perhaps, best be understood if we review how behavior is based upon action in the neurons, where changes from old to new patterns can be accomplished only when certain changes in neural association patterns occur.

Habits and Attitudes: Their Neural Basis

Neurologists have strong evidence that billions of neurons are present in the normal human nervous system and sense organs, that most of them form before birth, that many of them complete their development before birth, and that all of them have begun to form by the time the individual is one year old. Thereafter neurons may degenerate, but no new ones form. Their processes, axons and dendrons (dendrites)* grow as the body grows. This involves little growth on the part of some neurons and tremendous growth on the part of others. The brain, for instance, grows very little after 10 years of age, so that the millions of neurons in the cerebrum grow almost imperceptibly, whereas some of the neurons, whose cell bodies are in the lower part of the spinal cord, have axons and dendrons that are as long as the distance between the lower back and the tips of the great toes. Figure 8–1 is helpful in comprehending the differences in length of neuron processes.

Neurologists believe that habits, attitudes, and behavior in general are the outward expression of the passage of nerve impulses along neurons and from one neuron to another or to many others. Because the same neurons involved in childhood also function in adolescence and adulthood, we can understand how the habits, attitudes, and other kinds of behavior which the child has been developing since birth, continue to influence his behavior in adolescence and adulthood.

---

* The term *dendrite* is used frequently. For the sake of consistency, we prefer to use "neuron," "axon," and "dendron."

Nerve impulses are the physicochemical changes that take place in a neuron in response to a certain environmental change. The change at a dendron ending initiates similar change along the dendron through the nerve cell body, along the axon, and to any other dendrons which may be in contact with the axon or cell body. The

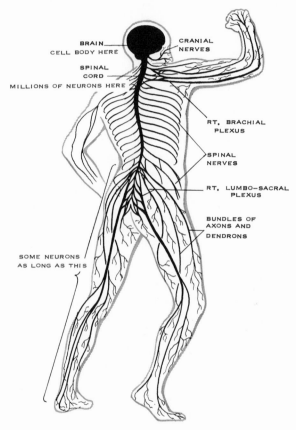

Fig. 8–1. The nervous system, showing different lengths of neurons, depending upon their location.

point of contact between dendrons and other neurons is called a *synapse*. The number of possible synapses between one neuron and others is incalculable, and the kind and numbers of such associations that an individual makes in his cerebrum may be the basis of what we call *intelligence*. As nerve impulses pass again and again over the same synapses, or again and again fail to pass over the same synapses, *habits* of behavior, including habits of thinking, develop. Nerve impulses pass over some synapses with little effort, whereas greater effort is required to make them pass over others. Wide variations among individuals exist in this respect. It is possible that special aptitudes are based upon the relative ease with which impulses pass over certain synapses.

No matter how much original aptitude an individual may have, he can never become an accomplished musician or mathematician, for example, without years of formation of certain habits. Each individual needs sound grounding in the tools (basic neuron combinations for the scale or number facilities) of music or mathematics if he is to become able to comprehend rapidly what his predecessors have developed in the field, so that he can perform what they have performed and be on firm ground to proceed from there. Nor can any individual become a responsible adult unless habits of independence and responsibility have been laid in his nervous system in early life.

Two Specific Examples of Habit Training

In the chapters on infancy and childhood, we referred to such things as the child's ability to pay attention and his increasing ability to concentrate his attention for longer periods of time, to control his emotions, and to develop habits of abstract thinking. In adolescence, the degree to which he has or has not developed these habits shows up more plainly than in any earlier period. Habits developed during infancy, childhood, and adolescence affect a primary aptitude that all normal people are assumed to have: the aptitude for becoming increasingly able to be independent of others and to abide by reasonable rules.

Let us compare Child A and Child B, who were born on the same date to hospital roommate mothers. From very early in his life, Child A was left with a reliable person while his parents went out to dinner now and then and to games, movies, and so on. The parents of Child B never left him. They went out only where they could take him with them. Both babies were healthy and had good sense organs. Child A had experiences which sent impulses over synapses in his cerebrum that associated the features, voices, and so on not only of his mother, but of other people also, with his physical comfort and his sense of security. Child B had no such experiences and hence developed no such synaptic connections in his cerebrum that associated anybody other than his mother with his physical comfort and sense of security.

The parents of Child A continued to go out during his early childhood, as they had previously. The parents of Child B began to get tired of taking him with them, because his presence limited where they could go. When they decided, however, to leave him with a reliable woman, he screamed at their leaving, and continued screaming throughout most of the evening, and fell asleep only when he had exhausted himself. He was so emotionally upset that his sense organs were in no condition to send impulses to his brain (he could not see the woman for crying, nor hear her voice). His physical comfort and sense of security were so utterly lacking in her presence that cerebral associations would not have helped him to associate her with comfort anyway. The parents of Child A continued to go out, and the mother, at least, of Child B continued to stay with him constantly, instead of leaving him with someone else.

In the community in which the two families lived, children were expected to enter kindergarten at 5 years of age. The mothers of Child A and Child B took their children to the school building and to the kindergarten room a few days before school started, to introduce them to their new surroundings. On the day of school's opening, they took them again. The mother of Child A introduced him to the teacher and told him she would be back for him for lunch. She said good-by, he responded, and stayed beside the teacher while she left.

The mother of Child B had watched the mother of Child A. She introduced Child B to the teacher, but he clung to his mother, begging to be taken home. She told him that she would be back for him at lunch time. He clung to her hand and skirt. She said good-by and started to leave, and he clung harder than ever and began to scream. The teacher asked the mother to stay in the room for a little while until she could get his attention and then the mother should leave. She did leave finally, but only with Child B's screams ringing in her ears.

During his early childhood, Child A continued to expand his world, free to do so because he was comfortable with different people, his parents, his teachers, adult neighbors, and peers, the milkman, the postman, the policeman, and many others. His sense organs were active, receiving signals from his world, and transmitting them to his central nervous system. A good many of his actions for which he once had to use his cerebrum, such as walking, were now reflex actions and his cerebrum was free to receive and to transmit impulses, thereby making all kinds of new associations. His parents talked about different kinds of things, so that among his other accomplishments, Child A learned to do some abstract thinking. When he was 10 years old, his father needed a part for his electric saw that could be obtained only at a downtown store. Child A was able to take a note and the money and go alone by bus to the store and manage the errand successfully.

Child B had never been on any kind of a public vehicle without a parent. What thinking he did was largely about himself. He did feel urges to do as some of the other boys his age were doing but always felt afraid, as he had that first day in kindergarten. Because he spent so much time and energy thinking about himself, he was less able than Child A to get acquainted with other people and with their ideas, and with the inanimate world about him. Both Child A and Child B entered puberty between their thirteenth and fourteenth birthdays. Child A had observed some of the changes taking place in some of his peers. This was easy for him to do because all his life his parents had talked about growing up. He had seen them both without clothing, now and then, and he knew that changes would have to take place in him if he was ever to be like his father. His parents had assured him he would develop.

With the onset of puberty, he began to take more interest in his appearance. He wanted to train his hair a certain way. He had noticed that his peers seemed to fall into two groups, one group that wore very tight-fitting pants and shirts deeply open at the chest, and another group, all of whom wore the same kind of trousers, although not such tight ones and all the same kinds of shirts, but open only one button at the neck. He was considering the difference.

Child B was not as well prepared for puberty. He had never seen his parents without clothing. He had a younger sister but had never seen a girl nude. He noticed hair growing in his pubic region (he didn't know what you called it), and hoped it was all right. The blemishes that began to appear on his face also made him wonder if he was all right. He couldn't ask anyone, and he just kept making the same circular neural patterns in his cerebrum which resulted in feelings that he learned to call *worry*. He, too, began to take interest in his appearance, although it was a worried sort of an interest. How should he comb his hair, for instance. He had his own ideas, but his mother thought it would be best combed straight back. His habit to date had been to do as his mother thought best. The impulses had been traveling over those same pathways for 13 years now, and it was difficult, even painful, to make them cross new synapses.

By 15 years of age, Boy A had decided against the tight pants and open shirts, and went to the store and selected his own clothing. He considered his parents' ideas; they had given him the money, but he chose what he liked, feeling that they would be satisfied. The mother of Boy B went with him to select his clothes. He was glad, for he would have been afraid to make his own selections because she might not have approved of them. However, he would have liked shirts that were more like those of his peers. But, as yet, it was more comfortable to keep the impulses going over the same old synapses than to force them over new ones.

In the state in which they lived, licenses to operate vehicles can be obtained after passing an examination satisfactorily after the sixteenth birthday. Boy A had been using his sense organs while watching his parents drive for more years than he could remember. They were wise drivers, careful to drive at reasonable and safe speed, to obey driving regulations wherever they happened to be, and they had explained their driving to him. By the time he was 16 he had a fair pattern for driving worked out in his sense organs, cerebrum, lower brain, spinal cord, and muscles. As he said, he could "sit at his desk and practice driving." He took some lessons, passed his examination, and began to be a reasonably wise driver.

Boy B had also driven with both of his parents. They had not explained things to him. Whenever he had asked questions, they had brushed him off with, "You're not old enough. You have to be 16 to drive." As his sixteenth birthday neared, he reminded them that he would soon be old enough to drive. His mother undertook to teach him. He learned, after many emotional outbursts on the part of both of them and a few near-wrecks. He took his examination and was passed after a stern lecture on the part of the examining officer, who detected a certain unreliability in him. He drives, and now that he need not, by law, have anyone with him, he goes without his mother. He speeds, he races traffic lights, and in general flaunts traffic regulations wherever he can get away with it. After all these years it apparently has at last become more satisfying—although still not more comfortable—for him to send impulses over new synapses than to keep them going over old ones.

We have used Child A and Child B to show that adolescence is a period of awakening and transformation, when the patterns of personality already laid down may be modified but not replaced. The adolescent furthers his independence from adult supervision in somewhat the same pattern he used as a young child. In the case of Child A, it was not difficult for him to enter early childhood or early adolescence, chiefly because his parents had prepared both him and themselves for his growing independence. In the case of Child B, it was difficult. As a child, he screamed and made himself extremely unhappy whenever his mother forced herself to put him on his own, so that he never gave himself a chance to learn the joys of independence. He showed that he was still unprepared for independence even at 16, for example, when he failed to follow reasonable rules for driving. Neither Boy B or his mother see the kind of behavior in him that either of them really wants. And we see what can happen to the aptitude for becoming increasingly able to be independent of others and to abide by reasonable rules.

PHYSICAL GROWTH AND DEVELOPMENT

General Physical Development

In the preceding chapters we have discussed the physical changes that occur in puberty. As Table 4–2 (pages 136 ff.) indicated, these changes slow down after the spurt of growth at puberty and the first years of adolescence, but continue at a slower rate during later adolescence. Most girls cease to grow in height by the age of 17, and most boys have about 99 per cent of their height by 17 years, although they continue to grow slowly for the next year or so. A normal balance of the somatotrophic and gonadotrophic hormones (Table 6–1, pages 190 ff.) is accompanied by the cessation of the growth of the long bones and the fusion of some individual bones into single bones.

It is during the years of adolescence that many of the fusions occur, or at least begin. As the skeleton becomes more bony in proportion to cartilage, it becomes stronger. Posture is still in the formative state, however, during early adolescence, and the adolescent's emotional health affects it. If he is confident that he is developing all right, he is more likely to hold his body comfortably erect than if he is dissatisfied or uncertain that his development is as it should be.

Changes in body proportions continue slowly in early adolescence. Both girls and boys are likely to be somewhat "gangling" in appearance, but toward the mid-teens both sexes begin to "fill out" as skeletal muscle and *subcutaneous* (under-skin) connective tissue grow along with the skin and the skeleton. Sex differences occur in the filling-out process, girls developing less skeletal muscle and more subcutaneous connective tissue (including *adipose* or fat-containing cells). Girls develop characteristic curves as fat deposits form, particularly in the hips and shoulders, and as the mammary glands cause the breasts to swell.

The nervous, digestive, breathing, circulatory, and excretory systems continue to grow, although more slowly than in the years immediately following the pubertal spurt. The appetite for food tends to increase. Sense organs function with acuity, although many adolescents are found to have defective vision. A high percentage wear glasses, and in recent years, contact lenses have become increasingly popular with young people of both sexes. Discrimination and judgment of the environment by way of the sense organs increases somewhat during early adolescence but more so in later adolescence.

The skin glands and hair follicles continue to become more active, with acne being a common nuisance to both sexes, and the hair tending to become darker. The balance of endocrine secretions affects the rate of general growth, particularly the development of the reproductive organs.

The reproductive organs continue their development. In girls, little change takes place in the external genitalia, other than the further growth of pubic hair. In boys, the penis approximately doubles in both length and girth concurrently with the growth of the testes and scrotum, so that it is likely that the early adolescent boy may begin to need an athletic supporter at approximately the same time that girls are beginning to need brassieres. Erections of the penis are likely to occur frequently.

Menstruation

The menarche is generally recognized as indicating the beginning, although not the full achievement, of the adult sexual status in the female. Menstruation is typically irregular during adolescence. Whatever the age of menarche, few girls ever become absolutely regular. As a practicing physician [225] quotes, "The only thing regular about menstruation is its irregularity." Changes of environment, such as leaving home for camp or school, emotional ups and downs, and general health all affect the rhythm of menstruation and the duration of the flow. Girls tend to be careless about keeping actual calendar records. Because most girls recognize only that they do menstruate once in each calendar month, they can easily be under the impression that they menstruate more regularly than they actually do.

Attitudes toward menstruation have changed considerably in the past 25 years. Better understanding of anatomy and physiology, concurrent with women's greater social, economic, and legal freedom, has led to the attitude that menstruation is a normal female function which need not incapacitate her at all.

During World War I, physicians pioneered in the development of pads and tampons for the comfortable and sanitary absorption of the menstrual flow, and commercial companies undertook to manufacture their inventions. Advertising of their products, based on sound medical advice, has probably done more to change attitudes toward menstruation than any other single factor. Today, whether or not parents teach their children about menstruation while they are little, the children of both sexes grow up reading advertisements in magazines and seeing the packaged products in drugstores and department stores.

Girls today often swim, dance, and carry on all their usual activities during their menstrual periods. In unusual cases where *dysmenorrhea*, painful menstruation, occurs, medical treatment can usually correct the difficulty. It is foolish for a girl to postpone medical examination if she is at all incapacitated by her feminine physiology. Mothers in increasingly greater numbers are taking their daughters to competent physicians early in adolescence, for advice and reassurance.

Infectious Diseases

Adolescents, while less susceptible to the typical diseases of childhood, are as susceptible to certain infectious diseases as at any other time of their lives. Some knowledge of these diseases could be helpful to them in developing habits of healthful living, which have considerable effect upon desirable psychological development.

Attitudes toward *venereal disease* have changed during this century. The word venereal is derived from the Latin *venereus,* "of Venus," the Roman goddess of love. The inappropriateness of the term becomes obvious in the discussion that follows. Children now read about syphilis and gonorrhea in popular magazines just as they read about poliomyelitis. Some schools teach pertinent facts about these diseases. Not all do, however, and since students ask many questions about venereal disease, we include a brief discussion of them here.

The most common venereal diseases are *syphilis* and *gonorrhea.* They, like other infectious diseases, are not inherited, although they may be transmitted from mother to child. If the transmission occurs before, during, or after birth, the disease is said to be *congenital,* and not *hereditary,* the latter term meaning received by way of the genes in the fertilized egg.

Syphilis is caused by infection of the body by the microorganism, *Treponema pallidum,* a minute, spiral-bodied organism which flourishes only in the living human body. It does not live well in other animals, nor does it live in air, water, or on inanimate objects such as plumbing fixtures and eating utensils. The organism must pass by direct contact or by immediate transmission from the tissues of the infected person to those of another person. Infected males may infect females, or vice versa, in kissing or in sexual intercourse; infected mothers may infect unborn children by way of the umbilical cord, or infected adults may infect children by kissing them, by wiping them with towels they have just used, or by feeding them food with utensils that they have just contaminated. The disease shows up about three weeks after contact at the site of infection as a *chancre,* something like a cold sore, only relatively painless and longer lasting. After this, the organisms migrate throughout the body by way of the blood. There may be a secondary stage of the disease characterized by fatigue, falling hair, and sore mouth and throat membranes. Then the disease may seem to be gone, but actually the organisms are concentrating at a site for active multiplication. The site may be anywhere in the body. That is why syphilis is sometimes called "The Great Masquerader." Tissues where the organism tends to settle are the linings of the heart and blood vessels and nerve tissues. Therefore, the late stages of the disease usually simulate other cardiovascular diseases or nerve diseases such as blindness, *paresis,* or degeneration of the brain tissues, and *locomotor ataxia,* or affected coordination of the muscles.

The laws of most of the United States and of Puerto Rico (the District of Columbia is a notable exception) now require a test indicating that syphilis either is not present or is noncommunicable, before a license to marry may be issued. At least 28 states require physicians to have a test for syphilis made upon women whom they are attending either prenatally or at delivery. When a test is positive (indicating presence of the syphilis organism), curative measures must by law be started immediately.

Gonorrhea is caused by infection of the body by another microorganism, *Neisseria gonorrheae.* In nature, the species is found only on or in the living human body. It can be cultivated artificially on special media, but does not long survive outside the living body. It causes inflammation and pus formation on the mucous membranes of the body such as those which line the male and female genital and urinary tracts, the linings of the heart and blood vessels, the coverings of the joints, and the transparent membranes (*conjunctiva*) of the eyes. Infection of the genitalia occurs almost exclusively through sexual intercourse with an infected person, but infants may be infected congenitally at birth, and people of any age, especially children, may be infected by recently used towels.

The causative organisms of both syphilis and gonorrhea are killed by adequate treatment with penicillin. The relatively easy cure has lulled the public into a false state of complacency about these diseases. Bacteriologists are aware that millions of cases of syphilis and gonorrhea exist that do not come to the attention of public health officials.[58] Education about these diseases in early adolescence, before the boys and girls become more emotionally involved with relations between the sexes, may prove to be more effective than it would be later on in life.

Tuberculosis used to take a heavy toll in adolescence. As late as the early 1930's, 3,000 girls and 1,750 boys between 15 and 19 years of age were dying annually from this disease in the United States alone. This disease is caused by a bacterium, *Mycobacterium tuberculosis.* Unlike the causative organisms of syphilis and gonorrhea, the tubercle bacillus remains alive for long periods outside any living body, human or other animal. It lives in food and in air as long as it is not exposed to direct sunlight. Tuberculosis is much more common even today than is generally believed. According to Frobisher,[58] it annually kills many more people in the United States than do diphtheria, scarlet fever, typhoid fever, mumps, measles, whooping cough, and poliomyelitis all together. In countries where public health measures and nutrition are less adequate than in the United States, the death rate from tuberculosis is high.

Infectious mononucleosis, which is thought to be caused by an as yet unidentified virus, is common in adolescence. It is characterized by fever, general lack of energy, sore throat, and enlarged lymph nodes and spleen. It usually lasts for a few weeks or months, and rest is necessary for the most speedy recovery.

Malaria is common in many parts of the world, and adolescents suffer as much as any other age group from it. This disease is caused by a single-celled animal carried by the female of a certain mosquito. Malaria-control programs are expensive, but are nevertheless being developed by the public health service in many countries throughout the world.

Non-infectious Diseases

Some of the non-infectious diseases which children have before adolescence change in character after puberty, and others may develop after puberty. Allergic diseases such as asthma, which children have exhibited before puberty, often subside in adolescence. Some of the diseases connected with hormone production such as diabetes and simple goiter, may first reveal themselves in adolescence.[194]

State of Physical Health in General

If heredity is good, if physical health during infancy and childhood have been reasonably good, and if habits of diet, rest, waste elimination, and so on continue to be reasonably good, the early adolescent's health is unlikely to cause him much trouble. In both sexes, there is increased need for vitamins, minerals (particularly calcium and iron), and protein. This is as might be expected, because the body is growing and changing rapidly. As we have mentioned, there is increased likelihood of temporary hormone imbalance. There is also likelihood of anemia, increased dental decay, pains connected with growing joints and muscles, and instability of the circulation, resulting in fainting, in some adolescents.[194]

Even if health conditions are good, adolescents tend to develop some poor habits. Their social activities easily lead them into poor dietary habits such as the excessive intake of carbohydrates in the form of candy and soft drinks. Some of their social activities rob them of sufficient rest and result in excessive output of energy. As a result, the medical and dental publications express concern about the possible long-range effects of the poor health habits of adolescents. They refer to their "marginal nutrition," for example, which results in their living in a twilight zone between the absence of actual illness and the possible level of buoyant health which liberates the body and makes enjoyment of living possible.[165]

EMOTIONAL DEVELOPMENT

General Characteristics

Emotional behavior in early adolescence is somewhat reminiscent of that of early childhood. The same kinds of emotions that developed throughout childhood are felt, but are felt more deeply, and they are more complex and contradictory than they have been in later childhood. Early adolescents are likely to lose themselves in anger, fear, love, hate, joy, and worry. They often appear to surrender themselves to emotion to a degree that seems out of proportion to the situation involved, at least as adults size it up.

Emotions which are still felt for some time after the stimulating incident has passed give rise to *moods*. Like the young child, the adolescent swings rapidly from one emotion to another, but, unlike the child, his moods tend to persist and color his next action or emotion. In angelic moods, nothing is too much trouble for him to do to be accommodating, but in less pleasant moods, nothing at all seems to please him.

Daydreams characterize early adolescence. They are often idealistic in nature, but just as often are a device that furnishes a means of escape from the less comfortable real world. As the years pass, the adolescent usually realizes the need to adjust his dream world to the facts of his real world, but sometimes reality is so unpleasant that facing it brings on moods of despair. Having fancied, for example, how he will act at a coming party, he dreams of great social success, but his social ineptitude at the party results in awkwardness and tactlessness, and he feels embarrassed, stupid, and disgusted with himself. Or he may dream of his relationship with a certain person whom he builds up to fit his ideal, and when the real person fails to live up to his dreams or to respond to his advances as he had dreamed, he feels "blue" and angry both with himself and the unsuspecting person. His disappointment both with himself and others results in his behaving in ensuing situations in what appears to other people to be a completely unreasonable manner.

He often needs a greater amount of patience and understanding from others than he gets. He may pretend that he is above trivialities and that he needs help or attention from no one. While we have been referring to "him," let it be stressed that girls are equally subject to these heights and depths of feeling. In the light of such understanding, it is not difficult to see why the moods of early adolescents are volatile, sometimes even a kaleidoscope of variations.

Nevertheless, during early adolescence, progress is normally being made toward greater stability of emotions and moods. Explosive expressions of emotion become less frequent, and the girls and boys become increasingly able to respond appropriately to stimuli which previously aroused them to unwarranted heights or depths of emotion. In the transition from childhood to adult emotional behavior, adolescents are likely to sulk instead of exploding in anger, or they may pout or withdraw from a social situation where, previously, they would have quarreled openly. They may express their feelings of elation more calmly than previously and may cease to laugh as raucously as they did earlier. Fears and anxieties which were previously openly expressed may "go underground," only to reappear in another form. A boy who previously would have said that he was afraid to stay at home alone may now pretend that "of course, he isn't afraid," and then go to bed with his hunting knife on one side and his rifle on the other, and a string tied from his big toe to the doorknob to wake him if any intruder should move the door.

Increasingly, the normally developing early adolescent realizes that emotional explosions are not only considered bad manners, but that they also lose friends for him and reveal that he has not yet left childhood behind. Emotional maturity, in the sense that the individual can manage his own affairs in a responsible manner and consider the feelings and needs of others, is not likely to be achieved in early adolescence, but in people in whom it is eventually going to develop, it is present in its essential outlines by 16 or 17 years of age.[65]

State of Mental and Emotional Health

Generally speaking, good mental and emotional health in early adolescence is the rule rather than the exception. Severe disorders in adolescence are rare, although many boys and girls go through periods of depression that cause their behavior to resemble mental illnesses such as some of the types of schizophrenia.* In most cases, these depressions are only transitory, and adults find it difficult to realize that young people can swing back to normal as quickly as they do.

States of anxiety are typical of adolescence. The boys and girls have many new ideas confronting them. They have many adjustments to make in their living, and many things are confusing. Gallagher [59] mentions among other things, the confusions that come from the adolescent's thinking about school, religion, vocation, the behavior of adults, and death. With sympathy and kindly humor on the part of parents, most early adolescents manage to feel reasonably comfortable a good part of the time, although it is not unusual for early adolescent girls, especially, to break into tears easily over seemingly trivial matters.

PERSONAL-SOCIAL DEVELOPMENT

Attitudes Toward Self

Like all attitudes, attitudes toward self have a history. The infant at birth has no concept of self. Only his needs and their fulfillment have meaning for him. But in infancy and childhood, the foundations for the adolescent's concept of self are laid and are built upon during the years of adolescence and adulthood. The adolescent's ability to think for himself and to evaluate himself with intelligence and judgment reflects what his parents, teachers, and other adults, but particularly his parents, have given him in the way of discipline and love. Either, like Child A mentioned earlier, the treatment he has received has made him a free, worthy, and self-respecting person, or like Child B, a dependent, uncertain, and undisciplined person.

---

* Schizophrenia, from the Greek, *shizo,* "split," and *phren,* "mind," is defined as a group of disorders characterized by disturbances in reality relationships, by a blurring of thought processes, and by disturbances in behavior.

In early childhood, the individual's concept of himself is largely molded by his experiences in his home. During later childhood and puberty, school and peer experiences and experiences with a greater variety of adults either confirm or cancel out his ideas about himself. Throughout these years, his concept of himself is influenced by the manner in which others respond to him. If they accept him, approve of him, and encourage him to keep on behaving as he is behaving, he tends to accept and like himself as he is, as a person who can be wrong now and then without being rejected, who can make mistakes and learn from them, and who can venture into new realms of experience with the attitude that new people and new things are likely to be interesting.

If, on the other hand, he has always been talked down to, punished unjustly, made to feel inadequate, or if he is ignored, he tends to develop feelings of inferiority and distrust of himself. Thus he is severely handicapped in meeting the tests, the introspections, and the adjustments needed in adolescence. Most children, of course, have some of both kinds of experience, and their concepts of themselves are molded by the interaction of experiences. On the whole, children are amazingly resilient, and can "forgive," as it were, many mistakes made by adults, at least if there is some let-up between mistakes. Children tend to feel that adults really mean well even though some adults behave fairly consistently as though they do not mean well. The examination of hundreds of case studies of adolescents leaves the authors with the conclusion that children, on the whole, want to think well of their parents in spite of what they report parents have done to them in the way of undesirable treatment.

In the adolescent years, the ideas and opinions of people outside the home receive serious consideration. The adolescent who has been actively developing his own ideas all along, as Child A was doing, is in a favorable position to continue to evaluate himself in the light of the ideas of others. He is not afraid to consider their ideas when they differ from his own. He may even try putting some of his new ideas into practice, but with the ability to retain what seem to have value and to discard those which lack value for him.

Adolescents like Child B, on the other hand, are on less firm ground when they become aware of new ideas. Child B is less able to evaluate himself and to consider the ideas of others calmly. He is more likely either to refuse to consider them at all because he is afraid to, or to go overboard and adopt them as his own without putting them to the test of judgment, which he lacks. Such adolescents are at the mercy of the social group with whom they happen to be at any particular time, and some of them may even be influenced by the behavior of chance passers-by in their lives. If we keep in mind the neural basis of behavior, it is not difficult to understand the differences in self-evaluation that habits of childhood bring about.

From the point of view of the adolescent, the "inner" part of his life is most important. By this we mean his feelings about himself; his ideas of his traits and of his assets and liabilities; his notions of his role in life, and his role in his family; his notions of his childhood and his past experiences; his beliefs and values; and his degree of conviction that he has a right to his own thoughts and a life of his own, and a right to make his own decisions and choices.

Depending upon the parents, the only child may or may not have a difficult time in evaluating himself. If he has been treated as Child A was treated, he is on as firm ground as if he had been a member of a family of children who were all treated the same way. Child B had a sibling, but his parents managed to treat him and his sibling in such a way that they both lacked ease in sending nerve impulses over new synapses.

The only child does have more responsibility in one way: his actions and his alone can reflect upon his parents. This was brought home to us recently when a 14½-year-old girl who had two brothers explained what she had in mind for herself. Her brothers were both going away to camp for the summer, and she and her parents were going on an extended trip by train. She explained to her parents that she must look very nice on the trip, that her clothes must be right and she must have her hair and nails done because "I shall be your only child, and people will judge you by how I look." She felt that, whenever she and her brothers were together, all three shared the credit or the blame for how they appeared to other people.

All the ideas and feelings that the adolescent has about himself make up his over-all degree of acceptance or lack of acceptance of himself. In this acceptance is incorporated an increasingly clear view of what, with reasonable effort, he might become.

The Survey Center of the University of Michigan [208] asked over one thousand 14- to 16-year-old boys what about themselves they would like to change, about their looks, their life, or their personality. The answers tabulated were as follows:

Nothing	38 per cent
Personal characteristics	28 per cent
Be nicer to my family	12 per cent
Control my temper better	6 per cent
Be more responsible	4 per cent
Physical characteristics	27 per cent
Social skills	21 per cent
Abilities	7 per cent
Don't know	3 per cent

These answers indicate that a good many of the boys were reasonably well satisfied with themselves. It is possible that some of them who answered "Nothing" were tired of answering questionnaires, but we assume that, on the whole, they were not greatly at odds with themselves or with their families. As a result, they were relatively free to meet the demands of the years in which they were living as well as those of the years ahead.

Attitudes Toward Others

As we have seen, the adolescent's attitudes toward himself are in many ways the product of his experiences with others. We have also implied that the individual's behavior toward others is a by-product of his attitudes toward himself. Because of uncertainties about themselves and about social technics, young adolescents may fail in their attempts to make friends. As a result, they may feel that other people do not like them. In homes where adolescents feel free to talk, "Why don't people like me?" is a common question. Sometimes it really is not a question, but a comment calculated to bring forth a parental denial of the idea. Adolescents gain comfort from being told, "People do like you; at least, some people do." Likewise they will say to a parent, "I know you don't like me," chiefly to have that idea denied, also.

Their reaction to their uncertainty about being liked takes various forms. Some affect the appearance of not caring what others think, and behave as if they are indifferent, being too busy with other "more important" things. This behavior may easily widen the rift between them and others, rapidly decreasing their opportunities to make friends. Others with similar uncertainties fawn upon their peers, running errands for them, giving presents, and voicing extravagant compliments. This behavior, too, may drive people away, although it may occasionally win the companionship of someone who enjoys being master to a slave.

Some early adolescents are sufficiently mature to find satisfaction in helping the "fringers" become part of a group. The Michigan study of 14- to 16-year-old boys [208] also asked them what gave them not just fun, but genuine satisfaction. Nineteen per cent of them listed "Helping others." This kind of adolescent realizes that other adolescents may have gotten off to a bad start, but, with encouragement, can learn how to get along in a group. These boys and girls go out of their way to be friendly and give hints and suggestions about what to do and say in order to be more comfortable socially. In doing so, they find satisfaction in helping others, and they themselves grow and enjoy knowing more different kinds of people, and understanding ideas different from their own. They develop a comfortable balance between self-assurance and awareness of the needs and feelings of others. They are often well liked and are chosen for positions of leadership in group activities.

Adolescents who are reasonably sure of themselves can live without too many defenses. Because they can afford to be generous toward the abilities and actions of others, they can also let others live without too many criticisms or too much direction from them. They are not concerned with competition for first place in all areas, because they recognize differences in aptitudes and abilities, and realize that there is room for many to excel. They can enjoy teamwork which involves the pooling of ability for the sake of accomplishing a task which an individual could not do alone.

Adolescents need to develop reasonable humility and reasonable confidence. Most of them are able to do so, especially if they have been growing along these lines in the past and have been given reasonable sympathy from parents and other adults as they go ahead. Delinquent behavior most frequently develops as a result of some interference with the development of reasonable confidence in one's self.[70]

Transition to Heterosexuality

One of the developmental tasks of early adolescence is the establishment of new relationships with peers of both sexes, or the development of *heterosexual* * as well as new *homosexual* relationships.

During childhood, as we have pointed out, boys tend to prefer boys' companionship, and girls tend to prefer that of girls. At

* Greek *heteros*, "other"; and *homos*, "same."

puberty, along with the changes in hormone balance interacting with social and cultural expectations, both sexes begin to view the opposite sex in a new light. Since the hormonal changes begin in girls earlier than in boys on the whole, the transition to heterosexuality begins in most girls before it does in most boys. The girl, who until this time has considered boys as horrid, dirty creatures who are generally a nuisance, begins to see boys who are a year or so older than she is as different beings, and begins to change her behavior accordingly. Early adolescent girls are ambivalent in this area as they are in others. They want males, including boys and their fathers, to notice them and their developing bodies. At the same time, they seem to resent remarks being made about them.

Early adolescent boys, about a year later than girls on the whole, also begin to view girls differently. They, who have for the past several years found girls to be silly things most of whom can't throw a baseball or climb trees well, now begin to see what they can do to attract the attention of girls by paying more attention to their toilet, dressing differently, and so on. At the same time, they sometimes experience strong feelings toward their mothers and antagonism toward their fathers. They often hug their mothers roughly rather than tenderly, but at the same time resent their mothers' interference with their attempts to interest girls.

For parents who understand what is happening to their adolescent girls and boys, this is an interesting time, and a time in which they can exert tremendous influence on their sons and daughters, for better or for worse. Parents who are happily married are likely to see their children's behavior for what it is and are able to be sympathetic and at the same time guide them in their judgments concerning their peers.

A husband who is sure of his wife's love is not upset by seeing his son embrace her. Likewise, a wife who is sure of her husband is not upset by seeing her daughter snuggling up to him. Husband and wife feel confident that their children are developing toward adult manhood and womanhood—which, of course, has been their goal in rearing them!

Trouble may be in store for adolescent boys and girls whose parents are not sure of each other's affection, or for those whose parents have either not had clear goals in the rearing of their children or who had goals that involved the rearing of the children to be chiefly their sons and daughters rather than future husbands and wives. It may be very comforting to a parent to receive such attention from a child. A middle-aged father can easily be flattered by his blossoming daughter's attention, and a middle-aged mother can easily enjoy and want to perpetuate her tall young son's attention. One of the sources of great difficulty in selecting a mate and in marriage is a woman's tendency to compare all men with her father, and a man's tendency to compare all women with his mother.[203]

If all goes well, parents help their children gently through this stage, and together watch them making their heterosexual adjustment with their peers, ready to help them regain their confidence when rebuffed and to give them gentle suggestions for greater success in the future.

During the period in which the transition to heterosexuality is being made, adolescents are also likely to feel new attractions to members of their own sex. They feel attracted particularly toward other adolescents who have been their friends during childhood, and who are easier for them to understand than are members of the opposite sex.

In these girl-girl and boy-boy friendships, which are less complicated, as yet, than are heterosexual friendships, adolescents learn more about control of their emotions and about consideration for the feelings of others. Because these friends are outside the immediate family, their disapproval has a sharper disciplinary effect even than that of parents or other members of the family. A University of Michigan Survey [209] of 12- to 18-year-old girls revealed that 60 per cent of them said they "needed and wanted" loyal girl friends to whom they could talk freely and in whom they could confide their innermost thoughts, questions, and feelings. Boys also have their best friends. Where telephones are available, long conversations cover all sorts of subjects from school work through problems with parents and with members of the opposite sex (Fig. 8–2).

The tendency to develop close friendships with members of the same sex is so characteristic of early adolescence that this period is sometimes referred to as the "homosexual stage" of psychosexual development. In this stage, some individuals participate in physical sexual activities with members of their own sex. In some cultures, homosexual activity is required practice in the process of growing up sexually.[187] In some cases, the relationship is with an older person of the same sex. In contemporary United States, Kinsey [106, 107] reports that homosexual relations occur within both sexes in early adolescence, in about 45 per cent of the boys studied and in a lower percentage of the girls.

Homosexuality in its broader sense is typically a relatively brief stage in the early adolescent period. As the normal adolescent gains experience with members of the opposite sex, he begins to feel more

Fig. 8–2. Long telephone conversations are important to the teenager.

at ease with them. The boy and girl both find heterosexual interests occupying increasingly more of their time and interest. Landis,[117] for example, found that 33 out of every 34 girl-girl homosexual friendships were discontinued, while the 34th remained in the early adolescent stage of psychosexual development and became overtly homosexual.

If parents too insistently and for too long a time (which varies with the boy and girl) refuse their early adolescent sons and daughters normal dating and boy-girl group experiences, they deny them the experience necessary for the development of judgment of boy-girl activities and of the character of individual men and women, at the time when their children's peers are gaining this experience. If not permitted to achieve this developmental task at the appropriate time, some boys and girls never become able to take the necessary steps into comfortable heterosexual relationships.

Some of the transition into heterosexuality is made through casual interchanges such as occur at the corner drugstore (Fig. 8–3) and in

Fig. 8–3. Transitions to heterosexuality: casual interchanges.

group dating (Fig. 8–4). In situations like these, the strain of keeping up a twosome date is absent, and getting the "feel" for boy-girl conversation and other activities is facilitated by the shifting of focus from one individual to another, by seeing how others handle situations, and by group games, singing, and similar activities. This transition from group-dating into "pairing off" is in many ways comparable to the shifting group play described for 4- and 5-year-olds. In time, early adolescents begin to feel secure enough to enjoy informal twosome conversations (Fig. 8–5).

Although serious boy-girl relationships may develop in early adolescence, and many marriages are taking place before the young people are old enough to marry without parental consent, the wisdom of doing so is questionable. Judgment of character is insufficiently mature, and vocational preparation is often interfered with by the coming of babies before the couple is sufficiently secure financially as well as emotionally.

Concurrent with the physical changes of puberty, the ensuing transition into heterosexuality, and the impracticality of early adolescent heterosexual contacts, is an increase in the frequency of masturbation. Kinsey and his associates [106, 107] report that of their sample of 8,000 women and 12,000 men, 20 per cent of the women and 82

Fig. 8–4. Transitions to heterosexuality: group dating.

per cent of the men reported masturbating to *orgasm* (climax of sexual sensation) by 15 years of age. These same studies revealed that most males masturbate with fantasies of imagined sexual situations. Fantasies also occur in females, but physiological satisfaction seems sufficient for some (36 per cent). If masturbation does not interfere with the procedure of the adolescent's transition into heterosexual relationships with his peers, there is no evidence that any physical, emotional, or mental damage results.[59] On the other hand, there is evidence that damage does result, particularly to the development of healthy heterosexual relationships, from worry about masturbation. The Kinsey Reports [106, 107] include excellent bibliographies on this subject.

The important task for the early adolescent in the personal-social area is the evaluation of his emerging self and the clarification of his

Fig. 8–5. Transitions to heterosexuality: informal twosome conversations.

role as a person living among other people. In this period, he is growing from the relative unawareness of his inner self which is typical of childhood to the insights and outlooks of the adult he is going to be.

INTELLECTUAL DEVELOPMENT

No obvious spurt of intellectual development occurs that is comparable to that in physical development.[153] Changes in intellectual growth consist of a continuing acquisition of knowledge and of a broadening and deepening of thinking and reasoning. Actually, if the early adolescent understands the physical, emotional, personal, and social changes taking place in him and in his peers, he is probably performing as much cerebral activity as at any other time in his life. Although school grades tend to slip during the early teens, exposure to school subjects, the mass media, discussions with peers and sometimes with adults, all add new information and ideas which challenge reasoning.

Development of Concepts

If their attitude toward intellectual growth is positive, adolescents of average or superior intellect greatly increase their capacity for abstract thinking. As in childhood, concepts in adolescence are limited by the individual's experience. With experience, the ability to make generalizations from specific facts, to comprehend abstractions, and to weigh values, along with the ability to communicate ideas, can increase rapidly. Historical events, for example, such as the economic depression of the 1930's and World War II cannot be meaningful to contemporary adolescents unless these events are presented to them in a realistic manner. If information is not meaningful and fairly concrete, superior adolescents have little advantage over other adolescents in concept formation. However, when information is meaningful, the adolescent who is superior in verbal intelligence shows higher scores on concept tests than does the individual with lower verbal intelligence.[83]

Even adolescents of superior intelligence can form misconceptions. In areas of information that, for various reasons, are not discussed or written about clearly, such as personal death or sex, misconceptions are especially likely to develop. Without sufficient background information and freedom of thought, the adolescent may easily misinterpret or accept uncritically what he hears and reads. It is common, for instance, for adolescents to get such erroneous concepts as "in women, sexual life ends at menopause," that "masturbation leads to insanity," and that "the worst thing that can happen to a person is to die." The fortunate adolescent can talk such things over with his parents. Since many adolescents do not feel free to talk to anybody other than their peers about such matters, they continue their state of intellectual and emotional confusion, circulate it and reinforce it among themselves, and hand it down to boys and girls slightly younger than they are.

Because adolescents have lived such a relatively few years, it is difficult for them to form concepts of the possible time ahead in their own lifetimes. They have also had little experience in living through the consequences of their own actions and choices, because most of these have been so much the result of other people's ideas of what is good for them. What they eat, where they live, where they *have* to go to school, and so on—these have not been entirely their ideas. It is not likely that they conceive of how different things would be if they had been born and lived elsewhere and, as a result, had different experiences.

Because of their lack of experience, it is difficult for them to make long-term plans. To stay in school after the years of compulsory schooling are over can seem to involve too great a sacrifice of immediate advantages, such as freedom from assignments and from being graded by teachers, and of having a job and the additional freedom that comes with having one's own money. The present is real, and demanding of satisfaction. The thrill of speedy driving, for example, is more real than its danger. Only when some adolescents see actual driving accidents can the realization of the danger outweigh the thrill. For some, only an unwanted pregnancy in one of their immediate friends can make real the dangers of premarital sexual intercourse. It is adolescents reared like our Child B who are more likely to have difficulty in forming long-term concepts. Child A has actually, all his life, practiced arriving at concepts which have involved increasingly long periods of time.

Imagination

During later childhood, boys and girls are so involved with actual experiences that they give less time to imaginary activities than they did in early childhood. In early adolescence, the imagination undergoes a kind of reawakening. New kinds of experiences and ideas abound. The imagination is stimulated by the physical changes themselves. "Now I am on the way to womanhood," the girl thinks, and the boy soon finds that he is on the way to manhood. Their concepts of womanhood and manhood undergo change, as the possible delights and responsibilities that accompany adulthood come into clearer focus. Some adolescents are moved to express their dreams and longings in poems, stories, plays, the dance, or other artistic media. Whether their activity in these media is original or a rendition of the work of others, the performance serves as an avenue for expressing their imaginative moods. Accuracy of rendition is less important to them than is the expression of their feelings.

Some adolescents express themselves in athletic activity. For some, science, or social service such as hospital work, offers them an outlet for their imagination, and gives them an opportunity to judge their possibly glamorous ideas against reality. All these expressions of their dreams and desires reflect their developing understanding of human life in relation to its surroundings.

In early adolescence, imagination often expresses itself in exaggeration. In their inexperience, adolescents are themselves impressed by overstatement of facts, and tend to assume that others are too. It often takes time and experience for them to discover that people with more mature minds are not impressed and that they discount some of what is stated. If exaggeration remains a habit beyond early adolescence, an individual may find, in some situation where he needs desperately to be believed, that no one takes him seriously.

Objectivity in Thinking

In childhood and early adolescence, the center of the universe is the individual himself. Early adolescents make some progress in thinking and feeling beyond themselves, but they still have too much yet to learn about themselves to be able to spend much thought on others. They are in the process of evaluating themselves—intellectually, personally, and socially. If they overestimate their intellectual ability, they may aspire to goals which are unrealistic. If they underestimate themselves, they may settle for less than they could do. They need the help of parents, teachers, and counselors to develop a realistic concept of their intellectual ability and aptitudes. Beyond that, they need encouragement to do their best along the lines of their best aptitudes, whether these be mechanical or more abstract. They need to appreciate the importance of whatever it is that they seem to be best fitted by heredity and experience to do.

DEVELOPMENT OF INDEPENDENCE

The typical early adolescent becomes touchy with members of his family and retreats from them in order to be by himself. He is not sure of himself, and wonders why he cannot get along with them

more smoothly. Parents are often hypercritical, and fluctuate between asking too much of an adolescent or not enough. Even so, the
early adolescent seldom voices criticism of his family. He may think
and feel it. His withdrawal from the family indicates an even
stronger need to assert his own individuality. The family typically
fails to understand him.

Early Backgrounds

During infancy, partly because of the individual's helplessness
and dependence upon adults, he is likely to experience a period of
omnipotence. As the early years pass, the child perceives his own
relative helplessness and dependence upon others, but still retains
his self-concept of independence and omnipotence because, to a
large extent, his wishes are still gratified even though he himself cannot always take care of his needs.

In most cultures, parents begin to take steps to lessen a child's
dependence as soon as they consider him able to begin to do things
for himself. This treatment tends to undermine his feelings of omnipotence and independence. There arises in early childhood a sort
of crisis at which most children recognize that they cannot compete
with or dominate adults any longer. Adults are bigger, and they
have control over him. The only way the child can retain a reasonably high level of self-esteem is to accept his dependence and adopt
a subordinate role in relation to the parents.

In early adolescence, girls and boys develop a clearer but still an
incomplete realization of their dependence relationship with their
parents. They know something of their physical relationship with
their parents, how intimate it once was (at least, with their mothers),
and how much less intimate it is becoming. They understand their
environment better; they feel that they "know their way around," to
a certain extent. They recognize, however, that for various cultural
reasons they are still completely dependent upon their parents for
financial support, and to a lesser extent, dependent upon their
parents for emotional reassurance that they are coming along all
right.

In cultures where adolescents are permitted to participate in
situations which carry social and economic importance, such as helping with preparations for adult entertaining, working for money, or

doing work which the family would otherwise have to pay to have done, girls and boys tend to develop mature and responsible behavior earlier than where they are not permitted to do such things.

In some complex modern cultures, where early adolescents find little opportunity to participate in status-giving activities, they often tend to substitute for such activity by identifying themselves with prominent figures in the worlds of entertainment or sports. In such cultures, the performance of routine home chores is helpful if the adolescents can feel that such performance is essential to the comfortable functioning of the home. But if the jobs seem to be "made" or unimportant, performing them does less for the development of responsibility.

Parent—Early Adolescent Conflicts

Conflict between parents and early adolescents is natural. In some cultures, the adolescent feels free to express himself directly to his parents. This, at least, brings the sources of conflict out into the open. In more adult-dominated cultures, the adolescent is expected to maintain the appearance of unquestioning obedience toward parents and other adults. With what we know of the need for developing independence, such obedience can result in severe emotional conflict. Resistance, even in thought only, may bring deep feelings of guilt and confusion. If the adolescent with such feelings can talk to his peers or to objective counselors, he finds that his feelings are, to a greater or lesser extent, shared by most adolescents. This knowledge itself is helpful. Common adolescent questions include the following: "Why do my parents boss me around as if I were a child?" "How much of my life ought I to tell my parents?" "Is it right for my parents to open my mail?" and "Why won't they let me grow up?"

A survey of boys from 14 through 16 years of age made by the University of Michigan [208] found that 44 per cent of the boys studied said that they never disagreed with their parents (it was assumed they meant they never disagreed openly). Of the 56 per cent who said they did disagree with their parents, the most frequent source of disagreement was control of hours and what was to be done with spare time. Twenty per cent of these boys still received physical punishments, 31 per cent were still scolded or "talked to," 83 per cent were punished by deprivation of privileges such as going out or being denied use of the family car. Three per cent were "always given a second chance, were never punished."

It is hard for any adolescent to understand many of these situations, and harder still for him to accept them. One of the strongest of the adolescent's ambivalences is about his parents. In his quest for independence, he has a vigorous need to react negatively to many of the requests and suggestions of all adults, and especially of his parents. Although deeply dependent upon and often fairly sure of his parents' love and approval, he nevertheless feels compelled to fight their suggestions. This not infrequently brings him to take stands which he does not really want to take.

Money and Independence

One of the most frequent disputes between parents and adolescents is over money.[208, 209] Should there be an allowance or not? If so, how is it to be spent? Should the adolescent be allowed to earn or not? If he does earn, must he pay board and room with his money, save it, or feel free to spend it as he wishes? Families differ in these matters.

We have seen earlier that allowances are usual for children of 5 or 6 years, in families in the United States. Having money and learning to handle it wisely is a worthy goal. We also saw that some children fail to handle their allowances with reasonable skill, with the result that their parents often discontinue them. Some families still have not resumed allowances even by adolescent years, having formed the habit of doling out money as the need arises. This leaves the adolescent deprived of the sense of freedom and of developing some skill in handling money. In the University of Michigan Survey,[208] about half of the boys between 14 and 17 years of age and two-thirds of the girls from 14 to 18 received allowances from their families on a regular basis, the amounts varying between fifty cents and five dollars a week; 85 per cent received from one to five dollars, the amounts decreasing as earning power increased.

A substantial majority of the adolescents between ages 14 and 17 worked at paid jobs of some sort doing either chores at home or work outside of the home. Eighty per cent of the 14-year-old girls earned money babysitting outside their own homes. This percentage declined to only 58 for the 16-year-olds, because by this age an additional 32 per cent were earning money at other types of jobs. Of the boys who worked, 18 per cent worked for their own families, and 77 per cent worked outside of the home.

Among the girls who worked outside their own homes during the school year, only a few of the 14-year-olds worked more than 13 hours each week. However, the majority of the 16- and 17-year-olds worked more than 13 hours each week. Of the 14- to 16-year-old boys who worked during the school year, about half worked 13 hours or more each week, about one-fifth worked from 21 to 30 hours, and a few worked more than 30 hours each week.

The girls in this study spent the greater proportion of their earnings on minor items of clothing (the major items still being provided by their families), on school expenses, and on personal dues; 20 per cent of the 14-year-olds and 12 per cent of the 16-year-olds saved some of their money; the rest was spent for entertainment and hobbies. Boys spent their money in much the same way, but with less for clothing and more for dating. The over-all picture gained from these studies is that substantial numbers of early adolescent boys and girls work outside of their homes. The boys work longer hours, on the whole, than do the girls, and have somewhat greater freedom than do the girls in deciding what they spend their money for.

It seems relevant here to raise a question about the wisdom of thirteen or more hours of work per week during the school year for early adolescents who are still growing and whose energy may not suffice for rapid growth, outside work, and good school record, as well as activity for gaining experience with peers. Some individuals probably do not have the energy, but others do profit greatly from the work experience and suffer in no observable way because of it.

New Parent-Child Relationships

Before the adolescent can achieve independence, former parent-child relationships must give way to new. This is often difficult. Some parents tend, as we have seen, to continue earlier patterns of discipline and other relationships with their adolescent children. If these patterns are overdominating or overpermissive, the adolescent's transition into adulthood is difficult. If, for example, his parents have been and continue to be overstrict, he may react with aggressiveness in order to break the chains; or he may seem to accept the situation, when actually his rebellion goes underground, there to affect his behavior in unexpected and seemingly irrelevant ways. Such parents are usually forced eventually to relax their control, but their children may not at this point be competent to use their freedom.

On the other hand, if overindulgence has been and continues to be the pattern, the overprotected adolescent may find himself unprepared for the preadult world, and his reaction to the first social failure, for instance, may be extremely painful. He may try to escape back into childhood, where he was safer, or he may have a personality sufficiently insulated from reality to allow him to feel comfortable about blaming his failures on someone else. If so, he may go on with this kind of behavior until he is fixed in this pattern of escape.

The achievement of desirable independence is a two-way process. It is one in which the parent finds it possible to free the child and to enjoy his growing independence, and in which the adolescent learns to like the feeling of self-discipline and independence of thought and action. Both parent and adolescent have to modify past habits, and both have to learn to appreciate the viewpoint and needs of the other.

SUGGESTIONS FOR FURTHER DISCUSSION

1. Consult sources in your library about the complexity and difficulty of adolescent adjustment in this country, as contrasted with other countries of the world, and with this country in the 1920's and 1930's. Report your findings to the class.

2. What do you consider to be some of the widely accepted standards for adult behavior in our society today? To what degree do you think today's adolescent should guide his behavior by these standards?

3. Some young people feel that democratic procedures between parents and children in the home are not good training for growing young people. Do you agree or disagree with this? Why?

4. It is recognized that long-standing poor habits yield slowly to better ones, even when the individual has good intentions in the matter. What suggestions can you offer for speeding up the acquisition of good habits?

5. How have your interests in other persons and your behavior toward them changed and matured since you were thirteen or fourteen years old? Should there be further change if economic adequacy and personal happiness are to be at an optimum in your life?

6. If you have younger siblings, what suggestions have you for helping them prepare for the adolescent adjustments and transitions?

7. Select from the class individuals to play the father, the mother, and a sixteen-year-old in a discussion of the following situations:

a. The adolescent (boy) wants the use of the family car on week ends.
b. The adolescent (girl) protests a 1:00 A.M. return from dances; a 10:00 P.M. return from midweek dates; a restriction of dates to two a week.
c. In each instance, have a second discussion in which the adolescent and one parent exchange roles.

8. Visit some community projects where young adolescents are working or playing in groups. Report to the class your impression of the adequacy with which the primary objectives of the project were being facilitated or impeded by the behavior and attitudes of the adolescents. Do you have any suggestions to make for improving their attitudes and behavior?

REFERENCES FOR FURTHER STUDY

Crow, L. D., and Crow, A. *Adolescent Adjustment and Development.* New York: McGraw-Hill Book Co., Inc., 1956. Ch. 6, changing emotional patterns; Ch. 8, importance of interests and attitudes; Ch. 16, home adjustment of adolescents.

Dewey, R., and Humber, W. J. *The Development of Human Behavior.* New York: The Macmillan Co., 1951. Ch. 11, adolescence, pp. 297–309 (social factors in adolescent development, influence of culture, conflict between role and status, personality adjustments). Case studies.

Frobisher, M. *Fundamentals of Microbiology.* Philadelphia: W. B. Saunders Co., 1957. Contains an up-to-date account of infectious diseases.

Gallagher, J. R., and Harris, H. I. *Emotional Problems of Adolescence.* New York: Oxford University Press, 1958. Discussion of these problems by kindly physicians who have made the study of adolescence their special concern.

Jersild, A. T. *The Psychology of Adolescence.* New York: The Macmillan Co., 1957. Ch. 6, adolescent fantasies, day-dreams, and dreams. Chs. 7, 8, and 9, emotional development; love and affection, joy; anger and hostility; fear and anxiety. Ch. 14, the adolescent at school.

Munn, N. L. *The Evolution and Growth of Human Behavior.* Boston: Houghton Mifflin Co., 1955. Ch. 17, pp. 484–493, changes in personality; in adolescence; problems of adolescent adjustment.

Seidman, J. M. *The Adolescent: A Book of Readings.* New York: Holt, Rinehart & Winston, Inc., 1953. Selection 15, principles of growth and development of intelligence in adolescence; Selection 22, age differences in religious beliefs and problems during adolescence; Selection 26, the moral beliefs of sixteen-year-olds; Selection 47, the sociology of parent-youth conflicts; Selection 48, the adolescent and his happy family; Selection 53, the jobs youth want and the jobs they get; Selection 54, satisfactions in work; Selection 55, dissatisfactions in work; Selection 63, a check list of facts about jobs for use in vocational guidance.

Seidman, J. M. *The Child: A Book of Readings.* New York: Holt, Rinehart & Winston, Inc., 1958. Selection 24, self concepts and delinquency; Selection 25, intrapersonal factors in delinquency.

Stone, H. M., and Stone, A. *A Marriage Manual.* New York: Simon & Schuster, Inc., 1953. A practical guidebook in question and answer form about sex and marriage. Very helpful to adolescents and adults.

For film suggestions see Film Supplement, in the Appendix.

CHAPTER 9

Later Adolescence

General Considerations

As Chapter 8 stated, we consider the period of later adolescence to extend from 16 or 17 years of age to the early 20's, when human beings are considered to be adults. It is true that most people are physically adult by 21 years of age. Criteria for emotional and intellectual adulthood are not as clearly discernible in most people, however, and by no means all people are economically independent by 21. We shall have more to say about maturity in the chapters to follow this one. Here we shall concern ourselves with the characteristics typical of people who have gone through the earlier periods of life, and have completed the developmental tasks of those periods with reasonable success.

Those in middle and late adulthood are inclined to look upon the period of late adolescence as a time when people are old enough to enjoy many of the pleasures of adulthood before being burdened with adult responsibilities. They look back at their own youth and at contemporary late adolescents, wishing they had known in their youth what they know in their later years. "If youth but knew, and age but could," and "Youth is so wonderful, it's a shame to waste it on young people" are typical thoughts of older people when they consider late adolescence.

This is, of course, an overidealized picture of late adolescence remaining in the minds of people who are reliving, in the neural pathways of memory, the fun and excitement of their youthful adventures, and possibly the sweetness of young love. Too often, they have forgotten the demands that study and the first job made on them when they were young. They no longer recall the bewilderment they experienced in deciding upon a vocation, in settling problems of religion, in learning what to believe about people, in acquiring or not acquiring a mate, and in analyzing the seeming contradictions that come with experience. Late adolescence, however, is a period in which young people tend to stabilize, following the turbulence of early adolescence, and when they can enjoy life as a continuing but not overwhelming challenge.

The young person at this stage may be thought of as taking over the paddling of his own canoe down the stream of life. This is the same canoe that he has been riding all along, but his parents have commanded the steering paddle throughout his life. The stream of life, like any other stream, has its quiet spots, its currents, its rapids and whirlpools, and its waterfalls—some of them high and dangerous ones. Most parents have realized, more or less consciously, that sometime, along about age 17 or 18, the young person would be taking over his own steering paddle. They have, it is hoped, given him some practice, first with the forward paddle then with the steering paddle. They have, it is hoped again, been pointing out what the water looks like in the quiet spots, where the helpful currents are and how to use them, that rapids sometimes mean hidden rocks which should be avoided unless one is willing to risk a hole in the bottom of the canoe. They have certainly been pointing out what the signs of a high waterfall are likely to be, and have advised that he portage around these falls.

If they have been wise they have been handing the young person the steering paddle in some of the quiet waters, and have given him limited practice over rapids and in some of the swifter currents. Thus, the young person will have learned not only how to handle his craft, but also about the force and pattern of the stream he must negotiate. If he has been well prepared and has had some experience, he will know how to use the currents in order to make rapid progress, how to rest in the quiet waters, how to detect the rapids and to avoid hidden rocks, and when to portage around dangerous falls. The parents will doubtless stand on the bank and shout a few directions for a time, but as the young person demonstrates his ability, knowledge and judgment his parents generally soon go about their affairs, in quiet confidence that he is now mature enough to manage his own affairs. If he is not well prepared, it will be wise for him to recognize this and to stick to the quieter waters until he gets the feel of his canoe and develops some skill in handling it. He needs also to learn the signs of trouble ahead. He may and probably will tip over occasionally in the process of learning. In this case, if his gear is well packed and the canoe a sturdy one, he can right the canoe, repack the gear and get on with his trip, being wiser because of his mishap.

PHYSICAL STATUS

Size and Proportion

During or by the end of later adolescence, both sexes complete body growth in height. Their proportions in height are those of adulthood (Table 4–2, pages 136 ff.). The average male is about 67 inches in height, the average female 64 inches. Considerable variation in weight exists, although not as much as exists in later years. The average male weighs about 140 pounds and the average female about 120 pounds.

Skin and Hair

The activity of the skin glands tends to stabilize; acne usually decreases and then ceases almost entirely. The hair of the head, face, and body tends to coarsen and darken, and acquires mature texture and character.

Trunk Systems

The appetite for food is likely to be great during the early years of this period, tending to subside toward the end. Digestion is usually excellent if emotional life is satisfactory. Breathing rate stabilizes to between 16 and 20 inhalations per minute, and most people notice greatly reduced susceptibility to infections of the breathing apparatus. The vocal cords continue to elongate, although more slowly, and toward the end of the period, most people develop the qualities of their mature voice. The heartbeat stabilizes to between 100 and 70 beats per minute at rest.

Bone and Muscle

The growth of the skeleton slows down, fusions of some bones continue, and by 21 years of age only about 206 separate bones exist, as contrasted with the 350 that were present at puberty. Posture and carriage of the body are still very flexible. In many ways this is the last chance at good posture. Sitting, standing or walking postures at this period fix not only postural habits but also the permanent structure of the individual bones and their relations to each other. Posture is to a high degree a reflection of inner feelings. In turn, it affects outward appearance.

Smooth and cardiac muscles are nearing the adult condition, and they function well if the emotional condition of the individual is healthy. Skeletal muscles continue to grow and strengthen, although these do not attain their full growth and strength until the individual is about 30 years of age. This explains partially why baseball pitchers and other athletes often improve in skill in the years following their late adolescence.

Nervous System and Sense Organs

Full growth of the nervous system and the sense organs is attained during this period. New synapses continue to come into function in the nervous system, especially if an effort is directed toward making them do so. The sense organs are functioning well in most people. Visual acuity reaches its highest level at about 20 years of age.

Reproductive Systems and Endocrines

The reproductive systems continue their rapid growth in the early years of this period and become fully functional in both sexes. This is also true of the endocrine glands. However, the irregular release of fertilizable eggs during the adolescent years of young women makes it uncertain whether the ability to reproduce develops earlier in one sex than in the other. In sexual responsiveness, the female matures much later than the male, the highest level in the male being attained in the late teens and early twenties, and in the female, in the late twenties and early thirties. Nothing that is known of anatomy and physiology accounts for this age difference. We venture the hypothesis that the difference is a cultural one which has developed as a result of the difference in the teaching of boys and girls, particularly about the psychological aspects of reproduction.

Physical Habits

People in late adolescence tend to have a tremendous amount of energy for what they want to do. They can get up early, work at a job all day, or attend classes and study during the day, and spend many hours in the evening either on social life, study, or anything else that they are highly motivated to do. Some, but by no means all, participate actively in sports, either in connection with school or college or on community teams. Some men make athletics their career, but few women become great athletes. As a rule, women discontinue active sports in late adolescence, although some retain an active interest in sports such as golf, swimming, and riding.

Habits that have been built in previously are likely to continue into late adolescence. If habits for efficient living have been developed, they are likely to be retained. If poor habits have been developed, they are unlikely to change now, although it is still within the power of the individual to change them if he is sufficiently motivated. When people who have grown up as Child B did (see Chapter 8), leave home or even if they stay at home, they are likely to manage their bodies as unwisely as Child B drives a car.

EMOTIONAL STATUS

Late adolescence, being a period in which people are somewhat if not entirely on their own, offers them more opportunities to test themselves in their ability to manage their own affairs. If they have been maturing satisfactorily, they are reasonably free from emotional reactions typical of childhood. If they have not been progressing satisfactorily, they have considerable difficulty in managing their affairs. Some of the latter kind of young people recognize their own retardation, and courageously set about catching up to the level of their peers. Others, more seriously retarded, may fail to recognize their own emotional level, or if they do, may be too much on the defensive to consider trying to improve.

Cultures and individual parents differ in how well they prepare their adolescents for the tests of approaching adulthood. Some observers feel, however, that the world is full of adolescents and adults who are arrested emotionally at a childhood or adolescent level, and that only a relatively small percentage of people are as fully adult emotionally as they are physically. The psychiatrist G. B. Chisholm has said that, so far in the history of mankind, there have never been enough emotionally mature people at any one time to manage the affairs of all the emotionally immature people. Let us look at some of the emotions as they are customarily expressed in late adolescence.

Anger

Several studies indicate that anger is a frequent and intensely felt emotion during these years.[87, 92] If we think of anger by dictionary definition as "violent, vindictive passion," or "sudden and strong displeasure," we may gain some insight into why it is frequent and intense during later adolescence, when all emotions tend to be vigorous. Not all adolescents are alike, and the conditions that arouse anger differ from one to another and are somewhat related to the individual's experiences in growing up. If a young man has grown up under rigid discipline in connection with politics, religion, or social prejudice, he may be infuriated when (in college or in the armed services, for example) he is expected to associate closely with people of different political conviction, faith, or race. An individual who has been reared in a more liberal environment may be angered by contact with ideas that are more conservative than his. Even the manner of speech or use of certain phrases may make some young people angry. One 18-year-old boy, who had grown up thinking of death as the natural end of life, asked explosively one day, "Why do people say 'pass away' when what they mean is 'die'?"

The stimulus to which adolescents react with anger may indicate that they attach some uncomfortable significance to it. A parent's simple question about a college student's courses may bring forth an angry, "I'll take care of my affairs! Let me alone, will you?" This is probably resistance to what seems to him a parental implication that he is not yet able to manage his own affairs. Similarly a young woman who, while growing up, has had little clear education about sexual matters, may state angrily, "Everything about this psychology course is related to sex." She is actually angry with her own lack of information and at the people responsible for it, but she vents her anger on "the course" which brings her own inadequacy to her unwilling attention.

A high proportion of anger responses are reactions to people, other than parents, who seem to be exerting pressure on the adolescent to do something he does not want to do, at least not at the moment. He knows he should take his suit to the cleaner's but he doesn't want to just then. She knows she should write that "thank you" note, but not right now, and so on.

From what we have said, it would seem that a good many instances of late adolescent anger are really the individual's anger at himself. This is understandable because his life is becoming increasingly complex at a time when he is trying hard to establish his independence. The individual can profit by studying his own pattern of anger, what causes him to become angry, why he becomes angry at particular stimuli, and what form of expression his anger tends to take. Some people fail to react angrily to situations which ordinarily arouse people to anger. This may be the result of punishment for displays of anger during childhood, so that this kind of anger has been submerged into the unconscious mind. Some people learn to fear the consequences of their violent expressions of anger and learn to control it before it gets out of hand. Some learn to suppress anger until they can take it out safely on a punching bag or a golf ball, or in cleaning their rooms, for example.

The late adolescent who is maturing accepts the fact that anger is a normal emotion, and that there are and will be situations in life which rightly provoke his anger. He realizes, however, that his right to be angry works toward his good, and that of other people, only if he learns to direct the energy involved rather than permit it to direct him.

Fear and Anxiety

If later adolescence is going forward satisfactorily, the sources of fears and anxieties change. Whether or not the fears and anxieties of childhood and early adolescence are being left behind or whether they are still operating, depends largely upon habits developed through the years. Just as the little child learned not to fear thunder, for instance, when he sensed his mother's comfortable attitude toward it, so also the adolescent learns not to fear such things as venereal disease and social rejection, as he gains in understanding of their causes.

If the adolescent has learned along the way to be interested in new information, to want to understand more of the facts of a situation, the murkiness surrounding hitherto incompletely understood areas tends to disappear, and he sees what the actual situations are. If this is his emotional condition, he learns to fear only those situations which can really cause trouble, and as a result, he may learn how to avoid them. If, on the other hand, the adolescent has not developed the habit of getting accurate information about the sources of his fears and anxieties, he may actually have learned to fear accurate information itself.

Members of both sexes may continue to worry about their acceptance in society and about their ability to find a suitable mate. Not many studies have been made of fear at this and later age levels. However, a study of university male students between 18 and 24 years of age revealed that they had more social fears than had boys between 11 and 16 years of age.[222] Social fears include exclusion from groups, committing a *faux pas,* and so on. Fears of animals such as insects, snakes, and horses had been dropped by the older group, but fears connected with sexual activities and with authority had increased. The fears connected with sex included the consequences of sexual intercourse such as discovery, pregnancy, venereal disease, and the consequences of previous masturbation and possible homosexual activity. Fears of authority include dread of parental criticism and failure in academic work or in a paid job.

A study of fears in late adolescent girls [232] showed the commonest source of their fears to be social situations. Fears of animals seemed to be the next in frequency, with fears of sexual activities and their consequences third. Girls seem to be less aware of their sexual physiology than are boys.

The expression of fears may be different in later adolescence than it was earlier, partly because later adolescents have acquired another relatively new fear, that of losing face among their peers or in front of adults. As a result, they may pretend to disapprove of some of the things or situations that they really fear. They may affect lack of interest in certain social or sexual areas, or they may hold that certain things are "unesthetic" or that certain activities are "vulgar." In some cases, late adolescents, as do individuals at any age, continue to make coarse, unfunny jokes about areas in which they have unresolved fears, such as sexual activities and religion.

Anxiety is related to fear, but it tends to be caused by less specific stimuli and to be more pervasive. One who may have been afraid of a specific situation may lose the fear, once the situation ceases to exist, but anxiety easily becomes a habit that needs nothing very specific to keep it operating. Anxiety is a more dignified term for worry. It involves the recurrent passage of nerve impulses over the same pathways in the brain and the stimulation of the same nerves in the autonomic nervous system. Because the fibers of the autonomic nervous system innervate most of the internal body organs, anxiety becomes a complex of several feelings, unexpressed anger, irritability, uneasiness, apprehension, depression, and often headache, stomach ache, abdominal pains, and so on. With all the uncertainties that accompany late adolescence, some anxiety is inevitable. Hopefully, most of it is transitory.

The late adolescent usually knows that he has about achieved his ultimate physical stature and general build and that his general level of intellectual and other abilities is pretty well known to teachers and others who have been rating them throughout his adolescence. He wants to be accepted socially, but he may not be quite sure at what socioeconomic level. He may not be sure as to whether or not he wants further formal education, or whether he is capable of it if he wants it. He is not quite sure of his status in connection with compulsory military service, whether to try to do it and get it over with, to try to defer it, or to try to avoid it. In most cases, he is not sure of what he wants to do for a living.

Later adolescent girls are spared some of the boy's sources of anxiety, but they have other sources. Shall they consider further education or not; shall they get a job, and if so, what; is marriage and children what they want or not. The more thoughtful ones wonder what marriage and parenthood actually involve, and if they really want to restrict themselves by marriage. If they decide they want marriage, they wonder how to go about getting the mate they want, and to whom they can be a good mate.

If the late adolescent decides to get further education, in college, for example, he has to consider what kind of college he is best fitted for. Even students who are well endowed intellectually may experience feelings of anxiety about their adequacy in academic and related social areas. College students who have been leaders in preparatory schools may not have questioned their adequacy before. When, in college groups, they find themselves in the society of people who possibly exceed them in ability and experience, their sensations may be more painful than any they have been accustomed to.

Just how prevalent anxieties are in later adolescence is not known because adequate means have not yet been devised to determine their extent. Most adolescents are anxious to a degree that interferes at times with the normal performance of their work, study, or other activities; some are habitually anxious. Figure 9–1 shows some of the college student's anxieties. One investigator [222] studied anxiety

LOVE AFFAIRS

GRADES

CHOICE OF CAREER

ATHLETIC SUCCESS

MARITAL OR FINANCIAL CONDITIONS (HOME)

FEELINGS OF GUILT

SHYNESS AND SENSITIVITY

EMOTIONAL TENSIONS

Fig. 9–1. College students have anxieties.

in 232 college male students, all of whom were selected for their good physical health, satisfactory academic status, and overtly desirable social adjustments. Seventy-two per cent of these students listed problems that worried them sufficiently to make them want to talk them over with someone. Seventeen per cent listed acute problems,

which included worries about career, emotional instability, tenseness, excitability, love affairs, marriage, and sex relations. Other
worries were connected with financial situations at home, siblings,
parental behavior such as marital quarrels, shyness, sensitivity, and
how to meet and get along with girls. Other studies of college students reveal worries about examinations, athletic ability, money, and
personal appearance.

Some adolescent anxieties stem from feelings of unworthiness or
guilt, because they do not work hard enough, because they do things
parents would not approve of, because they question social mores or
religious doctrines, and for many other reasons. Anxieties such as
these are usually relieved when the adolescent manages to face the
sources squarely, understand them, and adjust to them. Adolescents
often profit by hearing themselves tell their worries to a sympathetic
but objective listener. In doing so, they usually see their situations
in better perspective, which in itself is likely to reduce the importance of the situation.

Jealousy and Envy

Toward the latter part of adolescence, boys and girls begin to pair
off, if they have not already done so. Very frequently, they have
understandings and decide "to go steady." This means that the boy
takes no other girl out for the time being, and the girl accepts no
invitations from other boys. Since they are still learning about
people and various experiences, they are likely to tire of each other's
company, but often one tires before the other does, or one gets
opportunities that are attractive sooner than the other does. At any
rate, jealousy is likely to arise in the one who senses or has evidence
that the "steady" has inclinations in other directions. Jealousy can
occur in both sexes, but is more likely to develop in the girl, since in
most cultures she is expected to be less aggressive in the mate-
seeking process than is the boy.

Jealousy is generally expressed verbally at this age. The later
adolescent may become a master of sarcasm when speaking to the
person who is the cause of his jealousy. When speaking to others
about the person, he is likely to find faults with the individual's personality or character.

If the culture of which he is a part consists of different socioeconomic levels, adolescents may be stimulated to envy by the fact

that others have larger cars or more expensive clothing, or by the fact that others live in larger homes in more select neighborhoods, and so on. Some adolescents make themselves miserable through envy of other people. If they do, they are hard for their families to live with. On the other hand, some more mature late adolescents see the relative superficiality of material possessions and decide that their future is likely to be happier if they make their friends among people who are less concerned by such things.

Happiness and Gaiety

While late adolescence is obviously not the happy, carefree time it is often assumed to be, it nevertheless has its good moments. Between worries, sometimes things do go smoothly. When things are going smoothly for the adolescent, his autonomic nervous system stimulates his other bodily systems and sense organs to optimal activity. As a result, he feels "on top of the world." When things are right, the sky looks unusually blue, the clouds unusually white, the grass unusually green, the birds sing unusually sweetly, and "God's in His heaven, all's right with the world."

Sympathy and Compassion

In early adolescence, boys and girls are still fairly self-centered. There are so many things they have to learn about themselves that considerable concern with self is normal and desirable at that time. The normally developing later adolescent has learned to know himself well enough to begin to be somewhat more concerned with other people than he had been previously. This feeling is so typical that, to some extent at least, later adolescence is characterized by a somewhat naïve desire to be of service, especially in a glamorous way, although often in a genuinely religious way also.

Surveys [209] of the interests of older adolescents indicate that service in social agencies, settlement houses, hospitals, and so on, has a great appeal for them. In this kind of service, some young people see for the first time people less fortunate than they are, physically, financially, and so on. They see how physically ill or handicapped people of various ages react to their conditions, some with cheerfulness and courage and others with less desirable behavior. They discover that various degrees of happiness and of family unity exist in homes in a wide range of socioeconomic levels. They learn that neither desirable nor delinquent behavior is confined to any one level of society.

Some adolescents who get this kind of experience find themselves feeling deeply sympathetic toward others, and for the first time, grateful for their own condition in life. Some find themselves thinking, "There, but for the grace of God, go I," or "How ashamed of myself I ought to be!"

In these and similar experiences, the older adolescent, who does not have too much of the "unfinished business" of childhood and early adolescence still to take care of, begins to develop compassion; that is, fellowship of feeling with others. He begins to find himself able to share all kinds of emotional experiences, joy and grief, anger, fear, anxiety, hope, or despair. As his experience increases, he learns to be compassionate with human beings of a continually widening range of ages and conditions.

INTELLECTUAL STATUS

Growth of Intellect

Investigators are not in complete agreement as to the precise age at which individuals reach their highest level of intellectual growth because it cannot be measured as accurately as physical growth. If a record of an individual's height is kept along with his chronological age, there is no doubt about when he stops growing in stature. Intellectual growth cannot be measured in that way. Standardized tests, however, given to individuals at intervals over a period of years, indicate that the lower the native intelligence, the earlier the ceiling of intellectual growth is reached, and the higher the native intelligence, the longer it takes for the individual to reach his full intellectual stature. For example, children with an ultimate I.Q. of 80 based on the Otis test, reach their highest level of performance at about 12 years of age, children with an I.Q. of 100 reach their highest level between 15 and 16 years of age, and children with an I.Q. of about 130 reach their highest level at about 19. Using certain other tests, investigators have found that intellectual performance reaches its highest level at about 20 years of age.[232]

It seems reasonable from this kind of evidence to conclude that feeble-minded children remain feeble in intellect, and that average and superior-minded children remain so, respectively, unless accidents or illness damage nervous tissue, or a failure to make use of intelligence prevents some of its development. Generally speaking, full intellectual stature is attained by late adolescence. What use is made of intelligence remains to be seen in the years of life that follow. The use to which he puts his intellect determines the individual's degree of wisdom at any given time in his life.

A Critical Period

Later adolescence is a critical period in the use of the intellect. Just as new skills can be learned by the physical body after it has achieved its full growth, and as old physical skills can be improved and refined, so also can new intellectual skills be learned and old ones improved and refined. Few if any individuals, regardless of their level of intelligence, ever learn to do all the various things that they could do, or to think all the thoughts that they could think. Various factors interfere with the development of an individual's potentialities. The most obvious factor is *time*. No individual with average or better than average intelligence can find time in his lifetime to learn all the skills that he could learn, and if he gave all of his time to learning skills he would deprive himself of time to think.

Among other factors that influence the use of intellect is *motivation,* which, in the sense we use it here, may be defined as "the desire to do." For instance, even individuals with relatively low intelligence are motivated to cry when they are hungry, and, depending upon their experiences and degree of intelligence, learn increasingly effective ways of getting their hunger satisfied. An infant born with a defective cerebrum, however, may not be motivated even to cry for food. Children of near-average intelligence, or better, are motivated not only to get their basic needs satisfied but also to learn about themselves and their environment, and to learn various skills. Some children are highly motivated to do well in school and to learn through reading, radio, television, and any other media available. Others are motivated to learn only along the lines of their particular aptitudes. Since, however, so much of most kinds of information is disseminated by way of the printed word, motivation to learn to read is important for all normal people. Even the child who is not interested in reading for itself, but in mechanical things, must read directions for assembling and utilizing mechanical contrivances.

Motivation is so important in the use of the intellect that it has been and is receiving a great deal of study both in human beings and in other animals. As we have seen, basic physiological states themselves motivate us to attempt to achieve *primary goals* such as food, water, air, sleep, and affection. Normal human beings, however, begin to develop *secondary goals* early in life, and often these seem to have relatively little to do with the primary goals that remain with us throughout life.

The secondary goals of childhood, for instance, are typically playthings, bicycles, clothes like other children have, money, freedom to play and to watch television, knowledge beyond the immediate surroundings, and good grades. The secondary goals seem, on the whole, to be the result of a learned need, that of *status,* of having a feeling of importance in one's group.

Motivation for knowledge is not necessarily associated with intelligence or aptitude. Some children of high intelligence are highly motivated to learn. If they learn what their particular school or culture wants them to learn, they receive approval and good grades. If, however, they are not motivated to learn what the school wants them to learn and their learning is in other areas—nature study, for instance, in a school that teaches no nature study—they may receive disapproval and low grades.

A bright child in such a school might recognize and be able to name hundreds of species of insects in his locality, but if he did poorly in spelling, he would be penalized. Whether his low grade in spelling bothered him or not would depend on a number of factors, his siblings' grades, his parents' attitudes, and the degree of satisfaction he derived from his area of superior knowledge and interest.

Children of average intelligence may get high grades in school if they are sufficiently motivated to work hard at what the school assigns, get assignments done on time, and behave so that they cause no one inconvenience. Some of these children gain great satisfaction from their good grades and from the resulting teacher and parental approval. They may also enjoy learning. As a result of these interacting factors, their motivation may continue to be high and will carry them for a considerable distance through increasingly higher levels of learning. Some of these children eventually find a level where, in spite of their motivation, they can no longer perform the requirements. For instance, they may go through elementary and secondary school, college, and find themselves incompetent at the graduate level. Others may find their level of too great difficulty earlier, possibly in the freshman year of college.

Schools and colleges are also familiar with the student whose ability seems to be high according to test scores, but who does not perform in keeping with his apparent ability. These students differ from one to another. Some are motivated to do things that the particular school does not value, such as the insect study mentioned before, and are therefore in a school that is not suitable for them. Others are not motivated to do well in the particular school or college where they are, because the parents selected it for them against their will. Some people have developed such fear of not being "the best" in their group that they perform at a low level or not at all. Still others perform poorly in a subconscious attempt to punish their parents for reasons that they themselves do not know.

Health, both physical and emotional, is another factor that influences the development of an individual's potentialities. In earlier chapters, we have mentioned that the child is typically susceptible to a variety of infections and that his physiology is in the process of stabilizing. Many children, especially in the early grades, contract the typical childhood diseases which often keep them out of school for periods of two or three weeks at a time. In the meantime, their classes are going ahead. Since most children get these diseases, they usually even up over a period of time. If infections are not cleared up, however, secondary conditions such as rheumatic fever may develop, and these may keep children out of regular school for months.

Poor emotional health is even more likely to hamper intellectual development than is poor physical health. Poor emotional health usually expresses itself in behavior that parents and teachers call "nervousness." This can result from many kinds of situations, too much emphasis on grades, excessive jealousy among siblings, worry about parental quarrels, misconceptions about the body and physiological processes, fear of parents or certain teachers, and vague anxiety that prevents concentration on any subject for long enough to understand it.

If for the causes given, or for any other causes, young people feel that they are below their peers in intellectual development or "academics," as it is likely to be called in the United States, they are likely to begin to hate anything to do with school and even to hate reading itself. This feeling, of course, further interferes with their intellectual development and their possibilities for the future.

Whether or not the intellect continues to develop, the later adolescent characteristically uses the intelligence he has in a more realistic manner than he did previously. He tends to accumulate more facts that are relevant to his problems than formerly. He still daydreams, but his dreams are closer to reality. He thinks about practical matters such as a choice of vocation, and the means of obtaining money for his various needs. While some later adolescents plunge into actions without having thought out the possibilities connected with them, others imagine various ways of accomplishing their goals, thus avoiding some possible mistakes by envisioning them ahead of time. The individual who does this is likely to think, "Now, I could do this, or that, or the other. If I did this (or that, or the other), what would the outcome be? What would it mean to me tomorrow? A year from now? Five or ten years from now?"

Selection of Vocation

Among the developmental tasks of adolescence are those of selecting and preparing for an occupation and thus achieving assurance of economic independence. The vocation which the individual chooses has a great deal to do with the structure of his future life, the length of working day, the time of day spent in working, regular or irregular hours, the strenuousness of mental or physical labor, beginning remuneration, possibility of increasing remuneration, possibility of promotion, of greater responsibility, kind of relationships with other people, eventual socioeconomic level, whether or not he will marry, whom he might marry, and where he will live.

Some young people have little choice in the selection of vocation. Economic necessity, for example, may demand that they start to work at the minimum legal age at whatever job happens to be available. If they are sufficiently intelligent and motivated, and if they have enough energy outside of working hours, they may continue some sort of schooling. As a result, they may be able to get jobs better suited to their abilities and aptitudes as time goes on. If they have a level of intelligence suited to the tasks that their beginning job involves, and if they like those jobs, they may be happy at them or something similar throughout life. Society needs people of all levels of intelligence to do its work. The proper sterilization of glassware, for example, does not take a high level of intelligence, but it is absolutely essential to the combating of disease, and it does require conscientiousness on the part of the person in charge of the sterilizing.

The more fortunate young person has some time for selecting and preparing for a vocation. Preparation required varies with the job from short training courses of a few weeks or months, to two-year technical courses, or four-year college courses, or postgraduate work following college. The earlier in life an individual knows what he wants to do and what he is fitted by nature to do, the earlier he can begin to prepare for his vocation.

Adolescents often feel fairly sure that they know what they want to do, but as they learn of new possibilities, they are likely to change their minds. One 17-year-old boy, for example, had been thinking of forestry as a vocation until he visited a state university and learned about hotel administration, which also seemed to fit his ability and interests but which had not before come to his attention as a possibility. Some studies [92] show that adolescents are likely to dream of occupations for which their intellects and aptitudes do not fit them, or for which they lack the money and time necessary for the required training.

Over half of American high school students say that they want to enter the professions: medicine, law, teaching, nursing, and so on. Table 9–1 shows how unrealistic this proportion is when compared with the proportions of workers comprising the current labor force.

Table 9–1
Occupational Distribution of the Labor Force in the
United States in 1957

Professional and technical workers	about 10%
Proprietors, managers, and officials	about 10%
Clerical workers	about 15%
Skilled workers and foremen	about 15%
Unskilled workers	about 50%

SOURCE: Rockefeller Brothers Fund, Special Studies Report V, on Education, *The Pursuit of Excellence: Education and the Future of America.* New York: Doubleday & Co., Inc., 1958.

In countries where schooling is compulsory, some attempt is usually made to help pupils find work for which their inherent qualities and their socioeconomic circumstances fit them. Many high schools in the United States have arrangements for guidance and counseling, through which students may receive help in selecting vocations. These services make available catalogues of vocations and descriptions of jobs. Some of them give tests, the results of which the counselor helps the student to interpret.

On the whole, individuals who select occupations in keeping with their own real interests and abilities are not only more permanently satisfied but are better paid in the long run than are individuals who select occupations for other reasons, such as parental pressure, prestige, and so on.[87] Students are sometimes invited by business and industry to visit establishments where work is in progress, so that they can see what is involved and ask questions about preparation, satisfactions, and so on. The more thoughtful young people also investigate the experiences of others, who having faced similar choices earlier have selected one vocation or another. They do this either by talking among themselves about their parents and other adults whose lives they have been able to observe to a limited extent, or by reading, by discussions with parents, older siblings, teachers, and counselors, by attending conferences, and in any other way that comes to their attention.

There is no substitute for actual experience in working. By doing part-time work or by working during academic vacations, an older adolescent can often clarify his knowledge and feelings about the type of work he thinks he may be interested in. It is usually not easy to get this kind of work on a paid basis. As a result, some young people volunteer their services and achieve similar results in knowledge of the kind of work. Regardless of whether the individual is paid or not, the quality of the recommendations he gets from his employers has an effect on the quality of the job he will get in the future.

In considering a choice of occupation, girls face a situation which is more complicated, in some ways, than that faced by boys. Boys are expected to have an occupation which will be a very important part of their lives. Also, no field of work is completely closed to them. These things are not as universally true for girls. Some fields are closed to them, and in many fields men are more welcome than are women. Further, most girls are interested in marriage, and if so, in most cultural groups their marriage and family are expected to be the most important things in their lives.

Today, however, most girls need or want to be able to earn a living before marriage. In many cases, it seems desirable that the wife continue to earn during marriage, at least until the children come, and very frequently again after the children have grown up to a certain degree of independence.

A special report on *America's Resources of Special Talent* [231] pointed out the need for more women workers generally, and a special need for trained women in the various scientific fields. In the past, girls have not been encouraged to take enough mathematics and science courses in high school to prepare them for further training in science. Currently, however, girls with proven ability are being encouraged to take such courses.

In a nationwide survey in 1958, [210] one-third of the girls 11 to 18 years of age who were studied said that they "planned definitely" to go to college. About 13 per cent of these hoped to enter the professions of medicine or law or some field of science or art. About 50 per cent of them were thinking of the professions which are allied to the traditional feminine role: social work, teaching, and nursing. About 37 per cent of the total sample were interested in jobs that required no further academic training beyond high school.

Potential satisfaction in one's work is probably the most important criterion for selecting an occupation. The chances that any vocation will support the individual throughout his life and support his family also are good if he and his family select a standard of material living in keeping with their income. As we have pointed out earlier, happiness and family unity are found in families of all socioeconomic levels, and the same may be said of unhappiness and family disunity. The happiness of the breadwinner at his job is an important ingredient of family life.

Lifetime earnings and their relation to degree of education in the United States have been listed as follows: [176]

Table 9–2
Average Lifetime Earnings for Different Educational Levels

College graduate	$268,000.00
High school graduate	$165,000.00
Elementary school graduate	$116,000.00

This study concluded that a $10,000 investment in a college education pays back $103,000, the difference between the life earnings of the college and the high school graduate. These figures, of course, are average for men. Some earn more; some less. Women's earnings, to be compared with these figures, would have to be those of full-time workers on a lifetime career basis. The fact remains, however, that some of the happiest people would be found in all three categories, depending partly upon their fitness for their particular jobs and partly on the fitness of their standards of living to their incomes.

A special report on *The Pursuit of Excellence* [176] says:

> There are not enough young people interested in the fields of basic research, of teaching, of overseas assignments for our government. There are countless opportunities ahead for today's youth to participate in what many writers refer to as one of the most exciting eras in history. They can do so, nearly all writers agree, however, only if they learn to value intellectual excellence in whatever they undertake, whether that undertaking is freely chosen or a not-too-well-liked requirement in the preparation for a freely chosen career. The people who share the greatest excitement in vocational or professional life are those who demand the highest type of performance of themselves, who, in other words, have high standards of realization.

The danger in a report such as this one is that young people may misunderstand what is meant by "intellectual excellence." No matter what the level of intelligence, the individual only does his best when he keeps his mind on his job and when he realizes that his part is an important part of the whole, be it cleaning test tubes in the development of a new drug or the development of better international relations. We all have a need to feel pride in our work in order to perform it with intellectual excellence, no matter what its level.

PERSONAL-SOCIAL DEVELOPMENT

Later adolescence has sometimes been referred to as the "last chance" for achieving satisfactory personality adjustment. As long as an individual lives, of course, he still has the opportunity to make himself a pleasanter person for others to live with. It is true, however, that later adolescence and early adulthood offer the last relatively easy opportunities through which individuals can make major adjustments in personality. As we have seen, the longer the nerve impulses keep going over the same synapses, the more difficult it becomes to direct them differently and so to change habits.

Background of Personality

Changes in personality which are accomplished in later adolescence are changes within the personality rather than development of a new personality. An individual who has been quiet and somewhat self-contained during his childhood may learn in adolescence desirable social techniques and come to enjoy practicing them in the process of gaining friends, but he is not likely to become "the life of the party." Likewise, the individual who has been ebullient throughout childhood may, as an adolescent, learn some of the self-restraint needed to make him acceptable to others, but he is not likely to become quiet and reserved.

As we know, we are what we are as a result of the interaction of our heredity and the various environmental factors and experiences that came our way, as a result partly of circumstances and partly of our own initiative. By adolescence, we develop a central *core of personality* which persists throughout our lives, and around which other later-developing, peripheral traits cluster. In much the same way as the individual eliminates unproductive physical movements and unproductive sounds from his speech as he goes through childhood, the adolescent tends to eliminate certain minor personality traits and to strengthen other traits of his personality.

From what we know of neural physiology, it is understandable that the adolescent tends to change his peripheral traits more than his "core" traits. For example, he is less able to change such a core trait as customary optimism than he is to change a peripheral trait such as his manner of speaking loudly or quietly. No matter how seriously the later adolescent views international relations, for example, if he is a habitual optimist, he will still be hopeful of reasonable solutions. At the same time, he may realize that his voice fills the room when he is talking to someone only two feet away, and so he deliberately makes himself talk more quietly.

The older adolescent tries out ways of behaving which he feels may indicate differences in his personality, such as ways of standing, or selection of subjects that he brings into conversations, sometimes seeming to allow himself to be persuaded, and at other times making it seem that he cannot be persuaded to see an issue differently, sometimes having himself seem conventionally religious, and at other times agnostic. And so on.

The normally maturing adolescent is not so much concerned with Hamlet's well-known question, "To be, or not to be," as he is with "What to be?" and "Who to be?" He is clarifying for himself what kind of a person he is and what roles in society he is to play.

Students of human development are agreed that both heredity and environment are influential in shaping personality, but they are not agreed as to how influential each is in the shaping of the adult personality which begins to show clearly in later adolescence. In the 1930's, investigators were in fair agreement that physical development was least modified by environment, intellectual development somewhat more so, and personality development most of all.[160] More recent studies on animals such as horses and dogs shed some doubt upon the concept that environment plays the greater part in personality development.

For the purpose of studying the effects of heredity and environment, twins have proven most useful.[103] Identical twins, the results of the fertilization of one egg by one sperm, have identical heredity. Fraternal twins, resulting from the simultaneous fertilization of two eggs by two sperms, have heredity no more similar than that of any other siblings in the family. If identical twins are reared together, their environment is also likely to be very similar, but if they are reared apart, as adopted twins sometimes are, their heredity remains the same but their environments may be dissimilar. Fraternal twins reared together have dissimilar heredity but similar environment. Whatever the interplay between heredity and environment, the facts remain that, in later adolescence, the personality begins to assume its adult character, and that the individual can do much to modify certain peripheral traits.

Concept of Self

When they stop to think about their nearness to adulthood, some later adolescents become aware of what they consider their "scarred" personalities. Some realize that they have negative attitudes toward people in general, which they may think result from growing up under the domination of an overbearing parent, or because their fathers were absent from the home in connection with war service, business requirements, or marital problems. Some feel that their negative attitudes result from their own mistakes in choosing friends in early adolescence, and so on. It usually helps them to realize that just as no one grows up without a few physical scars, neither do most people attain adulthood without a few emotional scars or personality scars, however they wish to view them. If the individual appraises his personality assets as well as his scars, he is likely to be reassured in his movement toward adulthood.

Clarification of the Sex Role

Later adolescents have been learning some things about their sex roles as they have been growing up. Now in the late teens and early twenties, they are actually facing the major part of their lives when they will be living their sex roles in earnest. Some late adolescents may realize that their concepts of the sex roles are soon to be tested; others are relatively unaware of what will soon be happening, and stumble into the actual living of their roles. If their sex-role concepts were correct, they find themselves relatively well prepared to live their roles, but if their concepts were incorrect they may be in for rude shocks. Still others stumble on through life, never really clarifying for themselves answers to such questions as: what does it mean to be a man or a woman, what is my relationship to my own sex, what is my relationship with the opposite sex, what does it mean to be a son, a husband, a daughter, a wife, a father, a mother, a male member of society, a female member of society.

These concepts have been in the making for a long time, when later adolescence arrives. The boys and girls have learned chiefly from the adults who have been significant in their lives while they have been growing up. The boy, for example, has learned largely from the behavior of his father (and some other male adults) what they show it means to be a son, a husband, a father, in some cases, a bachelor, an employed man, and a male citizen. The boy has also learned what these adult men reveal of their attitudes toward women, and has seen how they behave toward different women: their mothers, their sisters, their daughters, and other women in society.

The girl has developed her concepts similarly from the men and women who have been significant in her life. Both boy and girl modify concepts learned from adults by learning also about what their peers believe the sex roles to be.

It may be obvious, but it seems to need saying that because most adults conceal portions of their actions, thoughts, and feelings from their growing sons and daughters, it is to be expected that boys and girls will enter adulthood with distorted or at least incomplete concepts of manhood and womanhood. Many later adolescent girls in the United States, for instance, have never done the family laundry for a week, and many boys have no idea how much it costs to run the family home for a week. In other areas, they are equally hazy.

As we saw earlier, one aspect of early adolescence is a sort of hero worship for older members of the same sex. This occurs in part because young adolescents are nebulous about what kind of adults they want to be. They, therefore, try out on themselves imitations of adults whose lives strike them as being what they would like theirs to be. As the years pass, they more or less consciously study older adults of their sex to discover patterns of masculine or feminine behavior and attitudes. They often choose parents, teachers, and employers for their models. In one survey of adolescent girls,[209] 80 per cent said that they wanted to be adults like their mothers, other female relatives, or teachers. Only 20 per cent were looking toward other women who represented more typically glamorous types.

As in the selection of vocation, the clarification of the sex role is easier today for boys than it is for girls. On the surface, at least, it is "a man's world," and boys are shown more clearly than are girls what is expected of them as adults. In countries like the United States, it is possible that the male role is not as clear as we have here implied, but since we shall have occasion to refer to this matter again in the chapters on adulthood, we shall leave it for the time being.

A 1951 study [54] has hypothesized that girls growing up today face new situations and have new expectations, in preparing for which they can find little or no guidance either in traditional folk mores or in their formal education. For this study, 300 typical adolescent girls in the United States were given a number of standardized tests in an endeavor to learn about their inner worlds, how they felt about themselves and their ways of living, and what they believed, fantasied, and expected.

The study revealed confusion on the part of the girls as they face changing masculine and feminine roles in family and adult life in general. The girl of today not only has to do the growing up common to all adolescents, but she must also clarify a role that is shifting even while she tries to focus on it. In addition, each socioeconomic group and each ethnic-cultural group passes on its traditional beliefs and patterns along with its characteristic defenses and reassurances. Some of these are adequate for the maturing girl, some are not. For example, an immigrant family in the United States may send their bright daughter through high school, but disapprove of college for her. The school guidance counselor and her peers disapprove of her concluding her formal education. She is confused and disturbed because she feels she must be loyal to her family, must develop her own potential, and must fulfill the expectations of the society of which she is a part. The study of the 300 girls concluded that personality problems and emotional disturbances tend to develop for each girl as she meets the often-conflicting demands of her particular subculture and of the broader culture of which it is a part.

Heterosexual Adjustment

Among the developmental tasks of this period of life, is preparing for marriage and family life, or for acceptance of the single life if this proves necessary. To some extent this task presents the late adolescent with his most difficult decision, to marry or not to marry. This is an especially difficult decision because, in most countries of the world today, monogamous marriage (one man to one woman as long as they both live) is the only legal kind of life in which natural heterosexual relationships can be maintained. According to law, the individual must either marry or channel in some other direction the energy that would normally go into sexual activity. As we pointed out earlier, however, some adolescents do engage in masturbation and homosexual as well as premarital heterosexual activities.

During early and late adolescence, most boys and girls "ease into" heterosexual relationships to some extent, as we have seen in group dating followed by single dating. In this manner, the younger adolescents gain some experience with the opposite sex in situations which protect them by the usual recreational activity and lack of privacy for any particular couple. By permitting this sort of safe social mingling of the young of both sexes, adults seem to hope that the boys and girls will gain enough experience by the time they begin single dating to manage their relationships with skill.

Experiences in dates may have deep and lasting significance in establishing general attitudes and feelings toward the opposite sex. Much depends upon the already partially formed concept of what it means to be a male and what it means to be a female. Some girls, for instance, are disappointed if a boy doesn't kiss them on the first date. Others are horrified if he does. Boys sometimes ask adults what they are supposed to do. As one 18-year-old boy said, "Girls fix themselves all up and act so that you sure want to kiss 'em, and then they slap your face if you do." When we tell girls this, some act as if they just don't understand what that boy could mean.

One factor which makes heterosexual adjustment in contemporary society difficult is the fact that the individual achieves physical maturity some years before he and she achieves sufficient emotional, intellectual, and financial maturity to be trusted with the full use of their physically mature bodies.

The restriction on the use of sexual capabilities is unique in the young person's life. In every other area of his being, physical, emotional, social, and intellectual, he is constantly encouraged to put his capabilities to full use. In the physical area, he is constantly encouraged to develop his body. In the emotional area, he is taught to control his anger but that some situations properly provoke his anger, to control his fears, but that some situations had better arouse his fear, to control his social contacts but certainly to develop desirable ones, to develop his intellect to its highest potential. But in the sexual area, he is supposed to do nothing until he is married.

It stands to reason that adolescents and even adults make mistakes in this area. The mistakes they make here have more serious results in terms of later life than do mistakes in most other areas. Unwanted pregnancies and venereal disease are probably the direct reasons for many of the cultural mores about sex. The cultural mores, however, themselves cause what may be the most serious result of a mistake in this area: the resulting damage to the individual's self-respect. The pregnancy will terminate, and the unwanted baby may be wanted by people who can give him a good home, the venereal disease can be cured if treated soon enough, but the wounds of self-respect are much more difficult to heal under the best of circumstances. Society, however, does not often provide the best of circumstances. In some cultures, of course, an unwed mother does not lose status, in that she proves by her pregnancy that she is fertile.

Adolescents are concerned about achieving heterosexual adjustment that will work to their greatest benefit in the long run. They are concerned about such problems as how much intimacy to permit on a date, "going too far," the "right" attitude about sex, and other similar matters. Every new date involves speculation on the part of each of the two people about the kind of behavior the other will expect.

Kinsey [106, 107] reported that, among the 8,000 women that he and his associates studied, of those married, nearly 50 per cent had had premarital coitus (sexual intercourse). The incidence of premarital coitus in the 12,000 men studied differed with their final educational level; that is, of the men who went to college, 67 per cent had premarital coitus; of those who went to high school but not beyond, 84 per cent had; and of those who did not go beyond elementary school, 98 per cent had.

While there is no question about the difficulty in the heterosexual area, young people who have been accustomed throughout their lives to thinking things through at the highest level of their ability and to regulating their lives with some regard for long-range values seem to manage in this area just as well as they do in others. Those who, like our Child B of Chapter 8, never have the chance to think their problems through independently and to take the responsibility of disciplining themselves, may have more difficulty.

Boys like this one often say that sexual abstinence is unnatural and unhealthy, and that they must have relief. They sometimes manage to persuade their girl friends also that this is so. While undoubtedly they are correct in that continual restraint from heterosexual activity is unnatural, evidence that it is universally unhealthy is so far not available. Married couples separated by war did in many cases abstain from coitus without apparent ill effects. They experienced discomfort, and in some cases resorted to less satisfactory forms of sexual activity such as masturbation, but many were able to resume natural heterosexual activity on their return to normal married life.

Young people who have their future in mind and who accept long preparation for a profession and the establishment of reasonable financial security before marriage, would seem to have a more serious problem than those who have no elaborate plans for the future. Kinsey's figures, however, do not bear this out, since a much higher percentage of those with the least education had premarital coitus than of those who went to college. It must be remembered that both sexes are involved in coitus, and the attitudes of the girls are as influential as those of the boys on the incidence of premarital activities.

Understanding why they feel the way they do probably helps

later adolescents as much as anything can. One study [13] of the physiological control of mating in mammals concluded that, with increasing evolutionary complexity, the sex hormones become less and less influential in the arousal of sexual behavior and the activity of the cerebral cortex becomes more and more influential. Human beings, high in the evolutionary scale, are more influenced than are other mammals by such cerebral stimuli as sensations, personal habits, and responses to social and cultural mores. A man, for instance, may be sexually stimulated by a whiff of perfume and sexually inhibited by being in church. A woman may be aroused by a touch and inhibited by wanting to protect her hair-do.

Mature love is a way of behaving between two people of opposite sex. A love relationship exists when a man and woman behave toward each other in a way that demonstrates that they know, care for, respect, and feel responsibility for each other. It is difficult for young people to know when they are developing that kind of love. The physical expression of affection is such a natural thing that it can easily mislead them. They may get further into sexual intimacy than they intend to if they are not familiar with the physiology of the sexual mechanisms. Nerve endings in the skin, especially in the erogenous * zones of the body: the lips, tongue, finger tips, breasts, and primary sex organs, under certain psychological conditions are easily stimulated. Their stimulation results in pleasurable sensations, which in turn stimulate some of the nerves of the autonomic nervous system, which innervate many parts of the body. This stimulation arouses both man and woman in preparation for coitus.

Students often ask questions about petting without making clear exactly what they mean by the term. Petting may be defined as any activity, usually involving physical contact, which arouses the sex organs, but students also seem to restrict the term to premarital activity. They need to realize that petting is normal and desirable throughout married life.

If unmarried people are aware of their increasing sexual arousal in a petting situation, they can understand what is happening in themselves and each other, and are equipped to govern their subsequent behavior accordingly. Talking about it at the time helps. It takes energy to think and to talk, and so some energy is directed away from the primary sex organs and to the cerebrum. Boys gen-

* Greek, *Eros*, "the god of love" and *genes*, "producing."

erally react more quickly to sexual stimulation than do girls. Consideration for the feelings of each other is, we know, an indication of maturing personality, and the lack of such consideration under the guise of passion is an indication of continuing adolescent behavior rather than emerging adulthood.

While premarital coitus has little if anything to recommend it as far as preparing men and women for their future life, either married or single, habits of satisfying each other by petting short of actual coitus carry some hazards also. Throughout this book we have stressed the neural basis of habit formation, and it is appropriate to mention it again. If habits are established over too long a period of time, over several years of engagement, for example, they can become more or less arrested at that level, so that, in marriage, the couple has difficulty in achieving satisfaction in complete sexual activity. What probably occurs in some of these cases is that, once the couple marry, they fail to engage in the same amount or kind of petting they had become accustomed to premaritally, and in attempting to have coitus without preliminary activity, they fail to achieve satisfaction. Married people need preliminary petting just as much as they felt they did when unmarried.[203]

Marriage relations are most complete when sexual activity is part of a deep and enduring love between man and wife. If young people make a practice of petting as a more or less casual part of dating, they may develop habits of physical arousal and release which have no association with love as a psychological experience between them. A preinduction booklet[211] for military personnel says, "A loveless intimacy which disassociates tenderness, respect, and admiration from the physical expression of sex, cheapens the individual and sometimes impairs the normal expression of sexual feeling."

Earlier in this chapter, we mentioned the possibility of the single life. It is true that some people of both sexes actually prefer the single life. It is also true, however, that many who would prefer the married life do not marry, for one reason or another. In addition there are many who marry young and are widowed, separated, or divorced early in life, and so live single lives after all. These people have sex drives also, although the strength of the drive varies greatly among individuals. They have to work out adjustments just as adolescents do, but theirs have to work longer. It is rarely possible to dam up sexual desire completely.

Individual Differences

We know that, in spite of cultural taboos, many people from childhood on through adulthood engage in sexual activity outside of marriage. Kinsey's records [106, 107] indicate the existence of a wide range in sexual capacity, in speed of arousal, in vigor of response, and in strength of sensation. At one extreme are members of both sexes who are quickly and highly responsive in sexual situations. These people, at times, may be preoccupied with sex to the point that they find it difficult to attend to other aspects of living. Some people, at the other extreme, are not easily aroused, and rarely if ever find themselves preoccupied with sexual thoughts or feelings. As in all other traits, most people fall between the extremes. It is reasonable to assume that psychological conditioning is strongly influential in modifying sexual desire. Children can be helped on the one hand to achieve some control over strong sexual feelings as well as over anger or fear; they can also be helped to develop appreciation of and means of expressing sexual feelings as well as of other feelings in creative activities of various kinds.

DEVELOPMENT OF VALUES

Factors Involved

In discussing the development of values at the later childhood level, we pointed out that the system of values which people eventually embrace as their own is dependent partly upon their inherent intelligence and partly upon their experiences in the culture or cultures in which they grow up. We have seen that between later childhood and later adolescence, physical and intellectual development reach their adult levels. By late adolescence, the typical individual tends to be somewhat seriously concerned with the development of his ideals, with clarifying his religious concepts, and with developing his own moral and ethical concepts.

Ideals, here, mean standards of excellence, as an all-around human being, as an expert professional of some kind, or as a glamour girl, but excellence, in any case. Religious concepts refer to the individual's beliefs in what binds the spiritual nature of man to some power beyond his own. The term "moral" is derived from the same Latin word, *mos,* the plural of which gives us "mores," defined in Chapter 3 as the manners and morals of a culture. Moral concepts are rules to which the members of a culture have become accustomed over a period of time. Ethical concepts are more inclusive than are moral concepts in that they apply to human conduct generally, rather than to that of any particular culture. They tend to disregard minor matters, such as whether or not one is expected to wear a hat, which the mores do concern themselves with. Also, a thief might consider his behavior "moral" if he is loyal to the gang of which he is a member, but this behavior could hardly be considered "ethical."

We have seen some of the difficulties involved in other aspects of adolescent development. In addition to these, what the adolescent observes in the everyday religious, moral, and ethical behavior of the adult life around him definitely affects his values. On the whole, adolescents tend to adopt the values and the conduct with which they are most familiar, without inquiring very deeply into what they really mean. Thus, adolescents growing up among people who value healthful habits of living, honesty, and so on, adopt these values themselves, and adolescents growing up among people who value pleasure for the present without regard to the future, cheating, and so on, adopt these values.

Most adolescents tend to accept values and to behave in ways that are most expedient. Just as most adults do, they often reveal substantial differences between the religious, moral, and ethical principles to which they give lip service and their actual behavior. Intelligence plays a part in the selection of values, but it results in different selections in different individuals. For example, an adolescent of superior intelligence may recognize the restrictedness of the values held by his family and adopt a different set for himself, whereas an equally intelligent young man may decide deliberately to follow his father in a life of shrewd, "just-under-the-line" business dealings.

Conscience

The development of a functional conscience is involved in the development of values for adult living. As a rule, the conscience of later adolescents either develops, or is arrested at an immature level, depending upon its development during childhood. If the individual has grown through his childhood and adolescence in an atmosphere of learning, with the concept that

> New occasions teach new duties
> Time makes ancient good uncouth *

he can see situations in better perspective and from more different viewpoints than he could formerly. As a result, he can form more adequate judgments, and in some cases but not in all, can expand his conscience. If, on the other hand, he has not been in the habit of learning different ways of looking at the same situation, his conscience may set firmly at an early age. For example, a child may grow up in a home where the parents and their friends make moderate use of alcoholic beverages. During his childhood, he learns that these beverages, like coffee, are not for him. However, he is now and then allowed to have very diluted drinks, less diluted as he reaches late adolescence. In this way, he learns from listening to and watching others and more recently from his own experience that alcohol affects the nervous system. At the same time, his judgment is developing and his conscience is setting up regulations about the use of alcoholic beverages that are acceptable to him and, hopefully, to society.

In contrast, a child may grow up in a home where no alcoholic beverages are served and where the parents believe the use of such beverages to be sinful. He sees advertising of beer and wine on television, he reads about alcoholic drinks, he hears his peers talk about drinks, he eventually sees people whom he knows drinking, and he is confused and bothered. His conscience hurts when he thinks about drinking, but in his mind he wonders why. Some children, reared like this, crystallize their consciences as their parents did earlier. Others, in spite of, or perhaps partly because of their painful consciences, drink too much for their good.

In such matters as smoking, drinking, cheating, and sexual behavior, adolescents vary widely. One 17-year-old boy says, "I gave up smoking at 12," while another says he has never smoked yet. One poll of 3,000 high school students in the United States [173] disclosed that "nearly all teenagers said they disapprove of high school students drinking . . . but a quarter of them admit they drink. More than three-quarters of them disapprove of smoking, but 38 per cent smoke." The investigator in this study concluded that a teenage

* James Russell Lowell, "The Present Crisis," 1844.

girl summed the situation up when she stated: "It's hard for a teenager to say, 'I don't care to' when all the rest of the gang are saying, 'Aw, come on.'" This problem of the adolescent sheds some light on juvenile delinquency, especially when we recall the adolescent's need to be an accepted member of a group.

Delinquency

Delinquency is talked and written about a great deal, but is seldom defined. In this book, so far, we have followed development from before birth to early adulthood, and we have assumed that normal people are born with the aptitude to become responsible, independent individuals who abide by the tested rules for living in society and eventually help to regulate the rules as times change. When a person's behavior over a period of time is such that it is damaging to individuals or to property, he is said to be delinquent. *Juvenile delinquency* is usually limited to the unlawful behavior of people under the age of 21 years.

Why do some people become delinquent? Obviously there is no one clear-cut reason. Delinquents are of both sexes, they vary in intelligence, and they come from all socioeconomic levels. In some families, all the children are delinquent, but in other families, one child is delinquent and the others are not. Studies of delinquents show that these individuals have certain concepts about themselves in relation to other people. These include feelings of being not wanted, of lack of acceptance, of being a disappointment to parents, of wanting to get even, of being continually thwarted, and so on. Glueck and Glueck [70] point out that delinquent behavior is one way of adjusting to a continually miserable situation. It is not a satisfactory way, but Kuhlen and Thompson [114] suggest that it may be healthier for an adolescent to join in with a delinquent crowd than to be a withdrawing "mother's boy" or to mope at home living a life of fantasy. However, not all adolescents with the troubles typical of the delinquents become either delinquent, "mother's boys," or live fantasy lives. Most of them have enough drive to regulate their own environments so that they can live normal lives. What we know of delinquency, however, can make us aware of how important it is for children to be born only into homes where an adult man and woman have achieved sufficient maturity to care for themselves and for their children.

The normally maturing older adolescent develops a set of concepts and values which provide him with strength and inspiration to enter adulthood. His concepts change as his experience increases and as he meets more people, but they continue to permit him to go steadily on his way without being jostled off his course.

SUGGESTIONS FOR FURTHER DISCUSSION

1. Think of various young persons you know who are now in their late twenties and who:
   a. Left school at the earliest leaving age.
   b. Got married in high school.
   c. Married when the girl was a freshman in college.
   d. Were engaged in college but got married only after both were graduated.
What is the life of each of these like now?

2. In the analogy about paddling one's own canoe down the stream of life what do you think is meant by:
   a. The quiet waters?
   b. Using the currents in order to make good progress?
   c. The dangerous rapids?
   d. The high waterfalls?
   e. Portaging around the waterfalls?
   f. Having one's gear well enough packed to withstand capsizing?

3. What do you think are the main differences in viewpoint today between your generation and that of your parents? Ask some members of your parents' generation what they think these differences are. Compare the two, and state your conclusions.

4. Discuss the effect of habitual cheating in academic work upon: future vocational adequacy, and upon ultimate strength or weakness of the personality.

5. How can some knowledge of the anatomy and physiology of sex in the human being help the older adolescent?

6. As you know older adolescents, what do you consider to be:
   a. Their most pressing anxieties?
   b. Their greatest satisfactions?
   c. Their attitudes toward working for the future versus living in the present?
   d. Their attitude toward religion?

REFERENCES FOR FURTHER STUDY

CROW, L. D., and CROW, A. *Adolescent Development and Adjustment.* New York: McGraw-Hill Book Co., Inc., 1956. Ch. 7, personal and social aspects of personality development; Ch. 9, sex behavior of adolescents; Ch. 16, vocational adjustment of adolescents.

JERSILD, A. T. *The Psychology of Adolescence.* New York: The Macmillan Co., 1957. Ch. 12, the adolescent and his peers; Ch. 13, heterosexual development; Ch. 15, vocational development; Ch. 16, the adolescent and his religion.

LANE, H., and BEAUCHAMP, M. *Understanding Human Development.* Englewood Cliffs, N.J.: Prentice-Hall, Inc., 1959. Ch. 13, the adolescent–young adult: achieving independence from home; establishing heterosexuality; achieving means for economic independence.

SEIDMAN, J. M. *The Adolescent: A Book of Readings.* New York: Holt, Rinehart & Winston, Inc., 1953. Selection 7, problems of normal college students and their families; Selection 23, the religion of the postwar college student; Selection 42, the sex information of younger boys; Selection 43, how to be a woman; Selection 44, dating behavior of college students; Selection 45, a slum sex code; Selection 50, anxiety in the college classroom; Selection 60, psychological counselling of college students.

THORPE, L. P., and CRUZE, W. W. *Developmental Psychology.* New York: The Ronald Press Co., 1956. Ch. 12, psychosexual development. Summarizes development up to and through adolescence; discusses sex-education methods.

For film suggestions see Film Supplement, in the Appendix.

CHAPTER 10

Achieving Personal Maturity

General Maturity

In the last six chapters we have been discussing growth, from birth through adolescence. In each chapter, growth has been traced in the physical, intellectual, personal-social, and to some degree, in the spiritual areas. Physical maturity is generally achieved when the individual reaches his adult height and weight and when his various systems have arrived at an adult level of development and function. We have seen that this development goes on for about one-fifth of the life span. Intellectual maturity is conceived of as not only speed and accuracy in sense perceptions and speed and comprehension in dealing with language, but also as the possession of knowledge. Perhaps most important in adulthood, intellectual growth consists of the ability to select and use knowledge to make it a force in the continuing development of the personality. Such intellectual development may go on for a good part of the life span. Personal-social maturing, as it reveals itself in the achievement of smooth, superficial social relationships, can develop to maturity fairly early in late adolescence or early adulthood. The development of a deep understanding of people, including oneself, and of a capacity for rich interpersonal relationships goes on or can go on well into middle age. Spiritual maturing, according to most religious faiths, may go on throughout life.

Personal-Social and Emotional Maturity

Much has been written in both popular and professional literature about the meaning of this type of maturity. Many points of view have been expressed and many definitions of "the mature personality" have been given. There has been general agreement, however, that parent-child relationships in the early childhood years play a fundamental role in laying the foundations of personality and in determining whether the individual's personality growth will be arrested at the childhood level or have the impetus to continue growing with the years.

In the professional literature,[19] there is a strong implication that an inner psychological constitution, based upon physiological factors, is one of the important determining elements in any given individual's personality make-up. It is of special significance in determining the strength of emotions and, therefore, the control of emotions. Both professional and popular literature emphasize the necessity for each individual to keep evaluating himself as a personality and to initiate within himself the drive toward eliminating less mature in favor of more mature habits and characteristics.

The very use of the word "maturity" or "maturing" implies growth. Gesell [65] has clarified what is meant by "maturity": "Maturity ceases to be a mystical concept when we use it to define the orderly sequence of behavior growth." In this chapter, we shall discuss some of the basic principles concerned and trace some of the patterns of development in personal-social and emotional growth toward maturity. These patterns do not appear to be as definite in sequence as are patterns of physical or of intellectual development. "Personality," Fosdick states,[52] "is not like a structure but more like a river for it continuously flows, and to be a person is to be engaged in a perpetual process of becoming." Personality grows in many ways, going through different stages in different people before it arrives at a satisfactory functional level.

Maturity is a relative term. Every individual is more mature in some personality areas than in others; no person is completely mature in all areas. There are, however, general levels of maturity below which no individual can function adequately. The effective individual, for example, is not constantly battling his impulses. He has come into sufficient harmony with them to be free to love, work, rest, and in other ways live fully. He has an inner assurance about himself and his relationships with others which makes it possible for him to express his drives constructively, using them for fulfillment of his own life and the lives of others. He has a perspective on life which permits him to let things happen, being able to make the most of what he has and what comes to him.

GROWTH IN UNDERSTANDING REALITY

One of the basic aspects of maturity is the achievement of an ability to understand and accept reality. What the individual believes to be true or not true, worth while or not worth while, plays a fundamental role in the determination of his behavior. We have seen the child's difficulty in understanding the difference between what is real and what he thinks of as being real. Having seen the play *Peter Pan* on television, for example, he may try to jump off some high place in an attempt to fly. Fortunately, most children do not try this from too high an altitude, hence are not seriously injured in coming to grips with the reality of the law of gravity. Once convinced that this law is a basic one and that Peter Pan did not fly without mechanical assistance, he probably will not again attempt to defy this law.

Most of the principles which govern human behavior, however, are not as clear as are the law of gravity and other laws of the physical world. Civil law is fairly clear. Most children are brought up to understand and respect at least the parts of it that operate in daily living. The "laws" of social convention are often not clear and in some situations seem confusing. They vary somewhat from culture to culture, even from family to family, and they change from generation to generation. They can be modified if enough individuals in any group agree to modify them. It is evident even to a casual observer that what any given individual accepts or rejects of his group social code modifies his behavior and consequently his adjustment to his group.

Acceptance of Basic Principles

Certain broad basic principles, however, govern human relationships. Even the gang-aged child learns that disagreeable, self-centered behavior drives people away from him, whereas pleasant consideration of others draws people toward him. In the long run, certain principles of loving and serving other people, of overcoming selfishness and other self-centered behavior, of tempering present behavior so that its consequences will serve long-range purposes, have been found to work well and have been passed on from generation to generation. Each world religion contains certain principles which have been found to benefit the individual and the group, breach of which has been found to be disastrous to the individual and to the group. One of the tests of maturity is the ability to grasp the basic principles which have been found to govern the long-range welfare of the human species, and to live with these principles in such a way that both the present and the future of the individual and of the species will best be served.

Believing What Is True

Whether the reality to be grasped, understood, and lived with is physical, intellectual, or spiritual, the mature individual eventually learns not only to believe what seems to be true, but also not to believe what becomes obviously not true. Failure in either of these directions interferes with effectiveness in living. It creates confusion in interpersonal relationships, causing misunderstandings and unnecessary deadlocks, and causes the misguided individual to make inappropriate emotional responses.

If the individual believes things that are not true, he acts as if they are true. For example, the paranoiac who falsely believes that someone is trying to harm or even to kill him is not only continually suspicious, but may even kill the person he suspects of intending to harm him. The schizophrenic who has false beliefs about himself and his abilities is so ill that he becomes totally unable to deal with life. Short of these conditions, many people who function as reasonably effective individuals believe many things that are not true, are ridden by superstitions, are continually distrustful of the motives of others, or are naïvely trustful of some even in the face of contrary evidence. Almost no one is entirely free of false beliefs, such as false beliefs about how the human body works or about what people from other countries are like. The mature person, however, gives up false beliefs with the knowledge and acceptance of facts.

Perhaps less disastrous to effective living than false beliefs, but still an interference with comfortable living, is the failure to understand and accept facts and principles which are basic to human living. This understanding and acceptance takes time, and comes about by a gradual process of growth. The young child, for example, accepts parental guidance of his behavior because he accepts his parents, and also because he senses that he is not old enough to judge for himself.[9] Gradually, however, he questions the dictates of his parents, tempering his behavior at least to some degree as he encounters opposing ideas about how to behave. The adolescent, because of his need to "grow up" and to judge everything for himself, sometimes tries to throw away most of the standards which have previously governed his life. If he does this, one reality he has failed to appreciate is the fact of his own inexperience in contrast to the greater experience of his parents and of past generations.

It is one thing for an adolescent to doubt, question, and weigh basic principles. It is another, if he casts them aside simply because he did not himself create them. If he does cast aside many of the basic time-tested principles, he demonstrates that he is not maturing even at an adolescent level. If, however, he can appreciate his own inexperience, he will doubt his parents' precepts, question them, investigate other ideas, and even try out some of them. Eventually, he develops a renewed insight into most of the ideas and principles concerned, sees them for what they mean, and hence becomes able to appreciate and to use them effectively.

Truth, Pleasant and Unpleasant

It is usually easy enough to believe and to accept the things in life that are pleasant; it is difficult to accept those that are not pleasant. "Wishful thinking," in which we believe what we want to believe and refuse to believe what we do not want to believe, is one of the marks of an immature personality. Unless the individual can face the unpleasant as well as the pleasant aspects of life, he exerts much effort in attempts to evade or to rationalize situations which, with better objectivity, he might change. Strangely enough, because of their inner confusion, some people are unable to grasp and to appreciate even the pleasant possibilities. They may, for example, even fail to appreciate the kindness and love of family and friends and in so doing lose much of the savor of personal happiness.

The maturing student attempts to understand and to adjust to life as it is, with joy and sorrow, success and failure, cooperation and conflict, generosity and selfishness, wealth and poverty, good and evil. As his insights deepen and his understanding broadens, his knowledge and strength grow. Unless his mind has been closed by indoctrination of a sort that precludes questioning, he moves from childhood's limited ideas and interpretations to a philosophy which accepts life and learns to live reasonably happily with it.

LEARNING TO LIVE WITH OUR EMOTIONS

General Principles

One of the most difficult of realities to be lived with is the fact that we have emotions, both constructive and destructive. Learning to live in a mature manner with emotion may be helped by some knowledge of how emotion is aroused and expressed. The physiological phenomena associated with emotions are pervasive, and under conditions of intense emotion or excitement are likely to be so intense that the individual has little or no control over them. They result from the action of the suprarenal glands of the endocrine system and of the sympathetic branches of the autonomic nervous system. Such phenomena include accelerated heartbeat and breathing; increased blood supply to the skeletal muscles; reduced blood supply to the digestive tract; release of reserve food from the tissues, providing an increased energy; control of behavior by the brain stem; and a temporary reduction of cerebral activity. These physiological changes prepare the body for instant, vigorous physical action.[138]

These reactions are associated with basic needs such as those for food, warmth, and protection from danger, the need to preserve the species, the need to be loved and appreciated, and the need to express inner capacities. Whenever basic needs arise, motivation to satisfy them follows. Strongly motivated behavior is emotional behavior. Many of the physiological accompaniments of emotion described above were necessary in primitive conditions for the immediate survival of the individual and, therefore, of the species.

Our existence today is not endangered in the same way as was existence in primitive times. Therefore, today's living requires a modification of the original responses, when emotion is aroused. Only in infancy are we permitted to express emotion in an uninhibited fashion. As we grow physically, we must also grow emotionally. We do this by gradually changing our responses to certain stimuli.

The young infant reacts emotionally only to broad, general stimulation. His expression is a general bodily activity lacking specific responses to specific stimuli. In later infancy he learns to react with specific emotions such as fear, anger, or love to more specific stimuli. For example, he becomes angry or frustrated when his physical movements are inhibited. In early childhood, he reacts still more selectively. He is afraid of the dark or of a dog, he is angry when a favorite toy is broken, or when he is forbidden to do something he wants to do. In middle and later childhood specific fears increase, and causes for anger, fear, or other emotion become associated more with the individual's own particular background and feelings.

In achieving emotional maturity, then, the individual learns to be increasingly selective of the stimuli to which he reacts emotionally. He learns, also, to be increasingly mature in his emotional responses, to ignore many of the trivial stimuli that aroused him in childhood. Whereas the young child is angered by not immediately getting what he wants, the emotionally mature adult learns to channel emotional energy into working for what he wants.

Maturing in emotional reactions involves both the nature of the reaction and its timing. The immature person tends to react immediately and explosively, without control. The mature person ignores trivial irritations or minor dangers, and restrains the reaction for an appropriate time and place. For example, a child does something requiring correction, and his emotionally immature father "bawls him out" before other people. A mature father would wait for an appropriate time to point out the error and discuss how it can be avoided in the future.

We see, then, that the maturing individual modifies his emotional reactions in two ways. First, reactions to many stimuli which arouse emotion in childhood are given up in favor of reactions only to stimuli that are appropriate for adulthood. Second, the form of the reactions is also modified so that control is achieved, and the reaction becomes one which anticipates long-range well-being and fulfillment. Becoming civilized means doing away with reactions to certain stimuli and replacing them with more subtle, constructive reactions. The culture controls the form of the emotional reaction in the sense that it determines largely what forms of expression are "permitted," the permitted forms in general being those conducive to well-being and happiness of individuals and of groups.

Part of the process of maturing is learning to overcome obstacles to the fulfillment of reasonable and desirable goals. We learn to wait, to resist immediate responses, and to mobilize the inner tensions which arise when we want something but cannot have it immediately. Thus we discover how to channel emotional drives into creative activity instead of allowing them to explode into useless or destructive behavior. We learn how to harness emotional drive so that it can work toward more worthy objectives.

Constructive and Destructive Emotions

Many people, in reading about emotional maturity, come to the conclusion that emotion of any kind is "childish," that the mature person has somehow arrived at a stage where he not only does not express emotion but feels none. This misunderstanding probably comes from the emphasis placed upon the danger of explosive and uncontrolled emotion, whether it be anger, fear, sexual drive, hatred, greed, envy, jealousy, enthusiasm, or even love. The necessity for control of the intensity of emotional reaction and of the manner of expression has been taught as one of the bases for sane, effective, and happy living. However, our controlling the emotions does not mean that we extinguish them, because emotions are basic to living. They provide motivation, inspiration, and concentrated dynamic drive for most of the worth-while work of the world.

There is an obvious distinction between the "dangerous" or negative emotions such as rage, anger, hate, greed, envy, jealousy, lust, and most fear, and the constructive, "full-of-grace" positive emotions such as affection, sympathy, joy, enthusiasm, fellowship, and fear which induces appropriate caution. The general assumption is that an emotion is categorized as negative because time has proved it to be destructive to the well-being and happiness either of individuals or the human species, though generally of both. In contrast, the positive emotions, if properly expressed, are conducive to well-being and happiness of individuals and of the human species.

Learning To Work and To Wait

Fortunately for the learning process, there is genuine satisfaction to be found in accomplishing the successive steps of growth. Both children and adults find much more satisfaction in the fulfillment of goals for which they have exerted continuous effort than they do in achieving goals with little or no effort. As a rule, more difficult objectives, once accomplished, bring deeper satisfaction, better rewards in money and in social approval, and they offer more adventure and more creative outlet. In helping young children to experience this type of growth, adults work along with them so that they learn to extend their attention span, and praise them for continually increased production as they achieve this. Older children win rewards for study in school grades, in recognition for superior skill in sports, in praise and awards for jobs well done. Adolescents gain recognition for superior accomplishments of various kinds. Adults reap satisfaction in human relationships, salary increments, security in position, and respect or prestige in the community. As the years proceed, individuals who have experienced these satisfactions along the way become increasingly able to work patiently for the achievement of their major goals.

Maturing in Anger and Frustration

Growth in maturity of anger reactions, as does increasing maturity in other emotional reactions, comes through a continuing substitution of stimuli to which the individual responds with anger. The infant or toddler is likely to be made angry by restrictions of bodily movement, by slight physical discomforts, by having to wait for what he wants, or by lack of attention. He reacts by being angry all over, kicking, thrashing, and screaming. He is likely to throw objects or himself down on the floor in a tantrum, or to hurt an animal, another child, or even attempt to hurt an offending adult.

The young child is learning some specificity in stimuli, and variations in form of response. He becomes angry at hard-to-handle toys or other objects, at having to change what he is doing, at failure to be understood when he tries to talk but is not yet fluent, and like the infant, when he cannot have his own way. As early childhood advances, verbal and other social stimuli and responses are added to the almost entirely physical stimuli and responses of infancy. At three and four years, he learns to use language in addition to physical violence to express anger. He calls names, is sarcastic, makes cutting remarks, and tattles. Language is useful not only for expression of emotion but also as a means of learning from explanations made about taking turns with toys. Through explanations and experience, the child learns better ways of getting along with others and has fewer occasions for being angry. When he wants something, he learns to ask for it instead of grabbing it. By age five, much of the physical reaction has come under reasonable control, although boys continue to fight at times. Continuation of temper tantrums beyond this age indicates a failure to take an important step in the maturing of anger responses.

In the later childhood period insults become as potent sources of anger as physical attack was earlier. To the gang-age child, unfairness, dishonesty, cruelty to younger children, and other such things stimulate anger. He regards these as situations which require his effort to correct. Quarrels will increase as group play increases, but the child who explodes into violent anger during a quarrel soon loses the respect of his peers. An important lesson of the gang is learning to maintain close personal relationships without quarreling. By seven or eight years of age, attempts to submerge physical and even verbal anger take the child into a stage of pouting or leaving the game as a way of expressing anger. The "hurt feelings" technique for expressing anger and for attempting to force others to one's will is sometimes employed to bring parents into surrender, but fortunately it seldom works in the gang and hence tends to be left behind in time. The child gradually learns to accept frustration of desires and to modify his behavior when frustrated.

In adolescence, personal insults are still potent stimuli for anger. Increasingly, the adolescent comes to feel the importance of the needs and rights of others and to be stimulated to a sense of indignation when he sees these rights and needs abused. When angry, he may still allow his tongue to run away with him. He may indulge in gossip, backbiting, name-calling, irony and sarcasm, but if he is maturing, these responses eventually join physical assault as discarded methods for expressing anger. Instead, he moves forward with desire and ability to defend less tangible values which he is beginning to recognize.

In mature adulthood, the individual develops a desirable balance in attitudes toward himself and others which keeps anger from being aroused by trivial or temporary situations. Basic principles of human relationships such as tolerance and understanding of others now function to keep his anger under control and result in more constructive emotions. He does what he can to remedy bad situations, and uses constructive devices to help him live with and work around what he cannot remedy. If his job is continuously frustrating, he may be able to change jobs. If this is not possible, he weighs the advantages against the frustrations, and in so doing often finds himself better off than he had believed. This alone does much to reduce anger. If frustrations are part of his family life, as they are to some extent in all families, he learns about the growth levels of the children and understands that much of what proves irritating about them is actually evidence of normal growth. This insight calls up the counter-emotion of parental pride. In frustrations that are part of the marriage relationship, a consideration of the needs and feelings of the two partners helps each to understand how to keep both of them reasonably happy.

There is need in the world for mature anger in an individual, who is roused by injustice, unfairness, brutality, and other destructive situations, and is led to work for their correction. Maturity in anger obviously does not mean that the individual is never angry; rather, it means that he is able to analyze stimuli, to react differentially to these stimuli, and to adjust his responses in such a way as to reduce the irritating quality of the stimuli.

In the discussion of anger to this point, we have been assuming that the growing child, adolescent, or adult has been conscious of what causes his anger and of his own behavior when angry. There are other reactions in the anger response—reactions which do not function on the conscious level. Because of this, anger may be directed not toward the offending person or situation but toward some convenient nonoffender. For example, the employed man may not dare to display anger on the job and may nurse it until he gets home, where he "takes it out" on someone there. One cartoonist made this situation into a chain reaction in which the father took his anger out on his wife who spanked the child who kicked the cat. The cat upset the family milk supply, which upset the milkman, who later accidentally spilled milk on the boss's doorstep. This made the boss's wife angry, and she took it out on the boss. The anger in a chain reaction does not, of course, usually get back to the original source, but the results of misdirected anger often boomerang on the person who expressed it.

We are not referring here to extreme anger sometimes expressed in delinquency. We are saying that although anger has its uses, on the whole it is a destructive emotion which decreases the individual's flexibility. It robs him of freedom to see and to choose among possibilities available to him, and it restricts his social horizons by limiting the number of people who will put up with his unpleasant behavior.

Maturing in Response to Frustration

Being thwarted in the fulfillment of desires results in what we call frustration. It may be expressed in several ways, toward situations or toward other persons. The frustrated person may *withdraw* from the frustrating situation, which may be the better part of valor in certain instances. However, if retreat from difficult situations becomes a habit, it may lead to retreat from life as a whole. In this case the individual may become useless in the accomplishment of the necessary tasks of life.

One variation of retreat is *compromise* with the thwarting person or situation. There are times when compromise is not only necessary but wise; there are other times when it represents unnecessary retreat from situations which might be corrected by an intelligent approach. Compromise sometimes saves a situation and makes a constructive relationship possible. Many businesses have thus been saved from collapse, as have many marriages.

Another reaction to continued frustration is retreat backward in the growth patterns, a return to outgrown, less mature levels of behavior. This is called *regression*. Young children, subjected to continuous frustration, regress on the average to behavior levels typical of children a year or a year and a half younger than their age. Older children and adolescents under continuing frustration also may display regressive behavior. Some people, who are adults chronologically, behave childishly if crossed even briefly. Others have more resistance to frustration, but display "childishness" only if frustration continues over a period of time. Few individuals of any age can take continuing year-after-year frustration without some damage to their spirit.

Among the immature reactions to frustration some are more harmful than others. *Direct attack*, for example, is hard on the other person; he may, however, hit back and thus make the situation hard on the initiator of the attack. Even though *withdrawal* (pouting, seeming hurt) may get results with parents, it seldom influences peers. Under any circumstances, withdrawal is dangerous to the person who withdraws. This is partly because aggression turned inward tends to result in self-accusation and depression, and partly because it means that the individual has surrendered and is no longer trying to preserve his individuality. Although aggressive children are more trouble to parents than are withdrawn children, they are usually healthier psychologically because they are actively preserving their individuality.

Maturing in Fear

We have seen that fear in the infant is a generalized response to situations such as falling or sudden loud noises. As the nervous and sensory systems develop to the point where perception becomes possible, the infant begins to develop specific fear reactions. Fear, as we usually think of it, arises only when we know enough to recognize potential danger. Many fears which develop in children come not only from comprehension of threatening objects but also from seeing other people reacting fearfully.

As the child grows older and becomes able to anticipate future events even briefly, he comes to fear imaginary things that have not yet happened, but which might happen. In later childhood, he also learns to fear things which he does not understand. If he is maturing in the emotion of fear, however, he is also learning more about how things work. He learns to use his knowledge as a means of overcoming fear. Some people never learn to do this, and remain for life at a childhood level of superstition.

In later childhood, most children still get into fights. Sometimes a child finds himself with his back against the wall in a situation where there is nothing else to do but face the danger and fight back at it. Physical courage has been born in some children under these circumstances. Some children learn physical courage through learning skill in boxing or other means of self-defense. This is true mostly of boys, but in many neighborhoods girls also become adept in ways of taking care of themselves in rough-and-tumble situations. Courage also develops as the child learns to defend another's reputation, or in telling the truth even when the outcome will be unpleasant for him.

In adolescence we saw that social fears exist, such as the fear of failing in school or in social contacts. These fears yield as the individual works conscientiously at his studies and learns social skills, thus achieving success in social and academic life. In these instances, he has learned to conquer fear by facing the situation and doing something to make himself more adequate in it. Again, in adolescence as in later childhood, courage grows in the form of willingness to work hard at difficult tasks or to defend a weaker person, or in the form of courage in holding to one's convictions in the face of differing opinions.

Maturity in the emotion of fear may perhaps be described, in part, as the ability to command adequate knowledge with which to eliminate fears that have no foundation in fact; in part, as an ability to overcome fear of failure rather than retreating from the situation; in part, as having courage in the face of physical danger while at the same time avoiding needless danger. Probably the most important test of maturity in fear is the presence or absence of psychological courage which gives one the power to look at one's innermost fears and anxieties and to face them. When an individual fears his own thoughts and feelings, he feels he must repress or escape from them. This leaves them as anxieties which distract attention and interfere with effective action.

Courage to face up to and do something about one's thoughts and feelings and to develop and release one's capacities is essential to the capacity to face life fearlessly. Such courage is an evidence of a healthy personality, of an emotional state that can reach out toward and become involved in the world without being submerged in it. The person who possesses such courage can afford new experiences. He is not afraid, for example, to love another person. Loving involves a merging of the self with that of another. Even though the rewards of loving another fully are among the greatest in human experience, it takes courage so to love. It takes a capacity to enjoy richly, to feel strongly, and even to suffer deeply.

Before leaving the subject of fear we should again call attention to the need for some fear and anxiety. In order to survive in threatening situations, there must be instant mobilization of physiological strength to fight or run. If the young of any species do not learn early to "fear" crossing a street in most contemporary communities, they may not live to do anything else. In human beings, a certain amount of anxiety, which causes us to restrain primitive behavior and to adapt to the reasonable demands of social living is not only normal but highly desirable. Maturity in fear, as in anger, does not mean a person should be without any fear. It means, rather, that he should possess a desirable amount of it for response to stimuli which threaten life, health, exclusion from vocational and social usefulness, or from continuing personal growth.

Maturing in Love

We have followed the basic lines of maturing in love fairly completely in other chapters, covering love both in its heterosexual areas and in its broader development. In general, we have seen that maturing in this emotion means a constant expansion of love from its concentration on self in infancy, to its identification with other individuals and even to humanity in general, which includes countless people we have never seen.

Specifically, we have inferred that the immature person, being preoccupied with himself and with his own reactions, is unable to see and to react to the needs and rights of others. Such a person "loves" others only as they serve his own needs. In order to love others freely and maturely, an individual must learn to feel beyond himself, to sense how others feel, and to react with sympathy to others. Mature love is freely given. It is not a commodity with which the individual "buys" favors, but a gift which asks nothing in return. Such love is accompanied by foresight that prevents overindulgence of children and the development of dependence, in friends or mates.

Jealousy is an outgrowth of a limited understanding of love. It is based upon the concept that an individual has only a limited amount of love to give, so that love given to one person is taken away from someone else. Love is not like this, but is something which grows as it is given or shared.

Maturing in Enjoyment

Increasing experience makes possible new enjoyments. As the young child gets out into the neighborhood, his life becomes more interesting. As his life proceeds, wider contacts increase the breadth of his ideas and interests. He leaves behind childish interests and comes to enjoy new skills and new ideas. He learns how other children live, think, and play. He goes to school, and learns to enjoy meeting people of various ages. He learns to read, and books open a whole new world to him. In the gang age, his skills and interests broaden tremendously.

In adolescence, the excitement of dating, parties, and of meeting new people and new ideas provides enjoyable experience. As adulthood develops and mates choose each other, the keen interest in numerous members of the opposite sex gives way to the far more satisfying interest of the developing relationship with the mate. Once the life work is under way and family life is a going concern, most families develop the ability to enjoy time spent at home. This is accomplished largely by being nice to each other at home, and through a further development of interests such as community affairs, reading, listening to and viewing selected radio and television programs, and so on. The wider range of interests tends to provide a community of interest with a widening range of friends and associates.

Maturing in Humor

Some people never get beyond the childish stage of humor where unhappy situations for others are funny, and where they continue to enjoy practical jokes which place someone else in a humiliating or painful situation. Mature humor includes rather than excludes others. Mature people are capable of enjoying jokes on themselves as well as enjoyable-to-all-concerned jokes on others. They appreciate repartee, skillful fencing with words, and situations in which no one is made unhappy, and in which characteristics which we all possess are shown in unusual ways.

Summary

When an individual matures in the sense that he has learned to live comfortably with his emotions, he leaves behind childish or adolescent behavior. He has achieved the capacity to ignore trivial stimuli and to react only to stimuli appropriate to an adult level of behavior.

He has learned to detect in himself and in others the early signs of emotional arousal and to behave accordingly. He understands something of how emotions work in himself and in others and has become reasonably skillful in encouraging constructive emotions such as enthusiasm, enjoyment, and happiness, and in redirecting or avoiding such destructive emotions as unprofitable anger, and fear, and jealousy.

He has learned to live with a certain amount of emotional tension. He inhibits some emotion before it gets out of hand and directs it into socially useful channels. He does not "blow up" on the spot but delays the expression of his feelings for a time and place appropriate for their expression. He can, in other words, not only largely select the stimuli which arouse his emotion but also regulate the time and manner of its expression.

He has learned some measure of control over his basic drives and is reasonably capable of ordering his existence. The mature individual can feel pleasure and pain more fully and hence can know a richness of living which the immature person is never free to experience. This is because he can gratify his needs through behavior that conforms both to the norms of his society and to his conscience.

LEARNING TO LIVE WITH ONESELF AND OTHERS

It has been said that maturity in feelings toward self is arrived at when the individual discovers that he is neither quite as wonderful nor quite as hopeless as he once believed himself to be. Nearly every person sometimes overestimates his assets and at other times overemphasizes his liabilities. One important aspect of personal maturity is achieved when the individual has learned to recognize and to use his assets and has also learned to recognize and either to live with or to correct his liabilities. This implies an objective evaluation—one that recognizes what is actually there rather than what the individual hopes or fears is there.

Personal Liabilities

Most people have at least three kinds of liabilities: those that do not exist except in their own minds; those that are there and cannot be corrected; and those that are there and about which something can be done.

Liabilities which exist only in the mind of the individual often do not need to be liabilities at all, but assets which are undervalued or as yet undiscovered. For example, many attractive and potentially charming girls develop feelings of inferiority because their mothers are so attractive and socially adept that they successfully and often unconsciously take the center of the stage on all occasions. Thus the mothers leave their daughters in the shadow, where the daughter, and often everyone else, concludes that she is neither attractive nor socially graceful. In such a case the girl's ineptness is real if in childhood or early adolescence she became convinced that she had not and never would have social charm. However, she *is* attractive to look at if she smiles and comes to life, and because she has been reared in a home where she has seen social graces practiced, she has a potential for success in social situations. Such a girl, with help in understanding her situation and practice in social situations where she is free of her mother's competition, often proves above average in her social skills.

There is also the boy who has good physical prowess but feels that he lacks it because he cannot keep up with top athletes. He therefore drops out of all athletic activity. With some help in correcting his evaluation of himself, he may become a good intramural athlete. Whether he goes out for teams or not, it is important that he learn to appreciate and use his body actively enough to maintain adequate health, now and later in his life.

We may also cite the person of high intelligence who gives up in college because he is not in the top 5 or 10 per cent of his class, and the potentially good musician who drops his music entirely because, in contrast to top performers, he feels that he lacks talent. As with the illustrations discussed above, these last two consider lack of top-flight capacity such a liability that they fail to use what are in reality strong talents. This is a loss to society. More important than this, however, is the fact that the young person has a sense of failure which would not continue to exist if he were to recognize rather than depreciate his capacities.

If an individual has a physical defect or an intellectual lack that cannot be changed, he can learn to live with it and to do whatever is possible to compensate for it. He may need help in developing desirable rather than undesirable compensations. For example, the short man who struts and brags, adds nothing to his height thereby. If, however, he becomes a reliable authority on any subject, he may earn a good living, and if he becomes a helpful person, he may win a place for himself in the community in addition to the love of family and friends. A person with a physical defect such as blindness may develop the power to listen and to remember which becomes the envy of the classroom or business office. Whatever the individual's liabilities, there are in most people assets which can be developed to provide a balance for liabilities which cannot be changed. Many individuals go to their graves with liabilities which might have been changed, and thereby have damaged their lives less, or which might even have been turned into assets. As Robert Browning in *Rabbi*

Ben Ezra says:

> Be our joys three-part pain!
> Strive, and hold cheap the strain;
> Learn, nor account the pang; dare
> never grudge the throe!
>
> For thence—a paradox
> Which comforts while it mocks—
> Shall life succeed in that it
> seems to fail:
> What I aspired to be,
> And was not, comforts me.

There comes to mind, for example, the bad temper that might have been brought under control, the selfishness that might have been outgrown, the nagging fear that might have been eliminated, the physical defect that might have been corrected or at least minimized, the superstitious attitude that might have been changed, the crude manners that might have been corrected. Weak muscles can usually be strengthened by exercise; an unpleasant voice, with training, can be improved. A good intelligence can with effort accomplish much that a brilliant but undisciplined intelligence may fail to do. However, no amount of effort will make an opera singer of a person with inadequate physical equipment, or a research scientist of a person with only average intelligence. Ambition needs to be compatible with the equipment of each individual.

Personal Assets

People in many cultures of the world are trained to be modest, even self-depreciating. "This most humble person begs to . . ." and "This unworthy person . . ." are formulas used in some **countries** whenever the individual refers to himself. In our culture, the "Look at me," "See me," "Hey, look what I can do" of the typical six-year-old child more often than not stimulate reminders that "We don't brag," "It's not nice to show off," "Let your deeds be worth noticing and they will speak for themselves." It is generally not acceptable to be cocky, to possess a too-obvious good opinion of oneself. In some homes, as we have seen, this is not true; rather, the child is adored and praised and is even considered cute when he boasts of his accomplishments. In the gang, however, such children soon "get put in their place," and often, because of the unexpected deflation of their egos, become unsure of themselves.

We are indicating here that many children are trained not to think about or emphasize their assets, but are painstakingly trained to search out their weaknesses and to correct their mistakes. Most adolescents and adults, when asked what they consider to be their liabilities or faults, could immediately think of a number of them. Asked what they think their assets or strengths are, they look blank, think hard, and name one or two things with an air that approaches apology for mentioning them. For most people, practice is required before they can make a ready evaluation of their assets. Awareness of one's own assets helps most individuals to think better of themselves and, therefore, to be emotionally healthier than they are when they believe their liabilities outweigh their assets.

An individual may discover unsuspected strengths when he finds himself in a crisis. Almost every individual possesses assets which remain undiscovered because he occupies himself with routines which he never bothers to improve, or because his thoughts travel in superficial channels and never explore new ideas. "Nothing ventured, nothing gained" is truest of all, perhaps, when the venturing is along lines of trying new interests, new skills, new ideas. Robert Browning in *Andrea del Sarto* says:

> Ah, but a man's reach should exceed
> > his grasp,
> Or what's a heaven for?

Failure and Success

Balanced attitudes toward failure and success are important to maturing of personality. As children grow, they can be helped to set goals for themselves which, with effort, they can achieve. Genuine self-confidence can be gained from doing things for oneself, from learning the satisfactions of work well done and especially from taking one's share in family and later in community responsibilities. Children can learn to focus attention on the job at hand rather than upon the praise and other superficial rewards they may gain from the situation. Thus they can learn to succeed with pride in the job rather than in the notice they get for doing it.

Everyone fails at something now and then. Most people at some time in their lives fail at something of basic importance to them. Children and young people can learn to realize that every human being makes mistakes, that people cannot learn or accomplish anything without trying, and that in trying out solutions to problems

some of the trials will fail. Failures are most valuable if they open
the way to further ideas. Minor mistakes often save us from major
ones—only, however, if we understand why we made the mistakes
and then learn from them. Growing children need to face their own
mistakes, but they also need to be protected from too-serious consequences of failure lest they learn to fear failure and hence stop
trying anything unless they are quite sure of success. A reasonable
sense of adventure is necessary for progress at any stage of learning.
In sum, everyone needs to *learn how to fail successfully*, and to go
forward in spite of some failure. In this way, the individual builds a
concept of himself as a person who is adequate, who may make
mistakes, but will not be defeated by them.

Learning Self-Confidence

Shyness may be the result of inability to meet certain situations.
As the shy individual learns skills in physical, intellectual, and social
areas, he becomes more self-confident. If, furthermore, he can learn
how to meet and introduce people, how to initiate and carry on a
reasonably sensible and yet pleasant conversation, these skills will
help to eliminate his shyness. Let us once more make the point that
an important aspect of social competence is the achievement of a
reasonably broad set of interests, so that one has a varied background
upon which to launch or continue conversations with others.

Shyness, however, often continues to exist in individuals of competence in some areas who, for some reason, have remained distrustful of themselves in other situations. Shyness may also be the result
of too much concentration on oneself—on "how I feel," and on "what
others think of me," rather than concentration on "how he feels" or
"what I think of others." Shyness has a way of disappearing when
the shy person looks around a social gathering for someone else who
is shy, and takes steps to make the other person feel at ease. This
accomplishes the miracle of self-forgetfulness and frees the individual to express himself. It also takes him out of the stag line (or the
wallflower group) and marks him as a participator rather than a
passive spectator.

Although active participation in group situations is desirable, the
mature personality does not exhibit excessive self-assurance. Few
people like others who have a tendency to "rush in where angels
fear to tread," who for example, dominate a class discussion in joy
at hearing their own voices expressing no-matter-how-trivial opin-

ions. Most individuals are not happy when faced with the necessity of spending a social evening dominated by one or two center-of-the-stage personalities. Social groups, however, pay little attention to the "mouse" or the "wallflower." Unless an individual can and will go half-way in making friends, he is likely to remain friendless. Unless he speaks up in classes or in meetings, he will lack an important way of clarifying his ideas.

Decision-making

Maturity in decision-making is closely associated with the kind and amount of independence and self-reliance achieved. If adults are to carry their responsibilities well, the ability to think and act quickly and accurately is necessary not only for meeting the crises but also the minor decisions of daily living. Overdependence upon the judgment of others wastes a great deal of time as one asks for opinions about and discusses minor details of the day. The indecisive person misses, for example, the advantage of using a full 50 minutes for study by using 30 minutes of it deciding just what and where to study. He may miss an opportunity for a job while he debates whether or not to apply for it, or he may lose the girl he thinks he might like while he decides whether or not to ask her for a date.

Some parents of college students welcome and even encourage long discussions (for which they pay long-distance phone rates) about what dress to wear to a dance or whether to come home by bus or by rail. Most people, however, are bored by prolonged "discussions" over minor details which do not concern them. They prefer to talk to people who have more stimulating things to discuss. In the world of employment, the indecisive person seldom lasts long in any but a repetitive job, and almost never gets advancement.

On the other hand, snap judgments made when a serious weighing of the situation is needed prove equally undesirable. The mature person recognizes the difference between minor questions which can be decided quickly, and major ones which need weighing more carefully. Once he recognizes that the situation requires serious thought, he begins weighing the pros and cons so that he can make a wise choice. In situations where the pros clearly outweigh the cons or vice versa, the decision is easy. It is when some of both the pros or cons offer advantages and disadvantages, that the decision becomes difficult.

Decision-making involves the ability to decide how important a matter is at the moment, and how it affects the future. The capacity and willingness to recognize when information or experienced judgment may be needed and where to get it, are important. If the decision must be made at once or in a short time, the exploration must of necessity be limited. In this case, the individual needs the courage to decide as well as he can with the information at hand, knowing that he may make a wrong decision.

Attitudes Toward Authority

Many people have difficulty in deciding when the judgment of another is better than their own, or not as good as their own. This involves their attitude toward authority, whether it be a contemporary or a historical authority. Some people are negativistic toward any opinion but their own; some are supinely dependent upon any kind of an opinion that comes to hand. A mature reaction to authority demands recognition of the difference between one that is competent and one that is incompetent. It involves the willingness to seek sound information and judgment with which to reinforce, or against which to measure, one's own information and judgments, and the capacity to accept and use the judgment of others when it is sound. The mature person is capable of judging his own opinions and actions with reasonable objectivity and of evaluating himself realistically. He remains, however, reactive to approval or disapproval from competent people.

Ideal independence is not an absolute condition, in which each individual lives, thinks, and acts only as an individual. It is, rather, one in which each person takes his share of the burden of society, in which he becomes an interdependent unit in the family or other social group. He does not take responsibility for others in areas where they should have the freedom to take responsibility for themselves. He is able to stand up for what he thinks is right and to act upon his convictions, but is also able to listen to the ideas and convictions of others and, when these are reasonable, to make necessary adjustments.

SUGGESTIONS FOR FURTHER DISCUSSION

1. Maturity in personality is relative to the age of the individual. What are some of the signs of satisfactory maturing on the one hand, and of immaturity on the other hand, in (a) a three-year-old? (b) a ten-year-old? (c) an eighteen-year-old? (d) a thirty-year-old?

2. Discuss the following quotation as an adequate criterion of personal maturity: "Those acts are mature which enhance personal relationships over the long run."

3. How would you help a child to learn increasingly mature ways of meeting the inevitable frustrations of life (a) at age six? (b) at age twelve? (c) at age sixteen?

4. How would you help an individual to develop the courage with which to meet the ordinary dangers of life (a) at age three? (b) at age six? (c) at age twelve? (d) at age eighteen?

5. How could you help some nonparticipant in social affairs to become more at ease? Explain the psychological principles underlying your approach to him.

6. Think about how you feel and act (a) in the classroom, (b) on a job where you are being paid, (c) on a date, and (d) while at home. Which of the various "yous" do you like best? Least? In each of the above situations, which characteristics do you think are the most mature for your age? The least mature? What could you do about the characteristics you like least? Those you think are least mature?

7. Have members of the class select items from the reading list below and report to the class for discussion.

REFERENCES FOR FURTHER STUDY

DEWEY, R., and HUMBER, W. J. *The Development of Human Behavior.* New York: The Macmillan Co., 1951. Ch. 12, pp. 316–330, adulthood: the mature personality.

JERSILD, A. T. *The Psychology of Adolescence.* New York: The Macmillan Co., 1957. Ch. 10, emotional maturity in the making.

JOURARD, S. M. *Personal Adjustment: An Approach Through the Study of Healthy Personality.* New York: The Macmillan Co., 1958. Each of the thirteen chapters deals with over-all definitions or specific phases of healthy personality.

LANE, H., and BEAUCHAMP, M. *Understanding Human Development.* Englewood Cliffs, N.J.: Prentice-Hall, Inc., 1959. Ch. 7, the meaning of character (goodness an active process, the goal of character education, goodness and conformity, motives, new conditions demand new characters); Ch. 16, know thyself.

MARTIN, P. C., and VINCENT, E. L. *Human Biological Development.* New York: The Ronald Press Co., 1960. Ch. 12, emotion in relation to physiology.

PRESSEY, S. L., and KUHLEN, R. G. *Psychological Development Through the Life Span.* New York: Harper & Bros., 1957. Ch. 10, moral, sociopolitical, and religious values and behavior. "The fundamental values of the American culture appear to be inculcated in children at a very early age. However, certain changes occur during later years." Well documented.

SEIDMAN, J. M. *The Adolescent: A Book of Readings.* New York: Holt, Rinehart & Winston, Inc., 1953. Selection 66, emotional maturity; Selection 67, manifestations of maturity in adolescents.

THORPE, L. P., and CRUZE, W. W. *Developmental Psychology.* New York: The Ronald Press Co., 1956. Ch. 17, maturity as a phase of development: advantages and disadvantages of maturity; criteria for maturity in various growth stages.

For film suggestions see Film Supplement, in the Appendix.

CHAPTER 11

Early Adulthood

Youth ended, I shall try
My gain or loss thereby °

The Age Span Covered

Early adulthood is generally considered the period from 21 years to the early forties. These ages are relative boundaries. Legally, the individual may vote and hold property at 21 years of age. Marriage laws differ by states, but in many states the boy may marry without parental consent at 21 years, in other states at 18 years. In many states a girl may marry without parental consent at 18. If married with parental consent the ages are earlier: for boys in most states it is 16, 17, or 18, but in New Hampshire it is 14; for girls in most states it is 16, but in New Hampshire it is 13. In most states, juvenile delinquency, with its protective legislation and its special approach to the prosecution of offenses, yields to adult court procedures at 16 to 18 years of age, in two states at age 21, the average for the states being 17 years. The trend is toward higher ages.

Thus variation exists in the age at which the individual is granted the privileges of adulthood on the one hand or is protected from his mistakes as a subadult, on the other. The later end of the early adulthood period is also flexible, some individuals showing signs of middle age earlier or later than the 40 to 45 years considered average.

THE EXPLORATORY PERIOD

The first few years of early adulthood are ones in which the young adult explores and tries out possibilities for the future. Most young

° Robert Browning, *Rabbi Ben Ezra*.

adults experience such an exploratory period in most if not all of the areas of living. They are, in a sense, for the first time sufficiently free from parental supervision to try things out for themselves. To the degree that they can choose experiences, this exploration may be consciously planned. To the degree that opportunities come along, the young adult must accept, adjust if possible, and learn from what happens. This kind of experience is characteristic of all stages of life. It is, however, likely to be most characteristic of the young adulthood period. Much happens then that is new and for which the young person has no ready-made solutions or answers, yet for which he is responsible and must develop answers.

Most young people live through a period in early adulthood when they are deciding upon or settling into their life occupation. Many of them have thought about and prepared for some occupation more definite than just "a job." What the first and perhaps the two or three ensuing jobs turn out to be depends upon the opportunities at hand when the time for taking a job arrives. The quality and variety of job opportunities which are open, and how close they are to the dreamed-of job depends upon demand-and-supply, and also, to an important degree, upon the type of training and the quality of the recommendations offered by the job-seeker. Few late adolescents realize in the high school or college years that with each day's work they themselves write the recommendations which will follow them. They determine these recommendations by the reputation they gradually build for dependability, reliable work, and ability to get along with others on the one hand, or for unreliability, mediocre performance, and difficulty in getting along with people on the other.

Other background factors are also involved in the experiences a young adult has in settling into his work, and in how long his exploratory period lasts. These are the factors of general maturity which were discussed in Chapter 10. One of the interesting evidences of this is to be found in the study of early- and late-maturing boys mentioned in Chapter 7. These two groups of boys, followed to age 33, were found similar in such matters as marriage status and the number and kind of friends. There was some difference, however, in their work experiences. The early-maturing men at 33 were pretty well stabilized in what they were doing and a few of them had already arrived in junior executive jobs. None of them were still unsettled in their jobs. The late-maturing group included a few who were still unsettled in their vocations, moving from one type of job to another in an attempt to arrive at the one they would pursue. None of them had arrived at a junior executive level. Most of them gave promise of settling eventually into some type of steady work pattern. Some of them, perhaps, like some of the people in an average-maturing group, will continue to be unsettled, taking any job that "turns up" in any line of work at which they are sufficiently competent to get a pay check.

Occasionally young adults, having prepared well in a given field, find themselves going into another, perhaps allied, field whose attraction for them has grown out of something which is at first only a side interest. One young adult, for example, majored in a field of his genuine interest, but in his junior year discovered a field which interested him enough that he took a summer job in it. He succeeded so well at this job that he took as many courses in the new field as the completion of his declared major would permit. He did so well in the second field that upon graduation he was offered a teaching assistantship with the opportunity to take graduate work in it. He and his fiancee agreed to delay their marriage for another year until he could complete his degree and see what happened then. At the end of the year, he was offered a university instructorship in what he then decided would be his profession, and began work toward his doctorate. He and his fiancee were married, knowing that there would be lean and hard-working years ahead. By 30 he had his doctorate, they had three children, and he moved into a good position on the university faculty. Thus an exploratory period in vocation usually involves some delay in immediate financial rewards and always involves the marriage partner if there is one. It often results in ample return in satisfaction in the later years.

Multiple Adjustments

Once the vocation is decided upon, the degree of success during the first few years determines to a large extent what the future opportunities for advancement will be. Here, as in the development of community participation and other aspects of adult life, what happens on the job revolves around whether or not the individual is married, and if so, how the marriage is working out.

Most divorces occur in the first five years of marriage. One of the most severe tests of young adulthood lies in the fact that launching into the life work and into marriage so often coincide. If the young people are mature enough to make the marriage a satisfying relationship, the vocation has a far better chance of success than otherwise. If, however, adjustment in the marriage proves to be distracting, and if, instead of providing mutual support and strength, the marriage proves to be a constant source of frustration and unhappiness, the work may suffer severely. Here we see the dual roles of worker and of family member either providing a means of integration or dividing attention and energy to such an extent that the individual is less adequate in either role than he might be in one or the other. There is much to be said for delaying marriage until after the wage-earner has had at least a few months to establish himself with reasonable security.

Final Weaning

In this connection, the question often arises about how much, if any, help the young person should have from his parents in the launching either of marriage or of the first serious job. Some parents feel that with marriage, aside from wedding presents and the financing of the wedding ceremony, the young people are "on their own." These parents assume that the young person beginning a job, having had a high school or perhaps a college education, requires no further help. Other parents continue financial help into their sons' and daughters' adult years. This assistance is often accompanied by advice.

Some young people, whether single or married, want both financial aid and preformed decisions, and the single or even the married ones may continue to live with or near their parents. Under these circumstances, the married couples often find that they are involved not only in adjustments with each other but with their own and each other's parents as well. Although marriage before the establishment of economic independence has become frequent, especially when long professional training is involved, mature young people carefully weigh the implications of continuing parental support.

Establishment of Adult Habits

As in any new situation, both on the job and in marriage, the individual has an opportunity to establish desirable habit patterns in the beginning months and years of the new activity. Habits of promptness, efficiency, and sound personal-business relationships on the job can, with thought and practice, become automatic. So also can habits of tardiness, of "getting by," of gossip and antagonism, uncooperativeness, evasion of responsibility, and compromises with honesty. In marriage, habits of consideration, sharing, talking things out, mutual support (or the reverse of these) begin to get established early, whether the young adult is aware of them or not.

If the individual is single he (she), like the married person, faces in the early adult years the problem of establishing work and living habits that fit together, and which will serve through the future. The young bachelor or single woman, for example, may be able to have a living situation that is attractive as well as efficient. This may be a room in an apartment hotel with a good dining room, or in one of the types of homes now available in most cities where groups of young people board and room much as if they belonged to a club. It may be an apartment shared with one or two others who, together, can afford cooperative housekeeping. The latter arrangement often proves especially suitable for women, who thus have a satisfactory place in which to entertain friends, which they will not have if they take a bedroom in a private home where there is no separate place for entertaining.

Wherever the living quarters are, or of whatever kind, the habits of living are likely to be those carried over from the childhood home. If these are habits of orderliness and reasonable efficiency, living is simple and agreeable. But if the habits are careless and untidy the young adult will soon find that most other people do not enjoy being in his home. If such a housekeeper is married to a mate who grew up in an orderly home, he (she) may find that disorder places a strain on the marriage. The early adult years offer a "last chance" to develop good habits of all kinds to replace unsatisfactory ones that may have been carried over from childhood and adolescence.

Adult Responsibility

Adult life means the assumption of responsibilities which test the level and quality of the individual's preparation for living. Many young people precipitate themselves or are by circumstance precipitated into these responsibilities so early that they seem to have little or no late adolescence, as that period was discussed in Chapter 9. When this happens they may flounder hopelessly and remain inadequate for the rest of their lives, or they may grow up rapidly, often learning to do things the hard way, but soon making a success of carrying the responsibilities they have no choice but to accept. The statistics on divorce, mental illness, and business failures indicate that many people fail in some aspect of adult responsibilities. Some, at least, of these failures occur because young people find themselves subjected to the tests of adulthood before they are ready for them. On the other hand, many late teenage people prove themselves ready to undertake adult responsibilities successfully. Many young adults bear extremely heavy responsibilities, such as those assumed by the jet pilot who has in his hands on each of his working days a hundred or more lives and equipment valued at millions of dollars.

Early and middle adulthood are the periods of peak responsibility in the life span. In babyhood there is no responsibility. During the growing years the individual learns to take some responsibility, and prepares for full responsibility for himself by adulthood. However, taking care of himself is not all that is required in adulthood, as Fig. 11–1 shows. The adult individual provides for his own and the oncoming generation and must make preparation for his old age, when he will not be able to provide for himself. Until recently in human history, the aged assumed that they would be cared for by their children. Today many countries are establishing and expanding government provision for old age, and private corporations and business concerns are providing pension plans for their employees. In large part, these are plans in which the individual contributes part of the cost by making payments at regular intervals during the years preceding old age. Thus he lays away funds out of his adult earnings. In countries where the aged are not provided for by public or other funds, adult sons and daughters provide for aging parents who have not made provision for their old age. It is not uncommon today for adults to be providing for themselves and their growing children, and at least partly supporting their aging parents, while at the same time trying to provide for their own old age.

But even this is not all that the adult must do. He must also help to support the feeble-minded, the physically incapacitated, the mentally ill, the incarcerated criminals, and the many others who cannot or are not providing for themselves. The more able citizens are, by circumstance, responsible for the care of the unable or the

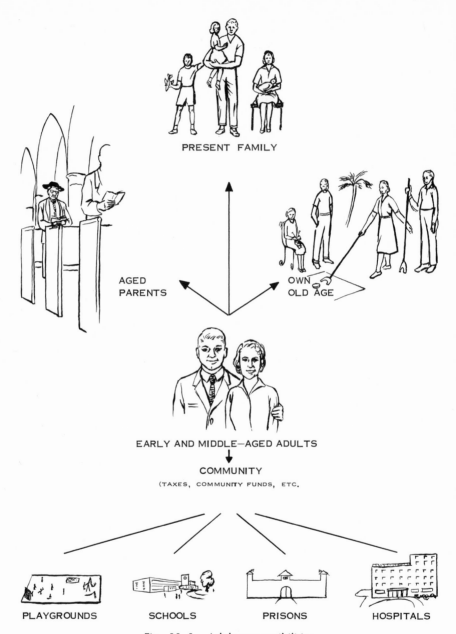

Fig. 11–1. Adult responsibilities.

disabled. In taxes, in contributions to charity, and in other ways, the adult cares for others than his own family. As time goes on, and population increases, this burden becomes greater.

Developmental Tasks

Financial care of self, family, and others is only one of the tasks of the adult period. For the great majority of people there are, in addition, tasks associated with establishing and maintaining the psychological as well as the physical welfare of a family. These tasks may be listed as: (1) getting a mate, often in late adolescence, but if not then, usually in the early years of adulthood, (2) learning to live as a married partner, (3) having and rearing children, and (4) establishing and maintaining a home which is an emotional as well as a physical haven.

Other tasks of early adulthood are: (5) getting started in an occupation, (6) accepting civic responsibility, and (7) finding a congenial social group. That adults have developmental tasks to accomplish surprises some young people. One young woman phrased her surprise as follows: "I never thought before that adults have adjustments to make or 'developmental tasks' to accomplish. I suppose I had thought that once adulthood was reached one was all set for life."

The Many Roles of Adulthood

Whether or not this awareness of tasks to be accomplished in adulthood comes as a surprise, few young people realize the complexity of adult life and the difficulty the young adult has in managing to perform all his roles at one time or in the rapid succession required. Children and adolescents play various roles such as being a child to their parents, a student to their teachers, a friend to their peers. This gives them some practice in playing varying roles to fit varying circumstances. In adulthood they must play the role of worker, of husband (wife), of father (mother), of citizen, of friend, and so on. In each of these roles they play subroles, being, for example, a worker on the job, a worker at the union meeting, a worker making out an income-tax form, and so on.

All-inclusive of these roles is the sex role of being a man or a woman. In Chapter 9, we discussed the formation through childhood and adolescence of the male or the female role concept, pointing out that multiple roles are involved in the role of both the male and the female. A man, for example, is a husband at home, displaying certain husband-father behavior, and feeling certain emotions in connection with his behavior. What he says and feels about this role when out for an evening at the club is known only to his friends at the club. In the same way, a woman has certain feelings about being a wife and mother at home, yet may express and feel different things about these roles at the bridge club. Many children learn something about this as they discover that their father is a certain kind of father at home, yet a slightly different father with each child. They hear that he is a different father at the P.T.A., where he may defend his child's behavior to a teacher, or at the businessman's luncheon, where he and other fathers boast about their children. Some children hear so much criticism from their fathers at home that they realize he is proud of them only when they hear, in a roundabout way, that he praises them elsewhere. So it is that there are varied husbands and fathers in the same man and varied wives and mothers in the same woman.

Sociologists have investigated and discussed this multiple-role phenomenon. They call attention to the fact that people tend to assume variations in role, depending upon the group they are with at the time. This occurs in response to the expectations of varying groups and because of associations with varying situations. For example, one group is boisterous, another quiet and serious. The church expects certain behavior, the civic club expects different behavior, the home something still different, and the individual expects still other things of himself. The adult needs the ability to play all of these roles without confusion.

As in most things we do in life, we do not always succeed as well as we wish in multiple role-playing. Fortunately, we perform most roles more or less unconsciously, so that we are often not aware of the cross-pressures arising from them, or with the inconsistencies they cause in our behavior. If we are fully conscious of these things, we may begin to "stutter" in our behavior, starting to play one role, hesitating in the awareness that another role is also involved in the situation, and, like the speech stutterer, becoming unable to proceed. Some business and professional men, for example, are conscious of conflicts in business or professional responsibilities they carry in several different capacities when they say, "What hat am I supposed to have on at this meeting?" Sometimes the varying roles are fairly compatible, but at other times they are directly opposed to each other as, for example, when the honest politician finds himself in serious conflict because his sense of ethics requires that he refuse to "do a favor" for a friend.

Complex as these roles are, sociologists find that "most of us most of the time manage to take different roles, as prescribed by the same or by different groups, without undue conflict. . . . Indeed, it is rather remarkable how many different roles most of us manage to take with a minimum of conflict." [159] It is true, too, that many roles are "nonoverlapping." Most men, for example, are business or professional men during working hours, family men in the morning and at night, club men at the club, or citizens-in-action at civic meetings.

In emergencies, such as community disaster, the first concern of any individual is usually his family's safety. Yet trained firemen, telephone operators, or policemen who are vital to the safety of many families usually remain on the job. The mayor or head of the Red Cross in a disaster-stricken area is expected to give all his immediate attention to the total situation.

Roles of Women Are Still Being Clarified

We have been discussing the general role situation where, on the whole, the culture is fairly clear about what is acceptable in adult life. Where woman's place in the society should be is still subject to debate. For example, should she be solely a homemaker? Should she be both a worker and a homemaker, but first a homemaker? Can she be, as men are expected to be, both a homemaker and a worker adequately?

History is still writing the answer to these cultural questions. Table 11–1 shows the change in status of women in relation to remunerative work, especially when they are married. Since 1890, with the exception of the year 1920, the proportion of women in the working force has been steadily increasing. The proportion of married women who are working has steadily and rapidly increased from 13.9 per cent in 1890 to 60 per cent in 1957. The jump in these figures is particularly noticeable between 1940 and 1950, this sharp increase being associated with World War II and the provision of government benefits for continued education of veterans of military service. During the War, many girls finished their education, married when the boys returned (or before their term of service ended),

Table 11–1

Marital Status of Women in the United States Working Force

Year	Number of Women Working (millions)	Percentage of Total Working Force	Percentage of Women Working Who Were:		
			Married	Widowed or Divorced	Single
1890	3.71	15.8	13.9	– *	86.1
1900	4.99	14.7	15.4	–	84.6
1910	7.64	25.2	24.7	–	75.3
1920	8.35	19.7	23.0	–	77.0
1930	10.63	21.8	28.9	–	71.1
1940	13.84	26.5	37.0	15.0	48.0
1950	18.66	29.0	54.0	16.0	30.0
1957	22.01	34.3	60.0	15.0	25.0

* Figures from 1890 to 1940 did not separate married from widowed or divorced. We are left to assume that a high proportion of those listed as married were widows, especially in the earlier years when the divorce rate was low. Data taken from *Statistical Abstract of the United States:* Historical Reports 1820 to 1940, and issues 1940 to 1958 inclusive.

and then worked while the husbands were finishing their training. In this process, the roles of men and women underwent considerable change. Men kept house and tended babies between their college or trade-school classes, while their wives worked. Any question about married women working seemed to be forgotten in the practical necessity brought on by the war. The situation effected a rapid shift in cultural expectations.

Once some women had proved that they could work for remuneration and be wives and mothers at the same time, other women became increasingly interested in doing so. Today, although most women who desire long-time careers consider seriously whether or not marriage will interfere, many of them are deciding to marry and to have families along with their work. Needless to say, making a successful job of this requires a high degree of native ability, physical and emotional health, and personal maturity.

Table 11–2 shows how many women in the total population of women in the United States are working for wages, and what percentage of each marital status is working. The percentage of all women over 14 years of age who work has risen slowly but consistently since 1940, as has the percentage of married and of widowed or divorced women. The decrease in the proportion of single women

Table 11–2

Percentage of All Women Fourteen Years or Over in the United States Who
Work for Wages, According to Marital Status

Year	Total Per Cent of Women Working	Per Cent of Married Women Working	Per Cent of Widowed or Divorced Women Working	Per Cent of Single Women Working
March 1940	27.4	16.7	32.0	48.1
March 1950	31.4	24.8	36.0	50.5
March 1957	34.8	30.8	37.6	46.8

Data from *Statistical Abstract of the United States*, 1958.

working from 1940 to 1950 is perhaps explained by the fact that the
age at marriage and marriage rate have both been changing, the age
at marriage having dropped in the later war years and the ensuing
years of economic prosperity. Therefore, more women of working
age have left the single for the married group. By 1955 and 1956, the
large numbers of wartime babies began to reach 14 years of age,
increasing in the "single" group the number who were too young to
work. In any case, the trend toward combining marriage and outside
employment seems clear. Women are currently performing this dual
role in large numbers, with decreasing cultural debate about their
right and ability to do so.

How well they do this is evidenced in *Who's Who of American
Women* (1958), which shows that there is almost no occupation or
profession which does not include a number of notable women, a
high proportion of them married and with children, and some of
them grandmothers. The largest group (15.7 per cent of the 20,000
women included in the book) is made up of women who are primarily club, civic, and lay religious leaders. Business women are next
with 12.7 per cent, college educators are next with 9.7 per cent,
artists with 6.7 per cent, and physicians and social scientists with 4.9
per cent.

In this discussion of dual roles for women, we do not imply that
homemakers do not work! If they have young children and no help,
they work harder than they would on an eight-hour paid job. In
doing this they carry far more than their own "weight" in the scheme
of things. Hard as this work is, however, until recently most women
would not have left it for the comparative peace of other jobs partly

because of cultural pressure against doing so, and partly because some of them prefer the work of the home. Table 11–2 shows, however, that circumstances force many women to become breadwinners and that even as late as 1957 the percentage of widowed and divorced women in the labor force was higher than that of married women living with their husbands. However, the percentage of married women with husbands who were working in 1957 was nearly twice as high as it was in 1940. The trend is toward a still higher proportion of women choosing to work for pay, doing this either to afford a higher standard of living and education for their families, or simply because they enjoy working.

THE ADULT AS A WORKER

Labor Supply Affects Who Works

In discussing the role of women, we have mentioned many aspects of the situation for women who work. Let us turn now to some aspects of the work life which affect both men and women. The basic principle of supply and demand applies to both men and women, and determines who may work. When an over-supply of labor exists, the culture tends to assume that the openings shall be filled by men, and by women who do not have a male breadwinner in the family; it also discourages the employment of adolescents. In periods of critical labor shortage, on the other hand, the culture encourages young people to work and finds a place for the marginal male workers and for aged workers. Under these conditions, women are also encouraged to work.

It is understandable that when labor needs can be met by men, who are traditionally the breadwinners for families, men should be preferred over women whose work may be interrupted by pregnancies. Men, being more likely than women to repay society for professional training, are also given preference in applications to professional schools.

When there is acute labor shortage, however, sex differentials tend to be eliminated. This fact can be seen in the 1958 figures (Table 11–3), on the employment of women in Russia, where labor was scarce, as opposed to the United States, where labor was plentiful. An additional difference between the two countries exists in the attitude toward women's traditional role in society, Russian women being expected to work. Table 11–4 shows the 1958 percentages of

Table 11–3

Percentage of Woman Workers in Three Professions in 1958 *

Profession	United States	Russia
Medicine	10%	75%
Law	5%	30%
College administration and teaching	25%	35%

* Figures taken from: Information and Research Notes, *The Education of Women.* Issued by the Commission on the Education of Women of the American Council on Education, Number 4. Washington, D.C., December 1958.

Table 11–4

Percentage of Higher Education Students Who Were Women in 1958 *

Type of Course	United States	Russia
All courses	35.2%	51%
Medicine	5.5%	69%
Engineering	0.6%	39%

* Figures taken from: Information and Research Notes, *The Education of Women.* Issued by the Commission on the Education of Women of the American Council on Education, Number 4. Washington, D.C., December 1958.

women students in all higher education courses, in medical courses, and in engineering courses, in the United States and in Russia.

The labor situation in countries other than Russia is enlightening, also. Table 11–5 shows that the United States has by far the lowest percentage of working people of both sexes under age 20; Yugoslavia has the highest among the countries for which figures are available. In all countries cited, over 90 per cent of the men between 20 and 64 are working. Belgium, New Zealand, and Italy have the lowest percentage of women aged 20 to 64 at work; France, Japan, and Yugoslavia have half or more at work, Yugoslavia having over 80 per cent. All these countries have substantial percentages of men over 65 at work, but the variation in percentages of women over 65 at work is wide, indicating that factors other than labor demand are influencing the situation. We have no data which explain what these factors may be.

Table 11–5

Percentage of Population in Three Age Groups in the Labor Force

	Males			Females		
	Age 15–19	Age 20–64	Age 65+	Age 15–19	Age 20–64	Age 65+
United States (1950)	44.9	90.0	41.4	26.3	33.0	7.8
Belgium (1947)	66.8	90.3	24.7	41.8	24.7	5.4
New Zealand (1945)	71.3	92.6	30.7	62.5	25.2	2.8
France (1946)	75.6	93.2	54.4	58.6	50.0	22.3
Italy (1951)	87.3	95.3	35.4	47.4	27.4	5.0
United Kingdom (1951)	82.9	96.8	32.0	78.2	36.0	5.3
Yugoslavia (1948)	90.0	98.6	82.8	86.7	81.5	59.0
Japan (1952)	58.7	99.4	55.3	53.8	54.4	22.0

From the International Labor Office, *Yearbook of Labor Statistics*, 1954, p. 8. Adapted by S. L. Pressey and P. G. Kuhlen in *Psychological Development Through the Life Span*. New York: Harper & Bros., 1957.

Job Security

Other factors are involved in the work life of adult men and women, factors which affect the smoothness of adult working life. Continuing opportunity to work depends not only upon the size of the working force in relation to the number of jobs open, but also upon the general economic health of the country in which the worker lives. An economic depression means fewer jobs with consequent unemployment of workers. Many people who were young in the 1940's and early 1950's had not experienced an economic situation in which jobs were hard to get. They tended to assume that any reasonably well-trained person could choose from among a number of job openings. The current generation of high school and college students is probably more realistic than this, having lived through periods when summer or other jobs were hard to find. Some economists warn that, although the type of depression that occurred in the early 1930's is not likely to be repeated in the foreseeable future, recessions may again occur.

Table 11–6 shows employment and unemployment for people who were in the "hire-and-fire" labor group in the United States from 1930 through 1958. In periods of economic setback (1933 and 1945 in the table), the people who suffer most severely from lack of income are those whose work is of questionable quality or whose business or professional practice is not as successful as that of their competitors.

Table 11–6

Percentage of Available Working Force Fourteen Years
of Age or Over Who Were Employed or Unemployed
Between 1930 and 1958 in the United States

Year	Per Cent Employed	Per Cent Unemployed
1930	91.7	8.7
1933	76.1	24.9
1940	91.9	8.1
1945	85.4	14.6
1950	95.1	4.9
1958	93.4	6.6

Data from *Statistical Abstract of the United States*, 1958. Years
chosen to show maximum years for unemployment (1933 and
1945), latest year available (1958), and three decade points.

In times when those seeking jobs outnumber the jobs to be had, the
superior, dependable, conscientious worker is (aside from labor union
seniority practices) the one last discharged and first reemployed; the
inefficient, undependable, lazy worker is the first discharged and the
last reemployed. During the depression of the early 1930's, among
the vast number of young people entering the labor market from
high school and college, nearly all of those who had a trained skill
or profession, and who had demonstrated reliability, dependability,
and other superior traits so that their recommendations were good,
eventually found and held jobs. Almost without exception it was the
unskilled, undependable group with mediocre or poor recommendations who remained unemployed.

During the 1940's and 1950's, vast expenditures for national defense and foreign aid created an exceptionally high level of economic
prosperity that made work available to everyone wanting it, almost
regardless of quality. Under these circumstances, as well as under
the competitive conditions of less prosperous economic periods, the
well-trained person with a superior capacity and mature behavior
still forged his way to financial security and to wide opportunities for
the use of his capacities, whereas the mediocre worker did not.

Work Life in City or Country

Many people feel an urge to live and work in the country. Others
prefer to live and work in the more populated areas. For many there
is little choice, since they must work where work can be had.

Although our concern here is largely with contemporary living, some perspective on the present may be gained from its contrast with the fairly recent past, as we look at Table 11–7. Whereas, in

Table 11–7

Proportion of Population Working in Agricultural and in Non-agricultural Pursuits Between 1820 and 1958 in the United States

Year	Working Population * (millions)	Per Cent of Population Employed	Per Cent of Those Employed Who Were in Pursuits	
			Non-agricultural	Agricultural
1820	6.5	44.4	28.2	71.8
1890	47.0	49.2	57.4	42.6
1940	110.0	47.2	82.9	17.1
1958	121.6	57.7	91.8	8.2

* Working population for 1820 to 1940 given in numbers of people 10 years of age or over. 1940 to the present in numbers of people 14 years or over. Figures taken from *Statistical Abstract of the United States,* 1958.

1820, only 28.2 per cent of the working population were in non-agricultural pursuits, in 1958, 91.8 per cent were so employed. The concentration of contemporary workers in non-agricultural pursuits is one of the reasons for the rapid expansion of cities. Cities have become too congested for comfortable living, with the result that their suburbs have expanded rapidly. People who live in the suburbs have added to their working day from one to three hours of commuting. Today's typical work week, of course, consists of eight hours a day for five days a week, in contrast to ten hours a day for six days a week in the 1890's.

THE ADULT AS A CITIZEN

One of the adult developmental tasks is "taking on civic responsibility," when at 21 years of age, voting privileges are given to the young citizen. Citizenship, however, includes not only participation in the governing of the community, state, and nation as a voter, but also participation in general community welfare.

Preparation for This Responsibility

In most democracies of the world, preparation for intelligent participation in government is considered one of the major responsibilities of the publicly supported school systems. In many of the newly emerging democratic nations, one of the most pressing needs is for general literacy to insure that all can read and write well enough to participate as intelligent citizens in government. In choosing methods for educating the young, in democratic countries, important consideration is given to training them to question, investigate, and decide matters for themselves as groups. This is thought of as a preparation for intelligent, independent adult living in all aspects, but one of the chief considerations is that it prepares the adult-to-be for intelligent participation in government.

One of the strong arguments in favor of self-government in schools and colleges and in the various types of youth organizations is that it gives the growing individual both "know how" and interest in government. Self-government among children and adolescents varies in quality and achievement of goals, depending upon the skill of the adult leadership and upon the initiative, interest, and ability of the participants. The quality depends, also, upon the attitudes toward community and government responsibility displayed in the homes of the young people.

Adult responsibility in citizenship involves understanding of certain principles of successful group participation in self-government, as follows:

1. Many benefits are gained from working together for the common good. Teams can accomplish much that individuals cannot accomplish alone.
2. Sharing of ideas and responsibility is stimulating, but requires steady work to produce worthy results.
3. Considerable skill is needed to lead rather than to boss. Self-control and long-range vision are also needed to win intelligent and reasonably speedy cooperation from a group.
4. If a boss develops in a group, courage, self-control, and determination on the part of the group are needed to cope with him, whether he has the best of intentions toward the group or whether he is a political boss motived by self or party interests.
5. Self-government works well only if most of the individuals governed take responsibility for the group. This means attending meetings and investigating issues (rather than only complaining or spreading rumors), whether one is an officer, a committee member, or simply a group member.
6. Self-government means learning that it is easy to be active in group affairs when the issue has an immediate effect on one's own life or on the lives of immediate family members. It is fairly easy to be

active when the issue concerns people whom we know or whose welfare ultimately concerns ours, and it is difficult to be interested or to enlist interest in an issue the benefits or consequences of which are not immediate or directly personal.

Acceptance of Responsibility for Citizenship

It is too much to expect preparation for citizenship to be completely successful any more than is preparation for any other area of adult living. This is especially true when success requires sacrifice to achieve results that may not become evident in the near future. A type of maturity is involved here that does not exist in the majority of individuals. For example, when school bonds which would necessitate a tax increase need to be voted, even some parents whose children are directly involved fail to vote for them. Non-parents are likely to vote against them, and big property holders, unless they have vision, may also vote against them.

One way to get a fairly broad vote in favor of present taxation or other implementation of long-range plans for community improvement is to point out the immediate advantages. For example, substandard schools, housing, health, and other conditions affect, indirectly if not directly, even the most privileged citizen of any community. Delinquency and crime have long been known to be frequently associated with substandard conditions of living. In one industrial city, for example, in which 25 per cent of the population was living in substandard housing, the following percentages of the city's social troubles come from the groups inhabiting the substandard area:

Adult arrests	62 per cent
Juvenile delinquency	57 per cent
Illegitimate births	55 per cent
Cases of tuberculosis	51 per cent
Commitments to state mental institutions	38 per cent

If only for the sake of protection from damage to private property, or from robbery or personal assault, citizens of any community benefit from the correction of such conditions. The values associated with doing so for humanitarian reasons are perhaps less obvious, but are equally real.

Failure to take civic responsibility, to keep informed about circumstances in the community, to vote, and to participate in community activities when needed, is probably one of the most serious faults in adult behavior in countries where freedom exists to be a force in community decisions.

On the other hand, most communities in such countries have at least some citizens who take their responsibilities seriously, and in doing so, find satisfactions such as friendships, the improvement of their libraries and schools, community health, and other facets of community living. The deepest satisfactions, perhaps, come from the knowledge that the community is a better place for everyone to live, including the individual's own family, and the satisfaction of having played a part in making it so.

On the national and international level, the individual often feels less able to function effectively. He may feel helpless in face of the complexity of the issues involved. However, radio and television broadcasts today cover issues well, as do many newspapers and magazines which also provide varying points of view. Thus it is possible to understand the issues and to make decisions when it comes time to vote. The voting records on presidential elections in the United States show that many citizens do not vote. In no presidential election since 1920 have more than 62.7 per cent of the voters exercised their privilege, until 1960, when approximately 65 per cent of the voters did so.

Wider Areas of Citizenship

Little that goes on in the world today fails to be of some significance to the citizens of each nation. Successful or unsuccessful as the League of Nations was or the United Nations now is, these organizations represent attempts to meet the responsibilities of world citizenship. Having seen how difficult it is for individuals to identify themselves with things beyond their own households, it is understandable why nations often find it difficult to see beyond their own borders. However, improved means of travel and communication have both caused and are helping to solve many of the world's problems. Travel and communication have bound the world into one interactive whole, and they also provide a means of broadening the interests and understanding of individual citizens. No generation in history has had the opportunity to see and to understand other nationalities and races that is afforded today's citizens. The effects of improved communication on attitudes toward, and participation in, world citizenship remain to be seen.

One further aspect of wider citizenship is that which looks ahead in time to the well-being of future generations. Scientists are concerned about man's future in relation to the resources of this planet. Current increase in population threatens to exhaust the earth's resources. Sears,[184] for example, points to the fact that modern man is drawing upon the world's known oil resources at a rate of one million times faster than these deposits have been accumulated.

Because of increasing productivity in agriculture, some people assume that the earth will support any number of people. In addition to agricultural productivity, they point out the advances in research which have increased the sources of energy available. It is estimated that the average American has at his disposal, through electricity and gasoline, the equivalent of the energy of three dozen human servants, and that atomic power will increase this. There is speculation also about the possibilities of harnessing energy from other planets.

It is easy for each of us to think in terms of what "science will accomplish." Actually, every one of us needs to be aware of his power as a citizen of this crowded world. The current great interest in the United Nations on the part of many people is an indication that some people, at least, are trying to understand the world's problems. If enough people see that it is in their power to control population, for instance, it can be done. We could guarantee that every baby would be welcomed because there is room and food for him and need for his talents. Certainly, if we control our own numbers, then "science" may well be able to provide the means of shelter, sustenance, and all the basic needs of human beings.

ADULT RECREATION

We have discussed the responsibilities of adults. Can the adult, then, have no fun? Yes, he can if he knows how. If later adolescence was a sequence of parties and excitement with little responsibility, the shift into adult life may be difficult. If, however, later adolescence was a normal balance of work and play, the realities of adulthood will not be unexpected.

For a good many people, one of the difficult transitions from adolescence to adulthood is in adjustment to the change in recreational activities. The greater amount of time that must go into adult work and home responsibilities reduces the time available for play. The change from the use of parental financial resources to reliance upon their own earnings may lessen the amount of money available for recreational purposes. Neither of these factors represents a difficult adjustment to young adults who have worked and who have been financing their own needs, at least partially, for some time.

Relation to Socioeconomic Status

The kinds of recreation the adult can afford vary, of course, with how much he has to spend on non-essentials. Adults of higher socioeconomic levels may have a more active and diversified social life than do those who cannot afford travel, theaters, night clubs, and parties. However, imagination and initiative are excellent substitutes for money in recreation. Almost every community offers either free or low-cost sports events, concerts, art exhibits, flower shows, and so on. The smaller communities are close enough to open spaces to provide hikes, picnics, and summer and winter sports. Resourceful young adults often solve the problem of home entertainment by pot-luck suppers to which each guest brings a dish, and in other ways keep parties simple and inexpensive.

Relation Between Health and Recreation

One important factor in how much pleasure an adult gets from life is the state of his physical and emotional health. If he has vigor for work, for his family, for neighborliness and community participation with some energy left over for hobbies, parties, reading, or other leisure occupation, his life will have zest. If, however, he lacks energy or if his psychological tensions consume excessive time, attention, and energy, he will lack freedom to give attention and energy to activities beyond work and the daily routine. In addition to zest and freedom for spare-time activities, the physically and psychologically healthy individual does a better and more satisfying job during his work hours.

Adult life tests earlier habits of eating, sleeping, relaxing, physical exercise, and the skills which have been acquired in such routines as self care and grooming. It also tests efficiency in the use and timing of movements, the handling of emotions, and the ability to execute plans. All these contribute to or detract from the success and the satisfactions of adult living and to the amount of free time and energy for play.

In adulthood, some changes from adolescent recreational patterns occur because of the circumstances of adult living. One of the most radical of these changes often occurs in the amount and kind of physical activity, and perhaps in other health situations. A number of factors are involved. For example, the young adult is typically occupied with the focal business of establishing himself in an economically sound occupation. He "goes where the job is," whether this is into a big city or a smaller community, in any part of the world. Wherever the place is, high on the list of considerations involved in the final decision is often what the place offers for use of leisure time.

Even with the best planning for recreation which involves use of muscles, however, the amount of time for physical activity available to office, professional, or management workers is usually limited. Some adolescents, in contemplating adulthood, fail to realize the abrupt change in the amount of vigorous physical exercise which typically occurs. Activity in sports or even just walking from one college building to another provided exercise in late adolescence, but the adult finds himself sitting, standing, or moving about in a limited space for 40 or so hours per week, driving both ways to work or riding a commuter train, having dinner and possibly settling down for an evening of theater, television, or other passive recreation. This involves no stretching of muscles or vigorous circulation of the blood, nor does it give an opportunity for physical activity to release emotional tensions. Dancing in a crowded place offers little real exercise; even bowling and roller skating is usually done in stagnant air. A house rather than an apartment provides such things as a lawn to mow, a garden to tend, sidewalks to keep clear of snow, space to play ball with the children, all of which offer an opportunity to use muscles, to clear the body tissues of accumulated wastes, and to clear the mind and nervous system of hang-over irritations and tensions of the day.

In spite of the lack of vigorous use, the adult body tends to run smoothly, and is at its peak of efficiency and of attractive carriage, poise, and form. The form and carriage, however, tend to deteriorate unless they are maintained by exercise and by a reasonable balance between the intake and use of calories.

Amount of Time Available for Leisure

In attempting to find out how much time the average adult has for leisure, investigators have looked for the average number of hours spent in work, sleep, and other non-leisure activities. They have found that, in order to maintain adequate health with which to live comfortably, most people need a fairly constant amount of sleep. Eliminating the hours used for sleep, work, community activity each week, what is left for leisure? The studies have shown that the average man or woman between 25 and 45 years of age currently has about three and one-half hours of spare time per day.

We saw earlier that the amount of leisure available to adults is increasing because of the shortening work week. Today's young adult will probably live to see a typical work week of thirty or even fewer hours. In discussing the problems associated with the use of increasing leisure, Lynes [130] has said: "In some industries it [the work week] is already approaching thirty, and the twenty-four-hour week is more than a dream, it is a threat." He goes on to say that time is a vacuum that has to be filled. If it is not filled with work, it is filled with alternatives. Too much leisure time may lead people into trouble, for lack of something better to do. It takes practice and thought to be a successful member, even a part-time one, of the leisure class. The goal is to find satisfying things to do with leisure. Success in doing this depends largely upon a person's emotional maturity, his previous experiences, and the degree to which he wishes to give his life purpose and direction.

Leisure time hangs heavily for a person who has few interests or who lacks initiative, but for many individuals it offers a chance to pursue interests and to serve the community. Some individuals "pursue their leisure" with such zest, however, that they find themselves with every evening of the week devoted to committees, meetings, or church work. Their week ends are tightly scheduled with work to keep up the garden, the house, the car, or to pay off social debts. Thus leisure time becomes scheduled work time, because the individual's own conscience and his feeling of need to keep up with his neighbors drives him to be active. The pressures which drive some individuals to over-schedule off-the-job time are what may be called "the social pressures of leisure."

The Ability To Enjoy Leisure

Strong as social pressures are, they are not as strong as the moral pressures of leisure. Individuals differ both in the way they structure their jobs and routines to create freedom for leisure pursuits, and in the effort they exert to make leisure pursuits available to themselves and their famiiles. They also differ in the way they feel about playing as opposed to working. Some people "live to work," others "work to live." These opposing attitudes have a history, not only in the life of the individual but also in the culture. There has been a change in fairly recent American culture from the Puritan taboo on pleasure to the current attitude that pleasure is a normal, even necessary part of living. Whereas, formerly, the individual was supposed to feel guilty when experiencing pleasure, today he tends to feel guilty if he does not have enough pleasure. This attitude has represented a swing of the pendulum from Puritanical severity to more enjoyment of life. Some people think this swing has gone too far, and that it needs to swing back somewhat toward a more balanced position.

Finding a Congenial Social Group

Among the developmental tasks of early adulthood is finding a congenial social group. In the earlier years of the twentieth century, people did not move frequently. Children grew up and became adults in the same town, often in the same neighborhood. Childhood friends grew up into adult friends and associates. The picture has now changed, and people are now far more mobile. Contemporary young adults belong to a generation which has moved often, this mobility being accelerated by World War II and ensuing world incidents, which have taken families into many new locations. Some of these young people have not spent more than two or three years in the same neighborhood; most of them have moved at least once before marriage and more than once since marriage. Few of them, as adults, have settled in the same neighborhood or even in the same town in which they grew up. This means that the majority of today's young adults need to find new friends, who in many instances are replaced in two or three years by other new friends. Such young people must prove adept at getting acquainted with people and at selecting and winning friends, or they remain lonely.

When the young adult is single, the problem is first one of establishing living quarters which make entertainment of friends possible. It then becomes one of finding the friends. Young people with initiative find ways of doing this, such as joining a church group, attending courses or lectures which attract people with similar tastes, and doing volunteer work in settlement houses or other service organization. Young men can "look over" the girls at their place of work and take the initiative in becoming acquainted with them. Girls can do this also, but the initiative taken is usually of a somewhat more subtle kind than that culturally permitted to the male. Not infrequently, the initiative is taken for the single people, either male or female, by some married adult who enjoys helping young people to meet new friends.

Other things being equal, friendships in adulthood, as in childhood and adolescence, tend to be established on a basis of propinquity. The pattern of new friendships, therefore, is likely to center around people encountered at work, or in the neighborhood if it is one of homes rather than of big apartment buildings. Even in apartment buildings, however, the factor of propinquity appears to function in the development of friendship. One study [169] of a multiple-dwelling housing area in a large city found that the nearness of apartment entrances to each other and the location of mail boxes and of stairways influenced the numbers of friendships, and with whom they were made. In families, any member, including the children, may become friends with someone in another family, thus bringing the families together. Husbands may, for example, become friends at work and eventually suggest that their wives meet, or wives may meet at the supermarket and later suggest that they and their husbands get together socially. Although such combinations do not always turn out well, some enduring friendships are thus formed.

Some neighborhoods are more conducive than others to finding friends. For example, in a newly built community made up largely of young couples with or without children, the young adults are all new and looking for friends. As a result, they manage to get together by bringing the babies to parties and putting them to bed while the party goes on. In older communities, the young adults tend to be outnumbered by more established family units, and therefore have a more difficult time finding congenial friends.

The single woman among married couples in an older community is often all but cut off from social life unless she becomes acquainted with some young couples who may find a young bachelor to accompany her to parties. Single women, as we saw earlier, outnumber bachelors. Since bachelors are usually in great demand socially, and since men customarily take the initiative in asking for dates, the social situation is probably more difficult for the single woman than for any other group of adult people. In spite of the social difficulties of single women, however, the marriage rate is higher between 30 and 35 years of age than between 25 and 30. As at any other age, much of the quality as well as the quantity of social activity in early adulthood depends upon the skill and resourcefulness of the individual, and upon his willingness to do his (her) share in planning and financing social occasions.

THE PERIOD OF RELATIVE STABILITY

Performance

In many areas of life the period from age 30 to the early forties is one of peak fitness and satisfaction in living. It is also a time during which the peak of skill and production is reached in many kinds of activities. In sports, the peak is earlier. Studies [126] show, for example, that the peak year in boxing is 23, in baseball 28, and in bowling 30. In literary and professional skills other than athletic, as in many areas of business and the vocations, the highest level of performance is around 35. This level is arrived at earlier than in former generations when background training and preparation were less thorough and, therefore, more had to be learned on the job.[127] As might be expected, people who find their life work and settle into it early achieve more, and are more successful in it than those who are slower to adjust to a career.[127] Because happiness is associated with adjustment in work, the more successful achievers tend to be happier people than the wanderers.

Citizenship

Many young adults find themselves too preoccupied with job, family, and friends to spare time and energy for community participation. However, those in the thirties-to-early-forties age range are often settled enough to permit time for participation in church work, P.T.A. (as the children enter and go through school), young businessmen's clubs, and comparable activities. Some single persons in this age range find in community participation part of the activity and satisfaction they might otherwise find in family life. Furthermore, the person in this age range who has served his community earlier often finds himself in positions of trust and responsibility in his volunteer work.

Marriage and Family Life

Married life, if it is to succeed, tends to arrive at a workable adjustment as the marriage passes the five-year mark. Although some old people recall the earliest years of their marriage as the happiest, these years are usually strenuous to the point of fatigue as the woman bears and cares for preschool children, and as the man struggles to meet the bills for a growing family. When the children are old enough to go to school, and are able to perform much of their own physical care and to help in household chores, and as the father becomes financially better able to provide family needs, fatigue tends to lessen, and the satisfactions in change of work pace and of extra-familial activities increase. These changes, along with the fulfillment of seeing children growing up satisfactorily, often draw the husband and wife closer together even than they had been previously. They may improve a marriage which has not been completely satisfactory. If the marriage is not and has never been successful, it may fall apart entirely when the parents no longer have the needs of the children to keep them together.

Studies [113] indicate that girls who in their teens looked forward to marriage as their life goal but who failed to marry early, tend, in the late twenties, to become emotionally disturbed because of this failure. As they pass thirty years of age, however, many of them gradually recover their emotional poise as they make adjustments to new goals and new patterns of living. The desire for marriage tends to decrease as the individual recognizes that marriage is not likely to occur, and accepts the situation.

Friendship

Between 30 and 40 years of age most adults have found a circle of friends whom they enjoy. They are, therefore, as active socially as they wish to be or can afford to be. At this age the baby-sitting problem is usually resolved because some of the children have reached an age when they no longer need someone or can "baby-sit" with younger siblings. The single person has often found congenial friends, though some single people may be lonely. Bachelors of this age sometimes find themselves in high demand socially and become thoroughly skilled in retaining their freedom to circulate socially.

Personality

As occupational success or success in marriage becomes evident between 30 and 40 years of age, the individual, who in the early years of adulthood may have felt unsure of his capacity to meet life, often becomes more self-confident. This is because he now has a realistic appraisal of himself and satisfaction with daily living. The individual who has arrived at this state has the assurance that he has met enough emergencies successfully to be able to meet anything that comes up. When older people look back on this period they tend to think of it as one when ability was challenged, and when they found themselves adequate to the challenge. They think of it as a period when the transition from dreams to reality was fairly well accomplished. This period may be looked upon as a period of seasoned adjustment to reality.

Not Everyone Succeeds

We have referred to the period from the 30's to the early 40's as one of relative stability. The word "relative" was used because not everyone succeeds equally well in making the many adjustments of adulthood. During a period of life when most people have found a measure of stability, many fail to do so. Although most people succeed in maintaining themselves and others, some people, because of physical, emotional, or mental difficulties, are unable to maintain even themselves. Among these are those who may appear normal and adequate, but who are emotionally unstable. Some break down completely; others limp along in their struggle to cope with life. Those who suffer from serious behavior disorders may lose contact with reality, a loss which makes it impossible for them to care for themselves and possibly makes them dangerous to themselves or to others. These are called psychotics. There are other people whose inner struggles, while affecting them socially, do not prevent them from participating in ordinary, daily activities. There are called neurotics. The neurotics suffer from behavior disorders that spring from their inability to adapt to stress and conflict, but which do not prevent them from maintaining contact with reality.

It is estimated that in the United States alone 750,000 persons are hospitalized in mental institutions; they occupy 55 per cent of the available hospital beds. Hundreds of thousands of other mentally ill individuals are treated yearly in psychiatric clinics or in private practice. Some sixteen to seventeen thousand persons in the United States commit suicide each year, and there are about 3,800,000 alcoholics in the adult population. In addition to these, it is estimated that there are from seven to eight million others in the United States who would benefit from psychiatric care if it were available.

One 1958 study [84] of an urban community of 240,000 in the New England states showed that in this industrial city the prevalence of neurosis among men was higher than among women, the greatest difference being during the years from 25 to 35. In the decade studied, the rate for women was approximately 3.5 per 1,000 population, but for men approximately 5.0 per 1,000 population. Only after 55 years of age did women have a rate equal to or higher than that of men and even then the difference was slight. For both men and women the incidence of neurosis increased from a negligible figure at 14 years to a sharp peak at 35 years, then descended sharply to only 1.25 per 1,000 population in each sex at around 55 years. Thus we see, that neurosis reaches a peak during early adulthood, when responsibilities also are at a peak. The psychoses, which are more related to basic physiological conditions in individuals, continue to increase throughout life.

SUGGESTIONS FOR FURTHER DISCUSSION

1. Think of three or four unmarried young adults, aged 21 to 30, whom you know. What type of work are they doing? Where and how do they live? What type of social life do they have? How well do they seem to be managing their money? Their time? Their energy? What seem to be their greatest satisfactions in life? Their greatest problems?

2. Do the same for three or four married couples in or near the twenties in age. Include at least one couple who do not yet have children.

3. Browse through the daily newspapers of the past week or so. List some of the incidents of tragedy or of special achievement that have occurred in the lives of young adults. These will not, of course, be representative of the daily lives of young adults, since they are exceptional enough to get into the papers. They may, however, serve to broaden your concept beyond that obtained from the samples of young adults in Questions 1 and 2 above.

4. Have members of the class report aspects of young adult life discussed in

the readings listed below. In view of these reports and the statements in this chapter:

    a. Do you think today's adolescent is being adequately prepared for the adulthood which lies ahead of him?

    b. What, if anything, should be changed in his preparation?

    c. What advice do you have to give the average college student as he prepares for his adult life?

REFERENCES FOR FURTHER STUDY

DEWEY, R., and HUMBER, W. J. *The Development of Human Behavior.* New York: The Macmillan Co., 1951. Ch. 12, pp. 310–316, adulthood: physiological characteristics and changes.

PRESSEY, S. L., and KUHLEN, R. G. *Psychological Development Through the Life Span.* New York: Harper & Bros., 1957. Ch. 6, the work life: gross data about workers and jobs, the course of work life, the "way of life" and work, major needs indicated from a "developmental" study of work. Ch. 9, satisfactions in life activities: gives data to contrast adult interests and satisfactions with those of childhood and old age.

For film suggestions see Film Supplement, in the Appendix.

CHAPTER 12

Courtship, Marriage, and Family Life

THE INSTITUTION OF MARRIAGE

In the preceding chapter, we directed our attention to the varied activities of early adulthood, leaving for more detailed discussion, in this chapter, the areas of courtship, marriage, and family life. The majority of people marry sometime during their lives. The United States Bureau of the Census discovered that of the male members of the population 45 to 54 years of age and older in 1958, 96.3 per cent were currently married or were widowed or divorced; and of the female members 45 to 54 years of age or older in 1958, 96.5 per cent were currently married or were widowed or divorced. High percentages of both single men and women past 35 years of age indicate that at one time or another they would like to have considered marriage, but for one or more reasons which we shall discuss later, they had not married. Obviously, the married state with all its demands and difficulties is attractive to the majority of people. It is relevant to look into why marriage came into being, what marriage is really like, and why it is an attractive but difficult relationship.

Why Marriage Came into Existence

All human beings die, and new individuals must continually be produced. It takes men and women together to have and to rear human children. We have seen that human infants are utterly helpless at birth, and that they remain relatively dependent upon other people for a long period of years. Because of this dependency, human mothers are for the most part pretty well occupied for many years caring for their children. As a result, they in turn are dependent upon somebody else for support. Because of this fact, some kind of arrangement is essential for the care and support of mothers and their children until the latter are able to take care of themselves and to begin the next generation. The various kinds of arrangements that human beings have worked out for these purposes may be collectively termed family life.

Man has tried many kinds of family life—as it develops in group marriage, with polygamy and with monogamy.[138] For most people, in most cultures, family life as it develops with monogamous marriage seems to work for the best interests of all concerned—for the woman, for the man, for the children, and for society in general. We may say, then, that the basic purposes for marriage as far as society is concerned are (1) the having and rearing of new generations, (2) the gratification of normal desires under optimum conditions, and (3) the giving of mutual companionship, help, and comfort by one mate to the other in good times and in bad.

Obviously, if the rearing of children is to be achieved, the gratification of desires within the framework of mutual companionship and support between a man and a woman before the birth and during the growing years of the children's lives must also be achieved. Therefore, each of the three purposes of marriage is of equal importance.

Individual Reasons for Marriage

Why do boys and girls and men and women marry? If we ask them, what do they say? In the United States, the most usual response from late teen-agers and those in the early twenties is a look of amazement that anyone should ask, followed by, "Because we're in love, of course!" What do they mean by that? If they are asked they respond variously. Some are speechless, some irritated, some giggle, and some are thoughtful. What do they really mean? It is difficult to find out, because often they are referring to feelings which they like and want more of, but are not clear about what more gratification of those feelings might involve.

After thinking about the questions, some of these young people come back with,

"Well, I want to be in my own home where I'm the boss."

"I'm tired of having to check in with my parents about everything I do."

"We're in love and we want to make it legal," usually referring to sexual relations, and

"We've been engaged for a year and a half, and we are tired of waiting."

The answer to the question, "Waiting for what?" usually is rather incoherent, but it generally conveys the idea that it is foolish to keep putting off normal physical relationships. It is as if to say that all other problems vanish, once physical intimacy is achieved.

There are other reasons given, of course, but they are more likely to come from people who are somewhat older. A few years makes a great deal of difference in the outlook of both men and women. People even only slightly beyond the early twenties are likely to mention that in addition to being in love, they want to marry to satisfy their needs for congenial companionship, for economic security, for having a family, and for sharing their lives with someone with whom they feel comfortable and able to be themselves. From these reasons, it is obvious that marriage is a relationship with many facets.

EMOTIONAL ASPECTS OF MARRIAGE

In relation to marriage, what we *know* about ourselves and others is important, but how we *feel* about ourselves and others is far more important. The majority of us live most of our lives, and particularly most of our married lives, not on intellectual or spiritual levels, but on emotional levels, that is, levels of *feeling* rather than levels of *thinking*. Therefore, if we understand how we ourselves and how others feel about things connected with marriage, we have at least a start in the complicated business of learning what it takes to live together in successful marriage.

Emotional Needs That Lead to Marriage

In preceding chapters, we have discussed at some length the emotional needs of human beings from infancy through early adulthood. What, then, are the particular emotional needs of mature men and women who look to marriage and the family as their way of living their lives? Simply stated, they may be listed as follows:

1. The need to receive affection from their mates and from their children.

2. The need to bestow affection upon their mates and upon their children.
3. The need for approval by their mates and by their children.
4. The need to feel approval of their mates and of their children.
5. The need to really belong to a mate.
6. The need to feel that a mate belongs to each of them.

The child and the immature person feel the need for receiving affection and approval and for someone belonging to them more strongly than they feel the need to give affection and approval and the need to belong to someone else. They want to get something from other people, just as the baby wants to get nourishment from the breast and as the adolescent wants a great deal of assurance from others that he is all right. If, as the early years pass, the child is secure and confident that he is loved and approved for just what he is, he begins to be less occupied with satisfying his own needs, and gradually begins to share. He is ever-sensitive to any real or fancied diminution of affection or approval for himself and, as a result, every now and then longs for babyhood where all was well and there was no doubt about his being loved and approved. If all goes well, he continues this now-advancing, now-retreating behavior for years until the feeling of confidence that he is all right is settled within him. When this has happened, he is well on his way to emotional maturity and to achieving the ability to bestow affection and approval and to have someone belong to him even as he accepts affection and approval and belongs to that someone else.

The foregoing is fundamental and it comes about only by a continuing repetition of receiving before we can give. Unfortunately for their married and family lives, many men and women arrive at the legal age for marriage lacking the conviction that they as individuals are satisfactory people, loved, approved, and needed in this world for what they are. Hence, they find it difficult to give of themselves in the manner and to the degree that marriage and parenthood demand.

Just why there is this failure to be convinced is not clear in all cases. Many different circumstances may result in convincing a person that he or she is not worthy of the love and approval of others. As a further result of this, a person so misled by such unhappy convictions actually becomes less worthy. We may mention here a few of the possible circumstances that may have these unfortunate results.

In the first place, not all infants are wanted by their mothers: some of them because of the mother's lack of physical or emotional fitness for motherhood, some because they interfere with the mother's other activities, some because the parents' marriage relationship is unhappy or because the mother was unmarried, some because the parents already have more children than they can provide for financially and emotionally, and some of them for various other reasons. We know that some mothers fear that they will "spoil" a child by paying too much attention to him and thus fail to give him the attention that any child really needs. Some mothers find themselves married to husbands who have never been fully convinced of their own worth. As a result, these husbands compete with their own infants for their wives' attention. Sometimes it is the other way around; that is, wives who have never been fully convinced of their worth become mothers and have difficulty in giving sufficiently of themselves to their children in addition to their husbands.

Thus innumerable vicious circles exist. This means that men and women who retain too much of the unfinished business of childhood themselves get into marriage and parenthood unable to give sufficiently to satisfy the basic needs of the generation they are producing. It must be recognized that some people are more difficult to satisfy than others. Some children seem to have needs for affection and approval that can never be satisfied, and we may as well recognize the fact that some children are easier to love than are others. The right kind of attention may work wonders with the less lovable, however.

It can probably be stated with considerable accuracy that mature men and women who are ready for marriage and parenthood are those who, while recognizing their own imperfections, are satisfied that they are pretty good people on the whole. They still feel the need to receive affection, especially from their mates, the need for approval from their fellow men in general, but especially from their mates, and the need to belong to some one person in particular. But they also feel an equally strong need to bestow affection and approval upon others and to have someone in particular who wants to belong to them. Because they feel these needs, they are equipped to enjoy living with their mates, their children, and with other people beyond their family circles.

They are people who may feel deep affection and respect for their own parents and others of their elders, but who are also independent of them. They are adult in every sense of the word. They can make wise decisions and compromises. They are willing to learn from the past experiences of others. At the same time they recognize that they are new adults, the exact like of whom have never before existed. They recognize that they are living in an old world which in many ways is also a new world, the like of which has never before existed.

In classes in education for marriage, two words have evolved which, while not euphonious, are full of meaning. These words are *marryability* and *marriageability*. Men and women who are able to get mates are marryable, but only those who can make their marriages last according to their vows, "until death do us part," are marriageable. The marriageable men and women either already know when they take their marriage vows or else very quickly learn what it means to say, "Therefore, shall a man [woman] leave his father and his mother, and shall cleave unto his wife [her husband]; and they shall be one flesh." * They understand also what "forsaking all others" means, and who "all others" are: parents of both, other friends, and even their own children when they have reared them to be independent people in their turn.

Reasons for Singleness

Since marriage seems attractive to most people, why do between 3 and 4 per cent of men and women not marry? There are numerous reasons, and an understanding of these reasons sheds light upon the difficulties that occur when people in similar circumstances fail to heed them and marry. So let us look into some of these reasons.

Some men and women do not marry because of lack of opportunity to meet suitable mates. Many factors bring about this lack of opportunity. Higher education may interfere with time and interest in seeking marriage partners. This factor brings people into the early twenties, after which other factors enter into the situation. People get jobs where contacts with the opposite sex are few. Some jobs take them to communities where people of their own social class, religious group, or of similar tastes and interests are few. Too rigid standards set by the individual or by parents or older siblings may make the finding of a suitable mate impossible. Some parents, who themselves have failed to mature with the years, cling to their sons and daughters in a last futile attempt (usually unconscious) at ful-

* Genesis 2:24.

filling their own unsatisfied needs, and find fault with all possible mates until the son or daughter gives up trying to meet people who might be possible marriage partners.

Men and women sometimes believe that they cannot marry because they cannot find suitable employment or because the income from the employment they have is too low and not dependable. Some feel that they cannot marry because they have dependents— aging parents, younger brothers and sisters, or invalid relatives. In some cases, personal or family reputation rules out thoughts of marriage. One otherwise most eligible college graduate, for example, felt that he could not marry because his father was an alcoholic. Differences in social, racial, or religious status cause some people to feel that they cannot marry, even though they might know someone whom they would like to marry.

Not infrequently people fail to marry because of their unwillingness to give up or to do certain things that marriage requires. Some are unwilling to give up their independence. Some feel that marriage would interfere with a career. This is not often true of men, since in most cultures men are expected to have both a career and marriage, but a few careers such as some in the military service and the priesthood in some faiths do put marriage out of the question. Women used to have to choose between marriage and a career, but this choice is becoming less and less necessary, although marriage is still likely to restrict the development of many careers. Almost any career open to women today with the exception of certain religious vocations permits not only marriage but parenthood also. Some men and women are unwilling to give up the acquisition of such things as clothing, cars, and jewelry, and the possibility of certain types of recreation and vacations that would be unattainable for most, at least in the early years of marriage-building.

Men and women are often unwilling to loosen parental ties and certain ties of friendship, such as a boy's ties to his fraternity brothers and a girl's to her sorority sisters. Some people do not recognize that ties such as these relax in normal growing up, with the result that more binding ties can be achieved with lifelong mates.

There are also chronologically adult people who are unwilling to undertake what have been called "the hardships and discomforts" of married life. For men, those are such things as assuming the financial responsibility of a family while it is growing up and of his wife and himself in their later years, helping with the care and training of the children, helping with or possibly doing the marketing alone, and the maintaining of the home and grounds. For women, some of the hardships and discomforts are things such as housework, laundry, for some even the sexual relationships, pregnancy, birth, the care and training of children, and for some, what seems like the daily grind of seeing a husband off to work in the mornings and seeing him return tired in the evenings. Needless to say, if this is how marriage appears to some people, it is understandable and wise that they avoid it.

Still other men and women remain single because of unwillingness to merge their personality with that of a mate. This merging is really the essence of marriage. Higher education used to make some women feel almost guilty at the thought of failing to preserve their educated selves intact. Currently, however, it is affecting fewer and fewer women in this way.

There are also men and women who feel deeply that they are unsuitable for marriage. A physical, mental, or emotional defect in themselves or in their families sometimes brings about this conviction. For example, it may be hereditary deafness or the loss of a part of the body as a result of an accident. It may stem from the fact that a person has spent some time in a mental institution, has a feeble-minded relative, or is frigid when it comes to bodily contacts. The realization that they are homosexually inclined makes some men and women shun marriage. There are apparently some people who are celibate by nature, who, in other words, lack sexual ability somewhat as some others lack musical ability. The recognition of some of these conditions, even though they might be corrected, understandably causes people to feel that they are unsuited for marriage.

The loss of a loved one is another reason why some people do not marry. The loss may occur as the result of death, as a result of the loved one's refusal to marry because of his or her becoming aware of any of the conditions previously mentioned, or simply because of a change of mind and heart.

Then too, there are some people who destroy their chances for marriage by an excessive and obvious desire for it. This occurs when a man or a woman finds an apparently suitable mate and talks too soon about marriage or pursues the individual too vigorously, thereby frightening him or her away.

One further reason why many women are unmarried is the fact that in most of the civilized world women of marriageable age outnumber men. In the United States, for example, the Census Bureau found that in 1958, of the total 58.5 million males 14 years of age or over, 17.6 million were single, widowed, or divorced; of the total 62.7 million females 14 years of age or over, 21.3 million were single, widowed, or divorced. This means that there were in the United States 3.7 million more women who were single, widowed, or divorced than there were men of similar status. Most cultures permit only monogamy, so it is evident that some of the more numerous sex must remain unmarried.

Obviously, some of the reasons for failure to marry are regrettable because they not only deprive individuals of happiness, but also deprive the human species of some excellent parents and offspring. On the other hand, some of the reasons indicate a lack of confidence or a fear of losing one's identity in sharing life with a mate, so that it is well for the human species that these people remain free from a relationship that demands so much in the way of giving of themselves. Some unmarried people, of course, particularly those engaged in the vocations of teaching, nursing, religion, and public service, give of themselves as freely as does anyone in marriage. A difference does exist, however, in that married people of their own free will enter into an "until death do us part" relationship with one other human being, while the unmarried enter into no such intimate contract, nor one so fraught with possibilities for both joy and sorrow.

Similarity and Difference in Marriage Partners

In order to live a successful married life, a man and a woman need a proportion of similarity and a proportion of difference, but just what the proportions are no one can say exactly. The statement frequently heard that, in human beings "opposites attract," may be true, but the attraction is rarely lasting unless there are likenesses too. People differ a great deal superficially, but it is the deep, subconscious, emotional likenesses and differences that determine the strength or weakness of the attraction. People often look at married couples and wonder,

"Now what in the world does she see in him?" or

"How can he stand her?"

The fact is that observers are simply not in a position to know what powerful likenesses and differences exist in the partners of a marriage. Observers can see only the superficial traits which are relatively unimportant to mature married people. Really adult men and women know what they want from their marriage, and they know when they have what they want. As a result they are unconcerned by what other people think they have or lack. Tests that reliably reveal the deeper emotional traits that are important in marriage have yet to be devised, although some tests have been developed that are used by marriage counselors, members of the clergy, and others in helping people to understand themselves.

In spite of what has been said here about superficial traits, human society has learned through long experience that certain relatively superficial differences often do cause difficulty in marriage. Many of the people who marry lack confidence in their own judgment and, therefore, are unduly influenced by other people's opinions. Because of this, they may be unappreciative of the less obvious, more worthy traits that may exist in themselves and their mates.

Society, that is, parents, relatives, and others, has learned to look with the greatest approval on what may be termed "unmixed" marriages. According to the standards more or less set by society, a marriage is unmixed and therefore acceptable when the man and woman concerned are of the same age, or the man is a few years older of the two; when they are of the same height or the man is the taller of the two; when the two have about the same social, economic, and religious backgrounds; when they are of the same nationality and race; when they are of about equal intelligence or the man is of slightly higher intelligence than the woman; when they have the same degree of formal education or the man has a more advanced degree than the woman; and when they are both married for the first time.

A "mixed" marriage is any marriage that deviates in any significant degree from the standards and traits that society expects. The wisdom of these standards, which are based upon the experience of the past, is in some cases questionable. The age standard, for example, dates back to the time when women aged early and died young as results of too frequent childbearing and inadequate medical care during pregnancy and childbirth. Nowadays wives, on the average, outlive their husbands by three to five years.

Greater size, especially stature, in the man was once important when he needed great size and strength of body to perform his roles of provider and protector. Nowadays, in the push-button world, size and muscular strength are not as important as they once were. Some very small women fear sexual relations and pregnancy if their husbands are large, but the nature of the reproductive organs and modern obstetrical skill render such fears unfounded.

Differences in social and economic backgrounds seem to be relatively valid reasons for society's disapproval of certain marriages. When a miner's daughter marries a millionaire or the chauffeur marries the heiress, so many superficial differences in behavior may be present in the individuals or their relatives that they may obscure important likenesses; or so much antagonistic pressure may be exerted against the marriage by relatives and acquaintances that the really worthy components of the marriage may never have a chance to develop.

Differences in religious background may make marriage difficult. Marriage is usually considered mixed on a basis of religion when the partners retain their own faiths such as Jewish and Catholic, Jewish and Protestant, Protestant and Catholic, Protestant and Moslem, or other combinations. The difference is significant depending upon the degree of devoutness of the partners. The beliefs of devout members of all organized faiths carry enormous emotional charge, much more powerful than most people realize until they find themselves in intimate relationships such as marriage where the beliefs really matter. It is difficult for a Christian husband to realize that Christ is rejected by his Jewish wife. It is difficult for a Jewish or Protestant spouse to realize that to his Catholic mate the Catholic faith is the only true faith.

Differences within the major groups may also be bases for mixed marriage. An Orthodox Jew and his Reformed Jewish partner have difficulties concerning food and its preparation. An Episcopalian wife may find the hymns that her Baptist husband sings quite unhymn-like. A Roman Catholic may find it incredible that his Orthodox Eastern Catholic mate's observance of Easter comes on a date different from the date of his Easter. The examples mentioned may seem trivial to someone not in a situation where they exist. They are only samples, and they scarcely indicate the tremendous emotional weight that such conflicts carry within marriage.

Society on the whole is not averse to marriages between people of different nationalities. Sometimes it even seems to encourage them, possibly for the glamour that may accompany them. Some such mixed marriages, however, do run into unanticipated difficulties. Again different attitudes toward food and its preparation, different manners, different language, or even in the same language such as the English of England and of the United States, different meanings for familiar words—such seemingly little things, when they turn up repeatedly in marriage, often stir deep emotional feelings that make compatibility difficult.

While it is well known that no sound criteria exist by which human beings can be clearly separated into races, society on the whole looks askance at so-called interracial marriage. While it is also well known that the children of such marriages are in no way superior or inferior to the children of unmixed marriages, those who dare to contract interracial marriages still have to expect disapproval both of themselves and of their children. The disapproval is expressed in ways that strike at the most basic feelings, in that restrictions are placed on where they may live, where they may eat, where they may go for education and recreation, and even where they may worship.

Men and women are likely to be attracted to others of about their own degree of native intelligence. However, through immaturity or poor judgment, an individual of high intelligence is sometimes attracted long enough to a person of low intelligence for them to be married. Whichever way the difference is, the attraction is usually short-lived, for it takes average intelligence even to keep house well, and men and women soon tire of living with someone with whom they cannot carry on a satisfactory conversation. Generally speaking, parents and friends are less aware of differences in intelligence than they are of other differences. In fact they sometimes refuse to recognize lack of intelligence if it happens to be accompanied by financial wealth or social or religious status that is desirable from their point of view. It is, nevertheless, a factor that people considering marriage themselves need to think about.

The difference that society looks for in degree of formal education is probably rooted in the concept of the husband's being the head of the house. If a wife is a high school graduate and the husband is a college graduate, this may be all right with parents and acquaintances, but if it is the other way around there is likely to be some question. Whether or not such differences as this cause trouble depends upon many factors, but particularly upon the individual's acceptance of self as a person of worth and upon the mate's acceptance and expressed approval. If a husband with a lower degree of education is successful in his vocation and if the pair have much in common that pleases them, the educational difference is not important. But if he or she or both of them are either consciously or unconsciously disapproving of the mate, unhappiness results and expresses itself in various ways. As a result of military service in the modern world, marriages such as this are common. In many cases, the husband resumes his formal education following his military service, so that this difference in the marriage is only a temporary one. Some wives whose educational level was lower than their husband's at the time of their marriage find themselves "left out" as their husbands rise in business or professional life. An intelligent woman, regardless of educational level, can read and otherwise inform herself so that she is able to converse with her husband and his friends and their wives.

In a monogamous society, the optimistic expectation is that most people will marry only once. When widowed or divorced men and women marry, the marriage is considered mixed on the basis of previous marital status. A widow or a widower who has had a happy experience in marriage is likely to feel the need to marry again; and having chosen wisely the first time, the chances for a second wise choice are good. Really the greatest compliment that a widowed person can pay to the deceased mate is to marry another who reminds him or her of the first.

Widowed people who were unhappy in marriage and divorced people who obviously were unhappy sometimes profit from their experiences, but recent studies indicate that they are likely to have unhappy marital experiences again and again with different mates. According to the United States Census for 1949, second marriages of divorced people are about 50 per cent more risky than are all first marriages, and divorced women in subsequent marriages are about 10 per cent poorer risks than divorced men in subsequent marriages. Divorce may indicate lack of preparedness for the first marriage and repetition of unfavorable habit patterns in subsequent marriages.

Other bases for mixed marriages exist, but certain generalizations may be made about them all. The obvious differences do present some difficulties, but on the other hand, these very differences may add interest and zest to the marital relationship. Mixed and unmixed marriages alike present areas where adjustments have to be made, but these areas usually occur at deep-seated emotional levels which are hidden from outsiders and are often unrealized by the married partners themselves. Mature people often make assets of their differences, provided they are not too numerous. For example, a married pair may well enjoy learning about each other's faiths if that were their one most outstanding difference, but if in addition to that difference, the woman was a divorced Republican chemist and her husband a divorced high school teacher who was also a Democrat, the coordination of their differences might be overwhelmingly difficult. Immature people lacking confidence in themselves often have difficulty in reconciling their differences because both tend to be rigid about what each thinks is best and right. Nevertheless, when a boy and girl marry with everybody's approval, they may be misled by the approval itself into believing that for them, who have selected so wisely, all will be easy. Actually, no one of all the approving relatives and acquaintances and not even the two people themselves realize what the areas are in which they each will have to become accustomed to new ideas and to new ways of doing things.

Areas of Emotional Adjustment in "Unmixed" Marriage

While the areas of adjustment differ from marriage to marriage, some are so common as to be easily overlooked. A few things that demand considerable flexibility on the part of married people will be discussed. Before they marry, men and women can easily be unaware of the basic needs of their partners-to-be. Take the need for sleep, for instance. Before marriage, motivation to be together is so high that both man and woman may forego sleep just to be with each other late at night and at other times. After marriage when they are together anyway, basic personal habits and needs soon show up. In one marriage, the husband may be ready for bed at eleven P.M. and ready to rise at seven A.M., while his wife could easily sleep until ten A.M., and not be ready for bed until two in the morning. Response to light is another situation where adjustment may be required. Before marriage, dating couples may spend a good deal of time in subdued light, at movies, dances, and in other evening diversions. In marriage, a wife who in this case is the early-rising type, may obey her usual impulse to open the shades and put on the lights as soon as she gets up. She may be married to a man who would like to be a late riser and who, even if he does have to get up to go to work, would prefer to get dressed in the semidarkness. He may have light blue eyes that actually hurt in sudden light, and through long experience may have learned to do many things in very subdued light. The switching on of a bright light for a man like this can really start the day off badly, and he will not be likely to restrict the bad start to himself. Surliness at breakfast time is not unusual in marriage, but most couples are likely to try to justify their bad tempers by something that seems more dignified and worthy of bad temper than window shades or lights, because those things sound childish even to them.

In one specific marriage of which we know, difficulty has arisen because the wife has taken up smoking. It seems that neither of them smoked before their marriage nor for about three years after. Now the wife has given up her job and has had a baby, and wants to associate more with the other wives in the housing development in which they are buying a home. The other wives smoke, and she finds she enjoys smoking also. Her husband is shocked and angry. He says she is not the woman he married. (This shows his lack of understanding of marriage. As the years pass, what mate *is* the one that the partner married?) He considers smoking as something evil, and says, "I was taught to avoid even the appearance of evil." This sounds silly, but it is from such seemingly trivial things that great difficulties grow. It is not a reasonable matter, but as we have said early in this chapter, marriage is lived on levels of feeling rather than on levels of thinking or reason. Such a thing as this husband's feeling about his wife's smoking is very deep and not easily overcome or changed.

This particular marriage is as unmixed as society could possibly plan a marriage if it set out to plan one. This man and woman belong to the same church, he is two years older than she is, two inches taller, their backgrounds are similar, socially and financially, they are both graduates of a small college, both white, both native-born United States citizens, both married for the first time, of approximately the same native intelligence, and now after four years of marriage, they are embattled constantly. She says, "My family didn't smoke either, but my neighbors do and I like it and I'm going to!" He says, "Not in my house, you won't!"

Now they are finding it impossible to be happy with their child and to have a normal married life, even to participating in sexual activity. He snarls, "I'm getting impotent, and it's your fault," and she retaliates with tight lips, "Have I ever refused you?"

This young man and woman have ceased to approve of each other over a seemingly superficial matter concerning which their feelings are powerful. Now that the battle lines are drawn, fear of loss of face has entered in and neither will risk losing face. There they are, still needing each other terribly, with the knowledge that their child needs them too, and they are desperately unhappy.

Probably the most difficult part of ourselves and of others for us to understand is this area of our feelings about all the different kinds of things that impinge upon our daily lives. Since it is in this area that most of our married living is done, we need to try to evaluate our feelings so that we can decide whether they really are worth the destruction of otherwise happy relationships with our mates. In earlier chapters, it has been pointed out that our early environment has a tremendous effect upon our ideas and our feelings, but it has also been pointed out that we can continue to grow and to change our ideas and feelings. We need to know what we have strong feelings about and if possible why we have them.

What are some of the things about which we feel strongly one way or another? The answer depends upon the person, but some people have strong feelings about the following: television, fishing, smoking, shades up or down, bugs and spiders, the use of credit, jazz, poetry, children running, and other such things. Why do we feel about these and other things as we do? Have we as individuals thoughtfully considered them, or do we consider a sin or a danger anything that we do not understand or feel uncomfortable with? People who stay married do a lot of this kind of evaluation throughout their lives.

PHYSICAL ASPECTS OF MARRIAGE

We have said that most of marriage is lived on emotional levels. However, emotions, as we understand them, occur only in living bodies. A living man and a living woman are essential to human marriage. The human spirit and the human mind are both realities which are essential to marriage, but communion of spirits and minds without bodies is not marriage. One may be faithful to the memory of a sweetheart or a mate, but still one is not married to that memory, nor to an ideal. It seems important to stress this fact because some people tend to minimize the part that the physical body plays in marriage.

Role of the Body

The body is wonderful, interesting, and important in marriage. In the eyes of a construction engineer, it is by no means perfect, and the engineer can see many possibilities for improvement. However, in spite of its imperfections of design, it performs its functions amazingly well for an amazingly long time if its owner understands it and cares for it well. As the owner of a car gets better performance from it if he understands and respects its construction, so the owner of the living body gets maximum satisfaction from it only if he or she understands its construction and operation and takes care of it accordingly. Married people need to understand, appreciate, and care for their own and each other's bodies.

The body is a unit composed of many parts. Each part has its function or functions, but each part can function only as a portion of the whole. Any one part is as important in the operation of the whole body as any other part. In other words, there is no "rank" among the parts of the body. The parts of the urogenital system are as important as are the parts of the circulatory and the nervous system. H. L. Mencken once pointed out that in the minds of society in general there seems to be a sort of hierarchy of respectability of parts of the body depending upon their location, so that the brain is more respectable than the heart, the heart more respectable than the kidneys, and the kidneys more respectable than the urinary bladder. He was obviously satirizing the ridiculousness of such a state of mind, but if it does exist it is almost fatal to happy marriage, which involves the satisfactory functioning of the total bodies of both persons.

Care of the Body

For successful marriage, both partners need good physical health, especially in the early years while they are building the foundation of their marriage. Both partners need good appetites for food and good digestion; breathing, circulatory, nervous, endocrine, and excretory systems that function smoothly; and skeletons, muscles, joints, and skin that work without calling attention to themselves by pain, stiffness, and other troubles. Obviously, also, the reproductive systems of both need to be in good working condition.

While most state laws for procuring licenses to marry safeguard individuals against marrying someone with venereal disease, for example, the wise man and woman contemplating marriage see a competent physician some weeks at least before the date set for the marriage. A competent physician checks all the systems—all the "standard equipment," as it were—answers questions that the man and woman may have concerning the structure and functioning of their bodies, the possible transmission of hereditary traits, methods of family planning, and anything that they may have questions about. All religious groups recognize the need for good health in marriage and recommend that each couple have only as many children as they can properly care for, knowing that child-rearing demands good health on the part of both parents.

People who marry need not only to be endowed with good health, but they need also to know how to conserve both their own health and that of their mates. This requires knowledge of the fundamentals of nutrition, waste elimination, and general physical and mental hygiene. People cannot avoid undue strain in producing and rearing children without a diet containing adequate but not excessive amounts of carbohydrates, fats, proteins, vitamins, minerals, and water. They also need adequate rest, exercise, and recreation. They need to understand and to satisfy each other's sexual needs and to feel free to express their love for each other by physical methods. This means that they need to learn how to regulate sexual appetite just as all people need to learn how to regulate appetite for food, drink, and sleep.

Marriage does not confer freedom from discipline of the sexual appetite, as some of the boys and girls who say they are marrying because they are in love seem to believe. When conception occurs— and it may even be on the honeymoon—it is not unlikely that the obstetrician will recommend abstinence from sexual intercourse for one or more months. He will probably recommend abstinence during the six weeks preceding and the six weeks following childbirth. There will be other times when the husband or the wife will be too fatigued to engage in coitus although they will probably never be too tired for some kind of physical expression of affection. Actually, nothing is more relaxing to the man or woman exhausted from earning the living or from caring for sick children, for instance, than the tender caress of a loving mate.

The Role of Heredity

People who are considering marriage and those already married usually have an interest in heredity. Each one brings to the marriage a set of genes which has been passed to her and to him from the parents. They in turn each pass on a set to each of their children. This transmission of genes from one generation to the next is accomplished by means of an orderly mechanism which we shall describe briefly. Every human being has his and her own *genotype*, a set of genes borne on chromosomes, one set of which comes from the father by way of the sperm and the other set from the mother by way of the egg. Once the union of the sperm and egg has been achieved, the sex and the physical and mental potentialities of the individual are determined. While they may be modified by the environment, they cannot be eliminated.

To see how the transmission of hereditary traits occurs in a given marriage let us take a hypothetical husband and wife who at 21 years of age decide to marry. Figure 12–1 shows that Joan and James have in their cells 23 pairs of chromosomes, one pair of which, *XX* and *XY*, are sex chromosomes. They received half of these chromosomes in the egg from their mothers and half in the sperm from their fathers. Joan is a female because she received an *X* chromosome from both parents, and James is a male because he received an *X* from his mother and a *Y* from his father. For some years, both of them have been producing sex cells. If in the first year of their marriage, one of Joan's eggs bearing an *X* chromosome (as they all must) is fertilized by one of James' sperms which also happens to bear an *X* chromosome, about nine months later, their first child, a little girl, Sally, will be born to them. If this same chromosome combination occurs about two years later, another little girl, Susan, will be born. If, however, two years or so later, an egg is fertilized by a *Y*-bearing sperm, they will have a little boy, Samuel.

It happens infrequently that both ovaries produce an egg at the same time, or that one ovary produces two eggs simultaneously. If this happens to Joan, she may have twin boys, twin girls, or boy and girl twins. These will be fraternal twins. Even less frequently, a single fertilized egg may begin to divide into cells but they may split into two groups of cells. If the split is complete, Joan would have

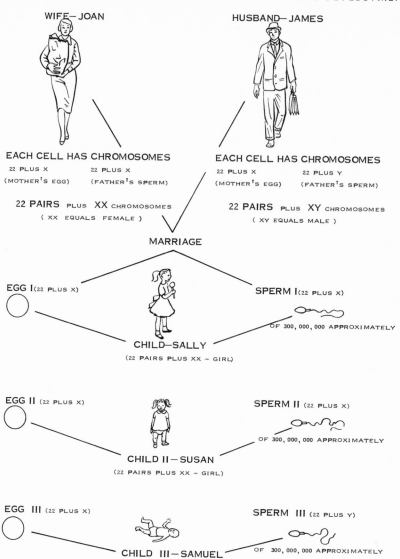

FUTURE CONCEPTIONS: BOY? GIRL? TWIN BOYS? TWIN GIRLS?
                    TWIN BOY AND GIRL?

Fig. 12–1. The mechanisms of heredity.

twin boys or twin girls, but not boy and girl twins because it would be the same sperm that started the lives of both of them. These would be identical twins.

We mentioned above that physical and mental potentialities are determined by genes on chromosomes. Let us suppose that Joan and James both have dark eyes, but that they each had one light-eyed parent. In human beings, dark eye color is dominant over light eye color. Let us suppose that both the egg and the sperm which began Sally's life each carried genes for light eye color and none for dark eye color. Sally then will have light eyes which will never turn dark brown or black. Suppose the egg and sperm that began Susan's life each carried genes for dark eye color and no genes for light eye color. Susan then will develop dark eyes probably fairly early in life.

Let us also suppose that the egg that began Samuel's life carried genes for dark eye color while the sperm which fertilized it carried genes for light eye color only. Since dark is dominant over light, Samuel will early in life develop dark eyes also.

This is the mechanism, highly simplified, of course, by which characteristics such as skin color, stature, tendency toward slenderness or stoutness, susceptibility to colds, sensitivity to sounds and colors, blood types, mathematical and musical skills, and many other traits are transmitted from parents to children. It is obvious why parents are interested in heredity.

Facts Parents Need To Know

In Chapter 7 we gave a generalized account of the development of the reproductive organs and how they function. It is important for men and women who plan to marry and to rear children to have a sound, even if not an extremely detailed knowledge of the human body of both sexes because it is their responsibility to inculcate in the minds and feelings of their children sound, comfortable attitudes about the body and its use. Practically everybody who has given the subject any thought agrees that whether parents are aware of it or not education about reproduction begins in the home. Such education is likely to be more satisfactory if parents feel comfortable about the subject themselves and are in command of an accurate and reasonably complete vocabulary.

A brief account of pregnancy and birth may be helpful here. Human lives begin only when the nucleus of a sperm fuses with that of an egg. Ovulation, the production and release of an egg from an ovary, occurs in most adult women once between each two menstrual periods. Intensive research indicates that it frequently occurs about two weeks before the onset of the next period unless conception (union of egg and sperm) interferes. Research indicates also that an egg is capable of being fertilized for only about 24 hours following the time of its expulsion from the ovary. Sperms have been found capable of living in the reproductive tubes of women for a variable number of days. Because no woman can be certain of the length of her future menstrual cycles, and because of the variability of time during which sperms retain their fertilizing power, it is very difficult for most couples to know when pregnancy can and cannot occur.

As a result of this uncertainty it is advisable for couples either (1) to wait to marry until they can welcome children, or (2) to marry and follow the instructions of a competent physician in the use of a reliable, harmless method of contraception. By employing the latter, they can space their children's births. In passing, it should be mentioned that the Roman Catholic Church favors the first of these two alternatives, but under certain circumstances sanctions the use of the rhythm method which depends upon the regularity of the woman's ovulation process. Most other faiths approve of reliable, medically tested methods.

The presumptive signs of pregnancy following coitus are: (1) delay of a menstrual period, (2) more than usual frequency of need to urinate, (3) tingling sensations in the breasts, and (4) uneasy sensations originating in the digestive tract. Any or all of these symptoms may occur in the nonpregnant woman, of course, but in an emotionally well-balanced woman who has engaged in coitus they usually indicate that she has conceived.

If this has happened, the couple soon notices other symptoms. Ordinarily no further, or very little, vaginal bleeding occurs, the woman becomes accustomed to the behavior of her digestive and urinary tracts, and her breasts and abdomen begin to enlarge. Wise couples follow a competent obstetrician's advice concerning diet, rest, exercise, and marital relations. Usually during the fifth month of pregnancy, the woman begins to be conscious of the stirrings of the fetus within her uterus. The positive signs of pregnancy are present in most cases by this time. They are: (1) the doctor's detection of the fetal heartbeat, (2) his being able to feel the fetal body, (3) and the mother's detection of fetal muscular movements.

Approximately 280 days from the date of the onset of her last true menstrual period, the signs of labor occur. They are: (1) the rhythmic contraction of the longitudinal muscles of the uterus at approximately 30-minute intervals, which gradually shorten, (2) the breaking of the membranes (water sac) surrounding the fetus, with a resulting gush of warm, amniotic fluid from the vagina, and (3) a pinkish discharge from the vagina, commonly called "the show."

Most obstetricians today instruct their patients to get in contact with them when any of these symptoms begin. Few doctors find it possible to assist at home deliveries today, and usually instruct their patients to get to the hospital as soon as the symptoms seem to be fairly certain to culminate in birth.

Most hospitals like the husband or some other relative with whom the woman feels comfortable to stay with her during the hours of labor. When the neck of the uterus is fully dilated, she is taken to the delivery room, and usually in a matter of minutes, the baby is born and the umbilical cord is severed. Soon after the placenta is delivered, and mother and baby leave the delivery room to meet the father.

Parents need this kind of information not only for their own comfort but also as a background from which to educate their children. If the parents do a good job at home, the schools, churches, and synagogues have something solid to build upon, and education concerning reproduction will be a cooperative undertaking.

"In Sickness and in Health"

While the need for good health in marriage has been stressed, we are all aware that illness of one kind or another is the common lot of men and women sooner or later in life. Most marriage ceremonies wisely recognize this by inserting the phrases, "in sickness and in health" and "until death do us part." For most healthy young people, the prospect of disabling illness is so remote and unlikely that they easily convince themselves that they would be faithful spouses should it occur. The statistics on increased life expectancy and conquest of disease by antibiotics have lulled modern men and women into believing that good health and long life is the normal expectancy

of everybody. This is an erroneous belief, as we see if we pay attention to the ages at which some of our relatives and acquaintances
are having heart attacks, developing ulcers, breaking down mentally
and emotionally, or being involved in traffic accidents. Even so, it is
probably the common cold, headache, nausea of pregnancy, and
upset digestive tracts that most frequently mar the joys of married
life, especially in the early years when children are being reared.
Emotionally mature married people are able to sustain each other
during periods of such trials.

ECONOMIC ASPECTS OF MARRIAGE

The phrase, "for richer for poorer" expresses a concept which in
some form or another occurs in most marriage ceremonies. It conveys the idea that marriage is also an economic relationship. Men
and women, with their children, have very tangible needs such as
food, shelter, and clothing. "Economics" is a term derived from a
Greek word meaning "the management of the household." In earlier
times, when each family unit was more or less self-sufficient, it meant
something different from what it means today, when every family is
absolutely dependent upon the activities of other people for producing its needs and making them readily available. Nevertheless, the
needs are fundamentally the same as they always were, and the
management of the household still involves provision, preparation,
and maintenance of daily and long-term needs.

Today, even though to a limited degree we are living in a "do-it-
yourself" era, provision, preparation, and maintenance require that
abstract something which we call "money" and we think of money as
"income" and "outgo." People who are contemplating marriage need
to have a fairly realistic idea of three main aspects of their economic
situation: the amount of expected income, the source or sources of
their income, and the uses to which their income will be put.

Amount of Expected Income

Attitudes concerning the premarital discussion of expected income
change with the times. At one time, no man would be expected to
marry a woman who could not bring to the marriage a dowry of
some substance, and no woman would be expected to marry a man
who could not keep her in the manner in which her father had accustomed her. Somewhat later, it became indicative of bad taste on the

prospective bride's part to mention or even to think of what her prospective husband could provide, such worldly matters being taken care of by discussion and agreement between her father and the young man concerned.

Nowadays any man and woman who do not consider their expected income are foolish and unrealistic. Men and women sufficiently mature to undertake marriage with its likely sequel, parenthood, discuss in detail how much money they can expect to take in. They decide whether or not marriage is feasible. If it is, they usually have to make some adjustments in their standards of living in order to make it work. Nobody can tell a man and woman just how much they must have, because their needs will depend upon many factors—their tastes, goals, skills in housekeeping, and their willingness to develop a flexible budget. In other words, their budget must be tailor-made to fit their particular needs. Just what they can do will depend to some extent upon where their income comes from and how reliable it is.

Source or Sources of Income

The most common source of income among married people today is the salary that goes with the man's job, but this is by no means the only source. Today many young people report that their parents are subsidizing their marriage entirely or in part. In some cases, especially where the young husband still has professional education to finish, it is the wife's salary that supports the marriage. In other cases, both married partners have salaries from jobs. Some young people report that they have investments which pay reliable returns, and some are recipients of veterans' benefits for education and home-buying. Whatever the source, it is important and enlightening for married people or people contemplating marriage to have a full understanding of the sources of the income upon which their marriage depends both at the present and on into the future.

Uses of Income

Where does the income go in marriage? The most realistic young adults usually think of shelter first. Marriage means among other things that a man and a woman who have been living in different homes now share a home. It is amazing how oblivious some young people are to this seemingly obvious fact. It is not unusual for a boy and a girl who are planning an elaborate wedding to be unsure as to where they will live. One of them may answer to the question,

"Where are you going to live?"

"Well, we aren't sure yet. Of course, we can always live with my parents."

But let us return to more realistic young people. Most of them today report that they have leased an apartment. These apartments may be in regular apartment buildings, in converted homes, in college or service housing projects, or over garages. They vary in size and facilities; some are furnished and some are unfurnished. Rents differ with size, utilities, furnishings, and location. Most married couples rent apartments near the job or school of one or the other, or of both if one can be found.

It goes without saying that not all couples live in apartments. Depending on their income and what is available, some build or buy homes, some rent homes furnished or unfurnished, and some live in trailers. Today's young couples tend to be ingenious in finding and fixing places up so that they are comfortable temporarily. What is even more important is that they are learning to work things out cooperatively.

The next item that a realistic young man and woman think about is food. They know that being in love does not destroy the appetite for food, but, rather, that it is likely to increase the need for food. They get hungry, and many of them do the marketing together, learning of each other's likes and dislikes, comparing prices of brands, and working out a mutually satisfying set of menus. Most of them find steak and mushrooms out of the question except for special occasions. They also find that if they are skillful at cooking and at judging the correct quantities, they can eat for much less than if they take meals out. In addition, they learn to know each other better while they are preparing meals, enjoying the results of their work, and sharing the cleaning-up activities afterwards.

Clothing soon becomes an item in the budget. Most young people enter marriage fairly well supplied with clothing, but things do wear out or become unfashionable. Women who sew have a great advantage over those who do not. They make garments for themselves and their children that give them much greater satisfaction and variety than if they have to buy everything ready-made. Many young men and women find it enlightening to calculate the cost of the clothing for each during the year previous to their marriage. Most women

spend more on clothing than most men do, but it saves many unpleasant surprises in marriage if the wife has known ahead how much
her husband's clothing costs and if he has known what his wife's
costs. In order to do this reasonably adequately, each one keeps track
of how many of each article, such as hose, underwear, shoes, etc.,
he buys in a year. If certain articles, such as overcoats, suits, and fur
coats, are expected to be used over a period of years, the cost is
divided by the number of years the wearer expects to use them.
Articles such as cosmetics and shaving needs may be included in the
clothing list, although some people have another category which
they call *grooming* under which they include haircuts, beauty shop
costs, and jewelry. Many prospective husbands who have been
opposed to their wives working for wages change their minds when
they see these lists, and this change may be all to the good.

Other avenues for the income are costs of transportation, house-
and clothes-cleaning and maintenance, insurance, medical and
dental expenses, education, needs of children, religious expenses,
gifts, contributions, luxuries, entertainment and recreation, taxes,
and, hopefully, savings. The realistic couple keeps track of these
various items before marriage and later on during the years of the
marriage. Some of these items are fairly constant, taking into consideration inflation and possible deflation. By the time most people
marry, they have a fair idea of how much smoking costs them, they
can have a fair idea of their annual dental expense and of their con-
tribution to their church or synagogue, for instance. On the other
hand, they have very little idea of what their medical expenses may
be, especially as children come along.

While it has been pointed out that the having and rearing of
children is one of the basic purposes for marriage, it is amazing how
many young people only vaguely recognize the possibility of a child's
coming in the first year of marriage and in some cases, another in
each subsequent year. Again realistic young men and women are
aware of this and discuss it before marriage. They decide together
how soon they can afford the first one and how frequently subse-
quently. If they feel that they cannot afford children at all for a
while, they decide either to wait to get married or to see a competent physician about a reliable, safe method of contraception. The
fact that many couples today either delay their marriages or marry
and delay having their children until professional education is completed and then have three, four, or more children should give us

faith in the discipline and forethought of at least some young adult members of the human species.

The Handling of Money as a Source of Harmony

When a man and woman marry, they establish a partnership that is as real as any business partnership and one that has as much if not more need for financial protection and security. Generally speaking, unless the income and property are very large, joint ownership of property and savings is highly desirable in marriage. To own a home jointly is a distinct advantage, for under the laws of most states, each partner is thus considered to own the property in its entirety. At the death of one partner, it is automatically the property of the other, since he or she owned it all the time. The same is true of checking and savings accounts, bonds, and so forth. The knowledge of this joint ownership to a man and woman of good faith, is a strong tie binding them closer together in the management of their economy, no matter how small or large it may be. Some people question the wisdom of this arrangement, but two people who cannot trust each other to the extent of the joint mingling of their *material* possessions will hardly be able to trust each other in the many varied and more subtly intangible areas that are present in every marriage.

Another source of harmony is the writing of wills by a man and his wife. A will may seem to be of remote importance in the days of the courtship or even early marriage, but it can be one of the most important and enlightening documents that the couple will ever prepare. When a good man and a good woman listen to each other's consideration for the other in the event of the death of one or the other and for their children in the event of both their deaths, an understanding and appreciation of each other develops more fully than it can through almost any other process.

In connection with the careful preparation of the wills of a man and wife, consideration and selection of insurance programs, guardianship for the children, the wise use of credit, and various other subjects naturally enter the minds of the couple. It is beyond the scope of this book to deal specifically with these matters. Most well-established banks employ individuals who are specially trained to help couples of all ages to see their way through these matters for their best good, which, of course, is also for the good of the banks, the insurance companies, and for society in general. Society does not profit in any way when married couples have financial difficulties; it suffers in terms of miserable people, broken homes, and juvenile delinquency.

LEGAL ASPECTS OF MARRIAGE

The only legal form of marriage in most of the civilized countries of the world today is monogamy—the union of one man and one woman who live together as husband and wife until one of them dies. Termination of marriage by divorce has become common, but it is still the exception to the rule. It is paradoxical that divorce has become common, since according to the terms of the legal contract of marriage, it is impossible. All marriage contracts either state or imply that the contract is for life regardless of the conditions of the man and woman concerned at the time of the marriage, and regardless of what may happen to them through the years. Most countries have devised laws which attempt to prevent men and women who lack the qualities necessary to carry out the terms of such a demanding contract from getting a license to enter it. These laws attempt to establish minimum standards of age; of physical, mental, emotional, and moral health; of relationship by blood or marriage; and of economic status.

Bronislaw Malinowski, a profound student of human relationships, has described the marriage contract well as follows:

Marriage is the most important legal contract in every human society, the one which refers to the continuity of the race; it implies a most delicate and difficult adjustment of a passionate and emotional relationship with domestic and economic cooperation; it involves the cohabitation of male and female, perennially attracted and yet in many ways forever incompatible; it focuses in a difficult personal relationship of two people the interest of wider groups: of their progeny, of their parents, of their kindred, and in fact of the whole community.*

Marriage involves specific responsibilities and obligations on the part of both partners, as well as rights and privileges. Mature people tend to be more aware of the former than they are of the latter. Immature individuals are more aware of their rights and privileges than they are of their responsibilities and obligations.

* *Encyclopaedia Britannica*, 1947, p. 945.

ETHICAL ASPECTS OF MARRIAGE

The civil laws under which we live teach us from very early life a good deal about what is acceptable and what is unacceptable behavior in group living, but most of the behavior of married people that really matters to the two of them is beyond the reach of legislation. It is in this area of intimate behavior that the real virtues (or vices) of married life develop.

In order really to fulfill the purposes of marriage, a husband and wife can hold nothing from each other; that is, nothing that concerns them as a unit. Some married people say, "We tell each other everything," which is both an impossibility and an absurdity. "Everything" means just that, everything they ever do or did. Then how much *do* married people tell each other, if it is a thoroughgoing marriage? The answer is: everything that matters.

Young and older people often ask, "What matters and what doesn't matter?" One fairly useful criterion is: anything upon which we find ourselves spending any appreciable amount of time or thought matters to our mates. Usually these things are not the most obvious ones, such as our activities before marriage, but things such as buying something without consultation, possibly on "time," then figuring out how to scrimp to pay for it without the other's knowledge, going to our parents' homes and talking over our own marital affairs, drinking secretly if the mate disapproves or more than the mate knows, or going out secretly with people whom the mate does not like. All these are clearly "vices" in the marriage relationship.

Some things that we may erroneously believe to be "virtues" occupy us and interfere with our marital harmony. For instance, a husband may have a difficult time with his superior on the job during the day. With the idea that he is sparing his wife worry by not telling her about it when he comes home (in a sour mood), he brushes off her welcome, is gruff during the evening meal with the children, spends a silent evening behind the newspaper, and retires sullenly to bed. He believes he is sparing his wife some uneasiness on his account, but how does she feel and what can she think? He would not have to share professional matters with her, but he could tell her that it has been a hard day, that he is tired and disturbed, but that as far as she is concerned, they are all right.

Similarly, wives often become preoccupied over one thing or another. A wife may get the idea that she has cancer, for instance. With all the publicity given cancer today, it is easy for anyone who spends a good deal of time at home to fancy that she has certain symptoms. Of course, she should have a check-up, but she is afraid to. The thought of cancer chills her. She fancies her days are numbered and feels that she must "spare" her husband the awful knowledge. But that she really spares him is unlikely. She is quiet and glum, she snaps at the children, and is tense and reluctant when her husband embraces her.

What we hope to convey is that it is a serious thing for married people not to keep their lines of communication open by conversing with each other. Some people may feel that what has been said here is ridiculous, but it is not unusual for students to report sadly that their parents live under the same roof but that they have scarcely spoken to each other for years. Each addresses the children but not each other, and when the children grow up and leave the home, the man and woman are almost or completely silent.

Married people have to learn fairness, justice, and forebearance with one another. Their relationship is so intimate that a goodly supply of these virtues is necessary. Tenderness means much, and gratitude for what they have is probably the most valued emotion married people can feel.

Former students remind us that writers on marriage usually omit what they themselves consider one of the most valuable assets in marriage, namely, a sense of kindly humor. This is true. Textbooks tend to be devoid of humor. A marriage that is devoid of humor must become unbearable. Humor is the sense which makes possible a kindly contemplation of the incongruities of life. Where more frequently and more intimately than in marriage, do we run into the incongruities of life? The husband and wife who can contemplate kindly the things that each does, enjoy each other's chuckles, and who can help each other to smile at themselves, have what it takes to reduce tension and to "pick up the pieces" and continue until the end of life, as their vows require.

Chastity and fidelity are virtues required of us by civil law, and they are infinitely wise laws that attempt to maintain these virtues. Chastity means virginity on the part of both men and women until marriage. Because men and women are human beings, there are many who fail to retain their virginity until their marriage. If they are fortunate and grow in wisdom, they may develop into happy married partners, but still it is desirable and possible for men and women both to enter marriage ready to learn with each other to be satisfactory partners in the most intimate of all relationships.

Although some marriages survive instances of infidelity on the part of one mate or the other, anything but complete fidelity is incompatible with both immediate and long-term success in marriage. A man and woman who understand and keep their vows are as much one when they are three thousand miles apart as when they stand together beside their first child's crib.

SUGGESTIONS FOR FURTHER DISCUSSION

1. How do you think the basic purposes for marriage listed in this chapter figure in the minds of people who applied today for licenses to marry? Find out what other members of the class think about this question.

2. Try to phrase your own definition of the different kinds of love: brotherly, filial, erotic, conjugal, and parental.

3. What do you think are the qualifications for "marryability" and for "marriageability"?

4. The phrase "forsaking all others" occurs frequently in marriage ceremonies. What does this mean?

5. What do you see as the advantages of the married life? Of the single life?

6. What do you see as the advantages of unmixed marriage? Of some kinds of mixed marriage?

7. A senior college student told her clergyman recently that she believed her fiancé loved her chiefly for her intellectual vigor. How realistic do you think she is about marriage?

8. What effect do you think the quality of the parents' marriage has upon children's concepts and attitudes toward marriage?

REFERENCES FOR FURTHER STUDY

HILLIARD, M. *The Woman Doctor Looks at Love and Life.* New York: Doubleday & Co., Inc., 1957. A warm, professional treatment of marriage, which helps both men and women to understand women.

MARTIN, P. C., and VINCENT, E. L. *Human Biological Development.* New York: The Ronald Press Co., 1960. Ch. 13, structure of adult reproductive apparatus, development of external genitalia; Ch. 14, preparation for adulthood, marriage and parenthood, pregnancy and childbirth.

PRESSEY, S. L., and KUHLEN, R. G. *Psychological Development Through the Life Span.* New York: Harper & Bros., 1957. Ch. 12, heterosexual development, marriage, and family relationships. Summaries of studies.

SCHEINFELD, A. *The Human Heredity Handbook*. Philadelphia: J. B. Lippincott Co., 1956. A clear and interesting account of human heredity, emphasizing matters that interest the non-specialist as well as the geneticist.

STONE, H. M., and STONE, A. *A Marriage Manual*. New York: Simon & Schuster, Inc., 1952. A practical question and answer guide to an understanding of marriage, particularly from the physical viewpoint, but not exclusively so. Excellent.

For film suggestions see Film Supplement, in the Appendix.

CHAPTER 13

Middle Adulthood

GENERAL CONSIDERATIONS

Middle adulthood is generally thought of as the period from 40 or 45 years of age to about 65, the latter age being the one when retirement becomes possible and in some instances mandatory. As in preceding developmental periods, both boundaries are flexible, varying from individual to individual.

We saw the transition in puberty and adolescence from the gradual development of the infant and child into the full powers of adulthood. Middle and old age is also a transition, a gradual decline from the peak physical and psychological powers of adulthood to the senescence of advanced old age. Some of the physical decline begins in certain of the systems around 40 years of age. Changes in other systems begin somewhat later. A fairly dramatic evidence of such changes is the menopause in women and the climacteric in men.

Middle Age Now Later Than Formerly

We have defined the beginning of the period of old age and hence the ending of middle age as being around 65 years. This definition is a useful one in the middle of the twentieth century in most countries of the world. It did not, however, define the beginning of old age at the beginning of the twentieth century. In 1900, for example, as Fig. 13–1 shows, the proportion of the population in the United States who lived to be 65 years old was only 4.1 per cent; in 1950 it was 7.6 per cent; in 1958 it was 8.6 per cent; the prediction for 1970 is 9.0 per cent.[190] Between 1900 and 1958 the percentage of the population over 65 in the United States more than doubled; the actual numbers of people over 65 nearly quadrupled, increasing from 3.1 millions in 1900 to 12.3 millions in 1958. Since 1800 the median age of the total population in the United States (meaning that one-half were over this age, one-half under it) was 16 years; by 1950 it was almost 31 years.[197]

The life span, then, has been increasing. Whereas in 1900 few people lived beyond 45 years of age, a substantial part of the population of the world now live to be 65 years old. Life expectation in the

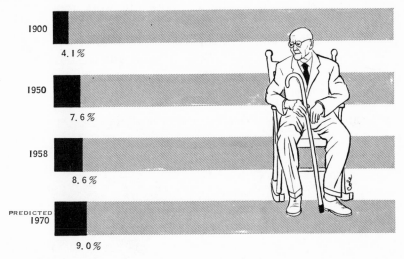

1900

4.1%

1950

7.6%

1958

8.6%

PREDICTED
1970

9.0%

Fig. 13–1. Proportion of population in the United States living to be 65 years old.

United States for the 40-year-old in 1955 was 33.7 years, being on the average about five years longer for women than for men. At age 60 in 1955, the life expectation was on the average 17.5 years, being about three years longer for women than for men. Health and usefulness of the 40- to 65-year-old person have been greatly extended, and the decline of old age has been greatly retarded. The years now referred to as the middle adult years were, until recently, considered old-age years in most countries of the world. In some countries, however, where nutritional deficiencies, disease, severe demands in living, and high maternal illness is general, many people still are physiologically old at 40.

There are, of course, wide individual differences in the onset and speed of the aging processes in all countries.[122] Such factors as heredity, illness record, nutritional history, the amount of stress and strain, of exhausting physical labor, and of good or poor physical and mental hygiene are important in determining how long any given individual remains in the "prime of life" and, therefore, the age at which the processes of decline set in.

Older adolescents often think of the 45-to-65-year period as one of aging, of out-of-date ideas, and of rigidity of habits. They sometimes feel sorry for the generation which is, in their minds, a group of has-beens. Some middle-aged people do give evidence of this and warrant pity. However, for those whose life work requires long training and experience, middle adulthood often represents a time of greatest usefulness and personal fulfillment, of top recognition for achievement (Figs. 13–2, 13–3, 13–4) in professional, business, and personal life. One reason middle adulthood is a period of peak performance in business or the professions is that top achievement in

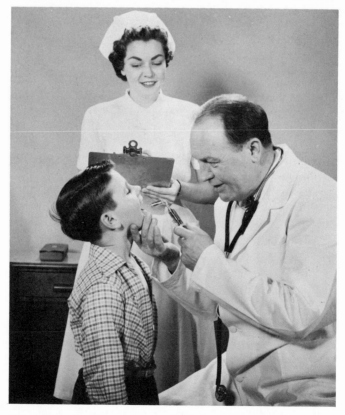

Fig. 13–2. Top recognition and fulfillment: in the professions.

Fig. 13–3. Top recognition and fulfillment: in business.

these lines is not usually possible without seasoned judgment and "know-how." This comes only with accumulated experience. Individuals, as a rule, are not trusted with duties involving great responsibilities until they have given evidence that they can handle such duties. Such responsibilities require sound judgment and skill in handling complicated programs and widely varied personal relationships. Only in rare cases do people under forty years of age possess these qualities.

We can see, then, why studies [125] show that the peak of recognition in the professional societies is in the fifties; leadership in governmental positions such as that needed by ambassadors, senators, top army officers, or judges of the Supreme Court, is in the late fifties or early sixties; and that even in the creative arts which require sound understanding of life and well-developed creative skills, the works of greatest merit are often produced in the middle to later years of the artist's life. For the average worker, regardless of achievement and fame, the peak of earning capacity comes between 45 and 54 years of age.[122] How much income this peak represents, as we have seen earlier, is closely associated with the amount and kind of the worker's preparation, those with higher levels of educational preparation having a higher peak than those with less education.

Fig. 13–4. Top recognition and fulfillment: in homemaking.

Feelings About Accomplishment

How the individual in middle adulthood feels about his achievement sometimes does not have much relevance to the quality of his achievement. In many ways the forties represent a period of testing of how the individual's career is progressing. By the forties and especially by the fifties, the individual who is not proceeding comfortably in his life work finds it increasingly difficult to change jobs. If he is dismissed from a job he is almost sure to find it hard to locate another, even in the field in which he has some experience. If, on the other hand, he is doing well in a career into which he settled soon enough to have built a successful experience, he may apply for other jobs and get them. If he is doing very well, his services are likely to be sought by others, and advancement in his career is likely to proceed at a fairly steady pace.

If an individual finds himself in a "dead end" job, he is almost inevitably forced to evaluate his progress in his work by the time he is forty. Even if he is moving forward in his career, he may and usually does evaluate where he is and where he thinks he may be going. In either of the above cases, he may conclude that he is a success, a partial success, or a failure. The feeling of partial success usually represents a partial achievement of goals once set, or the achievement of such goals, but not of succeeding goals which he has set later as success in previous goals was attained. It may represent a feeling that he has succeeded in some aspects of his work but not in others, or it may mean he feels he has succeeded in the goals he once set for himself, but that he chose the wrong goals. The feeling of failure is often relative. Failure may be recognized as such by people other than the individual, or it may exist only in his feeling about himself. Comparably, the feeling of success may exist only in the mind of an individual who overrates his performance; or his feeling of success may be a true evaluation of a performance judged successful by others as well as by himself. Some men, for example, may have succeeded in the eyes of their co-workers and of the public in general, yet may be failures in the eyes of wives whose ambitions are endless.

Adjustments to Feelings About Success or Failure

Criteria for success, of course, differ. To some people success means making money, to others it means advancing human welfare. To many people it means rearing a family of children who turn out well. One of the basic adjustments most people have to make in the middle adulthood period is an adjustment to the level of success they have achieved in life. Unless there are extenuating circumstances such as marital unhappiness or other personal tragedy, the feeling of success in the life work gives a feeling of personal fulfillment in life. A feeling of failure, however, often results in a sense of inadequacy. Much depends upon the personality developmental background and upon the presence or absence of love, understanding, and support. If an individual has a good personality background, love, understanding, and support he usually manages to find other rewards and other meanings and usefulness in life. If he lacks these he may go to pieces psychologically. In the latter instance he may try to escape his situation in one of the various forms of personality breakdown such as alcoholism or suicide, or he may develop physical conditions associated with intense inner conflict.

THINGS STILL TO BE ACCOMPLISHED

Developmental Tasks of Middle Adulthood

Late adolescents and young adults are often unaware that their parents may have problems of adjustment. It seldom occurs to young people that individuals over forty still have much growing to do and some developmental tasks to accomplish. College students frequently realize as they study the lives of those over forty that they have never before done much thinking about the later half of life and have never realized in a meaningful sense that they themselves would some day be forty, or sixty, or perhaps eighty years old. They are not even aware in a realistic way that the social security deduction from summer employment or from other pay checks is a payment for their own old-age security. Nor have they grasped the fact that their 45-to-50-year-old parents will, in another 15 or 20 years, be retired and "old," and that during these intervening years their parents are probably planning financially, and in other ways, for their retirement.

Taking Civic and Social Responsibility

Let us look at some of the developmental tasks generally thought of as needing to be accomplished in the middle adulthood period. As established citizens in their communities, the forty-to-sixty-year-old is expected to take civic and social responsibility. In early adulthood many people begin to serve on committees and to accept responsibility in civic and community organizations, but because they are climbing the ladder of economic advancement and rearing small children they are not expected to do so unless they can conveniently find time for such activities. At forty and later, having arrived at some stability in economic life and with the children now nearing adulthood, the community turns to the individual in middle adulthood for participation in activities needed to keep the community functioning. Churches, clubs, and volunteer social agencies need leadership, political offices need to be filled, and countless other jobs need to be taken by mature and responsible community members. Unless the mature but not yet aged members take on these jobs the community is left without adequate leadership.

The filling of such community jobs by people in middle adulthood is rewarding both to the community and to the individual. The use of experience and "know-how" in the interests of the community is personally fulfilling. Community work offers new and useful activities at a time when the daily routines are well in hand and offer less excitement than when they were new. Friendships made in such service are usually rewarding and lasting.

Developing Appropriate Leisure-Time Activities

Another developmental task of middle adulthood is the discovery and pursuit of appropriate leisure-time activities. If the individual gives time to the service of his community he accomplishes part at least of two tasks at the same time. As physical strength and speed decrease, the leisure-time activities pursued in middle age must be modified. Strenuous physical activities such as playing tennis or handball at a fast pace and for long periods of time usually have to be replaced by golf, bowling, and other less strenuous games. Dancing on crowded floors to the pound of percussion instruments into the late morning hours usually yields to evenings of reading, music, radio, television, or cards at home with two or three other couples.

Instead of pursuing many interests avidly, the middle-aged adult tends to concentrate on a few favorites.[87] Not only is more reading done because at this age there is more time to read, but there tends to be more discrimination in things read. In reading the newspaper, for example, greater attention is paid to editorials and world news and less to sports, crime, and disaster news than in earlier adulthood. When books are read there is greater preference for history, detective and love stories than for science and sports. There is less interest in reading or talking about sex than earlier,[21] and less about child rearing than when children were a commanding point of focus. More discrimination is also practiced in radio and movie selections. Television in recent years has become a primary recreational interest for middle-aged individuals partly because they have somewhat more time for it and partly because it can be seen with a minimum of effort. In general, however, the passive watching of television characterizes middle-aged adults of the lower socioeconomic brackets more than it does those who have more money to spend on theater, concerts, and other out-of-the-home amusements.[26]

Among the favorite enjoyments of middle age, when circumstances permit, is a vegetable and flower garden which offers gratifying activity and nutritional advantage at the same time. Church membership, along with social, business, and other club memberships rise sharply in the forties and fifties, but decline somewhat after sixty, and more so after sixty-five. This decline is associated with decline in general energy, and is also related to curtailment in income. Although church contributions are a priority in the budgets of many older people, dues for club membership are often beyond the limits of the income.

If, however, finances make continued social contacts feasible, middle-aged people, being more mature in adjustments to others and having more experience in social activities than younger people, are usually more successful in social situations than at any other time in life. There are exceptions. For some people, as they pass through the physical and psychological changes in middle age, energy may be lacking. The preoccupation of some people with their inner struggles may interfere with smooth adjustment to others, for a time. Unless the personality difficulties become fixed and the lost social contacts fail to be re-established, the interruption of social life is usually only temporary. The individual regains balance and again picks up the enjoyable pattern of social life. If the members of a social group are of the same general age, several members are likely to be experiencing the same difficulties at the same time. In this case, they usually understand and tolerate each other until the situation "returns to normal."

Looking Toward Retirement

Preretirement attitudes affect the individual's satisfaction or dissatisfaction with retirement. If the attitude is favorable, satisfaction in retirement is almost universal; if the preretirement attitude is unfavorable, it produces dissatisfaction in retirement. Preretirement attitudes of satisfaction or dissatisfaction occur whether retirement is financially well or not-so-well provided for. One of the important factors associated with satisfaction or dissatisfaction in retirement, then, appears to be the preparation made for living as retired people. Considerable education of the public about the facts of retirement and how to prepare for it has led to an understanding that one important way to prepare is to develop, in middle age, interests other than those connected with work.

Increasing numbers of middle-aged people are now conscientiously developing hobbies as a preparation for the time when retirement from the vocation or profession leaves them with time hanging heavily on their hands. Successful business and professional people have more hobbies in old age than do people who were less successful in earlier life.[213] This is probably because successful people are more likely than the unsuccessful to be forward looking. Women, whether working or not, have greater variability in their hobbies throughout the adult years than do men.

Relating to the Spouse as a Changing Person

One of the frequently listed developmental tasks of middle adulthood is the need to relate oneself to the husband or wife in the changing pattern of life. The implication is that as children leave home and as the pressures of supporting them and of maintaining a home for them reduce, the marriage partners need to learn to know each other as changing people rather than simply as husband or wife, father or mother.

Age changes personality, especially during early adulthood with its many pressing responsibilities. Marriage provides the most sensitive tests of maturity. In some marriages the task of adjusting to the spouse as a changing person is not difficult because the love underlying the marriage is sound and has stood the test of time. The two personalities have grown through the years along parallel rather than diverging lines. Such marriages have been growing relationships between two people. When middle age comes, it deepens and makes more enjoyable the personal relationship between the marriage partners. As the responsibilities of early adulthood lighten, the two individuals have opportunities to develop new interests both as individuals and as a couple. Such wives and husbands communicate with each other in ways that manifest a love that has far outgrown the ecstacies of the body alone—a love which somehow ennobles two human beings, each of whom knows that life without the other would be barren indeed.

Not all married couples, however, have grown together through the years. Some couples as young people, "fell in love" in a turmoil of physical feelings which at the time seemed to be "for all time." They married before they had time to know each other, to discover the basic ideas and values which governed their individual lives and set the direction for their future personality development. In middle adulthood such couples often look at each other and find that they are strangers. The physical excitement has given way to monotonous routine. As children leave home, there is nothing but convention and habit to hold them together.

In middle adulthood, with freedom from child care and with more time and money for recreation, there is often a renewal of social contacts. What form this social activity takes is likely to be affected by the patterns set in the earlier lives of the individual or the couple concerned. Sometimes middle-aged social life becomes an attempt to return to the excitement of an earlier gay and varied social whirl. Sometimes it is an attempt to capture the fun once longed and sought for, but never quite found. In either of these cases, if the marriage in middle age has little meaning, there are likely to be flirtations with other people. In some cases, these flirtations lead to divorce. Subsequent marriages under these conditions are often regretted, since the new alliance may prove to have roots no deeper than the original alliance and even fewer shared associations. This is especially true if the former marriage produced children who were, at least, one bond. The married person who too hastily sues for divorce, the partner who thinks he or she is in love with another, very often lives to regret this action. A partner's faith in the strength of a marriage, whatever its history, will often see that marriage through such a trying period and into the building of a new and more satisfying relationship.

Assisting Teen-Age Children To Become Responsible and Happy Adults

Another task of importance in middle age is the "freeing" of adolescent children so that they can grow into adult independence. In Chapter 8 we saw the struggle some adolescent young people have to free themselves of parental domination, in order to grow up. Adolescent-parent struggles are often complicated by middle age changes in the parents.

Let us look at this from the viewpoint of the middle-aged adult. We recall that at many stages in the infant and childhood periods parents fail to relinquish disciplinary techniques which work with the children at one age but do not work when the child grows into a new stage of development. The situation often becomes difficult when changes come as rapidly as they do in puberty and early adolescence, and when parents are also experiencing changes. It is an unhappy coincidence that often just as the mother begins to experience the symptoms of menopause, her children may be entering puberty or adolescence so that she is uncertain of her own feelings and symptoms and somewhat irritable, while her son is sulky or defiant and her daughter bursts into tears at the slightest provocation. The husband and father, who has his own troubles, centering around his job, financial problems, and approaching age of retirement, is also subjected to considerable strain because of the tensions at home. For the parents who have devoted a great deal of their attention to their children, it is difficult to get used to the feeling of being less necessary to the children than was once true.

At the same time that the parents are experiencing this feeling, the young people are trying especially hard to be independent individuals. The struggle is likely to be particularly difficult with the oldest, the first to leave the home, or the youngest child, the last one whose "loss" leaves the mother jobless in her accustomed field of child rearing. The father often becomes involved in these struggles as he attempts to reinforce the mother's position, or perhaps to defend the child's right to be free. In addition to the above factors there is the fact that the middle-aged parents, having reared the child, are greatly concerned for his welfare. They have lived not only through the mistakes of their own youth, but have had some 20 to 25 years to observe what happens to young people in a society which gives them unprecedented responsibility and freedom. The parents know that their sons and daughters are making choices that will affect the rest of their lives, and often making them without sufficient maturity or competent guidance. It is understandable that parents have difficulty in accomplishing the task of freeing adolescent children.

Assistance to Aging Parents

Another developmental task of middle-aged people is to accept and adjust to the fact that their parents are aging, and that in time they must find means of providing adequate care for them. In the middle of the nineteenth century, grandparents held an honored position in the center of the family, and their housing and support by the next younger generation was taken for granted. In the middle of the twentieth century, the situation is somewhat different. The expectation by the aging parents, by the younger family, and by the total culture is no longer that aging parents must live with the children. Today's families are increasingly making their decisions about how to care for aging parents without concern for what other people think of their decisions.[38] Older people in turn are seeing the advantages of freedom from the tensions of living in their sons' and daughters' homes, and are trying increasingly to make other arrangements for their later years. Peoples of all ages concerned seem to be acquiring a more flexible viewpoint about patterns of care for aging parents.

Populations today have become fluid in movement. The younger people have moved from their childhood homes. The older population has also been more mobile than it once was, but is still typically less mobile than the younger generation. Older people today tend to stay in the communities where they reared their families, or if they can afford it, move into "retirement" climates. Those who can so move are usually not financial problems to their middle-aged children. These are a small minority of the presently aging population. Today's middle-aged adult lives typically at some distance from his parents, at the time when they find themselves in need of physical, emotional, or financial help. If either of the aging parents has died, the other may be excessively lonely, which might not happen if the two generations were living more closely together.

Old Age Assistance programs, both federal and state, have alleviated to some extent the burden of financial support of aging people previously borne by middle-aged adults. An increasing proportion of the aging population will benefit in the future from pensions and annuities, which will in turn help to lighten the load of the middle-aged.

The majority of aging people today, however, either lack funds or receive inadequate funds from pensions, social security, and other sources. Generally speaking, because families today tend to be smaller than they used to be, it is more difficult for the middle-aged group to share the cost of support of the older generation. There are fewer sons and daughters to spread the care among them when the aging parents become infirm.

There is seldom an extra bedroom in the home that would give an aging mother or father or both adequate privacy and peace of mind. The extra expense of a larger apartment or additional rooms in a house is prohibitive for most families who have to meet or recently have met the costs of education for their children. Unless there is space for reasonable privacy in the home the strains which normally arise when two mature generations try to share the same home are multiplied until the emotional tensions may become intolerable for all concerned. Many older people recognize these difficulties and express a preference to be cared for in some way other than in the homes of their children.

Older people dread leaving old friends and familiar surroundings. Until they become actually unable to care for themselves, they much prefer remaining in their own home or in the community with which they are familiar. If this is impossible, they and the middle-aged generation often find themselves happier and more relaxed if the aged people can be housed near, but not in, the home of their children. Thus they can visit back and forth and share holidays together but can live their own lives without too much adjustment or interference. If this means a change of community for the aged parents, the middle-aged sons and daughters usually find that the effort to locate new friends for the parents, in churches or other ways, pays dividends in happiness and independence.

Let us look at the current housing situation for aged parents and their children. In 1952 about 50 per cent of persons over 65 years of age were married and living with their spouses. Of these older couples about 25 per cent were living with their children.[206] About 30 per cent of the men over 65 who were divorced or widowed lived with their children. About 45 per cent of the single, divorced, or widowed women over 65 years of age lived with a younger generation of their family.

In the homes where elderly couples lived with their sons or daughters, the senior couple was designated as head of the household in about three-quarters of the cases. The aging mother or father who lived with a son or a daughter was designated as the head of the household in only about one-third of the cases. In those cases where the older person was head of the household, the adjustment was most difficult for the middle-aged people who were living in households not basically their own. In those cases where an older person was not head of the household, the adjustment was most difficult for them. The aged person, who has for years been head of his own household, often experiences the strain of adjustment in a home where he does not have authority. Some elderly people manage to adjust successfully, especially where the middle-aged people and their children show an understanding of the situation and make a real place for them in the daily routine in the home.

When grandparents, parents, and children live in the same home, the home is called a three-generation home. Some such homes are composed of aged grandparents, middle-aged parents, and adolescent children; others have middle-aged grandparents, young parents, and young children or infants. In the former case, where the middle-aged people head the household and therefore are responsible for the harmony of family living, the youngest generation is usually in adolescence, with all this means in tensions normally experienced between adolescents and their parents. In such households there often arises a situation in which the grandparents tend to "take sides" with the adolescents. If the grandparent is a widow or widower, and hence feels somewhat alone, there is temptation to "buy" the affection of the youngest generation by using such money and influence as are available to support the wishes of the adolescent. Adolescents, in turn, are only human if they take advantage of the situation to promote their own wishes. This places additional strain on the middle-aged parents.

Accepting and Adjusting to the Physiological Changes of Middle Age

The gross changes associated with the aging process show an orderliness and a patterning comparable to that which characterizes the growth and development of the earlier periods of life.[122] They also show wide variations in age of onset and in rate of development from one individual to another. These individual differences have been present from the beginning of life and have been cumulative in effect, so that by 40 years of age some individuals are well along in the later aging processes, whereas others seem to be in the prime of life.

As we have seen earlier, men have a shorter life expectancy than women. There is some evidence [212] that men have somewhat lower general resistance throughout life and that physiological malfunctions strike men in middle age more often than they do women.

This may be associated with the fact that men usually take more of the strains of economic competition than do women. Women continue to have lower rates of heart disease and gastric ulcer, which plague many middle-aged men.

GENERAL APPEARANCE. Graying of hair has traditionally been regarded as a sign of aging. A few individuals have some gray hairs or are quite gray even in their twenties. Most people have some gray hair by 40 years of age; few are not gray by 60 years. By 40, reduction in the elasticity of the lens of the eye, along with other general eye changes, causes most people to find that they need glasses in order to read. Some people fight both of these evidences of aging, dyeing the hair, and refusing to admit that they need reading glasses. The ability to accept these changes and to adjust to them is an important aspect of maturing.

The "middle-aged spread" of the hips in the fifties often follows the menopause in women. Because of lack of exercise and too many calories in the diet, adipose tissue tends to accumulate in both men and women. Even in the forties many men and premenopause women lose their trim appearance and begin to sag in posture. If so, the postural defects of earlier adulthood become exaggerated. The elasticity of the skin decreases after 35 to 40 years of age, and wrinkles begin to appear. Some older adults give in to wrinkles and increasing weight, but the middle-aged adult, particularly the female, usually fights these signs of loss of youth, as the number and prosperity of beauty salons and slenderizing parlors testify. Middle-aged men often resist these changes, and take steps to keep physically fit.

SKELETAL CHANGES. Bone density is a measure of bone strength and efficiency. The peak of bone density occurs around 35 years of age.[89] From this age on there is a gradual decline which shows in a lightening of the bone in weight and an increase in its porosity. As age proceeds, the bones become more porous and lighter in weight, and gradually lose their original elasticity and capacity for resistance. By 50 years, for example, a broken or bruised bone recovers less rapidly than formerly. It usually comes as a shock to a person of 50 to be told after an accident that he is healing very nicely "for a man of his age." Such an incident may be the first time that he comes to grips with the fact that he is no longer young.

In pregnancy and during the first six months after giving birth to a child, the bones of a woman are likely to undergo rapid changes in mineral content. Unless adequate mineral nutrition is maintained, the bones during pregnancy and lactation may change sufficiently to show in X-ray pictures. Under good dietary conditions mineral losses are usually restored by six months after the birth of the child. Obviously, it is wise to permit ample time between pregnancies for the restoration of these losses. Mineral changes resulting from the aging process are usual after forty years of age, but a succession of pregnancies before or during this age may leave too little opportunity for recovery from such losses, so that advancing age may prove disastrous to the woman's health.

Although nutrition is generally believed to have a relationship to the aging process in bones, not much is yet known about the specific nutritional needs of people for maintaining health in other tissues as the aging process gets under way. It has been well established that hereditary, endocrine, and nutritional factors are all associated with the aging process. Whatever the factors associated with aging changes in the skeleton, there are as wide variations among individuals in the age of onset and in the rapidity of skeletal aging processes as there are in the elasticity, texture, and coloring of the skin, the hair, and other parts of the body.[25]

JOINT DISEASES. Many individuals of 40 years or over begin to experience some arthritis, often at first in a finger or foot joint or in the spinal column. If knee joints become involved, the individual's mobility may suffer. If elbows, wrists, and finger joints become stiff and painful, workers who are dependent upon hand skills may be genuinely handicapped.[66]

Much can be done in the treatment of arthritis to retard the progress of the condition. Bed rest and freedom from strain are important. There is some evidence that emotional factors such as general tenseness affect freedom of joint and muscle action and inhibit adequate circulation, and hence may be factors in the development of arthritis in some individuals. Studies [191] have shown, for example, that in certain kinds of arthritis there is a high proportion of histories which show early childhood overprotection and restrictive parental influences, thus creating in the individual a chronic state of rebellious hostility. In such cases, psychological as well as physical treatment is helpful. Courage is needed if the painful joints are to be kept in motion.

Health situations such as arthritis, bone fractures, and heart troubles test the fiber of the personality. If the individual has too little courage, or if he yields too easily to pain, increasingly poor health usually ensues. If, however, the past development of the individual has given him courage, determination, and a viewpoint which finds life worth while in spite of pain or handicap, the healing processes of the body proceed more rapidly so that some difficulties can be retarded or even arrested.

MUSCLES. Muscle strength is as a rule at a maximum between ages 25 and 30. After this a slow decline usually occurs. In such muscle groups as those concerned in hand grip, the decline is only about 10 per cent between ages 30 and 60; decline in muscle strength of the back and legs occurs more rapidly. Many coordinating mechanisms are involved in the use and maintenance of endurance in large-muscle activities. Reduction in the efficiency of some organs and of the body-regulating mechanisms as a whole takes place after forty years of age and is well advanced by fifty to sixty years. This results in a reduction of the ability to perform continuous muscular work.

However, wide individual differences exist in the age at which power and endurance in muscular performance declines. Such factors as the type of general hygiene followed and the amount and kind of over-all use of the muscles throughout childhood, adolescence, and early adulthood have a telling effect. One study [172] of Dutch men and women, who as a group use their muscles for work and for moving around far more than is usual in the United States, showed that their muscular strength at 40 to 45 years was still 96 per cent of the 30 to 35 year maximum for human beings, and at 50 was 92 per cent. The study concludes that the decline which is much more rapid in the United States occurs as a result of the push-button nature of housework and of industrial production, the sedentary nature of office work, and the two-car family.

Continued use of the body not only builds muscular strength during the early years; it stimulates and maintains the mechanisms involved in oxygenation and circulation of the blood and hence the nutrition of muscle cells. If the use of the body has been steady and not excessive, the individual usually enters middle age in fairly good muscular condition. Adjustment of exercise to less strenuous sports has been discussed earlier. Some middle-aged individuals, realizing that they are losing strength, and wishing to preserve erect carriage and youthful posture, frantically attempt to make up in middle age for lack of exercise in early adulthood. Often they exercise only on week ends and brief vacations, and then excessively. This does not accomplish the desired result, and sometimes results in heart attacks or other injuries.

The general set of the muscles tells the story of an individual's life. Use, disuse, abuse of the body, pride in it or dislike of it, continued joy in or lack-lustre expression of the self, serenity, or continued strain—these and many other things mold the musculature as life proceeds.

Since we express most of our emotions by contracting the various facial muscles, the facial skin tends to begin to wrinkle early in adulthood. Most people have parallel creases across the forehead by 30 years of age, and often one or two vertical creases above the nose depending upon how much frowning they do. Smiles raise the corners of the mouth, and scowls lower them. By 40 years of age, customary feelings, resulting in contraction or relaxation of the facial muscles, have molded the muscles and wrinkled the overlying skin so that the face tends to express the tensions of the individual both pleasant and unpleasant. Until we are 35 or 40, our faces are those God gave us; after that they are the faces we make for ourselves.

Middle adulthood is the period when the life history becomes particularly evident. Some people learn to cover up. They can force muscles to hold the body erect and to put on an animated facial expression. Sometimes a change of mood can, through a change of muscle set, erase years from an individual's appearance. Certain middle-aged people of volatile emotions can look 35 or 75, depending upon whether the mood is one of animation or of depression. The observer who tries to read the life story of such individuals must wait for the moment when the voluntary control of muscles is relaxed and the individual is unaware of his expression.

DIGESTION. One of the usual statements made about the physical condition of middle-aged people is that they are inclined to overeat and underexercise, hence to become too fat. One study [162] has shown that from 20 to 30 per cent of people over 30 years of age are obese (having more than 15 per cent excess over the desired body weight for the age). Since the obese tend to die earlier than do persons of normal weight, excessively overweight middle-aged people often do not live to become "old aged." Most of the very old are underweight rather than overweight, partly because of their nature and partly because of factors which result in malnutrition in the later years of life.

Overweight which results from overeating in middle age has both physical and psychological aspects.[66] The general glandular changes associated with the menopause in many women, for example, seem to predispose the body to store fats unless the caloric intake is carefully controlled. Combined with the lower rate of activity required as children grow up and need less care, the "middle-aged spread" becomes a reality. Although glandular changes are thought to be less pervasive and to come about more gradually in men than in women, middle-aged men are likely to reduce their physical activity without reducing their caloric intake. For example, many middle-aged men are at the top of their business or professional careers and are under considerable strain from heavy responsibilities. They tend to do business over the luncheon table, sometimes preceded by cocktails, ordering a menu to impress the guest with the generosity of the company expense accounts. Some reduce their breakfast intake; few of them reduce their dinner intake since at home dinner tends to be the main meal for the family, and at parties the food is too tempting to be resisted.

The incidence of diabetes, a disease associated with defective metabolism of carbohydrates, reaches a peak between 50 and 60 years of age.[111] The combination of strain and excessive eating and drinking is conducive to the development of this disease in individuals who are predisposed to it. Other diseases of the digestive system such as ulcer of the stomach or duodenum, and cancer of the stomach, liver, pancreas, and intestines occur in from 10 to 25 per cent of men between 45 and 65 years.[90] Men are more susceptible to diseases of the digestive system than are women. Cancer or other disturbances of the lower intestine are often associated with chronic constipation. Continued use of cathartics tends to increase the difficulties by irritating the tissues.

HEART AND CIRCULATION. The heart and blood vessels, like all organs of the body, undergo both structural and functional changes as age proceeds. In the cardiovascular system these changes are not as a rule marked before 60 years unless there has been a history of hereditary defect or disease of these organs.[226] As with all other systems, wide individual differences exist in the age of onset and the speed of aging.

In many of the cases in which "heart attacks" occur in middle age, there have been previous warnings that the heart was under strain.

The individual may then have avoided having a physical examination because, as in the case of suspected cancer, he dreads a confirmation of the trouble. Early and correct diagnosis is invaluable in clarifying what is or is not wrong and what can be done to avoid more serious difficulty. Adjustments in work load, frequent short vacations if possible, correction of family difficulties or of other psychological strains, often bring about improvement or full recovery. On the other hand, delayed diagnosis may leave the way open for increasing difficulty. Nervousness and uncertainty tend to increase the strain. Slight signs of trouble, for example, may cause panic in the individual, increasing the rate of the heartbeat and placing additional strain on the blood vessels.

How well the individual accepts a diagnosis that requires adjustment of his attitudes and his daily regime depends upon his previous ability to adjust to reality and upon the help or resistance he gets from family members. Four out of five heart cases in middle age are men. Therefore the cooperating members of the family in 80 per cent of the middle-aged heart cases are wives and sons and daughters who may have to give up time as well as some material things in order to free the husband and father from excessive financial worry. Many a young person has worked all or part of his way through college when he had not expected to because illness in the father or mother, with accompanying medical expenses, cut off or diverted money originally marked for education. Many wives and children make the necessary adjustments.

Whether the difficulty lies in the heart itself or in the blood vessels which supply it with oxygen and nourishment, the situation is much the same psychologically as that described above. Prevention is far better than curing or correcting damage once done. Hypertension in the blood vessels is often associated with emotional tension and excessive fatigue. The blood vessels which supply and drain vital organs, such as the heart, brain, and kidneys, are strategic. Damage to the heart or the brain resulting from inadequacy of the supplying or draining vessels is sometimes critical. Ruptures or clots in the blood vessels of the brain may cause death, temporary, or permanent paralysis of certain parts of the body (strokes). In or near the heart, and other organs, they may also cause critical illness or death.

When illnesses resulting from these difficulties arise, the ability to accept the situation and to adjust to it are important. Resentment, feelings of self-pity, unwillingness to make the necessary adjustments and to make the effort necessary to regain whatever capacity is possible, all contribute to continuing invalidism. Whether or not partial or total recovery is possible, the life of the invalid and of those who must take care of him is bright and cheerful or bitter and depressed, depending largely upon the attitudes of the invalid. Tensions occur more frequently in individuals who have not made fairly satisfactory adjustments in earlier life.

Excessively tense middle-aged individuals have often been so not only in the early adult years but also in adolescence and even in childhood. Studies [66] show that many individuals who have histories of hypertension are characterized as aggressive, ambitious, explosive, and active worriers. Correction of these traits would have been easier in earlier life, although it is still not impossible for some middle-aged people who are sufficiently motivated to learn to control their behavior. In some cases, professional help may be needed in the restructuring of attitudes underlying these traits. Important as psychological factors are in hypertension, they are not, however, always the cause of it. There are physical causes which, being primarily important after age sixty, will be discussed in Chapter 14.

CHANGES IN THE FEMALE REPRODUCTIVE SYSTEM. In Chapter 7 we discussed the changes in the reproductive system of girls in puberty. These changes which rendered the individual capable of reproduction are dramatic both in physical and in psychological aspects. In the period of her middle adulthood, a woman loses the capacity to reproduce. This change is referred to as the menopause or female climacteric. The decrease of hormone production and decrease in fertility are accompanied by the gradual cessation of menstruation.

Fertility wanes in most women as the fortieth year of age approaches, and even earlier in some. There is some evidence that the amount of ovarian hormone decreases after age 40 in all women.[142] Irregularities in menstruation usually occur for a year and a half to two years before its actual cessation. The last menstrual period represents the final link in a chain of events that may have begun some five to ten years previously. The sequence usually begins in the early forties with the decrease of the gonadotrophic hormone of the hypophysis. Menstruation usually ceases somewhere between 45 to 50 years of age. One study [106] found a range of 40 to 60 years, the median being 49 years. A small percentage of women cease to menstruate before age 40. Continuation of menstruation into the late 50's is more common than cessation before 40 years of age. There is a popular notion that women who have a delayed menarche (first menstruation) usually have an early menopause. This has not been substantiated by studies.[142] Rather, it has been found that there is little relationship between the age of menarche and of menopause.

Circulatory and other changes during menopause result in the hot flushes, dizziness, and occasional severe headaches which are characteristic of the menopause. Some women fatigue more quickly than formerly. Even a previously mild-mannered woman may have periods of irritability, nervousness, and emotional instability. Some women experience periods of forgetfulness and difficulty in concentration, and some experience severe depression and require temporary hospitalization.

When we consider the physical changes that occur during menopause, these psychological conditions are not surprising. For all women, single or married, the unaccustomed irregularity of menstruation indicates that the end of the reproductive part of adulthood is approaching. For single women who have always had a deep desire for motherhood, this signifies the futility of any hope for children that may have lingered through the years. On the other hand, some single women seem to lack any desire for biological motherhood. For them, the end of reproductive ability may be welcome.

These same reactions may be true for married women also. Fertile married women, however, have by this time probably had all the children they want or can properly care for. For them, especially if they do not use a reliable method of contraception, menopause can be particularly disturbing. A delayed menstrual period may make the woman wonder if she may be pregnant. Her concern can easily result in all the symptoms that she learned to expect in her previous pregnancies. She probably hesitates to communicate her uncertainty to her husband, and as a result, is irritable in her relations with him and also with her children. In addition, certain other fears may nag at her, fears inspired by old wives' tales about insanity, cancer, loss of sexual ability, and therefore possible loss of attractiveness to her husband.

More realistic sex education and marriage counselling have helped women to understand that they do not, because of the cessation of their reproductive function, lose their attractiveness for their husbands. In fact, some women become more satisfactory partners after the menopause because they no longer need fear pregnancy.

In recent years better medical therapy and clearer understanding have greatly reduced the incidence of excessive depression and of the many other symptoms previously common during and following the menopause. However, the emotional and physical symptoms discussed may make a few years of the menopause trying not only for the woman herself but also for those who have to live and work with her. These symptoms are general enough that physicians and lay people alike freely give a diagnosis of "menopause" to practically any physical or emotional disability or distress that occurs in any woman between the ages of 45 and 55 years.

After the menopause, there follows a gradual involution or shrinking of the reproductive organs. In some women, these organs become somewhat more susceptible to irritation, and cancerous growths may develop.[142] Physicians encourage all women, particularly during and after menopause, to have careful medical examinations not less than once a year, and to consult a physician immediately if there is any bleeding from the vagina or if any lump, no matter how small, appears in the breasts.

CHANGES IN THE MALE REPRODUCTIVE SYSTEM. Retrogressive changes in the male reproductive system are less dramatic than those in the female. Aging occurs gradually from about 35 years of age on.[48] In women, as we have seen, the cessation of the reproductive capacity does not severely affect the capacity to participate effectively in sexual activities. In some men, however, it is probable that participation in sexual activity decreases or ceases before fertility is lost. The problem of male impotence, when it occurs, is so complex that not much in the way of definite scientific findings is available. Such factors as physiological changes and psychological and cultural attitudes toward sexual potency complicate attempts to separate the physiology of the male climacteric from other aging factors. Much still remains to be learned in this area.

Studies [151] of the prostate (a gland which surrounds the neck of the bladder and the urethra) show that tissue changes, correlated with the aging process, occur in most men after 40 years of age. Whether or not this change and other physiological changes in the aging man produce sexual impotence is not definitely known. Cancer of the prostate occurs so often in middle-aged and older men that careful examination of this organ is a routine part of all thorough physical examinations of men over 40 years of age. Moore [151] found that cancer of the prostate was seldom present before 40 years of age, but that it was present in 17 per cent of the men studied between 40 and 49 years of age and that it increased steadily with each decade. In men between 81 and 90 years of age, 29 per cent had prostatic cancer.

Even though decline of the reproductive capacity in men is gradual and may not cease until very late in life, some men experience a set of symptoms including hot flushes, impotence, lethargy, and insomnia, which have led investigators [151] to infer that there is a phase of the male climacteric not unlike the menopause in women. However, the number of men in whom these symptoms are severe enough to bring them into clinics is very small in comparison to the number of women who seek clinical help for similar symptoms.

Mental and Emotional Disturbances

General mental or emotional disturbances are about as frequent in the middle-aged period as the general trends in the population would lead us to expect.[66] We saw in Chapter 11 that neuroses reached a sharp peak around 35 years of age and dropped in frequency from that age on. Psychoses appear much less frequently than do neuroses in the earlier years but increase steadily from early adulthood throughout the remaining years of life. Now that the control of mental and emotional illness is greater than it formerly was, the middle-aged period shows no more incidence of psychoses than any other period in the generally rising long time trend for psychoses.

Decay vs. Growth

One sage has quipped that "The chief thing you should try to save for your old age is you." * Another has said, in a hint on how to grow old gracefully: "People who can get along with themselves can get along with anyone." † Middle age requires much adjustment. In many people, preparation for this adjustment has been occurring throughout life. Situations arise which test courage, staying power, self-control, insight into the lives of others, and hence into one's own life and personality. We generally learn in early adulthood to grow out of adolescent dependence upon external and obvious values into increasing dependence upon sound internal values. Any one who has learned to adjust to life by early adulthood is likely to make a

* *Saturday Evening Post*, February 1959.
† Cornell University Bulletin No. 837: *Growing Older*.

satisfactory adjustment to the many changes which occur in middle age, but the individual who has failed to adjust earlier usually has a difficult time with his problems in middle and old age.

In middle age, after more than half a life-time of using certain habits and attitudes, it is not easy to change them. Having previously looked forward to the use of capacities at their peak efficiency, it is not easy to shift the perspective and adjust to the idea that satisfactions must increasingly be found with gradually decreasing capacity. Difficult as change of old habits or development of new ones is, many people in middle age do change. They develop new kinds of interests, and learn to enjoy less strenuous kinds of fun; they exchange the excitement of earlier years for quieter and deeper feelings. They become good companions to themselves. These changes bring to some individuals an almost mystic enjoyment of nature and a deep serenity.

Much depends upon the attitude with which the middle-aged person approaches his situation. Release from intense strain and overwork in exchange for increasing freedom to enjoy things other than work will be something to welcome or resist, depending upon the viewpoint of the individual who is making the transition. If the change represents to the individual only loss of prestige and power, this "loss" will dominate his thinking and feeling. On the other hand, if the change represents his successful training of younger adults and genuine pleasure in permitting them to take over, his satisfactions will be deep and rewarding.

The physical changes of middle age may mean the giving up of agility and youthful looks, but their replacement by skills and a look of some distinction. If the preoccupation in middle age is upon "lost youth," the individual will become bitter, antagonistic, and physically ugly. On the other hand, if the individual is aware of his growth in poise, wisdom, and understanding, he feels that life has been and is still worth while, and people will probably seek his company as much or more than they have ever done previously.

SUGGESTIONS FOR FURTHER DISCUSSION

1. Call to mind the happiest man of 45 to 50 whom you know, and answer the following questions about him:
   a.   What is his daily routine?
   b.   How well does he appear to be physically?
   c.   What strains and frustrations do you think are present in his life?

d. What seem to be his major satisfactions?

2. Do the same for a women of 45 to 50 years of age.

3. Do the same for the least well-adjusted man and for the least well-adjusted woman, each around 45 or 50, known to you.

4. How do the satisfactions and problems of the well-adjusted persons in 1 and 2 compare with those of the poorly adjusted persons in 3? Be specific. What conclusions do you draw from this about the problems and satisfactions of middle adulthood?

5. Have members of the class read and report to the class for discussion the references listed below.

REFERENCES FOR FURTHER STUDY

HILLIARD, M. *A Woman Doctor Looks at Love and Life.* New York: Doubleday & Co., Inc., 1957. A sympathetic treatment of single and married life by a physician with deep understanding of human aspirations, fears, and joys.

MARTIN, P. C., and VINCENT, E. L. *Human Biological Development.* New York: The Ronald Press Co., 1960. Pp. 468–471, the reproductive systems throughout postnatal life.

PRESSEY, S. L., and KUHLEN, R. G. *Psychological Development Throughout the Life Span.* New York: Harper & Bros., 1957. Ch. 10, moral, sociopolitical, and religious values and behavior (traces these throughout the life span, lending background for consideration of these developments in later life).

For film suggestions see Film Supplement, in the Appendix.

CHAPTER 14

Later Adulthood

Grow old along with me!
The best is yet to be,
The last of life, for which the first was made.*

GENERAL CONSIDERATIONS

Old age is often thought of as a period of loneliness, use-lessness, and unhappiness. Old people are often considered by younger people to be inflexible, untractable, and unteachable, pre-disposed to unreasonable childishness, predominantly unemployed, and in general a burden to themselves and everyone else. Thanks to the recently developed science of gerontology (Greek: *geron*, "old man" and *logos*, "discussion") and to the branch of medicine called geriatrics, old age is less and less characterized by such behavior and attitudes. People over 65 years of age are now referred to as being in "later maturity." The period is more often than not thought of as the age of retirement, with freedom to do as one pleases.

Today the spotlight is on youth. This does not mean that parents and grandparents are not loved and respected by their children and grandchildren. Nor does it mean that there is no concern for the well-being of aged people. It means, rather, that children, adoles-cents, and young adults are so in evidence in the population that their needs and activities get the most attention, whereas the affairs and needs of the elderly are generally less attended to by other age groups. Young people who have failed to envision elderly people as individuals with problems to solve and development still to be done say such things as: "that old age was a definite period in the develop-

* Robert Browning, *Rabbi Ben Ezra.*

443

mental cycle never before entered my mind," and "I'd never thought of old people very much, and had never before considered myself as being old some day."

Differing Views of Old Age

One view of old age is a political one, which sees the old-age population as a growing political force because it is steadily increasing in numbers and all of its members are voters, cognizant of their potential influence and of the need to voice their own needs.

Another view of old age is an economic one. Even though the funds of many old people are limited, their total buying power is considerable. Advertisers are finding it increasingly worth while to aim at them as potential buyers. Another aspect of the economic view is represented by the concern some writers have for the increasing public and private pension funds which, although paid for in part by the recipients of the funds, nevertheless are piling up increasing tax burdens for the oncoming generations. As we shall see, there is also a category of workers who are referred to as "old" from the point of view of the adequacy of their work.

In general, however, writers who discuss old age have no such categories or special viewpoints in mind. They are writing about old age as an over-all stage of development. They argue that no calendar age or partial aspect of aging can be set as "old age." Individuals who are useful and needed in the community, they say, should not be forced into industrial, political, or social retirement simply because they have passed a given birthday.

Increasing Proportion of Older Population

"Old age" is also receiving scientific attention because it is represented in an increasing proportion of the population. We discussed this increase in Chapter 1, stating that it is resulting from improved health conditions. As we saw in Chapter 13, in 1900, only 4.1 per cent of the population in the United States was 65 years or older; in 1958, 8.6 per cent had reached this age. There are varying predictions about how rapidly this percentage of older population will increase; they run as high as 18 to 19 per cent for the year 2000.[36]

These figures become more meaningful if we look at them from the point of view of how long any given person of any given age can expect to live. We saw in Chapter 1 that the life expectation at birth for men born in the United States in 1955 was 67.4 years, and for women born in the same year was 73.6 years. We also saw, in Chapter 13, that in terms of people who are now old, in 1955 in the United States the average life expectation for 60-year-olds was 17.5 years. In Table 14–1 we see that at 65 it was 14.2 years, and for 70-year-olds it was 11.2 years.[197] Table 14–1 contrasts these with life expectations in several other countries.

Table 14–1
Life Expectation in 1955

Country	At Age 65	At Age 70
United States	14.2 years	11.2 years
Israel (Jewish pop.)	14.0	11.2
Netherlands	14.1	10.8
Sweden	13.8	10.6
Japan	12.2	9.6
Hungary	12.2	9.6
United Kingdom	11.8	9.1
Portugal	11.6	8.7

Figures from *Demographic Yearbook,* 1957. Statistical Office of the United Nations, Department of Economics and Social Affairs. Data not available for the newly developing nations.

The implication in these figures is that people live longer than they used to. It must be remembered that these figures are averages for the given age level. In the total population, more people are living into and beyond these ages than previously. However, if we look at the number of years a given individual who has lived, say, to be 60 years old can expect to live, the outlook is different. An individual who has lived today to be 60 years old cannot look forward to as many years of life as could an individual of 60 years in the days of the Roman Empire. This is because medical science and better public health have kept alive today many individuals who, in the days of the Roman Empire, would have died early. If any individual lived to be 60 in those days, he was made of stern stuff and usually continued to live many more years past 60 than is usual today.

Claims of ages which are well over 100 years are difficult if not impossible to substantiate, since accurate birth registration did not exist until fairly recently. One oft-quoted example is an individual in Denmark who is said to have lived 146 years, being born in 1626 and dying in 1772. Records indicate that other individuals have actually lived to be well over 100 years old, but they are exceptions. Only about 65 people out of every 100,000 live to be 100 years old today.[41] Currently, the limit to the span of life, for practical consideration, is less than 100 years and is seldom over 90 years.

Factors Influencing Longevity

Length of life is affected by hereditary factors. The effects of these, however, can be modified by the quality of physical and mental hygiene throughout life. Longevity is somewhat affected by geographic locality. For example, people in the Prairie states live longer on the average than do those in the Mountain and Southern states. Married people, as a group, tend to live longer than those who are single, widowed, or divorced. The number and severity of illnesses experienced by an individual tend to affect his prospects for longevity. As we saw in Chapter 13, excessive weight tends to shorten life. Conversely, good nutrition, reasonable freedom from illness, and well-ordered living may add years to a given individual's life.[41]

RETIREMENT FROM LIFE WORK

Compulsory or Voluntary

We have defined the upper limit of middle age and the lower limit of old age as 65 because this is the age set by most businesses and professions as the age of compulsory or voluntary retirement. Until the late 1950's it was also the age at which United States federal old age insurance began to pay benefits. It still is the age for men, but women may now begin to collect from these funds at 62 years at a rate 25 per cent less than what is paid if they do not collect until they are 65. In Denmark, state old age pensions are available at 65, in Sweden at 67, and in Norway at 70. Sweden gives pensions regardless of the individual's income, the amount being about $335 per year to single people and $530 to a married couple. To those with no income other than the pension, additional allowances are given for housing, clothing, and fuel. Denmark gives about $320 per year to single people in Copenhagen, about $280 in smaller towns and about $240 in the rural areas. Married couples get 150 per cent of these amounts. Supplements are provided when necessary for housing, clothing and fuel.[80]

In the United States, some companies make voluntary retirement at 60 possible. State employees' retirement systems such as that of New York make voluntary retirement possible at 60 or even at 55 years if the individual elects to pay extra premiums into the system through his years of employment. Some educational or business retirement systems, however, do not make retirement compulsory until 68 or even 70 years of age. Labor unions tend to name 65 as the age at which pensions may begin. Although unions often oppose compulsory retirement as a general principle, a compulsory retirement clause is sometimes written into contracts.[36] When it is, the compulsory retirement age is usually stated as 68. Railroad contracts are usually written so that employees may stay in service "as long as they are physically fit," but they may retire at 65 if men, or at 60 if women, with full retirement benefits. Post Office employees may retire at 60; clerks and carriers must retire at 62, and superintendents at 70.[23] About 40 per cent of the companies with pension plans were reported by the National Industrial Conference Board to have compulsory retirement regulations.

Many people over 65 years of age prefer to continue working if this is possible, partly because many current retirement payments are inadequate for a good standard of living and partly because they have not prepared adequately for the use of their leisure time. Hence, they do not know what to do with themselves when not working. Some retirement systems permit the retirement payees to work for additional income while at the same time drawing retirement money. Restrictions are sometimes selective. For example, people on state retirement systems may sometimes earn money outside of the state or even within the state if not employed in any state-paid position. In the Federal Old Age and Survivors Insurance plan, the recipient may not, between 65 and 72 years, earn more than a minimum (in 1960, $1,200 per year) while receiving social security payments. After 72 years of age, however, there is presently no ceiling on earnings while receiving payments. Supplementations from other retirement funds are permissible under the federal Social Security system, and many of the larger business organizations provide their retirement systems as a supplementation of the expected federal retirement funds. Many retired federal employees receive Civil Service annuities in addition to federal Social Security funds, and some of them also receive state employees' retirement funds.[150]

When Is a Worker "Old"?

Retirement age is only one criterion of when a worker is considered too old to work. In many types of jobs, the worker who loses a job will find reemployment difficult because he is considered old at an age considerably below compulsory retirement age. In discussing "who is an older worker" some writers use biological age as the criterion, others use chronological age. When the biological age is used, the physiological definition is based on a composite measure of physical capacity. When chronological age is used, the assumption is that there is a correlation between that and physical capacity. Many workers, if measured by physical capacity, would be found to be "younger than their years" and might hold jobs to an age considerably more advanced, chronologically, than the usual age of compulsory retirement. Chronological age first affects employability for men at 45 years of age, for women at 35 years, these limits being used in certain work situations to define the lower limit of the "older worker." [23] Depending upon the type of employment involved, then, some people would have difficulty in finding new jobs at or soon after these ages.

The impact of unemployment in periods of economic recession differs greatly with age, the workers over 45 years of age suffering a higher rate of unemployment than younger workers.[23] During periods of high employment, such as those of World War II and the postwar years, older workers seem to have had as low rates of unemployment as younger workers. It is in the marginal employment situations that the older worker tends to be laid off sooner than is the younger worker. Once laid off in marginal employment periods, the over-55 worker has greater difficulty than the younger worker in finding reemployment.

Aging of workers depends somewhat upon the type of work done. One study [17] of mill workers showed that many die soon after retirement. Two theories are offered as an explanation of this: one, that work is the center of existence for the mill worker and when the job is gone, life crumbles; two, that the men are exhausted after too many years at excessively hard work. The latter theory seems to be fairly widely held, since there is a considerable push for earlier retirement at 55 or even 50 for men who do hard physical labor under grueling circumstances.

Economic Status of the Retired

As one would suppose, the economic condition of the retired varies from near-starvation to luxury, depending upon the economic preparation for retirement and many other circumstances. In 1956, a survey was made of retired people in and near a large industrial city.[2] It showed 135,000 residents over 65 years of age. Six thousand of these were on relief rolls. Many others kept off relief by making constant sacrifices. Some life pensions were as low as $60 per month. Other residents had federal Social Security payments but could not feed, house, and clothe themselves on these, much less pay medical expenses. Many people received only part of the top possible payment stated in pension systems because they had not been long enough under the system, or for other reasons. In this study, although the top possible payment under federal Social Security at the time of the study was $108.50 per month, it was found that the average payment was $60 per month. In 1956, this $60 was considered by the Department of Public Assistance in the locale of the study to be $4 below the amount needed for bare existence. In this community, railroaders' pensions were set by law at $166.98, plus other benefits, yet the average railroad pension paid was $101.81.

Some people on restricted retirement incomes manage to earn in spite of the general prejudice of employers against the old. A representative sample of 13,600 individuals over 65 years of age showed that annually 12.5 per cent of the couples earned from $1 to $499; 44.2 per cent earned over $500; but 43.3 per cent were without earnings and had to live on retirement income. The median income of these couples without earnings was $1,387 per year, and of those still earning, $2,162 per year. Single or widowed men had a median total income of $1,440 per year. Single or widowed women had a total median income without earnings of $273; with earnings, of $738 per year. Many of the older people in this study were not able to work, and many others would have liked to work but could find no employment.[198] This study included many individuals too old to have been able to participate in, and hence to benefit from, current pension and security plans. It seems evident that median old-age incomes will in the future be higher than in this study because a larger proportion of the aged populations will have participated in retirement or Social Security plans. There is speculation, even so, that these plans will increase payments in the years ahead as rapidly as inflation occurs.

It is estimated that about 25 to 33 per cent of the people over 65 years of age in the United States are wholly self-sustaining; the majority are dependent in whole or in part on their families or on public funds.[177] A number of those who are dependent had provided what seemed, in their earlier years, to be adequate retirement income for their old age. Since the 1930's, however, inflation has depreciated the dollar so much that each $1,000 of retirement income planned for in 1933, in 1959 purchased only $475 worth of the goods purchasable with those dollars in 1933. If the retirement plans were made in 1940, the $1,000 would, in 1959, purchase only $522 worth of the goods it would have bought in 1940. Twelve million people are now estimated to be attempting to live on such depreciated retirement dollars. One of the challenges of today is to halt the depreciation of retirement dollars, either by halting inflation or by establishing a rate of increase in retirement funds commensurate with economic changes (the "escalator" clause). If this is not done, it is estimated that the 21 million people who will be on retirement incomes by 1975 may be retiring on seriously depreciated dollars.

This is the least optimistic aspect of the retirement income picture. Let us look at a 1958 study [150] of the retirement incomes of older women who have been in the professions. We saw earlier that, in general, women's over-sixty-five incomes are smaller than are men's, and that as a result, more older women than men were living with relatives. For professional women, however, the picture is different. In 1958, over four million women in the United States were receiving monthly payments under the federal Social Security system. In addition to these four million women, almost another million were receiving retirement income from other governmental sources such as federal, state, and city retirement systems, and Armed Forces pensions. Public school teachers were included in this million. Women received 70 per cent of all death benefits from insurance companies. These were sometimes very large. They were often used for the support and later education of children.

In 1957, there were about 250,000 retired government employees, of whom about 50,000 were women. About three-fourths of both men and women in this group had additional sources of income.

Among these retired government workers in 1957 the average annual income was \$1,944 for women and \$2,900 for men. Information gained from a group of 1,250 retired women public school teachers, half of whom were single, showed that three-fourths of them had income from at least two other sources in addition to their public retirement income. This did not include the husband's income for the third of these women who were married and living with their husbands. Three-fourths of the retired school teachers in this survey owned their own homes; half of them had life insurance annuity payments; 40 per cent of them had income from investments; 25 per cent had some type of employment, most of them on a part-time basis; and a few received royalties from books, or other types of income. As a group, these retired school teachers were above the average of retired people in income. School teachers, however, are known as good planners in the use of money.

We should not leave this discussion without calling to mind the well-preserved older couples (as in Fig. 14–1) who, properly insured and now retired, happily stack their suitcases into the back of their car and set off for warmer climates. There are many of these, as any visitor to Florida, California, or other "retirement states" can testify.

PHYSIOLOGICAL ASPECTS OF AGING

When Is a Person Physiologically Old?

Every person who lives long enough begins to slow down and eventually stops living altogether. Whatever the viewpoints on old age discussed earlier, a person can be considered to be growing old when his physiological processes begin to slow down. He is old when enough of them have slowed down to the point where he is compelled to make substantial adjustments in his daily routines.[122] Somewhere between 60 and 75, most individuals experience physiological changes which reduce physical efficiency noticeably and which increase the prevalence of long-term disabilities.

Aging Tissues

Fundamental to the concept of physiological aging is the concept of a general senescence of the body tissues. If the tissues remained young in the sense of an ability not only to meet the normal demands of the body but also to resist diseases, to repair bone fractures, and in other ways to meet emergencies, the assumption would be that the body was not yet aged. An essential characteristic of a living system which sets it apart from the non-living is its capacity to maintain itself, to repair and to reconstitute itself. Just how tissues in living beings retain or lose the power to do these things is not yet

Fig. 14–1. Off for warmer climates.

definitely known even though many studies have been done on this, and several theories of biological aging have been developed. No theory is as yet based upon indisputable experimental evidence.[131] The following questions are still not answered: What is aging? When does aging begin? What cellular components are affected by the aging process? What are the age changes which eventually bring about the death of the organism?

It is known that, with aging, there occurs: (1) a gradual retardation of cell division and growth, and of tissue repair, and (2) a gradual lowering of the basal metabolic rate.[131] These changes result in gradual degenerative changes, decrease in elasticity in the elastic connective tissue, decreased speed, strength and endurance of nerve and muscle reactions, and decreased strength of skeletal tissues.

The Skin

One of the organs which suffers most, when tissues lose elasticity, is the skin. In fact, the skin is so susceptible to the rigors of time and exposure to the elements that, unless it is constantly cared for, it tends to reveal how old the individual possessing it is.[30] Elasticity of the skin is at a peak between 25 and 35 years of age. It decreases gradually between 35 and 60, especially in men. In women, however, skin elasticity between 50 and 60 years of age is almost as great as at 35 years.[108] Women give the skin much more cosmetic attention than do men.

In contrast to young skin, which is smooth and elastic, old skin is flabby and wrinkled. Cosmetic attention, dry or wet climate, dirty or clean air, and hereditary factors all affect the skin. Decrease of subcutaneous fat is a factor in wrinkling. The skin of the trunk tends to lose less of its elasticity and becomes less wrinkled and flabby than does the skin of the hands and the face, which are exposed to the elements.

Overexposure to sunshine is sometimes related to the development of skin cancer, the incidence of which increases with advancing age. In one study,[30] the median age for the occurrence of skin cancer was found to be 57 years for one type and 66 years for another type. Increased pigmentation in certain skin areas sometimes produces brown spots which look not unlike freckles. The causes of many changes in the skin which appear with age are still not understood.

Hair, as an appendage of the skin, tends to become gray and thin in later age. Baldness, however, seems to have little to do with advancing age. Many men become increasingly bald up to a certain stage of baldness around 40 or 50 years of age, but not much more bald after that. Baldness is a sex-influenced character, few women becoming bald, although women's hair as well as that of men tends to become thinner and less manageable as age advances.

Body Regulating Functions

Homeostatic processes are those processes which provide constancy within narrow limits in the temperature of the body and in the chemical composition and other properties of the blood. Changes in the external environment or in the activity of the person which affect body temperature or acidity, for example, must be counteracted by appropriate mechanisms within the body in order to reestablish the conditions conducive to cell activity. Continuity of life depends not so much upon the activity of any specific system as it does upon the integration of all the systems and the effectiveness with which they maintain stability of the cellular environment of the body.[191]

Since the homeostatic mechanisms of the body become less efficient with age, older people tend to find themselves more comfortable and better able to function when they live in mild climates and do not have to adjust to wide swings of temperature.[66] General body temperature in the aged is about the same as that in younger persons. However, in the aged, the body's response to high or low external temperatures is slower than in the young. Extremes of cold or heat cause more discomfort for the old than for the young. The death rate from heat stroke rises sharply after age 60.[191]

Vital capacity (the maximum amount of air which can be breathed out after taking the deepest breath possible) decreases after age 50.[232] Since it is in part dependent upon the elasticity of the tissues of the breathing apparatus as well as upon neuromuscular coordination of the chest movements, it deteriorates fairly rapidly after 65 years of age. In old age, there is an increase in the amount of air that remains in the lungs with each breath. This is the air that has received carbon dioxide from the blood. When any of it remains in the lungs there is less room for fresh, oxygen-laden air. Thus the carbon dioxide-oxygen exchange in the lungs is less efficient in old age.

For this and other reasons, older people tend to slow down, and therefore find it necessary to reduce the vigor and rapidity of movement. They cannot manage sports that require rapid changes of movement. They rest more often, even in quiet games, to recover from the exercise and to permit body temperature to adjust. They often take naps after meals, while the body is digesting food, and in other ways permit their bodies to have the longer time needed to adjust from one activity to another.

Heart and Circulation

One of the reasons why the body finds it more difficult to adjust to changes in activity or to strenuous demands of any kind is that, after 60 years of age, the heart increases in size and weight, its muscle becomes less elastic and tends to accumulate calcium deposits, and hence does not function as efficiently as formerly.[66] The walls of the blood vessels also lose elasticity, thicken, and harden because of the infiltration of calcium deposits, resulting in arteriosclerosis, popularly known as "hardening of the arteries." As the interior diameter of the blood vessels becomes smaller, the heart has to pump the blood through less space. As a result, heart failure may ensue.

In many cases, changes are more marked in certain blood vessels than in others, those supplying the cerebrum (upper brain) and the heart muscle itself being especially susceptible to change. Cerebral hemorrhage occurs when vessels in the brain break. In the heart, blood-vessel changes may result in what are referred to as "coronary attacks." Defects such as those induced by rheumatic fever in childhood seem in many cases to place only relatively slight burdens on the heart and circulation in the later years of life.[226] We saw in Chapter 13 that certain of the more severe circulatory diseases prove fatal to people under stress in middle age. Both men and women after 65 years of age are usually well past the major occupational strains. Therefore, the heart and blood-vessel diseases associated with continued stress are less likely to occur in old age than in middle age, when the strains of living were greater. However, the changes in the heart itself and in the blood vessels which supply the heart produce difficulties in many older people.

Weakness either in the heart itself or in the vessels supplying the heart or the upper brain are tested if the older person suffers an accident or an illness. In such instances, cerebral hemorrhage or coronary attack may be precipitated, causing acute illness or death. Older persons wisely avoid sudden, excessive strain whenever possible, and regulate their smoking and their intake of food and alcohol.[226]

Eyes and Ears

We referred in Chapter 13 to the decreasing elasticity of the lens of the eye, which necessitates reading glasses, bifocals, or trifocals for many people around 40 to 45 years of age. In the later years of life the eye suffers further changes. The most likely changes are a decrease in the area of the visual field, slower adaptation to twilight vision, and less distinctness of images in dim illumination.[57] These changes, accompanied by slower motor reactions in all parts of the body, are reasons for the restrictions on drivers' licenses for people over 80 years of age.

One fairly common eye defect which occurs in the later years of life is the formation of cataracts, in which the lens of the eye becomes opaque. The lens is dependent for its nutrition upon the capillaries in the small muscles which control the thickness of the lens as it adjusts to light from far or near objects. These capillaries, like other blood vessels, tend to become less efficient with advancing age. In addition to this, the lens itself becomes thicker, more dense, and therefore less efficient in transmitting light waves. At a given stage of these processes, vision becomes impossible in the eye affected. In this case, the lens may be surgically removed and the individual fitted with a lens set into eyeglasses, which provides reasonably adequate vision.

Research [57] shows that even though the capillaries of the small muscles which control adjustment to near and far vision suffer some deterioration with aging, the muscular power of these muscles does not seem to decrease noticeably. Some atrophy of the optic nerve usually occurs with advancing age. This is the result of arteriosclerosis of the blood vessels which supply it. In spite of the above accompaniments of advancing age in the eye and in the body as a whole, it has been demonstrated that in most individuals the normal life span of the eye exceeds that of the body as a whole.

Although some loss in the acuity of hearing is a frequent occurrence in the later years of life, more frequently in men than in women, little is known about the exact causes of this loss.[232] The loss in the ability to hear high tones which often characterizes the aged appears to result from deterioration in the cochlea, the tiny, coiled chamber which houses the endings of the auditory nerves. The eardrum may become less elastic in the aged and hence less responsive to sound waves. The channel from the outer ear leading to the eardrum may sag as the surrounding muscles and skin sag, and hence may interfere with the movement of sound waves. Modern hearing aids compensate to a large degree for certain kinds of hearing loss. Along with glasses for failing eyesight, hearing aids serve to keep older people in touch with the world.

Teeth and Jaws

Tooth enamel has little or no power of regeneration. As age advances, teeth lost from decay and other causes are not replaced.

Wear on the enamel of the remaining teeth is progressive, depending to some extent upon the texture of the diet, coarse diets causing more rapid wear. Diets that require too little chewing, however, fail to give the teeth enough exercise to stimulate an adequate flow of blood into the tooth pulp and the gums surrounding the teeth. Loss of teeth results from faulty nutrition or from disease resulting from bacterial invasion, rather than from old age, per se.[175] Artificial dentures may be accompanied by loss of chewing efficiency up to 50 per cent or more, with the result that the less efficient digestive system may be irritated by food particles. Dentures fitted by expert dentists, however, permit relatively efficient chewing throughout old age.

Changes in the form and size of the jaws and other facial bones, along with loss of elasticity of muscles and skin often result in the "caved-in" look of the very old face. Loss of teeth or ill-fitting dentures add to this appearance. The nose in old age may become somewhat bulbous, which, along with the loss of elasticity in the skin and connective tissues, gives the appearance of a lengthening of the nose. Combined with loss of teeth and changes in the jaw, this often produces the appearance of a nose and chin growing closer together.

Digestion and Nutrition

Deaths from digestive diseases in persons above 45 years of age are only one-third as frequent as deaths from diseases of the heart.[90] They are slightly more frequent than deaths from cerebral hemorrhage and paralysis. The chief cause of death from disease of the digestive system is cancer of the stomach, liver, gall bladder and bile ducts, which together make up about one-third of the total of all forms of cancer. Add to these the other cancers of the digestive system such as cancer of the pancreas, of the peritoneum, intestine, and rectum, and we find that cancers of the digestive system make up more than one-half of deaths from all forms of cancer. Sex differences exist in the number of deaths from cancer of the digestive tract. Cancers of the tongue and mouth cavity, for example, are six or seven times as frequent in men as in women, whereas cancer of the gall bladder is four times more frequent in women.[90]

In spite of these difficulties of the digestive system, most elderly people die with digestive systems capable of functioning beyond their life span. As distinguished from diseases of the digestive system, the sheer aging process seems not to affect the digestive system as much as it does some of the other systems of the body. This is interesting in view of the fact that, during the lifetime of many individuals, gastrointestinal disorders occur more frequently than do disorders of the other systems. Apparently, in the survival process, the digestive system has developed its own kind of resistance to deterioration.

In cases when the range of interests and satisfactions become greatly restricted, eating often becomes a central interest and major satisfaction for the old. Nutritionally, aged people need fewer calories than do younger people, the caloric requirement for them being about half that of late adolescence and early adulthood.[132] This is in part because the aged are less active than younger people, and hence burn up fewer calories. Although the caloric needs of the aged are less, their nutrient requirements are just as high as in earlier life. We learned in Chapter 13 that the bones of middle-aged people tend to lose calcium. This calcium loss tends to increase in the later years, partly because of aging itself, but often because the aged do not always eat what they need. The lack of need for calories, for example, tends to result for many aged people in a reduced intake of all foods. The decreasing ability to mobilize ready energy in the body tempts the aged to emphasize carbohydrates (starches and sugars) in the small amount they do eat. The two sources of energy which create the greatest danger to the nutritional well-being of the aged are excessive alcohol and sugar.[132] Next in order are fats and white bread.

Another aspect of aging in relation to nutrition is the fact that all of the nutritional deficiencies accumulated throughout life now affect the total aging process. An inadequate diet in old age further accelerates the aging process. It is therefore especially important for the aging person to have a well-balanced diet, with especial attention to vitamin and mineral needs.

Nutritional imbalance in the aged is associated with factors other than the above. Restricted budgets, as we saw earlier, are primary considerations for many older people. Because rent and taxes must be paid, diet often suffers, as meat substitutes and carbohydrates fill the stomach at minimum cost. Increasing infirmity reduces the energy needed to shop for and prepare meals, even if the budget permits well-balanced ingredients. In bad weather the neglect of proper meals may amount to near-starvation. This, in turn, further reduces ambition, invites disease, and tends to set up a vicious circle of depletion. If poor food habits carry over from earlier life, the impact is exaggerated both by habit and by accumulated nutritional deficiencies. Lowered nutritional status and lowered vitality give rise to discouragement, a sense of futility, and of depression. Adequate nutrition is basic to all aspects of the aging process, psychological as well as physiological.

However, even if older people have the same diet as younger people, their bodies vary considerably in the use of the nutrients. Even though their needs for nutrients are the same, their use of the nutrients is likely to be affected by the conditions under which the food is prepared and eaten. If meals are eaten alone by a person who longs for the younger years when he or she was surrounded by a family, or by an individual who is in an institutional setting while longing to be elsewhere, the body does not make as good use of the nutrients as it would under more enjoyable circumstances. McCay [132] has stated that the social conditions under which the food is prepared and eaten seem to be much more important to the aged than is the nutritional content of the food. For example, a woman who is planning, preparing, and sharing food with her husband will get much more nutritional value from the nutrients eaten than will the same woman served the same nutrients in an institutional setting, or in the home of a relative who does not want her around.

Muscular Strength

Decreasing efficiency of the carbon dioxide–oxygen exchange in the lungs, along with decreasing efficiency of the circulatory and muscular systems and the deterioration of motor nerves, makes for a decrease in the ability to endure sustained muscular effort in old age.[232] The reduction of muscular capacity, to which we referred in Chapter 13, proceeds into old age. The gait of the older person is less resilient and steady than formerly. Reduced tonus of muscles of the back and chest may result in a stooped posture which becomes evident in some individuals as early as age 50, but in most individuals by 75 or 80 years of age. Much depends, of course, upon the use of the muscles throughout life.

Each muscle group has its own pattern of growth and decline. We have referred earlier to the back and chest muscles as being particularly susceptible to decline in strength after 65 years of age. In contrast to these muscles, those of the wrist and hand decline the least in strength, some 25 per cent of 60- to 70-year-olds being able to perform with these muscles at a level equal to the average of the total population. Although the public at large is not aware of this fact specifically, great wonder as well as admiration was expressed when Martha Graham danced with precision and fine balance in her late sixties, whereas admiration but less wonder was expressed at the dexterity and finger-wrist strength of Iturbi, as he played the most difficult and demanding piano repertory at a comparable age. The differential rates of decline between the back muscles and the hand-wrist muscles are important in regard to the employment of older people. It is more reasonable to expect their continuing success in jobs involving hand strength and flexibility than in jobs involving long hours of standing, bending, or lifting.

General motor reaction time declines little before 60 years of age, except the decline in reaction to light and sound which results from deterioration in sight and hearing.[232] The relationship between re-action time and industrial accident rate has been studied, and old workers are found to have an accident rate not appreciably higher than that of workers as a whole.[110] This is contrary to what might be expected from the above discussion. It seems, however, that although the older worker may be slower, he is more cautious. Some older workers even make up in experience for decreases in motor dexterity, with the result that among older workers who have proved good enough to remain on the job there is often the ability to produce as rapidly as younger workers.[147] The workers whose dexterity has obviously declined are, of course, not retained in employment.

One set of muscles which eventually becomes less efficient is the set which controls the vocal cords. The voice tends to become higher in pitch and less steady in old age than it was in the younger years. The decline in lung capacity referred to earlier means that a reduced volume of air is available. Hence, older people lose in strength as well as range of vocal tone, and their voices tend to become monot-onous. That there are notable exceptions is evidenced by the number of actors and singers who, with the help of microphones, have staged strong comebacks after 70 years of age.

Muscle tremors sometimes occur when nerves involved in muscle action become impaired.[161] This aspect of aging is closely associated with hereditary factors which involve aging of nerve fibers. In very advanced age, however, changes occur in most individuals in the neurons involved in finer motor movements such as those of the hand. Handwriting becomes shaky and finally illegible, food gets spilled on the way to the mouth, and bathing and dressing become more difficult or perhaps impossible. In advanced senescence, loss of control of the urethral and anal sphincter muscles may occur. This loss of control over waste elimination adds to nursing problems.

Bone Conditions

We have said that calcium losses and other bone changes may occur in middle age because of inadequate nutrition. Even under good nutritional intake, they occur to some extent in all people of advanced age.[66] Loss of muscular strength and coordination increases the danger of falls for the aged. Icy walking conditions, loose rugs in the house, and stairs which lack hand rails are hazards to the old. Fractures of the thigh bone are fairly frequent because this part of the skeleton bears the weight of the body in a way that makes it particularly susceptible to aging changes. Fractures of the spine also occur and, along with thigh bone or pelvic fractures, are slower to heal than are most other types of fractures. Because of losses in strength and thickness as well as hardening of the blood vessels of the bones, all bones are harder to heal in old age than in the earlier years of life.

PSYCHOLOGICAL ASPECTS OF AGING

It is evident from the foregoing discussion that a good deal is known about the physiology of old age. Much less is currently known about the psychology of senescence and senility. We need to define these terms which are coming into common usage. *Senescence* refers to a relatively even decline in all abilities; *senility* refers to a more rapid decline of mental than of physical abilities. As is true of all ages, older individuals tend to come to the attention of physicians because people are accustomed to seeking professional help for their physical ailments. They are less likely to seek help for psychological difficulties. Studies are therefore easier to conduct in the physical areas. In recent years, the increasing proportion of the aged in the population has generated interest in psychological study of the old. Investigators have studied not only the aging who seek medical help, but have also sampled the total aging population. Such broad sample researches in the physiological areas of gerontology have been under way since the early 1930's; in the psychological areas, they were relatively few until the late 1940's. Many psychological studies are currently under way, and their findings may shed new light upon psychological aging.

Psychological Accompaniments of Illness

As would be expected, some studies in the psychological areas have grown out of the abundant research in the physical illnesses and deteriorations of old age. Some writers [24, 66] have suggested that unconscious emotional factors in the aged may play a part in their accidents, resulting in fractures as well as in the retardation of the healing of the fractures. For example, the old person may have an unconscious desire to express resentment against his caretakers by forcing them to take prolonged care of him. Feelings of guilt and a consequent need of self-punishment for his rebellious or hostile feelings may also be a factor. Wishes for death may be a predisposing element in the emotional picture. These factors are not, of course, to be assumed whenever an older person sustains a fracture. Old people who are healthy in both body and mind may slip on a rug or on ice. They are, however, most likely to do this at times when their muscle strength and nerve control are below par. In other cases, even when the old person is healthy in mind and emotions, he is susceptible to falls when recovering from any illness which leaves his muscle strength and nerve control in poor condition.

Many orthopedic surgeons trained to work with the aged are now alerted to the necessity to observe, evaluate, and assist in restoring the patient's emotional state as well as his broken bones. It is currently usual medical practice to try, whenever possible, to repair fractures in the old by means of pins or other mechanical devices which make some movement possible rather than to immobilize the patient by putting him in bed or a wheel chair.[66] Some mobility is helpful not only to the patient's interest in life and hence to his recovery, but is also helpful in promoting circulation and avoiding blood clotting, which results in serious complications.

Prolonged periods of inactivity resulting from fractures or from any prolonged illness sometimes lead to emotional complications. Timidity in movement, for example, may develop because of pain or from fear of future falls. If the patient refuses to try to get about, this adds to the handicaps to recovery associated with immobility.

General physical and mental hygiene, particularly adequate physical therapy, are usually effective in promoting physical and emotional healing. Perhaps most important of all factors is the attention and affection of family and friends, which enables the old person to feel that his life is not over, and that he is still wanted. Anything within his capacity that he can be encouraged to do for himself helps the aged individual to feel less of a burden to others and more of a participant in the life around him.

Changes in Intellect

Although a good deal is known about how intelligence develops, much less is known about how it changes in the later years of life. We have seen that intelligence, as measured by the standardized tests currently available, declines gradually between ages 25–30 and 60, and more rapidly thereafter.[74] There is, however, considerable evidence [161] that the symbolization processes which involve language, information, and comprehension are more resistant to the effects of aging than are memory or the ability to learn new materials.

As in all aspects of aging, wide individual differences exist in the way intellectual functions deteriorate. Some individuals, by 60 years of age or earlier, give evidence of fundamental failures in memory and association, in reasoning, and in other intellectual capacities. Others, like Senator Green who acted as Chairman of the United States Foreign Relations Committee when over 90 years old, and Justice Holmes who handed down some of his most famous Supreme Court opinions after 90, bear witness to the fact that some minds function brilliantly and remain highly useful into advanced old age. In private life most of us know such individuals as the old Quaker lady who taught herself Latin at 83, or the woman of 90 whose sound advice on personal situations made her one of the most sought after people in her community. Such individuals usually remain in good physical health as well, so that they can continue their intellectual and personal contributions to their communities.

Individuals differ, too, in the interrelationship between physical and mental decline. Certain men and women retain accurate memories and keen intelligence even though their skeletal or digestive systems show deterioration. Conversely, some people lose all semblance of intellectual capacity, becoming unable to react intelligently to their surroundings many years before the body deteriorates to the stage of death. In these latter instances, the cells of the cerebrum have lost their ability to function, and the individual is said to be in a state of senile dementia (loss of mind resulting from senility).

Between the extremes of complete loss of intellect on the one hand and the continued high degree of functioning on the other, are most of the people who represent the aging population as a whole. In general, advancing years affect intelligence in certain characteristic ways. Fairly extensive cellular alterations occur in the nervous system as a whole. When these changes occur in the cerebrum, which is made up largely of association neurons, mental functions which are dependent upon these neurons begin to fail. Memory suffers, and as forgetfulness progresses, the individual becomes increasingly less capable of making associations which assure the remembering of current situations. New telephone numbers, for example, must be written down where they can be looked up when needed: the grocery list must be written down and then, too often, hunted for, because the individual has forgotten where she put it. New names and new faces are not easily remembered; current events, personal or political, tend to be forgotten, or to be recalled only with concentrated effort. Former events, however, tend to be recalled easily. Thus, as failure of contemporary memory occurs, patterns of associations established in earlier years cease to be interfered with by recent associations. Hence, the individual experiences them again. The extremely old tend to live more and more in the past, and in the end may be entirely possessed by the memories of early life, which may be very pleasant.

The continued functioning of contemporary memory is affected by the life the older person lives. One of the central considerations in maintaining alertness of intellect is the maintenance in old age of a lively set of interests and activities (see Figs. 14–2 and 14–3) which employ the mind and reward the emotions. To the degree that the mind stays active and interested, it resists the tendency to decay. The situation can in many ways be compared to the body which, if kept mobile, tends to retain its usefulness and healing power at an optimum, whereas the body that becomes immobilized loses its strength and heals less well. With favorable attitudes, the aging person can often compensate for a reduction in the speed of his intellectual processes by a lively interest in the world around him, and by a prudent weighing of situations in the light of his long experience. To the degree that the present enjoyably occupies the mind, the cerebral neurons tend to associate contemporary events in addition to those of the past.

Fig. 14–2. A well-tended garden is a rewarding activity.

Personality Changes

There is no old age personality, as such. There are no special traits, attitudes, or habits which distinguish the old as a group from younger groups.[36] The personality changes which occur in old age, as in middle age, have their origins in the earlier life of the individual. However, personality as it reveals itself in daily living is affected at all ages by the situation in which the individual finds himself.

Old age, as does all developmental periods, requires that the individual make certain adjustments. We have already discussed the need for older people to adjust to decreasing strength and health, and the need to adjust to retirement and to reduced income. The need to establish satisfactory physical living arrangements has been implied in the discussion of the need to protect the aged from falls, the advantages of being near adequate food markets, and the difficulties of adjustment to living in the homes of others.

One of the most severe adjustments of old age is associated with the loss of the spouse. The long years of habits established in the day-by-day living patterns shared with a beloved person make

Fig. 14–3. The true fisherman seems never to grow old.

difficult the need to adjust to a new set of day-by-day habits of living. A review of our earlier population figures reminds us that women, on the average, must make this severe adjustment more often and over a longer stretch of years than men. Since there are fewer unattached older men in most retirement communities than there are women, the men are more sought after socially, hence usually are less lonely than are the unattached women. Widowers tend to remarry more often than do widows.

How well either men or women adjust to the loss of the spouse depends upon the quality of the marriage through the years. In occasional instances, the death represents release from an unhappy relationship. Much more often, it means a separation that is almost unbearable for the remaining individual. The adjustment also depends upon recent events. Sometimes, for example, the death represents the end of a long illness from which the one partner is now released from pain, the other from exhausting nursing care. The pain of the loss may be eased by the memory of the care it was possible to give, and by memories of happiness shared through the years. Although the marriage relationship of most mature individuals has been highly gratifying to both mates, they remain independent personalities. In some cases, they have contemplated the almost inevitable aloneness, and have helped each other to develop interests that prepare them for the time when only one of them will be left. True love guards against the unbearable loneliness of the surviving spouse. Success or failure in adjustment to this and other situations has a substantial effect upon the outlook and behavior, hence upon the happiness, of the aged person as well as of those with whom he is associated.

Personality Breakdowns

Mental and emotional illness resulting from an inability to adjust to life situations in old age is not essentially different from illness resulting from the same inability in earlier life. In any individual, the manifestations of this type of illness are the same as if it had occurred earlier in the individual's life. As long as any individual is able to control his environment to some degree and to manage an adjustment of some sort to his surroundings, he may escape mental and emotional illness.

With the advancing years the individual is often compelled to face more and more circumstances over which he can exercise little control. Many older people must meet several trying situations at once, and must do this at a time in their lives when the aging process has weakened them physically and psychologically. An individual may, for example, have to adjust to failing strength and health, to reduced income, to the loss of the spouse, and to the necessity of living with people who are not too happy to have him around, all within a few months or years. He must face these multiple adjustments, and other situations which seriously restrict his self-expression and require a surrender to the choices of others in such matters as what he is to eat, when and where he is free to come and go, and other routine details. In such a situation, frustrations sometimes intensify beyond his capacity to endure them or to adjust to them.

When this happens, a previously near-neurosis is likely to become a full-fledged one. Weaknesses of personality, which existed in earlier years and remained uncorrected, may flare into well-developed psychoses. Accumulated frustrations and grudges distort the viewpoint and exaggerate disagreeable personality habits, which in turn sharpen the conflict with the surrounding environment. The resulting vicious cycle may produce a final breakdown that has been years in the making.

Some writers [66, 161] have suggested that the completely involuntary development of a neurosis or psychosis may, in occasional instances, be the only way a hemmed-in aged person can get release from his tensions. It is not a happy means, of course, since it serves only to increase the strains in his environment with consequent further restrictions on the expression or satisfaction of his needs. In such cases, as in all forms of neuroses and psychoses, psychiatric or other counselling help may benefit the older person if he has sufficient intelligence. Such help may in any case help the people who are responsible for or who must live with him.

Senile dementia, one form of breakdown which is peculiar to old age, has been mentioned previously. A result of the deterioration of the cells of the cerebrum, it is associated with physiological aging processes which affect both the circulation of the brain and the brain cells themselves. With such "loss of mind" there are accompanying personality manifestations which tend to take a form dependent upon previous personality weaknesses. The condition may take the form of exaggerated jealousy, suspiciousness of the people who are closest to him, and often of the person previously most loved. It may be accompanied by depression or by agitation. In one stage of its development, the patient may continually run away unless watched, the most usual reason apparently being to find something exciting to replace intolerable monotony. In its advanced stages, the patient seems to return to the childhood stages of irresponsibility, needing to be fed and otherwise cared for as in infancy.

SUCCESSFUL AGING

We have stated earlier that the best way to prepare to age successfully is to meet life well along the way. By the time we are old it is usually too late to repair previous failures in growth. For the few, as we have seen, old age is too late a time to avoid a breakdown. For the many, however, much can and is being done by community and social agencies to make old age "the best of life" as Browning indicates it can be.

Importance of Optimal Health and Adequate Income

Two major factors in good adjustment in old age, both before and after retirement, are good health and satisfactory economic status. We have discussed the many current efforts to insure financial means adequate to provide the basic needs of the aging population. As we saw, much still needs to be done.

Community Assistance to Successful Aging

Medically, enough is now known about how to keep aging people at an optimum of their potential health. It is now possible for many older people, who would until recently have had to be hospitalized, to live independently or with a minimum of community support. In such countries as Great Britain, the United States, and the Scandinavian countries, adequate diagnostic and treatment centers for the aged have delayed the deteriorations of aging and have controlled illnesses among the old so that the amount of sickness and the number of hospitalizations and the length of hospital stays have been greatly reduced.[80]

In these countries, experiments are under way which are designed to increase comfort and adequacy of living for aged people who do not require hospitalization, but who cannot completely care for their own needs. Large housing units designed to meet both the physical and financial needs of the aged have proved not only financially feasible to the agencies sponsoring them but a blessing to the old as well. Central kitchens which prepare nutritious meals to be delivered to the homes of the aged have been equally successful. Visiting nurses, visiting housekeepers, day hospital care, a "friendly visitor" system, central recreation centers, and community gardens, are some successful features of community aid to the aged. Counselling services assist the aged to reassess their finances, to take stock of their health status, to evaluate their possible employment skills and their recreational skills and interests. Help is given each individual so that he can utilize his skills and interests to the best advantage.

A Bill of Rights for the Aged

Books and articles on assistance to the aged and to the people they live with are available in a constant flow. Such titles as *Aging Successfully*,[124] *Understanding Old Age*,[66] *How to Retire and Enjoy It*,[67] are characteristic. In them is found a modern new approach to middle and old age. For example, a widely quoted excerpt from one of these * is a "Bill of Rights" for the aged. It is directed to the attention of the younger generations who are responsible for aged people and who live with or near them, and reads as follows:

1. The right to be treated as a person.
2. The right to be treated as an adult.
3. The right to a fair chance on our merits.
4. The right to a say about our own lives.
5. The right to a future.
6. The right to have fun and companions.
7. The right to be romantic.
8. The right to your help in becoming interesting to you.
9. The right to professional help whenever necessary.
10. The right to be old.

Congenial Friends

Public and private agencies help older people to find congenial friends and to come together in groups or clubs, to share interests and fun with each other. These situations tend to stimulate the development of new interests and the revival of old ones. Clubs thus formed, or which come together without the help of agencies, often adopt names such as "The Over-Sixty-Fives Club," "Senior Citizens," "The Golden Age Club" or, humorously, "The Fossils' Club." The personnel of these clubs and changes in officership are affected by illnesses and deaths more often than would be true for younger clubs. There is, however, good fun, a lively pursuit of common interests and, often, genuine service to the community. The following excerpt from a 1959 issue of an English local paper indicates something of the flavor these clubs may have.

The committee of the "Good Companions Club" are glad to report another successful year. As is inevitable in a club of elderly people, we have lost one or two of our members, but have been able to welcome several new friends.

* G. Lawton, *Aging Successfully*. New York: Columbia University Press, 1951.

There follows a report of changes in constitution and officerships, and a report of the success of the entertainment committee. Among the events reported were the following:

> On 9th June two coach loads of us went for a lovely country drive and tea at Mary Mason's Tea Rooms. On 16th July another coach load went to see "Starlight," the Sandy Powell show on the Pier. On the 23rd July—our Birthday Party—some members of the Women's Institute entertained us with an amusing play. A successful Whist party increased our funds by 85s. 6d.

Under the supervision of educational institutions, adult education classes especially designed for older people are offered. These are growing rapidly in number and in range of material. They include such topics as "hygiene for the aged," "the aging process," and "further personality development." As trained personnel becomes available, these classes take the form of discussion groups in which there can be developed a gradual understanding and acceptance of the facts of aging. If the guidance is skillful enough, this may lead to insight into old habits which make living at this period of life difficult. Sometimes this insight can lead to a modification of the old habits and the development of different approaches to specific situations. When this occurs, life for the older person and for those around him may take on a new and happier aspect.

Personal and Spiritual Growth

One series of such adult educational discussion classes [216] developed a philosophy and outlook which seems to us a good summary for our unit on aging successfully. In the review of the series, class members made a report which, with their permission, we abstract as follows:

As people look forward to retirement, there are several different patterns of anticipation. One type of person anticipates retirement as a period free of routine demands; a period in which there will be time for leisure, travel, and hobbies. For these people, life may and often does go along relatively happily with a letting down of tensions, a simpler pattern of living, a development of old or, occasionally, of new interests which center around recreation and personal affairs.

Another type of person feels reluctant to face retirement, seeing in it only a lowering of income and a termination of accustomed activities and associations. For these people, life in retirement often becomes much reduced in interests and activities. Horizons narrow and there develops a fear of any enlargement of horizons or of any change at all. Neither of these two types of people do any real growing. They are either standing still or retrogressing.

There is a third type of older person, unfortunately all too rare, who finds challenge less in personal puttering or amusement than in community activities in which he has had some experience or for which he has previously had no time. He does many things, often making needed contributions to the life of his community, thereby enlarging his own ideas and skills and benefiting the life of his neighbors. In this he finds a new sense of inner satisfaction and development. His activity is creatively fulfilling. This third type of person is living satisfactorily for himself and for his community. He is usually happier than the relaxed noncontributor who is busy only with his own recreation and hobbies. He is, of course, far happier than the person whose horizons are increasingly constricted.

Even this third type of person, however, may be missing the type of personal and spiritual growth which can be possible in the later years of life. With a lifetime of living, of experiencing and of maturing behind one, the later years of life offer a unique opportunity for a person to review and to evaluate his life. In so doing, he may find it possible to understand his limitations and his capacities.

Since life for the old is largely in the past and cannot be relived, the pressures for outer accomplishments are less, and the possibilities for inner growth are greater. In the process of quiet and realistic self-evaluation, older people often feel a release from limitations which have stood in their way in earlier life. They may experience a greater freedom to develop capacities which have not previously been developed. If this occurs, they gradually find it possible to free themselves from previous unfortunate habits of mind and spirit, and to develop new and stronger attitudes and feelings. This process is of necessity slow at any time after childhood and youth, and is especially slow in old age. In old age, however, there is far less competitive distraction. The process sometimes moves forward with sufficient speed to enable the individual to appreciate his progress, and when this happens, the satisfaction with such progress is deep.

The group whose discussions led to the above conclusions stated one further conclusion based upon the others. Appreciating that life's "unfinished business" in the areas of personality and spirit are cumulative, they decided that old age offered not only a last chance to finish some of the unfinished growing which every individual carries with him, but that it also offered a unique foundation of experience from which to proceed with such growing. Although most people never get the "unfinished business" of life attended to before life on earth is terminated, this group of older people found from their own experience that progress in finishing some of it in the later years gave them a feeling that they were achieving the purposes for which they were living. In this, they found that they reduced or even eliminated their fear of death.

SUGGESTIONS FOR FURTHER DISCUSSION

1. Think of the people over 65 years of age whom you know personally.
   a. What do they seem to be like in health; in disposition; in range of interests?
   b. How do you think they compare with the averages given in the text? Be specific.
   c. As far as you can judge without asking personal questions, how are their financial needs being met?
   d. Where are they living? How satisfactory do the living circumstances seem to be?
   e. As nearly as you can judge from observation, how adequately are their emotional needs being met?
   f. What do you think their problems might be? Their major satisfactions?
   g. What, if any, do you think may be the problems of their nearest of kin in relation to them?

2. What provisions for or contributions to the welfare and happiness of the over-65's are being made in your home community? By your state government? By the federal government?

3. Visit some home for the aged in your community. Is there anything you as a young citizen can do to make the occupants healthier or happier? Did they teach you anything about old age?

4. Do you know of any old age recreational clubs? What are their names? Who may belong? What do they do?

5. Browse through the books listed below and other sources in your library for further information about the aging processes, both physical and psychological. Document your findings and report them to the class for discussion.

REFERENCES FOR FURTHER STUDY

DEWEY, R., and HUMBER, W. J. *The Development of Human Behavior*. New York: The Macmillan Co., 1951. Ch. 13, old age: physiological old age; old age in cultural perspective; changes in population of old persons; cultural provisions for the old; personality and old age.

DRAKE, J. T. *The Aged in American Society.* New York: The Ronald Press Co., 1958. A college textbook on the aged in America. Presents aged people as human beings rather than mere statistics.

DUBLIN, L. J., LOTKA, A. J., and SPIEGELMAN, M. *Length of Life: A Study of the Life Table.* Rev. ed. New York: The Ronald Press Co., 1949. History of longevity; factors influencing longevity; forecasts; applications of known data to known problems such as population problems, economic problems.

THORPE, L. P., and CRUZE, W. W. *Developmental Psychology.* New York: The Ronald Press Co., 1956. Ch. 18, senescence: the final stage of development (intellectual and personality changes).

For film suggestions see Film Supplement, in the Appendix.

CHAPTER 15

The Pattern of Life

General Background

As we have seen, human life is complex, presenting many facets which contribute to or detract from sound growth and development. We have discussed what people are like in their different stages of growth. They change, not only in physical characteristics, but in emotional, social, and intellectual characteristics as well. We have seen something of peer relationships at each stage of life, and how people in different stages react with others who are older or younger.

We have said that most human beings are born into homes maintained by a husband and his wife, who are usually fairly young adults. From the beginning of life for some individuals but sooner or later in most people's lives there are, living in the home, people in stages other than infancy or young adulthood. In most cultures, at any given time, a household may include a man and a woman, a late adolescent, an early adolescent, one or more children in late or early childhood, and a baby. Possibly an unmarried aunt or uncle or a grandparent or two may live with them also. With today's increasing longevity, there is even the possibility of a great-grandparent in the home. Since this is true, many young people in the study of human development are deeply and personally interested not only in the developmental period in which they themselves now are, but in questions which arise about all stages of development from infancy through old age.

In addition to the households described above, we have referred to those in which widowed, divorced, or never-married men and women of various ages live alone, with a single relative, with another person of the same sex and of about the same age, or in institutions of one kind or another. Children who have no relatives, those whose relatives do not want them, and those whose parents have not released them for adoption, usually live in institutions with large numbers of their peers and other people of various ages. In learning about human development, we need to broaden our viewpoint to include understanding of the lives of both people who do and people who do not live in so-called normal homes.

Life Is Both Struggle and Fulfillment

Living things have never had life as they would like it. Organisms strive to produce more of themselves against constantly destructive forces. Everything struggles for its place, young birds in the parental nest, young mammals for the maternal nipple. Conflict is normal from the beginning. Human life is no exception, and conflict in human life results in interesting and sometimes perplexing situations.

However, life typically has satisfaction and happiness for human beings at each stage. The very process of living, of fulfilling basic needs, of growing and developing, is in itself satisfying. We have discussed the basic needs of human beings and how fulfillment of these is conducive to growth and to constant development from birth to death.

All people are dependent for the fulfillment of their needs not only upon their families or other people with whom they live, but upon many others in the community. In addition to living in a community, most people belong to some kinds of groups, from the groups of childhood to the various religious, social, recreational, cultural, and civic groups which exist for people in the successive stages of life. Children in many parts of the world attend school, where they come into contact with other children both older and younger than themselves, and where they are under the supervision of adults other than their parents. Most adults come in daily contact with employers or employees, clerks in stores, neighbors, and with many other adults in business or personal relationships.

Characteristic Problems

Complex relationships develop among all these people who have the different traits that accompany sex and age. This makes personal relationships interesting and fulfilling. However, it also makes for conflict—good, healthy conflict for the most part, if it is managed intelligently. No matter how well the relationships are managed, however, they do give rise to characteristic problems.

By characteristic problems we mean the various perplexing situations that arise naturally in human relationships and which can either be lived with while they last or can be solved with reasonable effort on the part of the people concerned. The problems can, of course, be solved only if those concerned are motivated to solve them and have sufficient insight into the situations and into themselves as persons to make solutions possible. They require the adjustment by one or more individuals to others. In such adjustments there is growth not only in the personality of the individual or individuals able to make such adjustments, but usually in the quality of the interpersonal relationships between them.

Struggle which results in adjustment has value. The baby in the playpen drops his toy. If someone rushes to pick it up for him, he loses the muscular exercise, the perceptual experience, and the emotional satisfaction of struggling to recapture it for himself. The young child, with his inner urge to grow and develop, wants to "help" in dressing himself. If his mother is "too busy" and proceeds to dress him in spite of his protest, he loses a chance to fumble, miss, try again, and finally get his socks on or even completely to dress him-. self, depending upon his age at the time. She has deprived him of an opportunity to struggle with a simple solution to one of his own needs. The older child finds himself in conflict with one of his peers. If his father settles the matter with the father of the peer, an invaluable opportunity to learn something in peer adjustment has been lost. The young adolescent wants the income from a paper route, but his parents drive him around on his route in the family car, keep his books for him, and check the business with his superior for him. Or the older adolescent finds a college course difficult and drops it in favor of something easier. In each of these instances the individual has lost an opportunity to struggle in a situation that would have contributed to his satisfaction in achievement. He has lost an opportunity to exercise and hence to strengthen his faculties, and, therefore, to experience a growing fulfillment in their use.

This is not to say that no satisfaction or fulfillment ever comes without a struggle. Anyone can recall many of life's keenest delights that seemed to "just happen," or have come about because of careful planning for us by those who love us. Nor does it mean that struggle, per se, is good, since to be in a situation where help is genuinely needed and to find ourselves deliberately deprived of such help is a frustrating and faith-shaking experience for an infant, an adolescent, or an adult. Nor is a life of "all work and no play" likely to produce the desired balance between achievement and rest. Our point is that all play and protection, with no struggle or strength-giving effort, prove disastrous to both body and personality.

Problems, then, do arise in human as in other life, whether they are adjustments to picking up one's own toys, or the earning of a living. They are inevitable in any set of human relationships. They also accompany certain ages and stages of growth, being in many ways a by-product of growth itself. Since many of the questions young people ask about themselves and their families or friends concern this category of problems, let us look at them more closely. In tracing growth from birth to death we have marked certain periods or stages, each with certain growth characteristics. We have seen that each growth period has certain developmental tasks to accomplish. If these are achieved, growth proceeds more satisfactorily into and through succeeding stages; if not accomplished, "unfinished business" carries over into the next stages where, if at all, it can be finished. We have implied that no child grows up without behavior problems, that no adolescent or adult is entirely free of the need to adjust his behavior and feelings to the needs and rights of others, and to his own inner longings. Certain periods of growth and development, however, present characteristic problems which not only appear frequently but which nearly everyone experiences.

The periods in which such almost universal problems arise are the transition periods: early childhood is a transition from babyhood to childhood; early adolescence is a transition from the child's body to biological maturity; and middle age is a transition from the responsibilities of adulthood to retirement, and for the woman a period of loss of fertility. These universal adjustments, with their accompanying problems, are not to be confused with problems which eventuate from structural or functional defects and which are indications of basic difficulty with or deviation from normal growth. The latter problems are not ordinarily corrected without skilled professional therapy, whereas the former, if met with reasonable maturity of understanding, are corrected by growth itself as the individual moves from one step to another of development.

The characteristic, almost universal type of problems often appear to the individual as critical problems of the deeper-lying structural or functional type. Not being understood for what they are, these problems often cause genuine anxiety and may be treated as indications of basic defect. In such situations, they are not "solved" and may fix themselves into the personality, there to remain through ensuing years.

Figure 15–1 shows some of the interrelationships and opposites in mood and feeling among the age groups. Although perplexing situations at each age level loom large while they exist, most people do enjoy living, perhaps more than they realize, and quickly forget their problems as soon as they live through them or solve them. Most of us, however, might enjoy living more than we do and worry less than we do if we had more insight into behavior. Let us review each stage of growth briefly in the light of the perplexities and fulfillments of each.

THE PERPLEXITIES AND FULFILLMENTS OF EACH GROWTH STAGE

Infancy

Most expectant parents look forward eagerly to their first child, picturing the satisfactions and pride they will feel in his presence. Unless they have seen newborn infants, however, they are seldom prepared for the appearance of the wrinkled, red bit of humanity, whose head may be temporarily molded out of shape by passage through the birth canal, and whose eyes for the first few days may be inflamed as a reaction to the antiseptic solution dropped into them to prevent infection. Knowing in advance, however, that the infant may look like this, they know that in a few days he will look much better. Normally mature parents adjust quickly to his temporary appearance and rejoice in the fact that "this is their baby" and that he is normal.

In Chapter 4, it was pointed out that even though the mother may wish to breast-feed her infant she may not prove able to do so, and that formula feeding is more beneficial for the child than attempts to continue breast feeding that prove unsatisfactory. It was also said that many infants need some help to suck satisfactorily.

Infants in the home require adjustments in the family routines, and they prove expensive additions to the family budget. However, they soon begin to react to the world around them, and if healthy and lovingly cared for, provide a kind of delight and emotional ful-

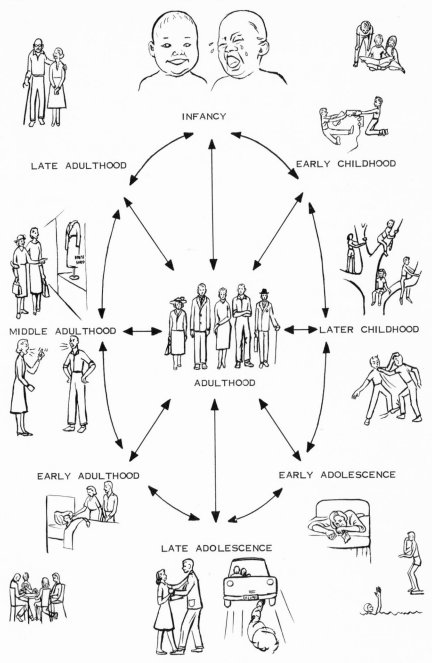

Fig. 15–1. All age groups are interrelated, and these interrelation-ships are affected by variations of mood and circumstance, as well as of age.

fillment found only in the growing young. It soon becomes evident that the infant himself both suffers (when hungry or otherwise uncomfortable) or contentedly and delightedly enjoys his days. As he begins to react to the environment outside of himself, his gurgles and squeals of joy upon learning to grasp a toy or to play hide-and-seek with a friendly adult are as much pleasure to others as to himself.

Young mothers typically undertake the care of their baby at home within a few days after giving birth. The frequency of feeding periods interrupts night rest, and adjustment of household routines often results in profound fatigue for the mother. She suffers a consequent feeling of discouragement over a period of days, which some physicians call "baby blues." If she and her husband know beforehand that this is likely to happen, they can recognize the symptoms and, rather than being frightened by the tears, can arrange their lives to counteract the situation. If they are not aware of what is happening, they may assume that there is something seriously wrong with her as a wife and mother and become increasingly tense, until this characteristically temporary adjustment to the presence of a baby becomes a serious family problem.

If young parents understand such characteristic but temporary situations, and if they are mature in their acceptance of the responsibilities as well as the joys of parenthood, the period of infancy can become a joyous and fulfilling one for them and a sound growth period for the child. When this is true, the period is remembered by the parents in later years as a wonderful one in which they knew exactly where their children were all of the time, and when each day brought new delights in growth accomplishment and in an unfolding development of personality.

We have said that the infant not only learns to walk, but walks into trouble. The toddler, with his imperfect motor controls, his incessant mobility, his unending curiosity, becomes a source of fatigue and discouragement to the mother who tries to keep ahead of his activities. With a second child, she knows that this toddler stage will end, and that toddlers who are hard to manage will not actually become preschool children who are impossible to manage. She knows that they will eventually develop motor controls and at least some self-control to match their activity and their curiosity. She will see, too, that the activity and curiosity have eventuated in rapid intellectual growth, and she will discover ways to provide this essential growth in a physical and emotional setting offering adequate opportunity to grow without too much cost to household belongings and human tempers.

If grandparents or other adults live with the family or see them often, they may be helpful or troublesome, depending largely upon the degree of real adulthood they themselves have attained. Most young couples and their children seem to work out their problems best if other adults do not know about them. On the other hand, a really adult grandparent can be a tower of strength to a young family.

Early Childhood

In this transition period from infancy to childhood the child is moving outside of the home and into the immediate neighborhood. Here he meets the neighbors' children's germs and self-centered interests, as well as their mothers' different ideas of discipline. In the primitive state of the young child's social development, pushing, grabbing, and hitting are characteristic. Playing beside rather than closely with peers predominates in the first years of this period; shifting-group play comes only when gradually increasing social skills and self-control make adjustment to others possible.

The two- to four-year-old's developing personality and awareness of himself lead him to resist adults and to fight for his right to act and to decide immediate situations for himself. Negativism to adult and older-child authority reaches a peak around three years of age. Although sense perceptions are rapidly becoming more accurate, many misjudgments continue to frustrate the child. Temper tantrums are characteristic of three and four years of age. As capacities develop and self-control begins, the causes of tantrums gradually diminish and the child learns more constructive ways of meeting frustration. That is, he does if the tantrums are understood for what they are, namely, an evidence of unevennesses in growth which in time smooth out.

Although three- and four-year-olds evidence some exceedingly trying behavior (as trying to themselves as to adults) they also experience hours on end of delighted, even exhilarated conquest of the things around them as they learn to go down a slide, to steer a scooter, to enjoy simple games and jokes. They are deeply and contentedly happy in the assurance of parental support and pride in their achievements. Their conversation as well as their behavior reveals the freshness of their new ideas, their puzzlements and wonderings and eagerness to learn. They are fun to have around.

Later Childhood

We have called this period the gang age and the school age, thus typifying the child's further exploration of his community and the major adjustments he is called upon to make. We have said that, in growth, this is a fairly calm period, physical growth tapering off, intellectual growth moving forward steadily under school training and varied community experiences. Personal-social growth centers around adjustments to the peer group where experiences are characteristically realistic, often difficult, and occasionally cruel. They are, however, often interesting, amusing, and educational, depending upon the gang, the neighborhood environment, and the individual child's own growth background. Success or failure in school or gang are fundamentally influential in the development of realistic adjustments to work and to personal relationships, to self-confidence, and to the development of childhood's values. Parental attitudes toward such success or failure are even more instrumental than the actuality of the success or failure in determining the child's future attitudes and feelings.

Concepts of honesty and truth are becoming more generalized. Because conscience is still in the making, instances of misappropriation of property and compromises with truth characteristically occur around eight to ten years of age. As we saw in Chapter 6, if these instances are understood by parents and other adults as evidences of as-yet-incomplete growth, they may be dealt with wisely. Misunderstood as evidences of a stealing or lying nature, they may be dealt with unwisely, with disastrous consequences to the personality of the child.

Although later childhood is a time when the child is increasingly away from home, being in school or with the gang, it is a period in which many children enjoy their families a great deal and learn much from them. Dinner-table conversations and family council discussions offer occasions where each member of the family participates, clarifies his own thoughts and feelings, learns to understand and to respect the views of others than his peers, and broadens his ideas and appreciations. It is often a time when family companionship is solidified in a way which fortifies both parents and the child for the almost inevitable differences of opinion and feeling which occur during adolescence.

In later childhood, some children enjoy doing things for and playing with some of their younger siblings some of the time, but most of them are annoyed by them a good deal of the time. Hearing sibling squabbles is one of the most wearing (and characteristic) problems for parents of children of a range of ages.

Many parents expect performance of a certain number of household chores during this age period. Where earlier, the ability and freedom to set the table or empty the rubbish baskets was pleasant, now these activities have lost their novelty and it takes real persistence on the part of parents to see that each child does his share of the running of the household.

Puberty

This is one of the transition periods in which much occurs that is temporarily disturbing to the child and to his parents. The transition from the child's body to sexual maturity, as we saw, begins in individuals at widely varied ages and proceeds at widely different rates. There is a marked difference between the sexes in average onset and speed of development of these changes. There are two groups of adolescents, namely the very early- and the very late-maturers, in which the fact of earliness or lateness produces characteristic temporary problems of self-attitudes and personal-social behavior. An understanding of these individual differences by parents, physicians, and other adults who live or otherwise come in contact with young people is of importance. Willingness to help the other-than-average-developers to understand the over-all picture of development and their place in the sequence helps greatly to reduce the tensions and anxieties or the personal-social frustrations of the early- or late-maturers of both sexes. An understanding of the sex differences in onset and rate of biological maturing makes possible insight into the personal or social problems which characterize the junior high school period of growth. It helps to adjust school and community agency programs to the needs and interests of this group.

Whatever the age of onset or the rate of biological maturing, understanding the exact nature of the changes taking place is generally agreed to be important to the way they are accepted, and to the quality of the adjustments made to them. Such understanding or the lack of it determines in large part the quality of feeling toward the body and its functions, and the wisdom or lack of wisdom with which young people guide their behavior as they come into sexual maturity. Lacking understanding, both the individual and the other people concerned with him tend to suffer anxieties about this phase of development, and to become strained in interpersonal relationships. With understanding, however, and with appropriate maturing of behavior, puberty can be a time of glad acceptance of the fact of maturing, and of mutual parent-child sharing of each evidence that such development is taking place.

The child entering puberty may be helped greatly by his somewhat older siblings, especially if they feel that they themselves are maturing satisfactorily. Sometimes a younger sister in a family begins to menstruate before her older sibling, and this situation takes considerable patience and sympathy on the part of the parents.

Children entering puberty sometimes take a lot of ribbing from younger siblings. Remarks about sister's hairdo and sweater fit and brother's shaving and hair style may give younger children much amusement, while being painful for the older youngsters to take. They often lack the grace to ignore the remarks, and break into tears or strike out at their torturers.

Adolescence

Early and late adolescence represent a continuing development not only from a child's body to biological maturity but also from childhood's feelings and behavior to the adult's sense of responsibility and self-determination. As we have seen, the individual throughout the teens is characteristically ambivalent in his feelings about himself and life. He longs to be financially as well as personally independent of his parents, but in most instances must continue to be at least in part dependent. He typically suffers conflict within himself because of his desire to make his own decisions and to lead his own life on the one hand and his feelings of obligation to comply with his parents' wishes on the other. He resists their concern for him, yet senses his own need for their approval and affection.

He realizes with varying degrees of clarity his need to choose and to prepare for a life work, but finds confusion in the vast range of possibilities and in his doubts about his own aptitudes. He finds support in his group because they, too, suffer his confusions and his ambivalences of feeling. Together they tend to express their protest against authority in sloppiness of dress and manner, and in exaggerated ideas and behavior. During the early adolescent years the individual is typically moody, unpredictable, and often rebellious. But he can also be lovable, responsive, and responsible, depending upon the circumstances and upon his mood. The new and compelling urge to establish an enduring heterosexual relationship through subsequent marriage creates conflicts while at the same time, if managed maturely, providing emotional satisfaction and happiness.

As adolescence proceeds toward adulthood, a continuing succession of decisions and behavioral choices tests the adequacy of previous growth and development. If the background of growth and of personal choices and actions is favorable, the problems of adolescence are usually met successfully. Horizons widen, opportunities are met, and new and desirable experiences are acquired.

With all the ambivalences and perplexities of adolescence, the high school and college periods are for most young people filled with a succession of good times and with new experiences in personal contacts. For some, it is a time of adventuring into new realms of knowledge, of the expansion of intellectual horizons, and of creative awareness and expression. For these individuals and for many others it is a time of serious preparation for the future, both vocational and personal.

Usually, the characteristic perplexities and decisions of adolescence are resolved and the individual moves into adulthood, carrying with him the accumulation of strengths and weaknesses, of knowledge and false notions, of standards and values, of habits and feelings acquired up to this time.

For parents and other adults in the home, the teen years of the children may be satisfying and highly interesting or largely years of worrying. If the young people are maturing biologically and emotionally, they often amaze adults with their resourcefulness and insight into their own problems. If they are not maturing satisfactorily, especially emotionally, their behavior is really cause for concern. If they remain in the home excessively, they are failing to learn to live with their peers, and if they are outside the home there are many opportunities for foolish behavior, with far-reaching results.

Early Adulthood

Early adulthood brings full responsibility not only for oneself but for others as well. If the individual is well prepared for it, it also brings a maximum of freedom of choice and of self-determination. Often referred to by the elderly as the happiest period of life, it is usually the busiest. Establishment in the life work, marriage and the rearing of children, setting up a home, and finding roots in a community leave relatively little time for leisure as such. However, when individuals are prepared for the responsibilities of adulthood, the daily living of a responsible life provides deep satisfaction and inner fulfillment. Countless conflicts and genuine causes for worry arise, but for the mature adult the solving of the conflicts and finding solutions of the worrisome situations give meaning to life which it would otherwise lack.

In many ways, early adulthood is the one period young people look forward to, the time they have so long been preparing for. It gives them full scope to prove themselves, to meet life, as nearly as one may at any stage, upon their own terms. For most individuals early adulthood proves a disappointment in some ways, yet in other ways it may surpass their fondest dreams. It is not the end or the complete fulfillment of life, but only the first stage of adulthood in which, full as it is in itself, preparation needs to be made for the succeeding two periods of life. Such matters as laying aside money and insurance for retirement and making a will (and keeping it up-to-date) receive attention, and help people to know each other's ideas and goals. Like most problems in life, economic problems in early adulthood become less serious if handled wisely, but more serious if handled poorly.

If the individual has sufficient motivation and patience, habits, attitudes and feelings can be and often are changed in early adulthood, from poor ones to more desirable ones. Much depends upon his insight and his determination to succeed in his job, his marriage, and in his own personal growth. Much, too, depends upon the mate he chooses, or upon the circumstances which cause him to remain single. Happiness and fulfillment do not become one's lot by chance —they are created from the behavior, attitudes, feelings, and beliefs which predominate in one's day-by-day living.

Middle and Later Adulthood

We have seen that middle adulthood can be a really delightful period of life, when the children are reared and launched, when the peak of responsibility in vocation and of income have been arrived at, when usefulness in the community lends interest as well as satisfaction to so-called leisure hours. Few people today, with the healthful vigor made possible in middle age, regret becoming grandparents because the term no longer carries the implication of physical old age. Today's grandparents, as a rule, are well enough to enjoy their grandchildren, although they are also well enough to be living active lives of their own. As a result, young parents can no longer, in all cases, rely upon their parents for baby care.

As a transition period in which the reproductive capacity ceases for women, children become independent, and the eventual laying aside of full responsibility becomes imminent for men, middle age is characteristically a period of physical changes and psychological stresses. Chapter 13 pointed out that if these changes and stresses are not understood and are allowed to assume too great significance, they may precipitate physical and personal situations from which there is no recovery. However, as the woman's physiology becomes readjusted after the changes of menopause, and as the man accepts and adjusts to a gradual waning of physical vigor, mature persons typically make a successful and usually happy adjustment to life.

Difficulties are common today though for middle-aged people, because with today's increased length of preparation for vocation and of life itself, the middle-aged often find themselves still partially responsible for their young adult children as well as for the care of their own aging parents.

Old age, as we have seen, is not the end of life, but a final stage of development. If it is not well prepared for, or if previous stages have left too much "unfinished business" in the personality, old age can be a burden both to the individual and to those who must care for him. If, however, adequate finances, appropriate living quarters, reasonably good health, a reasonably lively set of interests, and the affectionate regard of one's family are present, old age can be and often is a final period of growth and personal fulfillment. Final illnesses still cannot be avoided, however, and death needs to be approached as a last natural event in a successful life.

RÉSUMÉ

It is our hope that students of human development and behavior will understand that growth does not cease when the body achieves its maximum height; that growth can go on throughout life. It does go on if aliveness, usefulness, purposefulness, and thoughtfulness for others continue through the years. Life becomes meaningful only if it is met with increasing maturity of awareness, understanding, courage, productive effort, appreciation, and affection.

There are both problems and fulfillments in each growth period. The following story may show the importance of perspective in the solving of problems and the finding of fulfillments. A young honeymoon couple from the Midwest were driving through the Colorado Rockies. They encountered one of life's perplexing problems on their trip, and in the process found a bit of useful philosophy. Let the girl, now a middle-aged woman, tell the story:

We were in the last week of our month's trip. The scenery was glorious beyond description, but what a road! We had been two hours on a one-way shelf road, a mere gash in the mountain indicated by a fine line on the map. It was well advertised by the local community for the scenery it would reveal. Bob was not used to mountain driving though he had had practice at it for a week before we struck this. He was not always sure of the speed needed to keep the car in motion up the steep grades. We stalled a number of times and he had to struggle to keep the car from slipping backward while he got the engine started again. The potential drop off the edge was terrifying. I was on the point of tears, struggling to keep Bob from knowing how anxious I was. He seemed to be in the same frame of mind I was.

We reached the beginning of a particularly terrifying hairpin turn, from which we could see the road twisting for miles above us. We stalled again. Bob sighed, "I know this is a one-way road, but there isn't much traffic. How about turning around at the first chance and seeing if we can find our way down?"

I agreed.

It seems that human nature doesn't differ too much in this world. As we turned the bend we saw a large sign obviously needed at this particular point by many of the drivers on this road.

O! YES! YOU CAN!
MILLIONS OF OTHERS HAVE DONE IT.
JUST KEEP GOING!

It was amazing what this did to us. Suddenly we were in possession of ourselves. We did keep going, and in the next half hour, because of the mood of confidence engendered by that sign, we kept our momentum. No more stalling of the engine, far better time made, and we were at the top. The view was worth it. But the real experience we both have carried through the years was that sign. How often we have recalled it at critical moments in our lives, when we were at our wits' end as to how to proceed. We have always said to each other, "O! yes! we can! Millions of others have done it. Let's just keep going."

APPENDIX

Bibliographical Supplement

1. ABEL, J. M., and JOFFEE, N. F. Cultural backgrounds of female puberty. *Amer. J. Psychother.*, 1950, **4**, 90–113.
2. Allegheny County survey of retired people. *Pittsburgh Press*, July 8, 1956.
3. AMES, L. B. Development of the sense of time in the young child. *J. genet. Psychol.*, 1946, **68**, 97–125.
4. AMES, L. B., METRAUX, R. W., and WALKER, R. N. *Adolescent Rorschach Responses: Developmental Trends from Ten to Sixteen Years.* New York: Paul B. Hoeber, Inc., Medical Book Department of Harper & Bros., 1959.
5. ANDERSON, J. E. Dynamics of development: System in process. In D. B. HARRIS, (ed.), *The Concept of Development.* Minneapolis: University of Minnesota Press, 1957.
6. ANDERSON, J. E. *Psychology of Development and Personal Adjustment.* New York: Holt, Rinehart & Winston, Inc., 1949.
7. ASHLEY-MONTAGU, M. F. The existence of a sterile phase in female adolescence. *Complex*, 1950, **I**, 27–38.
8. AUSUBEL, D. P. Perceived parent attitudes as determinants of children's ego structure. *Child Develpm.*, 1954, **25**, 173–183.
9. AUSUBEL, D. P. *Theory and Problems of Child Development.* New York: Grune & Stratton, Inc., 1958.
10. BALDWIN, A. L. *Behavior and Development in Childhood.* New York: Holt, Rinehart & Winston, Inc., 1955.
11. BAYLEY, N. Growth curves of height and weight by age for boys and girls, scaled according to physical maturity. *J. Pediatr.*, 1956, **48**, 187–194.
12. BAYLEY, N., and ODEN, N. H. The maintenance of intellectual ability in gifted adults. *J. Geront.*, 1955, **10**, 91–107.
13. BEACH, F. A. Evolutionary changes in the physiological control of mating in mammals. *Psychological Rev.*, 1947, **54**, 297–315.
14. BENEDICT, R. *Patterns of Culture.* Rev. ed., Boston: Houghton Mifflin Co., 1948.
15. BENTON, A. L., and MENEFEE, F. L. Handedness and right-left discrimination. *Child Develpm.*, 1957, **28**, 237–242.
16. BIESANZ, J., and BIESANZ, M. *Modern Society.* Englewood Cliffs, N.J.: Prentice-Hall, Inc., 1959.
17. BLOOMBERG, W. J. Automation predicts change: For the older worker. In W. DONAHUE and C. TIBBITTS (eds.), *The New Frontiers of Aging.* Ann Arbor: The University of Michigan Press, 1957.
18. BRECKENRIDGE, M. E., and MURPHY, M. N. *Rand, Sweeney and Vincent's Growth and Development of the Young Child.* 6th ed. Philadelphia: W. B. Saunders Co., 1958.
19. BRECKENRIDGE, M. E., and VINCENT, E. L. *Child Development.* 4th ed. Philadelphia: W. B. Saunders Co., 1960.

20. BRIDGES, K. K. B. Emotional development in early infancy. *Child Develpm.*, 1932, **3**, 324–334.

21. BROZEK, J. Personality changes with age: An item analysis of the Minnesota Multiphasic Personality Inventory. *J. Geront.*, 1955, **10**, 194–206.

22. BUEHL, C. C., and PYLE, S. I. The use of age at first appearance of three ossification centers in determining the skeletal status of children. *J. Pediatr.*, 1942, **21**, 335–342.

23. BURNS, R. K., and BROWN, L. B. The older worker in industry. In A. I. LANSING (ed.), *Cowdry's Problems of Ageing.* Baltimore: The Williams & Wilkins Co., 1952.

24. CAVAN, R. S. Personal adjustment in old age. In A. I. LANSING (ed.), *Cowdry's Problems of Ageing.* Baltimore: The Williams & Wilkins Co., 1952.

25. COBB, W. M. Skeleton. In A. I. LANSING (ed.), *Cowdry's Problems of Ageing.* Baltimore: The Williams & Wilkins Co., 1952.

26. COFFIN, T. E. Television's effects on leisure-time activities. *J. appl. Psychol.*, 1948, **32**, 550–558.

27. COFFIN, T. E. Television's impact on society. *Amer. Psychologist*, 1955, **10**, 630–641.

28. COHEN, F. J. *Children in Trouble: An Experiment in Institutional Child Care.* New York: W. W. Norton & Co., Inc., 1952.

29. *Conference on Participation of Women in Science.* Annual meeting of the American Association for the Advancement of Science, Washington, D.C., 1958.

30. COOPER, Z. K. Ageing of the skin. In A. I. LANSING (ed.), *Cowdry's Problems of Ageing.* Baltimore: The Williams & Wilkins Co., 1952.

31. CROW, L. D., and CROW, A. *Adolescent Development and Adjustment.* New York: McGraw-Hill Book Co., Inc., 1956.

32. DANIEL, R. S. *Contemporary Readings in General Psychology.* Boston: Houghton Mifflin Co., 1959.

33. DAVIS, A., and HAVIGHURST, R. J. Social class and color differences in child rearing. *Amer. Sociol. Rev.*, 1946, **11**, 698–710.

34. *Demographic Yearbook 1957, 1958.* New York: Statistical Office of the United Nations.

35. DENNIS, W. (ed.). *Readings in Child Psychology.* Englewood Cliffs, N.J.: Prentice-Hall, Inc., 1951.

36. DEWEY, R., and HUMBER, W. J. *The Development of Human Behavior.* New York: The Macmillan Co., 1951.

37. *Dictionary of Occupational Titles.* Vol. 1; and *Occupational Outlook Handbook.* Washington, D.C.: U.S. Department of Labor. Published yearly.

38. DONAHUE, W. T., and TIBBITTS, C. (eds.). *The New Frontiers of Aging.* Ann Arbor: University of Michigan Press, 1957.

39. DOUGLAS, J. W. B. Mental ability and school achievement of premature children at 8 years of age. *Brit. Med. J.*, 1956, **1**, 1210–1214.

40. DRAKE, J. T. *The Aged in American Society.* New York: The Ronald Press Co., 1958.

41. DUBLIN, L. I. Longevity in retrospect and in prospect. In A. I. LANSING (ed.), *Cowdry's Problems of Ageing.* Baltimore: The Williams & Wilkins Co., 1952.

42. DUBLIN, L. I., LOTKA, A. J., and SPIEGELMAN, M. *Length of Life: A Study of the Life Table.* Rev. ed. New York: The Ronald Press Co., 1949.

43. DULANEY, D. E., JR. (ed.). *Contributions to Modern Psychology.* New York: Oxford University Press, 1958.

44. *Educator's Guide to Free Films.* Randolph, Wis.: Educator's Progress Service. Published yearly.

45. *Educator's Guide to Free Slidefilms.* Randolph, Wis.: Educator's Progress Service. Published yearly.

46. EDUCATIONAL TESTING SERVICE OF PRINCETON, N.J. *A Report to the National Science Foundation.* 1955.

47. ELLIOTT, M. A. Perspective on the American crime problem. *Soc. Problems,* Winter, 1957–1958, **5** (3).

48. ENGLE, E. T. The male reproductive system. In A. I. LANSING (ed.), *Cowdry's Problems of Ageing.* Baltimore: The Williams & Wilkins Co., 1952.

49. ERIKSON, H. E. *Childhood and Society.* New York: W. W. Norton & Co., Inc., 1950.

50. FLEEGE, U. H. *Self-Revelation of the Adolescent Boy.* Milwaukee: Bruce Publishing Co., 1945.

51. FORD, C. S., and BEACH, F. A. *Patterns of Sexual Behavior.* New York: Paul B. Hoeber, Inc., Medical Book Department of Harper & Bros., 1951.

52. FOSDICK, H. E. *On Being a Real Person.* New York: Harper & Bros., 1943.

53. FOSTER, R. G. *Marriage and Family Relationships.* Rev. ed. New York: The Macmillan Co., 1950.

54. FRANK, L. K., *et al.* Personality development in adolescent girls. *Soc. Res. Child Develpm. Monogr.,* 1951, **16**, No. 53.

55. FREUD, A. *The Ego and the Mechanisms of Defense.* New York: International Universities Press, 1946.

56. FREUD, A. The role of bodily illness in the mental life of children. In R. S. EISSLER, *et al.* (eds.), *The Psychoanalytical Study of the Child.* Vol. 7. New York: International Universities Press, 1952.

57. FRIEDENWALD, J. S. The eye. In A. I. LANSING (ed.), *Cowdry's Problems of Ageing.* Baltimore: The Williams & Wilkins Co., 1952.

58. FROBISHER, M. *Fundamentals of Microbiology.* Philadelphia: W. B. Saunders Co., 1957.

59. GALLAGHER, J. R., and HARRIS, H. I. *Emotional Problems of Adolescents.* New York: Oxford University Press, 1958.

60. GARRETT, H. E. *Statistics in Psychology and Education.* 3d ed. New York: Longmans, Green & Co., Inc., 1947.

61. GESELL, A. L. *Infant Development: The Embryology of Early Human Behavior.* New York: Harper & Bros., 1952.

62. GESELL, A. L., and ILG, F. *The Child from Five to Ten.* New York: Harper & Bros., 1946.

63. GESELL, A. L., and ILG, F. *Infant and Child in the Culture of Today.* New York: Harper & Bros., 1943.

64. GESELL, A. L., ILG, F., and AMES, L. B. *The First Five Years of Life.* New York: Harper & Bros., 1940.

65. GESELL, A. L., ILG, F., and AMES, L. B. *Youth: The Years from Ten to Sixteen.* New York: Harper & Bros., 1956.

66. GILBERT, J. G. *Understanding Old Age.* New York: The Ronald Press Co., 1952.

67. GILES, R. *How to Retire and Enjoy It.* New York: McGraw-Hill Book Co., Inc., 1959.

68. GINSBERG, E. The changing pattern of women's work: Some psychological correlates. *Amer. J. Orthopsychiat.,* 1958, **28**, 313–321.

69. GLASS, B. H. Chromosome count. *Sci.,* March 22, 1957, **125**, 542.

70. GLUECK, S., and GLUECK, E. *Delinquents in the Making: Paths to Prevention.* New York: Harper & Bros., 1952.

71. GOODENOUGH, F. L., and TYLER, L. E. *Developmental Psychology: An Introduction to the Study of Human Behavior.* 3d ed. New York: Appleton-Century-Crofts, Inc., 1959.

72. GUTTMACHER, A. F. *The Story of Human Birth.* New York: Penguin Books, Inc., 1947.

73. HARPER, R. A. *Psychoanalysis and Psychotherapy.* Englewood Cliffs, N.J.: Prentice-Hall, Inc., 1959.

74. HARRIS, D. B. (ed.). *The Concept of Development.* Minneapolis: University of Minnesota Press, 1957.

75. HARSH, C. M., and SCHRICKEL, H. G. *Personality: Development and Assessment.* 2d ed. New York: The Ronald Press Co., 1959.
76. HARTLEY, R. E., and GOLDENSON, R. M. *The Complete Book of Children's Play.* New York: Holt, Rinehart & Winston, Inc., 1958.
77. HARTUP, W. W. Nurturance and nurturance withdrawal in relation to the dependency behavior of preschool children. *Child Develpm.,* 1958, **29,** 191–201.
78. HAVIGHURST, R. J. *Human Development and Education.* New York: Longmans, Green & Co., Inc., 1953.
79. HAWKES, G. R., *et al.* Pre-adolescents' views of some of their relations with their parents. *Child Develpm.,* 1957, **28,** 393–399.
80. HILBOE, H. E. A modern pattern for meeting the health needs of the aging. In W. T. DONAHUE (ed.), *The New Frontiers of Aging.* Ann Arbor: The University of Michigan Press, 1957.
81. HILDRETH, G. H. Development and training of hand dominance: Developmental problems associated with handedness: Training of handedness. *J. genet. Psychol.,* 1950, **76,** 39–144.
82. HILLIARD, M. *The Woman Doctor Looks at Love and Life.* New York: Doubleday & Co., Inc., 1957.
83. HOFFMAN, H. N. A study in an aspect of concept formation, with subnormal, average and superior adolescents. *Genet. Psychol. Monogr.,* 1955, **52,** 191–239.
84. HOLLINGSHEAD, A. B., and REDLICH, F. C. *Social Class and Mental Illness.* New York: John Wiley & Sons, Inc., 1958.
85. HOOKER, D. *The Prenatal Origin of Behavior.* Lawrence, Kan.: University of Kansas Press, 1942.
86. HORNEY, K. *Neurosis and Human Growth.* New York: W. W. Norton & Co., Inc., 1950.
87. HURLOCK, E. B. *Developmental Psychology.* 2d ed. New York: McGraw-Hill Book Co., Inc., 1959.
88. *Information and Research Notes: The Education of Women.* Washington, D.C.: Commission on the Education of Women of the American Council on Education, No. 4, December, 1958.
89. INGALLS, N. W. Observations on bone weights. *Amer. J. Anatomy,* 1931, **48,** 45–98.
90. IVY, A. C., and GROSSMAN, M. I. Digestive system. In A. I. LANSING (ed.), *Cowdry's Problems of Ageing.* Baltimore: The Williams & Wilkins Co., 1952.
91. JERSILD, A. T. *Child Psychology.* 3d ed. Englewood Cliffs, N.J.: Prentice-Hall, Inc., 1954.
92. JERSILD, A. T. *The Psychology of Adolescence.* New York: The Macmillan Co., 1957.
93. JOHNSON, W. *Stuttering in Children and Adults: Thirty Years of Research at the University of Iowa.* Minneapolis: University of Minnesota Press, 1955.
94. JOHNSON, W., *et al. The Onset of Stuttering: Research Findings and Implications.* Minneapolis: University of Minnesota Press, 1959.
95. JONES, H. E. Adolescence in our society. *The Family in a Democratic Society,* 70–82. (Anniversary Papers of the Community Service Society of New York.) New York: Columbia University Press, 1949.
96. JONES, H. E. The development of physical abilities. In *The Forty-Third Yearbook of the National Society for the Study of Education.* Part I. Adolescence. Chicago: Department of Education, University of Chicago Press, 1944.
97. JONES, H. E. The study of patterns of emotional expression. In M. L. REYMERT (ed.), *Feelings and Emotions.* New York: McGraw-Hill Book Co., Inc., 1950.
98. JONES, M. C. The later careers of boys who were early- or late-maturing. *Child Develpm.,* 1957, **28,** 113–128.
99. JONES, M. C., and BAYLEY, N. Physical maturing among boys as related to behavior. *J. Educ. Psychol.,* 1950, **41,** 129–148.

100. JONES, M. C., and MUSSEN, P. H. Self-conceptions, motivations and interpersonal attitudes of early- and late-maturing girls. *Child Develpm.*, 1958, **29**, 491–501.

101. JOURARD, S. M. *Personal Adjustment: An Approach Through the Study of Healthy Personality.* New York: The Macmillan Co., 1958.

102. JUNGCK, E. C., *et al.* Constitutional precocious puberty in the male. *J. Dis. Child.*, 1956, **91**, 138–143.

103. KALLMAN, F. J. *Heredity in Health and Mental Disorder.* New York: W. W. Norton & Co., 1953.

104. KANNER, L. *A Word to Parents About Mental Hygiene.* Madison: University of Wisconsin Press, 1957.

105. KING, G. Some observations on nutrition today. Paper presented to the Pittsburgh Nutrition Council Conference, Pittsburgh, November, 1958.

106. KINSEY, A. C., *et al.* *Sexual Behavior in the Human Female.* Philadelphia: W. B. Saunders Co., 1953.

107. KINSEY, A. C., *et al.* *Sexual Behavior in the Human Male.* Philadelphia: W. B. Saunders Co., 1948.

108. KIRK, J. E. *Biology and Medicine.* In N. W. SHOCK (ed.), *Problems of Aging.* New York: Josiah Macy, Jr. Foundation, 1951.

109. KIRKPATRICK, C. *The Family: As Process and Institution.* New York: The Ronald Press Co., 1955.

110. KOSSORIS, M. D. Relation of age to industrial injuries. *Labor Rev. Monogr.*, 1940, **17**, 789–804.

111. KOUNTZ, W. B. *Degeneration and Regeneration.* In A. I. LANSING (ed.), *Cowdry's Problems of Ageing.* 3d ed. Baltimore: The Williams & Wilkins Co., 1952.

112. KRALJ-CERCEK, L. The influence of food, body build and social origin on the age of menarche. *Human Biol.*, 1956, **28**, 393–406.

113. KUHLEN, R. G., and JOHNSON, G. H. Changes in goals with adult increasing age. *J. consult. Psychol.*, 1952, **16**, 1–4.

114. KUHLEN, R. G., and THOMPSON, G. *Psychological Studies of Human Development.* New York: Appleton-Century-Crofts, Inc., 1952.

115. LANDIS, J. T., and LANDIS, M. G. *Building a Successful Marriage.* Englewood Cliffs, N.J.: Prentice-Hall, Inc., 1958.

116. LANDIS, P. H. *Adolescence and Youth: The Process of Maturing.* Rev. ed. New York: The McGraw-Hill Book Co., Inc., 1952.

117. LANDIS, P. H., *et al.* *Sex in Development.* New York: Paul B. Hoeber, Inc., Medical Book Department of Harper & Bros., 1940.

118. LANDRETH, C. Parent-child interviews and children's behavior. In *Physical and Behavioral Growth Report of the 26th Ross Pediatric Research Conference*, San Francisco, October, 1957. Columbus, Ohio: Ross Laboratories, 1958.

119. LANDRETH, C. *The Psychology of Early Childhood.* New York: Alfred A. Knopf (a division of Random House, Inc.), 1958.

120. LANE, H., and BEAUCHAMP, M. *Understanding Human Development.* Englewood Cliffs, N.J.: Prentice-Hall, Inc., 1959.

121. LANSING, A. I. (ed.). *Cowdry's Problems of Ageing.* 3d ed. Baltimore: The Williams & Wilkins Co., 1952.

122. LANSING, A. I. General physiology. In A. I. LANSING (ed.), *Cowdry's Problems of Ageing.* Baltimore: The Williams & Wilkins Co., 1952.

123. LAWRENCE, D. H. Sex, literature, and censorship. In H. T. MOORE (ed.), *Sex, Literature, and Censorship.* New York: Twayne Publishers, Inc., 1953.

124. LAWTON, G. *Aging Successfully.* New York: Columbia University Press, 1951.

125. LEHMAN, H. C. Ages at time of first election of presidents of professional organizations. *Scientific Mon.*, 1955, **80**, 293–298.

126. LEHMAN, H. C. Chronological age versus proficiency in physical skills. *Amer. J. Psychol.*, 1951, **64**, 161–187.

127. LEHMAN, H. C. Man's most creative years. *Sci.*, 1943, **98**, 393–399.

128. LEVINE, J. Responses to humor. *Scientific Amer.*, 1956, **194**, 31–35.
129. LEVY, D. M. Maternal overprotection. In N. D. C. LEWIS and B. L. PACELLA, *Modern Trends in Child Psychiatry*. New York: International Universities Press, 1945.
130. LYNES, R. The pressures of leisure. *What's New*, 1958, **208**, 12–17.
131. MACNIDER, W. DE B. Ageing process considered in relation to tissue susceptibility and resistance. In A. I. LANSING (ed.), *Cowdry's Problems of Ageing*. Baltimore: The Williams & Wilkins Co., 1952.
132. McCAY, C. M. Chemical aspects of ageing and the effect of diet upon ageing. In A. I. LANSING (ed.), *Cowdry's Problems of Ageing*. Baltimore: The Williams & Wilkins Co., 1952.
133. McGRAW, M. B. Maturation of behavior. In L. CARMICHAEL (ed.), *Manual of Child Psychology*. New York: John Wiley & Sons, Inc., 1946.
134. MACCOBY, E. E. Television: Its impact on school children. *Publ. Opin. Quart.*, 1951, **15**, 421–444.
135. MACCOBY, E. E., NEWCOMB, I. M., and HARTLEY, E. L. (eds.). *Readings in Social Psychology*. 3d ed. New York: Holt, Rinehart & Winston, Inc., 1958.
136. MALM, M., and JAMISON, O. G. *Adolescence*. New York: The McGraw-Hill Book Co., Inc., 1952.
137. MARKEY, F. W. Imaginative behavior of preschool children. *Child Develpm. Monogr.*, No. 18. New York: Teachers College, Columbia University, 1935.
138. MARTIN, P. C., and VINCENT, E. L. *Human Biological Development*. New York: The Ronald Press Co., 1960.
139. MARTIN, W. E. Quantitative expression in young children. *Genet. Psychol. Monogr.*, 1951, **44**, 147–219.
140. MARTIN, W. E., and STENDLER, C. B. *Child Behavior and Development*. Rev. ed. New York: Harcourt, Brace & Co., 1959.
141. MARTIN, W. E., and STENDLER, B. C. *Readings in Child Development*. New York: Harcourt, Brace & Co., 1954.
142. MASTERS, W. H. The female reproductive system. In A. I. LANSING (ed.), *Cowdry's Problems of Ageing*. Baltimore: The Williams & Wilkins Co., 1952.
143. MEAD, M. *Male and Female*. New York: William Morrow & Co., 1949.
144. MERRY, F. K., and MERRY, R. V. *The First Two Decades of Life*. Rev. ed. New York: Harper & Bros., 1958.
145. MEYER, A. Television, radio, films: Barrier or challenge. *Childh. Educ.*, September, 1957.
146. *Midcentury White House Conference on Children and Youth: Chart Book*. Raleigh, N.C.: Health Publications Institute, 1951.
147. MILES, W. R., and MILES, C. C. Principal mental changes with normal aging. In E. J. STIEGLITZ (ed.), *Geriatric Medicine*. Philadelphia: W. B. Saunders Co., 1943.
148. MILLARD, C. B., and ROTHNEY, J. W. M. *The Elementary School Child: A Book of Case Studies*. New York: Holt, Rinehart & Winston, Inc., 1957.
149. MILLER, D. R., and SWANSON, G. E. *The Changing American Parent*. New York: John Wiley & Sons, Inc., 1958.
150. MITCHEL, A. W. Ladies in retirement. *J. Amer. Assn. Univer. Women*, October, 1958.
151. MOORE, R. A. Male secondary sexual organs. In A. I. LANSING (ed.), *Cowdry's Problems of Ageing*. Baltimore: The Williams & Wilkins Co., 1952.
152. MORE, D. M. Developmental concordance and discordance during puberty and early adolescence. *Soc. Res. Child Develpm. Monogr.*, 18(1). Lafayette, Ind.: Child Development Publications, 1955.
153. MUNN, N. L. *The Evolution and Growth of Human Behavior*. Boston: Houghton Mifflin Co., 1955.
154. MURPHY, G. *Human Potentials*. New York: Basic Books, Inc., 1958.
155. MURPHY, L. B. *Social Behavior and Child Personality*. New York: Columbia University Press, 1937.

156. MUSSEN, P. H., and JONES, M. C. The behavior-inferred motivations of late-and early-maturing boys. *Child Develpm.*, 1958, **29**, 61–67.
157. MUSSEN, P. H., and JONES, M. C. Self-conceptions, motivations, and interpersonal attitudes of late- and early-maturing boys. *Child Develpm.*, 1957, **28**, 243–256.
158. NATIONAL MANPOWER COUNCIL. *Womanpower.* New York: Columbia University Press, 1957.
159. NEWCOMB, T. *Social Psychology.* New York: Holt, Rinehart & Winston, Inc., 1950.
160. NEWMAN, H. H., FREEMAN, F. N., and HOLSINGER, K. J. *Twins: A Study of Heredity and Environment.* Chicago: University of Chicago Press, 1937.
161. O'LEARY, J. L. Ageing in the nervous system. In A. I. LANSING (ed.), *Cowdry's Problems of Ageing.* Baltimore: The Williams & Wilkins Co., 1952.
162. OLSON, R. *Studies of Obesity.* Pittsburgh: Pittsburgh Health and Welfare Conference Council on Nutrition, University of Pittsburgh College of Medicine. Not yet published.
163. OLSON, W. C. *Child Development.* Rev. ed. Boston: D. C. Heath & Co., 1959.
164. PEASE, D., and GARDNER, D. B. Research on the effects of noncontinuous mothering. *Child Develpm.*, 1958, **29**, 142–148.
165. PECKOS, P. S. Nutrition during growth and development. *Child Develpm.*, September, 1957, **28**, 284.
166. PIAGET, J. *Judgment and Reasoning in the Child.* New York: Humanities Press, 1952.
167. POPE PIUS XII. L'alta parola del Sommo Pontefice agli studiosi della Genetica. *L'Osservatore Romano*, September 9, 1953.
168. *Population Reference Bureau Bulletin*, November, 1959.
169. PRESSEY, S. L., and KUHLEN, R. G. *Psychological Development Through the Life Span.* New York: Harper & Bros., 1957.
170. RAGSDALE, C. E. How children learn the motor types of behavior. In N. B. HENRY (ed.), *Learning and Instruction.* 49th Yearbook Nat'l Soc. Stud. Educ. Part I. Chicago: University of Chicago Press, 1950.
171. REDL, F., and WINEMAN, D. *The Aggressive Child.* Vol. 1. *Children Who Hate.* Glencoe, Ill.: The Free Press, 1957.
172. REJS, J. H. O. Über die Veränderung der Kraft während der Bewegung, Pflüg. *Arch. ges. Physiol.*, 1921, **191**, 234.
173. REMMERS, H. H., and RADLER, D. H. Teen-age attitudes. *Scientific Mon.*, 1958, **198** (6), 25–35.
174. REYMERT, M. L., and JOST, H. Further data concerning the normal variability of the menstrual cycle during adolescence and factors associated with the age of menarche. *Child Develpm.*, 1947, **18**, 169–179.
175. ROBINSON, H. B. G. Teeth and jaws. In A. I. LANSING (ed.), *Cowdry's Problems of Ageing.* Baltimore: The Williams & Wilkins Co., 1952.
176. *Rockefeller Report on Education: The Pursuit of Excellence: Education and the Future of America.* New York: Doubleday & Co., Inc., 1958.
177. RUCKER, A. W. The coming economic challenge of longevity. In W. T. DONAHUE (ed.), *The New Frontiers of Aging.* Ann Arbor: The University of Michigan Press, 1957.
178. RUSSELL, D. H. *Children's Thinking.* Boston: Ginn & Co., 1956.
179. RUSSELL, I. L. Behavior problems of children from broken and intact homes. *J. educ. Sociol.*, 1957, **31**, 124–129.
180. SANDERS, I. T. *The Community: An Introduction to a Social System.* New York: The Ronald Press Co., 1958.
181. SCHEINFELD, A. *The Human Heredity Handbook.* Philadelphia: J. B. Lippincott Co., 1956.
182. SCHEINFELD, A. *The New You and Heredity.* Philadelphia: J. B. Lippincott Co., 1950.

183. SCHONFELD, W. A. Inadequate masculine physique as a factor in personality development of adolescent boys. *Psychosom. Med.*, 1950, 12, 49–54.

184. SEARS, P. B. The steady state: Physical law and moral choice. *The Phi Beta Kappa Key Reporter*, January, 1959, 24 (2).

185. SEARS, R. R. Discipline and behavior of the preschool child. In *Physical and Behavioral Growth Report of the 26th Ross Pediatric Research Conference*, San Francisco, October, 1957. Columbus, Ohio: Ross Laboratories, 1958.

186. SEARS, R. R., MACCOBY, E. E., and LEVINE, H. *Patterns of Child Rearing*. Evanston, Ill.: Row, Peterson & Co., 1957.

187. SEIDMAN, J. M. *The Adolescent: A Book of Readings*. New York: Holt, Rinehart & Winston, Inc., 1953.

188. SEIDMAN, J. M. *The Child: A Book of Readings*. New York: Holt, Rinehart & Winston, Inc., 1958.

189. SHAFFER, L. F., and SHOBEN, E. J., JR. *The Psychology of Adjustment*. Boston: Houghton Mifflin Co., 1956.

190. SHELDON, H. D. *The Older Population of the United States*. Census Monogr. Ser. New York: John Wiley & Sons, Inc., 1958.

191. SHOCK, N. W. Ageing of homeostatic mechanisms. In A. I. LANSING (ed.), *Cowdry's Problems of Ageing*. Baltimore: The Williams & Wilkins Co., 1952.

192. SHOCK, N. W. (ed.). *Problems of Aging*. New York: Josiah Macy, Jr. Foundation, 1951.

193. SHUTTLEWORTH, F. K. *The Adolescent Period: A Graphic Atlas. Monogr.* 1951, XIV, No. 1. Evanston, Ill.: Society for Research in Child Development, Inc.

194. SILVER, H. K., KEMPE, C. H., and BRUYN, H. B. *Handbook of Pediatrics*. Los Altos, Calif.: Lange Medical Publications, 1959.

195. SIMMONS, K. Brush Foundation Study of Child Growth and Development: Physical Growth and Development. *Soc. Res. Child Develpm. Monogr.*, 1944, 9, No. 1.

196. SMITH, U., and SMITH, W. M. *The Behavior of Man*. New York: Holt, Rinehart & Winston, Inc., 1957.

197. *Statistical Abstract of the United States* (annual). 1958, 1959 issues. Washington, D.C.: Department of the Census.

198. STEINER, P. O. Income and employment: Basic factors. In W. T. DONAHUE and C. TIBBITTS (eds.), *The New Frontiers of Aging*. Ann Arbor: University of Michigan Press, 1957.

199. STENDLER, C. B., and YOUNG, N. The impact of beginning first grade upon socialization as reported by mothers. *Child Develpm.*, 1950, 21, 243–256.

200. STEWART, R. S., and WORKMAN, A. D. *Children and Other People: Achieving Maturity Through Learning*. New York: Holt, Rinehart & Winston, Inc., 1956.

201. STOLZ, H. R., and STOLZ, L. M. *Somatic Development of Adolescent Boys*. New York: The Macmillan Co., 1951.

202. STOLZ, L. M., *et al. Father Relations of War-born Children*. Stanford, Calif.: Stanford University Press, 1954.

203. STONE, H. M., and STONE, A. *A Marriage Manual*. New York: Simon & Schuster, Inc., 1953.

204. STONE, L. J., and CHURCH, J. *Childhood and Adolescence: A Psychology of the Growing Person*. New York: Random House, Inc., 1957.

205. STRANG, R. *An Introduction to Child Study*. 4th ed. New York: The Macmillan Co., 1959.

206. STRIEB, G. F., and THOMPSON, W. E. Personal and social adjustment in retirement. In W. T. DONAHUE and C. TIBBITTS (eds.), *The New Frontiers of Aging*. Ann Arbor: University of Michigan Press, 1957.

207. STUART, H. C., and STEVENSON, S. S. Physical growth and development. In W. E. NELSON (ed.), *Textbook of Pediatrics*. 7th ed. Philadelphia: W. B. Saunders Co., 1959.

208. SURVEY RESEARCH CENTER: INSTITUTE FOR SOCIAL RESEARCH. *A Study of Adolescent Boys.* Ann Arbor: University of Michigan Press, 1955.
209. SURVEY RESEARCH CENTER: INSTITUTE FOR SOCIAL RESEARCH. *The Needs and Interests of Girls.* Ann Arbor: University of Michigan Press, 1956.
210. SURVEY RESEARCH CENTER: INSTITUTE FOR SOCIAL RESEARCH. *The Program of the Girl Scouts of the U.S.A.* Ann Arbor: University of Michigan Press, 1958.
211. SWEENEY, E. E., and DICKERSON, R. E. (eds.). *Preinduction Health and Human Relationships.* New York: American Social Hygiene Association, 1953.
212. TAUBER, C., and TAUBER, I. B. *The Changing Population of the United States.* New York: John Wiley & Sons, Inc., 1958.
213. TERMAN, L. M., and ODEN, M. H. *Genetic Studies of Genius.* Vol. 4. *The Gifted Child Grows Up.* Stanford, Calif.: Stanford University Press, 1947.
214. TERMAN, L. M., and ODEN, M. H. *Genetic Studies of Genius.* Vol. 5. *The Gifted Group at Mid-Life: Thirty-five Years' Follow-up of the Superior Child.* Stanford, Calif.: Stanford University Press, 1959.
215. THORPE, L. P., and CRUZE, W. W. *Developmental Psychology.* New York: The Ronald Press Co., 1956.
216. THURSTON, F. M. Courses offered under sponsorship of Whittier College, Calif., 1959. Unpublished material. Cited by permission.
217. TRANKELL, A. The influence of choice of writing hand on the handwriting. *Brit. J. Psychol.*, 1956, **26**, 94–103.
218. TURNER, C. D. *General Endocrinology.* Philadelphia: W. B. Saunders Co., 1955.
219. UNESCO. World literacy at mid-century. *Fundamental Educ.* (Paris, France), 1957, **11**.
220. U.S. DEPARTMENT OF LABOR. *Handbook on Women Workers.* Bulletin 261. Washington, D.C.: Government Printing Office, 1956.
221. VAN RIPER, C. *Speech Correction Principles and Methods.* Englewood Cliffs, N.J.: Prentice-Hall, Inc., 1954.
222. WAKE, F. R. *Changes of Fear with Age.* Unpublished doctor's dissertation, McGill University, 1950.
223. WALTERS, J., *et al.* Perceptions concerning development of responsibility in young children. *Elementary Sch. J.*, January, 1957.
224. WATSON, J. B. *Psychological Care of Infant and Child.* New York: W. W. Norton & Co., Inc., 1928.
225. WECHSLER, S. M. Pittsburgh: Personal communication. 1960.
226. WHITE, P. D. The Heart and Great Vessels in Old Age. In A. I. LANSING (ed.), *Cowdry's Problems of Ageing.* Baltimore: The Williams & Wilkins Co., 1952.
227. WHITING, J. W. M., and CHILD, I. L. *Child Training and Personality: A Cross-cultural Study.* New Haven: Yale University Press, 1953.
228. WINCHESTER, A. M. *Genetics.* New York: Houghton Mifflin Co., 1951.
229. WITMER, H., and KOTINSKY, R. (eds.). *Personality in the Making: Fact Finding Report of Midcentury White House Conference on Children and Youth.* New York: Harper & Bros., 1953.
230. WITTY, P. A. Some results of eight yearly studies of TV. *Sch. & Soc.*, 1958, **86**, 287–289.
231. WOLFE, D. *America's Resources of Specialized Talent: A Report of the Commission on Human Resources and Advanced Training.* New York: Harper & Bros., 1954.
232. ZUBEK, J. P., and SOLBERG, P. A. *Human Development.* New York: The McGraw-Hill Book Co., Inc., 1954.

Film Supplement

ADDRESSES OF FILM SOURCES

E. C. Brown Trust Co., Portland, Oregon
Coronet Films, Chicago, Ill.
Encyclopaedia Britannica Films, Wilmette, Ill.
International Film Bureau, Chicago, Ill.
March of Time, Time, Inc., New York, N.Y.
McGraw-Hill Book Co., Inc., Text-Film Department, New York, N.Y.
Medical Films, Inc., San Francisco, Calif.
Mental Health Film Board, Film Service Department, New York, N.Y.
Museum of Modern Art, New York, N.Y.
National Film Board of Canada, New York, N.Y.
New York University Film Library, New York University, New York, N.Y.
Schering Corp., Audio-visual Department, Bloomfield, N.J.
Social Security Administration, Department of Health, Education and Welfare, Washington, D.C.
United World Films, New York, N.Y.

SUGGESTED FILMS

Chapter 1

Principles of Development (Child Development Series), 17 minutes, McGraw-Hill Book Co., Inc. Principles of growth and change from early infancy; growth factors common to all human beings; variables that contribute to individual differences.

Heredity and Family Environment (Psychology for Living Series), 9 minutes, McGraw-Hill Book Co., Inc. Limitations set by heredity; effect of environment in developing inner capacities. Each person has a hand in developing his own nature.

He Acts His Age (the first of the Ages and Stages Series), 13 minutes, National Film Board of Canada. An over-all view of the fact that children do what they do and are what they are at given ages because of the stage of growth which characterizes each age period.

Chapter 2

Preface to a Life, 29 minutes, United World Films. How personality is affected by the attitudes and actions, the dreams and wishes of father and mother and by contacts with family, friends, and neighbors.

Baby Meets His Parents (No. 1 in the Personality Development Series), 11 minutes, Encyclopaedia Britannica Films. Shows the influence of early parental contacts upon the baby's personality development.

Bathing Babies in Three Cultures (Character Formation in Different Cultures Series), 9 minutes, New York University Film Library. Mother-child relationships during the infant-bathing process in New Guinea, Bali, and modern America.

Sibling Rivalries and Parents (Child Development Series), 11 minutes, McGraw-Hill Book Co., Inc. Some sibling conflicts; the role of parents in causing and in handling them.

Chapter 3

The City, 33 minutes, Museum of Modern Art. Portrayal of certain impacts of city living upon human beings in unplanned cities as contrasted to cities planned to meet human needs.

Problem of Pupil Adjustment. Part I—The Dropout: A Case Study (Educational Psychology Series), 20 minutes, McGraw-Hill Book Co., Inc. When the school fails to meet the needs of an individual child: a case study.

Angry Boy, 33 minutes, Mental Health Film Board. How a guidance clinic helps a boy whose hidden hostility is expressed through stealing.

Chapter 4

Life Begins, 60 minutes, Encyclopaedia Britannica Films. Dr. Gesell's work at the Yale University Clinic of Child Development. A classical record of infant development from birth to eighteen months.

Life with Baby, 18 minutes, March of Time. A shorter film showing motor and other types of development from birth to five years. Dr. Gesell serves as commentator.

The Embryology of Human Behavior, 18 minutes, color, International Film Bureau (produced by Medical Film Institute). Traces development of eye-hand coordination and the patterning processes of behavior from a few weeks after conception through the early years of life.

Chapter 5

Terrible Twos and Trusting Threes (Ages and Stages Series), 20 minutes, National Film Board of Canada. A well-run nursery school showing characteristics of twos and threes, and how to provide for their needs. Home scenes and suggestions for parental guidance.

Frustrating Fours and Fascinating Fives (Ages and Stages Series), 22 minutes, National Film Board of Canada. Group as well as home scenes showing characteristics of fours and fives and how to provide for their growth needs.

When Should Grownups Help? (Studies of Normal Personality Development Series), 14 minutes, New York University Film Library (see below).

When Should Grownups Stop Fights? (Studies of Normal Personality Development Series), 15 minutes, New York University Film Library. This film and the one above show specific episodes with introductory sequences designed to stimulate class discussion.

Children's Emotions (Child Development Series), 22 minutes, McGraw-Hill Book Co., Inc. The major causes of fear, anger, jealousy, and curiosity in young children. The parental role in the handling of each, including both the avoidance of habits of fear, anger, or jealousy and the development of the habit of happiness.

Chapter 6

From Sociable Six to Noisy Nine (Ages and Stages Series), 22 minutes, National Film Board of Canada. Interests, activities, and personality characteristics of boys and girls of these ages; suggestions for parental guidance.

From Ten to Twelve (Ages and Stages Series), 26 minutes, National Film Board of Canada. Characteristics of ten- to twelve-year-old boys and girls; sex differences in development; suggestions for parental guidance.

Learning Is Searching (Studies of Normal Personality Development Series), 30 minutes, New York University Film Library. A third-grade schoolroom situation showing desirable methods of helping children search for information and solve some of their own problems.

Sibling Relations and Personality (Child Development Series), 22 minutes, McGraw-Hill Book Co., Inc. The relationship of siblings as they grow up; individual differences.

Chapter 7

The Teens (Ages and Stages Series), 28 minutes, National Film Board of Canada. Family life with teen-agers. Stresses parental role in guiding teen-agers.

Physical Aspects of Puberty (Adolescent Development Series), 19 minutes, McGraw-Hill Book Co., Inc. Physiological growth processes in boys and girls; some of the usual growth problems, such as those of late-developing boys and early-developing girls.

Human Growth, 19 minutes, color, E. C. Brown Trust Company (Oregon University School of Medicine). Explanations to a high-school biology class of what occurs as the body matures into adolescence.

Human Reproduction (Health Education Series), 21 minutes, McGraw-Hill Book Co., Inc. Explains human reproduction at a more advanced level than does *Human Growth;* functions of male and female organs, which are illuminated when under discussion.

Chapter 8

Discipline During Adolescence (Adolescent Development Series), 16 minutes, McGraw-Hill Book Co., Inc. Problems between adolescents and their parents are presented. Effects of too much and too little discipline are considered.

Social Acceptability (Adolescent Development Series), 20 minutes, McGraw-Hill Book Co., Inc. Concerns a high-school girl who is not accepted by her classmates and the effects of this on her personality.

Meeting the Needs of Adolescents (Adolescent Development Series), 19 minutes, McGraw-Hill Book Co., Inc. The story of a fourteen-year-old boy and his seventeen-year-old sister; what parents can do to help. In discussing basic needs of the adolescent, the film indicates that some parental worries about adolescents are needless.

Parents Are People Too (Health and Safety for You Series), 15 minutes, McGraw-Hill Book Co., Inc. Designed to show adolescents the parental point of view.

The Physiology of Normal Menstruation, 20 minutes, sound, color, Schering Corp. Self-explanatory. Free of charge.

Chapter 9

Toward Emotional Maturity (Psychology for Living Series), 11 minutes, McGraw-Hill Book Co., Inc. An eighteen-year-old girl faces a decision which involves not only herself but also her parents and a boy whom she likes. Shows something of the nature of emotion and factors involved in emotional growth.

Emotional Health (Health Education Series), 20 minutes, McGraw-Hill Book Co., Inc. A psychiatrist helps a college freshman to become better adjusted by seeing what causes his emotional upsets. Assures young people that emotional upsets are common but that, if they are prolonged, professional counsel and care are as important as with any physical illness.

Improve Your Personality, 11 minutes, Coronet Films. How personalities can be developed and adapted. Suggestions designed to encourage thought about and discussion of the individual's own personality.

Human Reproduction (Health Education Series), 21 minutes, McGraw-Hill Book Co., Inc. Explains human reproduction at an adult level: functions both of male and of female organs and how menstruation, fertilization, pregnancy, and birth occur.

The Male Sex Hormone, 20 minutes, sound, color, Schering Corp. Detailed endocrinology, helpful in understanding male psychology. Free of charge.

Chapter 10

It Takes All Kinds, 20 minutes, McGraw-Hill Book Co., Inc. In spite of the old model cars and fashions which appear in it, this film portrays differences in reaction to a stereotyped situation by various types of personalities. It leads the viewer to check himself against each type.

Chapter 11

Leaving It to the Experts, 8 minutes, McGraw-Hill Book Co., Inc. Concerns the individual's responsibility to keep informed of events in his local and his wider community. Stimulates group discussion.

Public Opinion in Our Democracy, 11 minutes, Coronet Films. The importance of public opinion; how it is formed and determined on a given issue. Shows the importance of individual opinions and the obligation to express and to act upon them.

Who's Boss, 16 minutes, McGraw-Hill Book Co., Inc. Problems arising in relation to management of money, friends, and home in adult life.

Office Teamwork, 12 minutes, Encyclopaedia Britannica Films. Valuable suggestions for successful relationships in the work life.

Chapter 12

When Should I Marry? 19 minutes, McGraw-Hill Book Co., Inc. Describes the experiences of two couples who married at an early age. Leads into discussion of the situations which arise.

Marriage Is a Partnership, 16 minutes, Coronet Films. A positive approach to the realities of marriage, not only as romance but as a sharing of responsibilities, decisions, and loyalties. Raises questions for discussion.

Marriage Today, 22 minutes, McGraw-Hill Book Co., Inc. The film shows two couples who are making marriage work. The keystone of their marriages is the companionship, physical and psychological, which they offer each other. A very meaningful film.

The Education for Childbirth Series, Medical Films, Inc.

A. *Prenatal Care,* 23 minutes, sound. An excellent film emphasizing the need for physical, emotional, and economic maturity preceding parenthood. Shows useful exercises.

B. *Labor and Childbirth,* 18 minutes, sound. Carries on where Film A leaves off. Birth occurs partially hidden from audience.

C. *A Normal Birth,* 11 minutes, sound. Shows the actual birth as the doctor sees it. Many students who see A and B are dissatisfied if they do not see C. A and C can be shown to advantage without B if labor is explained.

D. *Postnatal Care,* 30 minutes, sound. Shows up-to-date care following childbirth.

Chapter 13

Community Responsibilities, 11 minutes, National Film Board of Canada. In good citizenship, where does the individual's duty to the community begin or end in relation to personal freedom?

The Menopause, Its Significance and Management, 20 minutes, sound, color, Schering Corp. Very helpful for understanding the pleasant as well as the less pleasant aspects of menopause.

Chapter 14

The Steps of Age, 25 minutes, International Film Bureau. Emotional problems faced by a man and his wife when he is forced to retire because of age. Realistic although students often find it difficult to believe.

Life with Grandpa, 17 minutes, March of Time Forum Film. Discusses the problems of old age and suggests some solutions.

Your Social Security, 20 minutes, Social Security Administration. How Federal Old Age and Survivor's Insurance works. Who is covered, how applications are made, and how payments are processed.

Index

Page numbers in heavy type refer to illustrative material.